NEWS FROM THE WHITE HOUSE

NEWS
FROM THE
WHITE
HOUSE

The Presidential-Press Relationship
in the Progressive Era

George Juergens

The University of Chicago Press
Chicago & London

GEORGE JUERGENS is professor of history at
Indiana University the the author of *Joseph
Pulitzer and the New York World.*

The University of Chicago Press, Chicago 60637
The University of Chicago Press, Ltd., London

Library of Congress Cataloging in Publication Data

Juergens, George.
  News from the White House.

  Bibliography: p.
  Includes index.
  1. Press and politics—United States—History—
20th century.   2. United States—Politics and
government—1901–1909.   3. United States—Politics
and government—1909–1913.   4. United States—
Politics and government—1913–1921.   5. Progressivism (United States politics)   I. Title.
E743.J83   353.03'5   81-7634
ISBN 0-226-41472-8   AACR2

For Jane

Contents

Acknowledgments

It seems hardly sufficient merely to acknowledge all of the help I have received in writing this volume, but I am grateful.

A faculty fellowship from the National Endowment for the Humanities that enabled me to devote an uninterrupted year to research was critical to the project getting under way at all. Similarly, Robert Goldmann of the Ford Foundation provided an essential boost when he took an interest in what I was doing and arranged for a grant so I could have a semester off for writing. I am also indebted to James Elliott and the Indiana University Foundation for coming to the rescue when expenses associated with the book started to soar.

The efficient and friendly secretaries of the History Department at Indiana University have been a boon. Debbie Chase, who typed most of the manuscript, deserves special thanks. Others who assisted in various ways (some of them unfortunately no longer with the department) include Lori Bell, Elizabeth Gitlitz, Wendy Jensen, Diana Scroggins, and Connie Strange. Not the least of the reasons I feel warm-hearted toward them is the continual and genuine interest they showed in how the work was progressing.

I am indebted to John Moe, now of Ohio State University, with whom I have exchanged ideas over the years about the presidential-press relationship. Craig Tenney, with whom I have also spent many a pleasant evening talking about journalism and journalists, provided the benefit of his experienced newsman's eye in helping me to choose illustrations for the book. William Loeb, publisher of the *Manchester Union-Leader,* generously supplied a cartoon of William Loeb, Sr., and shared with me by mail interesting reminiscences about the Roosevelt family and his father's role in the Roosevelt administration. Thanks are due also to Cornell University Press for inviting me to duplicate a photograph from one of its publications.

Among the friends and colleagues who read portions of the manuscript are Roger Brown of American University, Robert Cross of the University of Virginia, Richard Dorson of Indiana University, John Garraty of Columbia University, and W. A. Swanberg, someone I am proud to call a fellow student of journalism. Several members of my own department read the entire manuscript and helped in a variety of ways. Without elaborating on their respective contributions, I want William Cohen, William Harris, Richard Kirkendall, and Lewis Perry to know that I appreciate all they did. I appreciate as well the contribution of Mark Wert, a former student now reporting for the *Rochester Democrat and Chronicle,* who gave the manuscript a close and astute reading that resulted in many improvements. James Patterson of Brown University provided encouragement and wise counsel at each step along the way, but then he has always been that kind of person—as was Nancy Patterson, whom we will miss. In particular I am indebted to Janet Rabinowitch for her help in bringing an overly long first draft down to manageable proportions. Although she is sponsoring editor at another publisher, and had no personal stake in this volume, out of friendship she went through the entire manuscript carefully to point out places where cuts could be made. She was always on target, and her contribution led to a tighter and better second draft.

There are many others I will not even attempt to name. They include friends in Bloomington and elsewhere, who whether or not they shared my fascination with the press, listened patiently as I held forth on the subject, consoled me when the work was going badly, and felt happy for me when it was going well. They include the students whose enthusiasm for the history of the presidential-press relationship fanned my own enthusiasm. Not least, they include the many librarians who by their professionalism made the work so much easier. To all of them, a deeply felt thank you.

I save for last the people who matter most. No one could possibly ask for more love and encouragement and support than I have received from my late father, Georg Ødegaard Juergens; from my mother, Magnhild Julin Juergens; and from my sister, Randi Louise Juergens. They have been a source of strength throughout my life, and an influence feeding into whatever I accomplish in my life.

And to prove that some of us are truly blessed, the love and encouragement and support have come also from my wife, Jane, and my two sons, Steven and Paul. It doesn't say enough, and yet it says everything, that we are a happy family. I wrote this book in that atmosphere, which was the greatest gift of all.

1

The New Era

On an evening in late September 1901, shortly after dusk, President Theodore Roosevelt beckoned to two friends waiting outside his office on the second floor of the White House and asked them to join him for a walk through the darkened streets of Washington. Lincoln Steffens, who would soon emerge as one of the foremost of a school of investigative journalists known as "muckrakers," and William Allen White, who had already achieved national prominence as editor of the *Emporia* (Kansas) *Gazette*, were on hand to help their friend through the earliest days of his presidency. Now, after hours of being besieged by callers and with no chance for privacy in his own office, Roosevelt wanted some time for himself. "Let's get out of this," he said to Steffens and White, taking them by the arm and leading them out of the White House.

The country was still mourning the death of Roosevelt's predecessor that September evening. A Polish-American anarchist named Leon Czolgosz had shot and critically wounded William McKinley on the afternoon of September 6 while the president was greeting well-wishers at the Pan American exposition in Buffalo. For several days it seemed that McKinley would pull through. The vice-president rushed to Buffalo on hearing the news, but was assured that the situation had stabilized and that he could safely join his family, who were vacationing in the Adirondacks. On September 13 he received a telegram telling him the president had taken a turn for the worse and that he must return immediately. When he arrived the following afternoon McKinley was already dead, and at 3:30 in the afternoon Theodore Roosevelt was sworn in at the home of a Buffalo resident as twenty-sixth president of the United States. He was still one month shy of his forty-third birthday, the youngest man ever to hold the office.

Roosevelt returned to Washington to a scene of predictable chaos. While he tried to catch up on matters of state and establish an office routine, a stream of visitors clamored for his attention, all of them intent on advising the young president on how he should conduct his administration. The fact that he commuted each night from the White House back to his Washington residence while Mrs. McKinley's belongings were packed and the mansion made ready for the new first family added to the sense of turmoil. It was certainly no time for quiet reflection. Nor, for that matter, would it have been seemly for Roosevelt to acknowledge publicly the emotions he felt. But he had to tell someone, and for the purpose he sought out his two trusted confidants, Steffens and White.

According to Steffens's account, Roosevelt on reaching the street did not even try to contain himself in describing his delight at being president. He meant no disrespect for McKinley, a good and honest man. It was just that the chance to govern was so exhilarating. And it was all such good luck. He had been put in the vice-presidency at the insistence of Thomas Platt, the old guard Republican leader of New York who had been appalled by Roosevelt's reform record as governor and wanted to get him out of the way. McKinley and his closest advisor, Mark Hanna, initially resisted the idea. They trusted Roosevelt no more than Platt, and only gave in after long argument. "Don't any of you realize," Hanna is reported to have said after the deal had gone through, "that there's only one life between this madman and the White House?" For his part, Roosevelt understood that he was being exiled, but went along because he had no real alternative if he intended to stay in politics. His friends tried to comfort him that the vice-presidency might after all be a stepping stone to the presidential nomination in 1904, but neither he nor they could have attached much hope to the prospect. The truth was that he had been maneuvered into a dead end, and could do nothing about it. And now suddenly, however tragic the circumstances, the prize had come to him. Roosevelt walked the streets with Steffens and White for over an hour, laughing aloud at the trick of fate that had foiled Platt's design and put him in the White House.[1]

The glee that Roosevelt had been barely able to suppress in public and that now burst forth on a walk with friends had to do with far more than comeuppance for a rival and ambition satisfied. Also central to his reaction was the sense of possibility in the air in 1901; the feeling that after decades of inertia in the White House opportunities now beckoned for a president to exercise bold, energetic leadership. Roosevelt exulted because he had come to the office at the precise juncture in the nation's history when he could be true to his own temperament in the way he governed. He was, and he sensed it, the man for the moment.

The country's rapid emergence as a world power, giving it a new role to play in international affairs, offered one area for leadership. When the *Times* of London bordered in black the columns carrying McKinley's obituary and British reactions to his death, the first time in history it had so honored a foreign head of state, the gesture spoke as much to the significance of the United States in British eyes as to the president's personal popularity.[2] Roosevelt never doubted that the twentieth century was destined to be the American century, as truly as the nineteenth century had belonged to Great Britain. Indeed, Alfred Mahan's *The Influence of Sea Power upon History,* published in 1890, had the impact it did on the circle he moved in precisely because it represented a blueprint for the transition to occur. Now that he held power, Roosevelt was eager to get started.

Just as exciting were the possibilities for a new vigor in domestic policy. After decades of allowing the builders of American industry to operate without constraint, years of neglect that resulted in slums, abandoned farms, class cleavage, people had started to awaken by the early 1890s to the price of progress. They were asking questions about individual responsibility in an industrial society, and about how traditional values and rights could be preserved under new circumstances. As a previous generation had almost sanctified the concept of laissez faire, now social justice as a concept was becoming a key to thought and action. The shift in values influenced broad areas of American life. The settlement-house movement associated with Jane Addams was a symptom; so was the rise of the Institutional Church and the stirrings of the Social Gospel in American Protestantism; so were the new themes in literature introduced by figures like William Dean Howells and Stephen Crane.

Almost inevitably the reform impulse also moved into politics. Theodore Roosevelt had indicated something of what lay ahead during his tenure as governor of New York, as had Hazen Pingree as mayor of Detroit and governor of Michigan. In 1900 Robert La Follette came back from political defeat to sweep into office as governor of Wisconsin, prepared to convert that state into a model of progressive reform. The political orthodoxy of the nineteenth century was like a dam starting to crumble before the rising level of discontent and restlessness. By 1901 the dam was about to burst. The voters wanted change, and were looking for leadership. They would follow with almost religious enthusiasm a president who showed the way.

For his part, nobody had ever accused Roosevelt of timidity or reluctance to lead. His zest for being at the head of the parade was one of the characteristics that most sharply distinguished him from McKinley. Roosevelt also understood that in twentieth century America the leadership had to come from the top. In earlier years the politics that mattered most to people, and therefore absorbed their attention, took place at the local and state levels. Presidents entered the lives of ordinary folk only in times of war, and otherwise could count on having the spotlight only every four years when they ran for office. Even then the interest had to do far more with the entertainment value of the race than with the sense that the outcome affected voters in significant ways. But this was increasingly less true in the modern era. Part of the reason is that industrial development had created problems that local and state jurisdictions could no longer handle. It also made the regions far more interdependent than they had been previously. Industrialization was a nationalizing influence in the benefits it bestowed and the price it exacted, which meant that the focus for political leadership almost had to shift from communities to the federal government. And as far as Roosevelt was concerned, it had to shift in particular to the president, who alone among public officials was elected by all the people.

For him to resolve in 1901 that he would be a strong leader was one thing. The harder question was how to do it. After all, a president cannot rule by fiat. Under the separation of powers in the Constitution he does not even have any formal authority to set legislative priorities, save for the negative authority of the veto. How, then, was Roosevelt to stir the country to follow him? The obvious answer, an axiom in political theory, was that he would have to lead through the extraconstitutional mandate of popular support. This much was conventional wisdom, something Abraham Lincoln had expressed as well as anybody almost half a century before in one of his debates with Stephen Douglas. "Public sentiment is everything," Lincoln said in discussing the Dred Scott decision. "With public sentiment nothing can fail; without it nothing can succeed. He who molds public sentiment goes deeper than he who enacts statutes or pronounces decisions. He makes statutes or decisions possible or impossible to execute."[3] For Roosevelt, as for any democratic statesman, his authority would depend, finally, on his being able to communicate with the people and persuade them.

But to invoke public sentiment represented only the beginning of an answer, for it did not explain how one went about communicating with, and persuading, a nation of 78 million. Roosevelt certainly could not rely on precedent, since no previous president—at least back to Jackson—had tried to assume direct leadership of a domestic reform movement. In the few cases since Jackson when presidents had acted strongly to carry out a mandate (Polk and Lincoln come to mind), they generally did so in times of war or threat of war when patriotic fervor provided its own momentum. Roosevelt had little to learn from them because his goals were different, and of course because he functioned in a different age. Nor did he have available the devices later presidents used to reach the public directly. Radio was still twenty years in the future, and television would not become a practical possibility for another half-century. Roosevelt even lacked the outlet men like Jefferson and Jackson had built their leadership on, a semiofficial newspaper that could be counted on to relay the presidential message as delivered in return for lucrative government printing contracts and privileged access to news. These personal organs went into decline in the mid-nineteenth century and expired with the establishment of the Government Printing Office in 1860. In short, Roosevelt faced an unprecedented challenge in communication at a time when old devices to reach the public had outlived their usefulness and new ones had not yet been invented.

What Roosevelt did have, however, an instrument he used to help shape the modern presidency, was an American newspaper that had undergone radical transformation in the two or three decades preceding. The fundamental change, from which everything else followed, was that journalism had evolved into a branch of big business, with millions of dollars of investment capital at stake and the pressures of the marketplace weighing heavily in the formulation of editorial policy. No longer was it possible for a would-be newspaper proprietor to start out as James Gordon Bennett had done in 1835 when he founded the *New York Herald,* with $500 in cash, a basement room on Wall Street for an office, and a plank laid across two barrels for a desk. As late as 1851 eyebrows had been raised when a trio of investors put up the seemingly extravagant amount of $100,000 to launch the *New York Times.* Half a century later the same sum would have barely sufficed for a paper in a medium-sized community with no pretensions to national coverage. The newspaper industry now dealt in altogether different figures. *Editor & Publisher,* the trade periodical, estimated in 1901 that anyone wishing to enter the field in New York City would have to start with a minimum investment of $1,000,000.[4] Even that amount was risky, and suitable only for marginal participation. One of the major dailies in New York City described by Lincoln Steffens in an article on the economics of the industry, presumably Joseph Pulitzer's *New York World,* operated on an annual budget of $2,000,000 in the mid-1890s, and had 1,300 full-time employees on its staff.[5] The return on investment in journalism was equally impressive. James Gordon Bennett, Jr., for example, his father's basement room on Wall Street now only a matter of family memory, netted annual profits of about $1,000,000 in the early 1890s from the *Herald* and *Telegram.*[6]

The shift from personal journalism to the newspaper as monolith occurred in response to the economic transformation of the nation in the last decades of the nineteenth century. Production on a vastly wider scale required equivalent innovations in distribution, not least a new reliance on advertising in newspapers and periodicals to reach the national market. The result was a revolution in scale and mode of operation for the press as sweeping as the revolution going on throughout the economy. In 1879 newspapers and magazines took in about $39 million annually, or forty-four percent of their total income, from advertisers. Ten years later the amount had almost doubled to $72 million, and comprised slightly more than fifty percent of total income. By 1914 newspapers alone totalled $184 million in advertising accounts, almost two-thirds of their total revenue.[7]

One of the immediate consequences of this development was that publications came under extreme pressure to increase their circulations in order to attract advertising accounts. Many reasons explain why newspaper sales exploded as they did in the late nineteenth century, but they finally all reduce to the new way the industry balanced its books. Part of the boom can be traced to the launching of new dailies in an industry offering obvious opportunities for profit; just as important was the avid push among papers already in the field to attract additional readers. The average readership of American newspapers almost doubled between 1880 and 1900, and by the time Roosevelt left the White House in 1909 had almost tripled.[8] Because of the particular attraction of large cities as an advertising market, the trend was most marked there. In the early 1890s only ten newspapers located in four cities had circulations in excess of 100,000. By 1914 thirty newspapers serving a dozen different cities had reached that plateau.[9]

The thrust for circulation in turn affected the editorial policies of papers, and in ways Roosevelt and his successors would be able to exploit. One consequence was to encourage the shift from an old-fashioned journalism in which news and opinion were virtually indistinguishable to a journalism based on the objective news principle. The appearance at mid-century of wire services had been an early influence in that direction. Dispatches sent to papers of every political conviction had to be written in a dry, unbiased, fact-oriented way offensive to none of them. Now with the industry undergoing structural change the reasons for objectivity became all the more urgent. Papers depending heavily on ad lineage, and under pressure to qualify as outlets to the entire community, couldn't afford to antagonize potential subscribers by allowing a blatantly partisan bias to color their news coverage. The only way to attract readers of different backgrounds and conflicting points of view was by sticking as closely as possible to a neutral rendition of facts. A style that journalists eventually elevated into one of the ethical principles of their craft (until McCarthyism caused some second thoughts) was motivated at least as much in the first instance by commercial considerations. To be sure, as the record of the Hearst and McCormick papers attests, slanted reporting did not disappear from the American daily. With each decade, however, it became less common and less overt.

A further consequence of the new journalism was increased stress on human-interest material, in reporting on government as well as in other areas. Newspapers had to respond to the reality that by and large readers are more interested in personal detail about figures in the news than in dry matters of statecraft. The wisdom applied above all in the case of the president of the United States. Scandal and gossip about chief executives had always been grist for the press, but now what can only be described as a kind of domestic chatter became a staple of White House reporting. The intense coverage of Grover Cleveland's marriage and honeymoon in June 1886 vividly illustrated the trend. Not only did newspapers all but suffocate the story of the wedding day in their attention to trivia (even the august *New York Times* devoted five full columns on its front page to an account of the ceremony), when the couple tried to slip away to their honeymoon cottage in Deer Park, Maryland, a small army of newsmen tagged along, filing an estimated 400,000 words over the next five and a half days while keeping the president and his bride under round-the-clock surveillance.[10] The intrusion enraged Cleveland and shocked those who still subscribed to the old proprieties. If such journalism is to be justified on the grounds that it sells newspapers, Joseph Bishop growled in *Forum* magazine, then "the profession becomes the lowest of human callings—lower than brothel-keeping or liquor-selling, for these make no pretense to respectability."[11] Whatever the merits to that argument, his appeal that newspapers conduct themselves by the same code a gentleman would follow in his private behavior was almost certainly unrealistic under modern conditions.

The key to Roosevelt's leadership was that he succeeded, as Cleveland could not, in making these characteristics of modern journalism work for him. A press obliged (at least to an extent) to report objectively, and eager for its own purposes to personalize the presidency, offered obvious opportunities for a publicity-minded leader to exploit. The trick inhered in knowing how to take advantage of opportunity. On that score Roosevelt demonstrated a shrewdness that made him virtually unique among public figures of his time, and went far toward explaining his achievements in office.

Roosevelt based his strategy on several tenets about the uses of mass communications in politics. To begin with, he assumed that the news that appears in a daily paper, and the way it is presented, does far more to mold public opinion than editorials. If he could seize the headlines and influence the way reporters wrote about him, it would not matter a great deal what the press might have to say about him on its inside pages. From this followed the further insight that the definition of news as a daily chronicle of official activity was much too passive and limiting in its implications. With any sort of imagination a modern president could generate news on demand to insure continued domination of the front page. And the more he did so, monopolizing public attention, the more he established his credentials as national leader, which in turn made it easier to keep on generating news about himself. His final insight was that a strong president must not only make news, he must pay close attention to how the news is disseminated. There are different ways to release information to the press. Roosevelt understood that using the correct technique in different circumstances would have a major bearing on the amount and kind of coverage he received. Indeed, handled adroitly, news could be his most telling weapon in the struggle for specific political goals.

Each of these points, which seem so self-evident in the modern era, were far from conventional in Roosevelt's time. Particular controversy surrounded the first and key premise, that news is more important than editorials in molding public opinion. It is true that students of journalism had been questioning the impact of editorials for decades before Roosevelt reached the White House. James Parton, a biographer whose list of works included one on Horace Greeley, came out strongly on the subject as early as 1866. "The prestige of the editorial is gone," he wrote in *North American Review.* "Our journalists already know that editorials neither make nor mar a daily paper, that they do not much influence the public mind, nor change many votes, and that the power and success of a newspaper depend wholly and absolutely upon its success in getting and its skill in exhibiting the news."[12] But few were as decided as Parton, and certainly not politicians who had most to lose if it turned out that editorials did matter. There was even something faintly heretical about questioning the importance of those who over the years had had the courage to speak out boldly on issues of the day. From Zenger to William Allen White, they belonged among the heroes of American history. This is why the romantic stereotype of the journalist was still of the lonely figure working by kerosene lamp to have ready for the next day's paper a statement inveighing against injustice or talking sense to an inflamed populace. Only later did we get the stereotype, an interesting change, of the brash reporter with a press card tucked in his hatband calling in to "stop the presses" because he had a "scoop" to deliver.

It took a Roosevelt to recognize that not only had newspapers changed over the decades, people were reading them in a different way and for different purposes. In the modern America of bustling cities and diverse populations, the public wanted facts, not opinions, bulletins, not discourse, and it wanted them quickly and tersely. The sensible recourse in that case was to be the source of the bulletins, and since they were critical in forming opinion, to exercise as much control as possible over what they contained and when they appeared. "President Roosevelt," a veteran reporter remarked, "knew the value and potent influence of a news paragraph written as he wanted it written and disseminated through the proper influential channels better than any man who ever occupied the White House, before him, or since."[13]

He also understood—something Cleveland and McKinley with their old-fashioned virtues and old-fashioned expectations failed to see (or at least to act on)—that the avid interest in him as a personality could itself be a source of strength. It opens the way for a president to dramatize himself, to become a symbol of state as well as political leader. When every detail of a person's life is a matter of public concern, something for the press to dwell on, he achieves an almost semimythic status, and puts precious distance between himself and those who would challenge his authority. And since a president always has the option of appeasing curiosity on his own terms, voluntarily making available all sorts of trivia about himself and his family, even orchestrating the publicity, he is better able to slam the door on the occasions when he does not wish to be on display. Of course it is impossible to exercise complete control. All modern presidents have suffered moments of outrage when newspapers ventured into areas that were supposed to be off-limits, and sometimes compounded the offense by being garbled or inaccurate in their intrusions. Presidents discover, as do monarchs and movie idols, that there are burdens as well as benefits in being put on a pedestal. Nevertheless, one of the ways to distinguish between those who succeeded as publicists and the others who failed is that the former made the personalization of the office work for them. Theodore Roosevelt was the first one to try, and in doing so set a standard for his successors to follow. Partly through natural colorfulness, partly through artifice, he kept newspapers filled with stories about his enthusiasms and eccentricities, his feuds and friendships, his sheer zest for living. In the process he succeeded to a remarkable extent in stamping his personality on the age and confirming his primacy as national leader.

Fundamental to all of Roosevelt's other accomplishments was his recognition that American journalism had entered the age of the reporter. The editors like Greeley and Dana and Bennett who had made their papers extensions of their own considerable personalities belonged to a simpler time. With the stress on news as opposed to opinion, the concern that the news be delivered accurately and objectively, and what would become more conspicuous with each decade, the insistence that news must be aggressively pursued rather than simply received through handouts, a changing of the guard was under way. In place of the editors who dominated a previous era, the new giants would be people like Oscar Davis, Richard Oulahan, Herbert Bayard Swope, Arthur Krock, reporters who earned their reputations by digging up the story.

The shift in status began well before Roosevelt took office. One of the early breakthroughs came with the Civil War, if only in offering battlefield correspondents a modicum of recognition and glory. Previously, the reporter was unrecognized, untrained, underpaid, so uncertain in job tenure as to be something of a vagabond, and perhaps because of the noise of the presses and erratic hours and pressures associated with the job, likely in his drinking and other personal habits to deserve his reputation as a wastrel. The flourishing in the decades after the Civil War of newspapers that emphasized sprightly writing, notably Charles Dana's *New York Sun,* and the improvements in pay and tenure and hours of work that followed as journalism became a major business enterprise, also helped to undo some of the onus attached to the craft. Indeed, those years saw the appearance of the earliest reporter-celebrities. Jacob Riis won fame as well as handsome monetary reward for his reporting during the 1890s on slum conditions in New York City, and later in the decade the war with Spain elevated a figure like Richard Harding Davis into almost as much a news presence as the people he covered.

This trend toward respectability, and what followed, pride in craft, was particularly evident among reporters in the two major news centers, New York and Washington. They regarded themselves as elite groups who had little time for the tom-foolery still associated with journalism in other sections of the country. As late as the 1890s in cities like Chicago and San Francisco, reporters influenced by the cult of bohemianism tended to equate the life of the writer with hard drinking and defiance of convention, and by their carousing provided material for the kind of stereotype popularized by Ben Hecht and Charles MacArthur in "The Front Page." But Washington reporters, in particular, had always been more sedate types, and by the turn of the century—conscious of their dignity, mindful of their credentials as political experts, perhaps encouraged by the bylines just starting to creep into American newspapers—they were becoming downright serious-minded. Ralph McKenzie, a veteran of the capital press corps, looked back in 1903 at the changes he had witnessed over the years, and remarked wistfully on the disappearance of the easy-going style of his youth. "The delightful Bohemian life of the Seventies and Eighties among Washington correspondents has, to a large extent. . . passed away," he wrote. "The witty coterie of newspaper scribes which one might find at almost any time during off-duty hours in the lobby of the old Willard Hotel—when statesman, pencil pusher and officeseeker met cheek-by-jowl and exchanged compliments, swapped lies and told stories—have vanished from their old haunts to reappear no more in our time. They have been replaced by a newer and younger set who are less Bohemian in taste, but of equal influence in public affairs and the force has been greatly augmented in number, including many young men who have yet to win their spurs."[14] Without fully realizing it, McKenzie was describing a Washington press corps starting to come of age.

An important factor in explaining the new style was the sharp upgrading in educational background of those now entering the field. Whereas reporting had once been a craft learned through apprenticeship, the print shop doubling as school house, the general expansion of education in the United States after the Civil War meant that many more people were coming in equipped with high school diplomas and sometimes even college training. Whitelaw Reid claimed as early as 1875 that virtually all of the writers on his *New York Tribune* were college graduates, and pointed also to the high educational attainments of the reporters on the *World, Times,* and *Evening Post,* citing only the *Herald* as a paper that preferred on-the-job training for its staff.[15] The claim seems far-fetched considering that only about two percent of the American population even held high school diplomas at the time.[16] But Reid's broader point, that journalism was starting to attract better qualified candidates, could not be denied. Indeed, by the time of Roosevelt's presidency some of them were even receiving university training in their field. An important breakthrough occurred in April 1903 when, after much soul-searching, the trustees of Columbia University—an Ivy League institution—agreed to accept a $2,000,000 grant from Joseph Pulitzer to establish a graduate school of journalism.[17] Before the school opened its doors in fall, 1912 the University of Missouri preceded Columbia by launching the first graduate program in journalism in 1908. Clearly, reporters had come a long way from being what President Charles Eliot of Harvard once called them, "drunkards, deadbeats, and bummers." They had every reason to take themselves seriously when educators took them seriously enough to make their craft a subject for professional study.

Nobody needed to tell Theodore Roosevelt that reporters mattered. He could not have had the insights he did about how modern journalism worked without recognizing that the newsmen on the beat were the key. If presidential leadership depends upon communicating with the people, and the press was Roosevelt's major instrument for communication, it followed that the correspondents who filed the dispatches about him would have considerable impact in determining the success or failure of his administration. "In our country," he once remarked, "I am inclined to think that almost, if not quite, the most important profession is that of newspaperman."[18] They were certainly a group well worth cultivating.

One of the keys to the Roosevelt years was that for the first time in American history reporters became part of the White House operation. The fact of having a White House press corps at all traces to Roosevelt providing permanent quarters for newsmen close to his own office. He further shattered precedent by making himself available to correspondents on an almost daily basis, and speaking to them with a candor that almost frightened those who shared his confidences. Which is to say, in responding to the important role they played in the system he made the role all the more important.

The reverse side of the coin is that in the process he also helped to groom potential adversaries. Presidents and reporters have fundamentally different priorities that are almost bound to set them at odds. Any chief executive will insist occasionally on confidentiality, while the job of the press is disclosure; presidents seek to highlight accomplishments and consensus, while journalists find their material in conflict and corruption and failure. The emphasis on news in the Roosevelt years meant that reporters took giant strides to becoming what they are today: part of the Washington establishment. It meant, too, that presidents and reporters embarked on the long train of confrontations that is another characteristic of contemporary American government.

What the one president began continued to good and ill effect in the administrations of the two who followed. As Roosevelt demonstrated the potentialities of publicity in presidential leadership, so his successor demonstrated how blunders in the same area can destroy an administration. William Howard Taft came to the office with impressive credentials as regards the qualities one ordinarily looks for in a president. He was honest, intelligent, highly experienced as an administrator, fair-minded, fundamentally decent. All he lacked was political sense, which meant in part the capacity to interpret and influence public opinion. He did not know how to use the modern American newspaper as an instrument of governance. It indicated how much the office had changed in just a few years that the failing rendered him almost pathetically unsuited to serve.

Woodrow Wilson certainly did not suffer from that handicap. He demonstrated in a variety of ways in his two terms that he was at least as gifted a publicist as Roosevelt, and perhaps more so. His innovations with the presidential press conference, the personal appearances before Congress, and most notably, the creation in the administrative branch during World War I of a vast bureaucracy to trumpet the government's message, all carried forward substantially what Roosevelt had started in making the White House the focus of national attention and crucible of national leadership. Where Wilson faltered was in his dealings with individual reporters. Personal and philosophical differences drove a wedge between them that eventually had destructive consequences. Wilson's bad fortune, and the country's, was that presidential leadership should turn out to be a matter of technique, but also of style.

It is no coincidence that the modern presidency and modern Washington press corps both came of age during the Progressive period, because each had much to do with the emergence of the other. Without minimizing the many institutional reasons why power flowed to the White House in the first two decades of the century—the added responsibilities devolving on the executive branch because of regulatory legislation, the country's new role in international affairs—everything else depended finally on strong leaders being able to assert their position at the top of the governmental hierarchy. For that the press was essential, which meant that presidents and reporters were of necessity thrown into a relationship of mutual need and mutual antagonism that continues to the present day.

A good place to begin in tracing how it happened is on a rainy day in the first months of Roosevelt's administration.

2

The News-maker

The story is told that on a chilly, wet day in early 1902, Theodore Roosevelt happened to look out the window of his office on the second floor of the White House and saw a cluster of sodden newsmen huddled by the pillars on the north portico waiting to interview the visitors passing in and out of the executive mansion on official business. He took pity on the group and ordered that a small anteroom adjoining his ground floor study be set aside for the press as a lounge and place to write their stories. More important, the room was conveniently located to monitor traffic through the foyer so newsmen could catch their subjects before they left the building rather than having to wait for them outside. Roosevelt's thoughtfulness in bringing reporters in out of the rain is commonly accepted as marking the birth of the White House press corps.[1]

Reporters had waited seven years to receive the recognition a press room implied. Until the mid-1890s there was no point in having such a room since the press did not cover the White House on a regular basis. Capitol Hill offered a far richer source of news, and in any event the best way to find out about the activities of the president was to rely on contacts with the congressmen and cabinet members who saw him regularly. Presidents had neither the inclination nor the facilities to make the information available themselves.

The change came in 1896, late in Grover Cleveland's second administration, when Harry Godwin, city editor of the *Washington Evening Star*, tried to rid himself of a persistent job-seeker by suggesting that he go to the White House and see if he could dig up a story for the paper. Considering the president's ill-concealed hostility toward reporters, Godwin assumed that it would be a long time, if ever, before he saw the applicant again. The thirty-five-year-old William "Fatty" Price, a rotund figure of almost 300 pounds, set out on the assignment fortified mainly with the saving grace of naïveté. Before coming to Washington he had edited a

14

South Carolina weekly for which his major reporting function had been to drop by the local depot and interview passengers arriving or departing on the two trains that stopped in town each day. He decided he would follow the same routine on this occasion. The idea of rounding up news simply by standing outside the White House and interviewing visitors as they arrived and departed was at once obvious and inspired.[2]

Price immediately struck a rich lode. It may be that the people he accosted opened up to him because of the sheer surprise at being asked questions under such circumstances. Within a few hours he had accumulated enough material to scrawl hurriedly a story that appeared in the *Star* that evening under the headline "AT THE WHITE HOUSE," the first installment of what would be a regular Price feature in the paper for the next two decades.[3]

The arrangement worked even better once McKinley took office. Far from sharing his predecessor's grudge against the press, the new president actively went out of his way to court journalists. And by this time there were more than a few to be courted, since Price's success had brought other reporters to the White House to join him in covering the newly discovered beat. McKinley instructed his secretary—John Porter, and, starting in early 1900, George Cortelyou—to brief the correspondents each evening on the day's events. With the outbreak of the Spanish-American War, when the flow of news picked up significantly, the president even allowed the correspondents to use an outer reception room as a place to deposit their hats and coats and pass idle time in relative comfort. Almost certainly the people who saw the president felt freer in talking with the press in this atmosphere of good will. The important point, however, is that interviews with visitors to the White House remained at the heart of the news-gathering operation, and as had been the case since Price first took up the assignment, they occurred outside the building. On cabinet-meeting days, for example, when reporters turned out in particularly large numbers, they usually waited in the reception room for the meeting to end. As soon as the signal came they would rush out to "newspaper row" by the north portico to intercept the department heads as they left. By convention the only individual immune from questioning when he appeared through the front door was the president himself.[4]

Roosevelt made an important gesture when he formalized what McKinley had started by establishing a separate room for the press inside the White House, and a few months later by providing permanent quarters. He had been appalled on moving into the mansion to discover how ill-suited it was as a home for a large and lively family. Since the ground floor consisted mainly of ceremonial rooms, and the president and his staff had their offices on the second floor, not a great deal of space remained as living area for the family. Older couples like the Harrisons and

McKinleys may have been able to make do, but it was an altogether different matter with six young children, the oldest still in her teens, and none of them of a retiring nature. Roosevelt found the situation impossible, and since few people—least of all he—liked the suggestion that the family live elsewhere and the White House become an official building only, Congress moved quickly by appropriating $540,000 in June 1902 to renovate the main quarters and build a new west wing for office space. In describing how he wanted the wing laid out, Roosevelt specified that one room off the main foyer, next to his secretary's, should be set up for the press.[5] This was a convenience, because it meant that for the first time reporters would have telephones available to call in their stories, rather than having to rely on the messengers and telegraph boys whose bicycles, parked in a long line on Pennsylvania Avenue, had been a fixture since the pack first joined Price outside the White House.[6] But the room the newsmen moved into in mid-October 1902 mattered also because it conferred a sort of legitimacy on their presence. It suggested they were no longer there just as guests of the president; they were filling a public function.

The fact that Roosevelt meant to be helpful by these arrangements does not mean that his motives were entirely, or even primarily, altruistic. His major purpose in bringing the press into the White House and later institutionalizing the relationship by providing permanent quarters, was to make it easier to generate publicity about himself. As long as he intended to dominate the headlines, it made sense to arrange that reporters be conveniently on hand; in a way almost extensions of his own staff. The same logic explains why he immediately set out to be the most completely accessible president America had known until that time. An appointment he arranged after returning from McKinley's funeral is revealing in this regard. He telephoned the Washington managers of the three wire services and asked them to come right over to see him. Charles Boynton of the Associated Press, David Barry of the *New York Sun*'s Laffan Agency, and Ed Keen of the Scripps-McRae Press Association (later to become United Press International) were particularly important in his plans because their dispatches appeared in hundreds of papers across the country, and because they tended to be the bellwethers for other journalists in deciding how the news would be presented.[7]

As Barry recalled the meeting with Roosevelt, which took place seated around the cabinet table, the president did most of the talking in laying out how he proposed to deal with the press. He pointed out that since he had known Boynton and Barry for years, and trusted them, they could expect his complete cooperation. "I shall be accessible to [you]," the president said, "I shall keep [you] posted, and trust to [your] discretion as to publication." Keen, on the other hand, whom Roosevelt had never met before, would have to prove he could be relied on. When Boynton and Barry vouched for their colleague, Roosevelt agreed that he would take him also into his confidence. According to one source, he put Keen to the test right away by using the meeting to deliver a scathing indictment of the Old Guard in his party. "If you even hint where you got it," Roosevelt warned when he had finished, "I'll say you are a damned liar."[8] He would do more than that. Roosevelt reminded the wire representatives that a reporter who violated his trust would be mercilessly cut off from further access to news. He would even take steps to deny legitimate news to the paper or agency which employed the offending reporter. This was too much for Barry, who protested that a grievance against a particular individual should not be escalated into a government vendetta against an entire news organization. But Roosevelt was firm, and even somewhat amused at his friend's unhappiness. "All right, gentlemen, now we understand each other," he said adjourning the meeting.[9]

Roosevelt proved to be as good as his word over the next seven years. He divided newsmen into distinct groups of insiders and outsiders, and was unforgiving in banishing those he felt, justifiably or not, had betrayed him. The fact that he could get away with such high-handedness goes far to explain why he received the favorable coverage he did. It did a journalist's career no good to be on the outside, not to know what was going on. The reporter had every reason to play along if that was the price for being informed. Of course the coercion only worked because of the unequal relationship between Roosevelt and a not yet fully mature press corps. Reporters in a later era, conscious of their own prerogatives, would not have tolerated a president telling them who could have access to the news and on what terms. But this was a different game played by different rules. And to Roosevelt's credit, the rewards for those who cooperated were considerable. His accessibility and candor with the insiders almost staggered newsmen who had learned the mechanics of their craft in the gray days of Cleveland and Harrison.

One of the occasions Roosevelt liked to see the press, often in groups of five or six, was at 1:00 each afternoon when a Treasury Department messenger who doubled as his barber came over to the White House to shave him. They used a small room between his office and his secretary's for the purpose. As Roosevelt settled in an arm chair to be lathered, the reporters would gather around and take turns throwing questions at him. It was a convenient arrangement for the president, enabling him to use constructively time which might otherwise have been wasted, and assuring the press that a period would be regularly set aside for them. If anything, they regarded it as a particularly desireable period, because Roosevelt had a tendency to filibuster when he spoke, and under the circumstances he had to be rather more restrained than usual. Not that he could ever be entirely tamed, but that too was part of the appeal. The reporters loved to watch as the president periodically jumped up to make a point just as the barber was about to draw the sharply honed razor across his face. Somehow the expected catastrophe never happened. As Louis Brownlow recalled, "A more skillful barber never existed. 'Teddy' in an ordinary armchair would be lathered, and, as the razor would descend toward his face, someone would ask a question. The President would wave both arms, jump up, speak excitedly, and then drop again into the chair and grin at the barber, who would begin all over. Sometimes these explosions interrupted a shave ten or a dozen times. It was more fun to see than a circus. . . ."[10]

But there were also quieter moments for conversation with the president. Oscar K. Davis, head of the Washington bureau of the *New York Times,* made it a point to drop by two or three evenings a week for private talks in the hour Roosevelt signed his correspondence before going back to the main building to dress for dinner. The two were close friends (the president called him by his nickname, "O.K."), and Davis was always welcome. The fact that the *Times* often opposed the administration editorially didn't matter, particularly since the paper played fair in its news columns. In these evening sessions Roosevelt demonstrated again his capacity to make every minute count. Davis marvelled at his ability to keep a conversation going while scanning letters, making occasional corrections or insertions, and signing his name.[11] Roosevelt pretty well had to be adept in that skill if he was to set aside as much time as he did for daily visits with newsmen.

So important did Roosevelt regard his press contacts that he regularly squeezed in extra time during the day for background sessions, and even arranged to see on an individual basis reporters who by any normal reckoning did not have the reputations to warrant a president's attention. Brownlow remembered his first meeting with Roosevelt in 1904 only a few weeks after he arrived in Washington as a correspondent for the *Louisville Evening Post* and *Nashville Banner.* At the time he requested and received an appointment he was twenty-four years old, nervous at being away from home, in awe of the White House and its occupants, and as a staunch Democrat, not at all approving of Roosevelt's politics. He had barely settled in the cabinet room to await the president's pleasure when Roosevelt came bursting in, "flying coattails, flying eyeglass cord, gleaming teeth, squinting eyes, outstretched hand, and 'Dee-lighted!' "[12] Within moments the young man found himself chatting as if with an old friend about his family and life back in Kentucky. The president brushed aside as insignificant the political difference between them. The important thing, as Brownlow soon recognized, is that they were both interested for their respective reasons in how the news got out.

This kind of access to the president of the United States was remarkable enough, but it meant all the more because of Roosevelt's openness when he spoke with the press. Reporters were amazed, and sometimes a bit concerned, at the things he told them. Isaac Marcosson, a veteran journalist, found an "almost astonishing frankness" on his visits to the White House.[13] The president talked freely about the most delicate matters of state, and seemed at times to be courting danger by the bluntness with which he discussed personalities in Washington. According to William Allen White, occasionally he even liked to discomfit officials trying to discuss private matters with him by speaking in a purposely loud voice so that reporters waiting outside his office could follow the conversation.[14]

For a press corps accustomed to finding presidential words about as revealing as an oration on the Fourth of July, the Roosevelt style was delightfully unsettling. They probably even exaggerated how far down the barriers fell. It is always enticing to be taken into another person's confidence, particularly one who wields power, and the things said can easily distract attention from the many other things consciously left unsaid. Roosevelt was outspoken, but he was no fool. Astute correspondents noticed that although he talked a great deal, in a way the words were like a smoke screen protecting him from exposure. He didn't engage in dialogues with the press. He lectured to them; endlessly lectured. "Few could stand up against the Roosevelt barrage of words," Isaac Marcosson recalled. "When he talked no one could get in a word edge-wise."[15] This made for strange presidential-press confrontations. Reporters learned to slip their questions in during pauses, and then scribbled furiously to keep up with the fast-paced monologue that followed. "I always came into the room," Lincoln Steffens said of his interviews with Roosevelt, "primed with a question that I fired quick; and he went off."[16] In fact, considering that there was no give-and-take in these sessions, no opportunity to probe or ask follow-up questions, it is probably inaccurate to call them interviews at all. Charles Thompson, who preceded Davis as head of the *New York Times*'s Washington bureau, shrewdly noted how Roosevelt always managed to command the situation. "It belongs to this side of his character that he was never interviewed, in any proper sense," Thompson wrote. "A real interview is an unpremeditated thing, in which the reporter asks what questions he pleases, and takes the answers with merciless accuracy. . . . No one ever heard of an interview being given by Roosevelt . . . he had himself under an iron control, no matter how exasperating or exciting the state of affairs might be. Impulsive? The thousand reporters who have tried to catch Roosevelt off guard and make him say something he did not expect to say will laugh at that idea."[17] Clearly the talkative president was not as naked as he sometimes seemed.

Moreover, his sessions with the press were governed by strict rules that no reporter ever had the chance to violate twice. He could not be quoted directly. When he said something was not for publication he meant precisely that; it remained a secret, and therefore a kind of bond, between himself and the press. (His off-the-record remarks were also a convenient way to put the lid on stories that might otherwise have come out independently.) The last and most difficult rule was that the journalist must have the good sense to know even without being told what sort of things were inappropriate to print. Roosevelt did not anticipate seeing some of his more pungent observations in the morning newspapers, any more than John Kennedy who also spoke to reporters with remarkable freedom expected his irreverences or profanities to be quoted. Breaching a confidence may have been the worst sin, but lack of discretion also constituted grounds for consigning a reporter to the Ananias Club, named after the New Testament character who lied about holding back part of a gift to the Church, and rebuked by Peter, fell dead. Members of the Ananias Club, and their numbers grew by the years, were dead in the eyes of the White House.

To say that Roosevelt had his defenses does not diminish the fact that he went much further than previous presidents in taking trusted reporters into his confidence. Certainly they appreciated his candor. "It was all or nothing with him," Oscar Davis recalled. "He either talked, with entire frankness and freedom, about anything and everything, or he didn't talk at all."[18] If much of what the president told them could not be repeated, that was a small price to pay. Almost by definition, a well-informed journalist always knows more than he can print. The information is still valuable, however, in providing perspective on present developments and depth for future reports. "You might have an hour with the President," Davis explained, "and talk all around the horizon, politics, diplomatic affairs, military, naval or congressional situation, money trust, labor, undesirable citizens, or what not, and yet not get out of it all a word that you could write that day. Then, within a week, something might happen that would be trivial and unimportant to one who had not had such a talk with the President, but which furnished a good story to one who had."[19] Of course in the process Roosevelt's purposes were also served. Since the information passed on represented the truth as he saw it, his sessions with the press helped to shape the version of truth that went out to the public. Both sides benefited by the arrangement: Roosevelt in getting the publicity he wanted, the press in enhancing the quality of its reporting and enjoying the excitement and status gain which closeness to power brings.

Roosevelt had a way of treating reporters close to him as virtually members of his administration. When he traveled he referred to the press contingent as his "Newspaper Cabinet," a status they were delighted to accept. J. Frederick Essary of the *Baltimore Sun* tells of an incident in Chicago when the president went there to address the annual banquet of the Illinois Bar Association which vividly illustrates this close tie. Shortly after the dinner began one of his aides pointed out to him that no settings had been laid out for the newsmen who had accompanied him from Washington, and that they were eating by themselves in a grill below the banquet hall. Roosevelt immediately rose to his feet, announced that since the correspondents belonged to his party he proposed to join them downstairs for dinner, and would return in time for the speeches. To the consternation of his hosts, he thereupon stalked out of the hall. Not until profuse apologies had been made, and a table set up for the press, did Roosevelt agree to return.[20]

This spirit of being in league with journalists colored his entire dealings with the press. It is seen again, for example, in a courtesy he showed while on his periodic speaking tours. Roosevelt, more than any previous president, endeavored to dramatize himself and his program by whistle-stopping across the country to reach the people in their own communities. The presidential train would make several stops a day, sometimes in cities where Roosevelt would be motored to a nearby auditorium for his talk, often in small-sized towns where he spoke from the rear platform of his car to the crowds who came down to the depot to see him.[21] The tours were another indication of Roosevelt's flair for publicity, and much more than a gimmick at a time when presidents lacked any other means to present themselves in person before the public and deliver their message without the filtering effect of the press.[22]

Reporters obviously wanted to go along on these "swings around the circle" because important news came out of them. They were also fun. In long days on the road a camaraderie developed in the press car which took form in boyish exuberances, in-jokes, memories of mishaps down the line, just the male atmosphere of stale cigar smoke and half-finished whiskey bottles. For all the complaints about lack of washing and laundry facilities, about writing stories through numbing fatigue and then worrying where to file them, reporters welcomed the assignment. But it was also exhausting work, and they appreciated Roosevelt's efforts to lighten the burden. The hardest part would have been having to clamber down from the press car at each stop, up to twelve a day, and fight their way through to a good position to hear the president speak, even though they knew he was likely to repeat the same familiar lines he had used dozens of times before. Still, they would have had to check the speech out and then rush back to the press car and prepare to start all over at the next stop.

To simplify this bone-wearying routine, Roosevelt made it a practice regularly to brief the newsmen on the talks coming up, telling them which they could ignore as rehashes of old material and which were worth covering. He sometimes even outlined in rough terms what he intended to say at the important stops so they could start thinking about their stories ahead of time. The briefings had the further advantage of enabling reporters to alert their papers when to expect copy, thus easing the problems of make-up in the home office and assuring that the stories, when filed, would get the best possible display. Charles Thompson had these briefings in mind when he wrote that "of all the candidates I have ever traveled around with on campaign tours, Roosevelt was the most thoughtful and forehanded; he made our work several tons lighter."[23] Of course in the process he also made his own work much easier. The result of helping the press can only have been to win their good-will, which in turn had to influence the tone of their reporting.

This is not to say that Roosevelt accommodated the press entirely out of ulterior motives. He obviously knew what he stood to gain from the friendship of reporters, but the further fact is that he genuinely liked many of them. No one could convincingly sham the affection he demonstrated in years of close association with the press, and certainly not a person like Roosevelt whose emotions were never far from the surface. He happened to be a gregarious individual who enjoyed the company of other gregarious types, particularly those who had something to say. Reporters fit the bill perfectly. Charles Thompson recalled an occasion, for example, when on the last leg of a thirty-day campaign tour in 1912 Roosevelt walked in on the press car as the reporters were having fun mimicking stock phrases from his speeches. With a straight face he strode to the center of the car, raised his finger, and then topped everyone with the best burlesque of all. " 'Comrade, you who wear the [Grand Army] button,' he began, pointing his minatory finger at Colonel Cecil Lyon. Then, exaggerating his own voice and gestures, he tore through the 'social and industrial justice' paragraph, warned us with great intensity about 'the Barneses, the Guggenheims and the Penroses,' and finally, with an expression of anxiety and alarm, he leaned toward Jack Pratt and Lucius Curtis and implored them piteously, 'Children, don't crowd so close to the car; it might back, and'—in his highest falsetto—'we can't afford to lose any little Bull Mooses, you know.' "[24] The newsmen howled through the performance. It was the kind of moment only friends can share.

Just as important, Roosevelt respected the judgment of the reporters in his entourage. He loved to talk politics with them, doling out information but at the same time picking their brains to find out what they had learned. And he didn't mind being contradicted if the reporter knew what he was talking about. On one occasion Roosevelt invited a group of newsmen into his office to tell them about a policy he had decided on regarding the railroads. When he had finished he asked in a perfunctory way what the group thought. To everyone's surprise a young man just recently arrived in Washington, Judson C. Welliver of the *Des Moines Leader,* spoke up and said he thought it was a bad idea, politely explaining why. The reporters held their collective breath as this newcomer in their midst lectured the president of the United States, but Roosevelt was impressed. He invited Welliver to dinner the next evening so they could talk at greater length, and later included him in a commission sent to study transportation problems in Europe. The Iowan joined the inner circle of White House reporters that first afternoon in the Oval Office because he demonstrated he belonged with a group worthy of presidential respect.[25]

One reason why Roosevelt admired reporters, and got along so well with them, was that journalism fascinated him. The parallel in this regard between him and two other presidents who also proved to be highly effective publicists, Franklin Roosevelt and John Kennedy, is interesting. The three men cared about far more than the personal publicity they received. They were also deeply interested in the inner workings of the craft: the office politics, the gossip, the personalities, the techniques in tracking down and writing good stories. Journalism was an avocation for them as much as an instrument of politics. Indeed, they each at some point in their lives tried their hand at newspaper work: Franklin Roosevelt, whose proudest achievement at Harvard was his editorship of the *Crimson;* John Kennedy, whose first job after being discharged from the navy was as a reporter for Hearst's International News Service; and Theodore Roosevelt, who thought seriously about running a New York daily after he left the White House and instead became contributing editor for *Outlook* magazine and later the *Kansas City Star.*[26]

As a journalism buff, Roosevelt took pride in knowing what was going on, and occasionally even liked to show off a bit. In the spring of 1907, when Charles Thompson decided to leave the *New York Times* and accept an offer to head the *New York World*'s Washington bureau, he went directly to the White House to inform Roosevelt of the decision. He dreaded having to tell him. The *World* was Roosevelt's bitterest newspaper critic, and Thompson had every reason to believe that the move meant his days of easy access to the Oval Office were over. He barely had time to get out a greeting before the president launched on a lengthy monologue full of the juicy tidbits he liked to share with friends but would not want an enemy like Pulitzer to hear about. Despite Thompson's embarrassed attempts to cut in, Roosevelt would not be interrupted. He said what was on his mind, and concluded, "of course, what I've been telling you is not exactly in accordance with the view your people on the *World* take. . . ." It had all been a game, but a nice one to assure a friend that nothing between them had changed. Thompson expressed amazement that Roosevelt knew about a move that had just taken place, and added that he had been trying to tell him for the past fifteen minutes. "I knew you had," the president responded with a smile. "As for how I know [about the move], I know those things."[27] He might have added that it was his hobby as well as business to know.

Journalists were obviously flattered by this interest in what they did, and in themselves as people. Isaac Marcosson noticed the trait the first time he met Roosevelt. He had been commissioned to do a story on the president for *The World's Work,* a monthly owned by Walter Hines Page, later to be American ambassador to Great Britain. As soon as he sat down Roosevelt opened the conversation by saying that he had been hearing excellent reports about Page's two sons at Harvard. It is true that the president moved enough in the same social circles as Page to know about the young men, and even that they attended Harvard. To be abreast of their scholastic progress, however, was something else. Still, as Marcosson recognized, "the editor of *The World's Work* would be pleased to know that the President of the United States was interested in his sons and had spoken about them. It was a typical Roosevelt performance."[28]

Even more flattering, if sometimes a nuisance, was Roosevelt's intense interest in what journalists wrote. He read voraciously, as much probably as any president. He also had strong opinions about what he read, which he was constitutionally incapable of keeping to himself. Mark Sullivan, later to become a leading columnist, remembered that his acquaintance with Roosevelt began when he wrote a mildly disapproving editorial for *Collier's Weekly* about one of the president's judicial appointments. He received back an eleven-page typewritten letter in which Roosevelt reviewed all of his appointments to the bench over the past six years and explained the sound reasons supporting each.[29] It was done in the spirit that even a misguided observer deserves having his errors pointed out to him. On the other hand an article that won presidential favor would often inspire a glowing letter of praise, and sometimes even an invitation to drop by and have lunch at the White House. Either way the press had no reason to feel that Roosevelt was not paying attention.

A president like this—concerned about the well-being of the press, accessible to them, candid, friendly, convinced of the importance of what they did—could not help but win an almost worshipful following among the newsmen in his entourage. He was the first chief executive to recognize that American journalism had entered the age of the reporter, and by responding to the change, help to hasten it. That by itself would have been enough to secure him a special place in the memory of journalists. But the Roosevelt phenomenon went much further, because he also turned out to be among the most colorful of all presidents. After years of reticence and starched dignity in the White House, reporters to their immense gratification discovered in Roosevelt almost more material than they could use. It was an intoxicating experience. The excitement in journalism, after all, inheres in having exciting things to write about. A dull administration deadens everything connected with it, not least the job of reporting. The press comes alive only when strong figures are at the helm, and controversial things are happening. In these terms, Roosevelt was an ideal subject. He made the White House hum with activity, and in the process gave the correspondents who covered him the best ongoing story in generations. They probably appreciated that as much as anything else about him.

Part of the reason he sparked excitement was sheer force of personality. "Roosevelt," one critic wrote grudgingly, "has the knack of doing things, and doing them noisily, clamorously; while he is in the neighborhood the public can no more look the other way than the small boy can turn his head away from a circus parade followed by a steam calliope."[30] He took such obvious pleasure in being president, in the clamor and excitement of fighting for good causes, in meeting interesting people and denouncing wicked ones, that the country almost despite itself had to become involved. Certainly nobody quite like him had come along in living memory.

It is interesting Roosevelt had this almost physical impact on contemporaries, because judged in conventional terms he didn't present a particularly impressive figure. His friend, William Allen White, described him as about five feet ten, stocky in build, with torso disproportionately shorter than legs.[31] Because of his extreme near-sightedness—while in the White House he lost vision in his left eye altogether as a result of a blow to the head while sparring with a military aide—he depended on thick lensed glasses which he wore in the pince-nez style popular at the time. White remarked on how mild his grayish blue eyes seemed when he took the glasses off. His other prominent facial characteristic, objects of caricature for a generation of cartoonists, was a gleaming double row of oversized teeth.

Not much in the description suggests a towering presence, and yet the people who met him were almost always impressed. Of course he was a cultist on the subject of physical fitness and kept in superb condition. He also had a reputation for heroics. One did not come into the Roosevelt presence without recognizing the cowboy who had knocked out a bully in a barroom fight, the hero of San Juan Hill, the big game hunter. But the quality that most struck people was the energy that radiated from him, exaggerating his every gesture and response. His eyes, mild when the glasses came off, glittered behind the pince-nez. He spoke in sentences punctuated with exclamation marks. When excited, which was most of the time, his voice rose several pitches to a falsetto. He walked always at a trot, as if trying to make up for five minutes missing in every hour.

He did not enter rooms; he burst in. He did not shake hands; he pumped them. He did not smile; he flashed his teeth and beamed.

So overwhelming was Roosevelt's vitality that he had to contend throughout his political career with gossip about his drinking. It seemed inconceivable that any normal being could maintain the pace he did without the aid of stimulants. Lincoln Steffens remembered an occasion when Roosevelt on his way to a cabinet meeting expressed concern about the rumors on Wall Street that he was habitually drunk, and even took drugs. "Now what should I do about that ?" he asked. "Should I take it up and fight it or should I ignore it?" Steffens offered the sensible advice that Roosevelt should follow his own first rule in such cases: "Never deny anything unless it is true." The president thought that just the right response, and a few minutes later laughingly repeated the line to his cabinet. As Steffens noted wryly, nobody else seemed to be amused.[32]

Most of the time Roosevelt was able to be philosophical about the gossip. "What difference does it make?" he responded when his aide, Archie Butt, commented bitterly on the talk. "Only that which is true is going to last. The people have their own methods of finding out the truth."[33] But it clearly did bother him, as was evident when he raised the subject on his own with two newspaper correspondents, James Creelman and David Barry, and earnestly described his drinking habits to them, saying that he only took an occasional glass of white wine because he found it good for the digestion.[34] The president was telling the truth, and once out of the White House enjoyed public vindication of a sort when he brought successful suit for libel against a Michigan editor who said of him that he "lies and curses in a most disgusting way; he gets drunk, too, and that not infrequently, and all his intimates know about it."[35] They knew no such thing, although they would have been hard put to deny that his behavior did not always accord with what is conventionally taken to be a sober manner.

One way Roosevelt's exuberance manifested itself was in his apparent interest in everything and everybody. No president has ever quite matched his catholicity of taste in friends and interesting people to have as guests in the White House or at Oyster Bay. They included reporters and politicians, of course. But also novelists like Owen Wister, educators like Charles Eliot, historians like James Ford Rhodes, artists like Frederic Remington, even prize-fighters like John L. Sullivan and cowboys from the days back on the ranch. He bubbled over with enthusiasms and almost like a child reached out for others to share them with.

Edward B. Clark, who arrived in Washington in 1904 as correspondent for the *Chicago Evening Post,* noticed the trait when a friend took him to the White House for the first time to meet the president. Roosevelt immediately recognized Clark's name from a monograph the journalist had written ten years before on a southeastern bird with a name "as long as the moral law," the prothonotary warbler. An amateur ornithologist himself, Roosevelt was delighted to meet the author and insisted that Clark come into his office for a chat about their mutual hobby. They spent forty-five minutes closeted together talking about birds.[36] Some time later Clark received an urgent message to come right over to the White House. Assuming that major news was breaking, and that he might even get an exclusive, he alerted the *Evening Post* to save space for a bulletin. When he arrived, Clark was ushered straight in to the president's office. Roosevelt jumped up from his desk, took the reporter by the arm, and hurried him out to the south lawn. It turned out that the reason for urgency, something he could not waste any time sharing with a fellow bird-lover, was to point out a nest of newly hatched owls that had just been discovered.[37]

This kind of constant, high-keyed enthusiasm made Roosevelt easy for reporters to write about. To say that he was colorful is almost an understatement. He was like a force of nature. And all the more interesting a news subject because his combination of personal qualities—caring deeply about everything, strong-minded, headlong in his rush through life—had him constantly embroiled in public squabbles that provided juicy copy for the press. He reveled in controversy, and if major issues were not available to fight about he made do with small ones. Whether the subject was simplified spelling, violence in college football, the evils of divorce, the declining middle-class birth rate, the writers he castigated as "nature fakirs" who imputed human characteristics to animals, he felt strongly on most questions and insisted that everybody else know how he felt. In the process he generally raised such a din that the country pretty well had to pay attention. "Roosevelt's fighting was so much a part of the life of the period," Mark Sullivan wrote, "was so tied up to the newspapers, so geared into popular literature, and even to the pulpit (which already had begun to turn from formal religion toward civic affairs), as to constitute, for the average man, not merely the high spectacle of the Presidency in the ordinary sense, but almost the whole of the passing show, the public's principal interest."[38]

There is another side to the coin, however. To say that the Roosevelt personality fascinated the country is not to minimize the care he took to see that the country remained fascinated. When dealing with exciting public figures it is often difficult to distinguish between the things they do spontaneously that make them special and the acts that are carefully contrived to achieve an effect. This was certainly true of the young president fate had put in the White House. He was a person of extraordinary gusto and enthusiasm who just in being himself made news. The further fact is that publicity was so essential to his style of leadership that he worked constantly to generate it. Roosevelt the news-maker was part natural man and part manipulator. He probably did not know himself where one aspect of his personality ended and the other began, but both are important in understanding his hold on the popular imagination.

The complexity is nicely illustrated by an incident in 1912 during his campaign for reelection on the Bull Moose ticket. On Monday evening, October 14, just as Roosevelt was leaving the Gilpatrick Hotel in Milwaukee to address a political rally, a fanatic, apparently deranged by the threat to the two-term tradition, stepped out of the crowd and put a bullet in the former president's chest. Neither Roosevelt nor his aides realized immediately that he had been hit. Not until the would-be assassin had been overpowered and Roosevelt and his party were in their car on the way to the hall did someone notice that blood was seeping through his overcoat. His aides pleaded that he be rushed immediately to the hospital, but Roosevelt refused. "I will deliver this speech or die, one or the other," he was quoted as saying.[39]

When he reached the hall the scene was one of high drama. The crowd, informed about what had happened, sat rigid with tension as Roosevelt slowly advanced to the podium and in a low, halting voice said, "It's true [that I have been shot]. Friends, I shall have to ask you to be as quiet as possible. I do not know whether you fully understand that I have just been shot, but it takes more than that to kill a Bull Moose. I don't know who the man was who shot me tonight. . . . He shot to kill me. He shot the bullet. I am just going to show you. (Whereupon Roosevelt unbuttoned his jacket and vest and exposed his blood-soaked shirt.) The bullet is in me now, so that I cannot make a very long speech. But I will try my best."[40] And for the next half hour, disregarding pleas that he stop and receive medical treatment, Roosevelt delivered his set speech. At the hospital later an examination revealed that the bullet had entered his right lung. He escaped more serious injury, perhaps death, only because its velocity had been slowed in passing through his overcoat, eyeglass case, and the folded manuscript of the speech.

By any sensible standard he had acted in a bizarre way. Even if the Milwaukee appearance had been a climactic event in the campaign, it would not have been worth the risk in going through with it. As it is, the rally had little significance. But in politics as in other areas of life, things are not always judged on rational grounds. His courage, if it was that, thrilled the country and injected new life into the campaign. A gesture later generations might regard as histrionic or immature struck his contemporaries as inspirational. It was a public relations triumph. Was it also calculated? Did Roosevelt go ahead with the speech only out of impulse, or because he recognized the potential for drama in presenting himself as a soldier wounded in the Progressive cause? Certainly he played on that theme two days later in his bedside statement from Chicago, where he had gone to recuperate. "It matters little about me, but it matters all about the cause we fight for," Roosevelt declared. "If one soldier who happens to carry the flag is stricken another will take it from his hands and carry on. One after another the standard bearers may be laid low, but the standard itself can never fall. . . . Tell the people not to worry about me, for if I go down another will take my place. For always the army is true. Always the cause is there. . . ."[41] Stirring words, and possibly entirely sincere. Sometimes it is impossible to tell with a gifted news-maker where spontaneity leaves off and calculation begins.

But in other instances the fine hand of the public relations expert is inescapable. Roosevelt was constantly alert to ways of getting his name in the papers, and knew all the tricks. He used to laugh, for example, that he had "discovered Monday."[42] The scarcity of news developments on Sundays leaves editors of the Monday editions with more space than they can easily fill. The president took advantage of that fact by timing many of his releases for Sunday evenings. He knew that even minor fare would get much wider play on the front page than he could expect for more important stories at mid-week.

No occasion for publicity was too trivial to pass up. Arthur Dunn of the Associated Press thought the president extremely kind when he delayed signing a Thanksgiving proclamation until Dunn could get a photographer to the White House to record the event. Even nicer, when the photographer arrived Roosevelt interrupted a meeting with the secretary of state so the equipment could be set up and the picture taken. Dunn cited the incident as an example of the president's thoughtfulness to the press, which of course it was.[43] But it is foolish to suppose that he kept Secretary Hay waiting, and put aside whatever matter of state concerned them, just to be a nice fellow. The real interest of the story is in demonstrating Roosevelt's attention to the smallest detail in arranging favorable publicity for himself.

He also knew about the importance of "image" long before Madison Avenue introduced the term to the vocabulary. He had been the butt of some laughter in 1902 when he returned empty-handed from a bear hunt in Mississippi. Apparently particularly sensitive on this subject, he took pains that the laughter was never heard again. When planning his next hunt, to occur in Colorado while on a western tour, he carefully arranged everything ahead of time. "As I understand it you would have five dogs," he wrote to the director of Yellowstone Park. "That number is ample if they are good ones. Could you try them—or at any rate try the two dogs you have on the ground at once and let me know the result? There must be no slip-up if I go hunting at all, and we must be dead sure we get our mountain lion. . . ."[44] Indeed, for appearance's sake he wanted more than just a kill. In orchestrating another hunt in 1905 he explained to a friend that "the first bear must fall to my rifle. This sounds selfish, but you know the kind of talk there will be in the newspapers about such a hunt, and if I go it must be a success, and the success must come to me."[45] Hardly the words of one oblivious to appearances.

This same concern with image helps to explain his uncharacteristic reticence when the Booker T. Washington affair exploded early in his administration. Roosevelt entered office determined to heal the sectional breach caused by the Civil War, and by showing good feelings toward the South to challenge Democratic dominance in the region.[46] As he explained in a talk with Francis Leupp of the *New York Evening Post* four days into his presidency, he intended to be far more responsive to southern problems than previous Republican presidents, and even to appoint southern Democrats to federal positions when qualified members of his own party were not available. As part of the same desire to normalize relations, he hoped to defuse the racial issue by consulting with responsible black leaders in formulating his policies. The most obvious such person in his view was Booker T. Washington, the respected head of Tuskegee Institute and, since the publication of *Up From Slavery* earlier that year, a figure of international renown. On September 14, 1901, the day he took the oath of office, Roosevelt wrote to Washington inviting him to come to the White House to discuss appointments. They met later in the month, and on October 7 Roosevelt acted on Washington's recommendation by naming Thomas Goode Jones, a conservative Alabama Democrat, former governor, and ex-Confederate, as United States District Court judge. The appointment won warm praise in the South.

Under the circumstances it did not occur to Roosevelt that he was doing anything controversial when he asked Washington to return to the capital for another meeting on October 16. When the educator arrived in the city this time he found waiting for him an invitation to dine at the White House. Washington accepted, and spent an apparently pleasant evening with the president and members of his family discussing matters pertaining to the South.[47] Afterward he took a night train to New York City.

Washington, the soul of discretion, had come into town and left unobtrusively, telling no one about the dinner engagement. The news filtered out when a correspondent for the *Washington Post* picked up his name on the daily list of White House guests and filed a routine report. Evidently neither he nor his editor realized who was involved, because the one sentence story that "Booker T. Washington of Tuskegee, Ala., dined with the President last evening" was buried on the bottom of an inside page.[48] When capital correspondents for southern papers spotted the item that day, however, they immediately recognized its significance. Their dispatches, which appeared in flaming headlines throughout the South on

October 18, brought down on Roosevelt some of the most savage criticism of his presidency.

The gist of the attack was that in sitting at the same dinner table with a black man, the president by implication had affirmed the social equality of the races. From this it followed that Roosevelt in effect countenanced black men making approaches to white women, even miscegenation (a strange assumption in view of Roosevelt's own racial views). "We do not believe that the people of the North are prepared to accept that doctrine and to put it into practice," the *Richmond Times* declared in one of the relatively moderate editorials; "as for the people of the South, they will not tolerate it, and they have nothing but contempt for any man who advocates social equality and miscegenation. This is not a question of racial prejudice, it is a question of racial instinct, which can be trusted when the strongest individual intellects are at fault."[49] Roosevelt's deed was not only an insult to every white southern man and woman, it threatened serious consequences by putting unacceptable ideas into the heads of blacks. "The action of the President in entertaining that nigger," Senator "Pitchfork Ben" Tillman of South Carolina is said to have warned, "will necessitate our killing a thousand niggers in the South before they will learn their place again."[50]

Roosevelt, who spoke his mind freely when it came to nature-fakirs or reformed spelling, was notably restrained in the face of this kind of provocation. It is true that he demonstrated a characteristic truculence in his private correspondence. "As far as I am personally concerned I regard their attacks with the most contemptuous indifference," he wrote to a congressman friend from New York. "There are certain points where I would not swerve from my views if the entire people was a unit against me, and this is one of them. I would not lose my self-respect by fearing to have a man like Booker T. Washington to dinner if it cost me every political friend I have got."[51] He was even more defiant in a letter to the editor of the *Boston Commercial Bulletin*. "I am sorry to say that the idiot or vicious Bourbon element of the South is crazy because I have had Booker T. Washington to dine. I shall have him to dine just as often as I please, exactly as I should have Eliot or Hadley."[52] Still, the interesting thing is that he said nothing in public, preferring to lie low as the storm raged about him. The failure to justify his action, to use the opportunity to speak out on tolerance, was not for want of allies. By and large northern papers found the campaign against him overblown and were responding with some of the things he might have said on his own behalf. One of the strongest rebuttals came from the *New York World*, which editorialized: "In eating with [Washington] the President is charged with having insulted the South. This man may cast a ballot but he may not break bread. . . . He may preach our Gospel, but not be our guest. . . ; die for us, but not dine with us. Truly liberty must smile at such broad-minded logic, such enlightened tolerance. Or should she weep?[53]

Roosevelt had his own reasons for avoiding such rhetoric, or any like it. As one who courted popularity, he realized that he had committed a serious blunder by venturing into an area where emotions were so intense, particularly if he hoped to make inroads for his party into the South. Under the circumstances good public relations inhered in knowing when to retreat. Any attempt to justify the dinner would only have impressed the people who saw nothing wrong in what he had done, while compounding his offense in the eyes of southerners and those who thought like them. By doing or saying nothing the storm would eventually blow over at minimal cost to himself. He chose the least heroic, but given racial attitudes in 1901, also the safest course.

There are some indications that he even tried to minimize the damage in private conversations by giving distorted versions of what happened. In his account of the episode, Mark Sullivan devoted a long footnote to detailing the conflicting versions of whether Washington had lunch or dinner at the White House, and whether he was actually invited ahead of time or asked to stay out of politeness because the meal had been served.[54] If the various authors are to be believed, the confusion came about because Roosevelt told different things to different people.[55] It was an unnecessary confusion, however, since Washington's formal acceptance of the dinner invitation appears in the Roosevelt papers. The major interest in Sullivan's footnote (a moral he did not draw himself), is in suggesting that the president was not above a bit of prevarication in protecting his public image. Certainly he never committed the same mistake again by inviting Washington or any other black to dine at the White House. Nor did he so much as mention the incident when writing his autobiography.

Roosevelt's skills as an image-maker were apparent again in the way he made news by finding innovative or unusual things to do. To a remarkable extent, many of the tricks subsequent presidents used to dramatize themselves they borrowed from him. In 1932, for example, when airplanes were still at a relatively early stage of development, Franklin Roosevelt excited his party and the nation by flying through a rain storm to Chicago to accept the Democratic nomination. It was a shrewd way to play down the importance of his paralysis and to suggest a capacity for bold, forceful leadership at a time when the country was gripped by depression. Still, the method of conveying a message about leadership is reminiscent of what Theodore Roosevelt did twenty-seven years before, in August 1905, when he descended to the bottom of Long Island Sound in a naval submarine, a type of vessel that had been in commission for only five years. He stayed down for three hours, much of the time handling the controls himself as the boat was put through its maneuvers. "I believe a good deal can be done with these submarines," Roosevelt wrote later to his friend, the German ambassador, "although there is always the danger of people getting carried away with the idea and thinking that they could be of more use than they possibly could be."[56]

In 1918, after the Germans had gotten carried away, another artful publicist dramatized his commitment to the Fourteen Points by going in person to Europe to negotiate the treaty ending World War I. Woodrow Wilson scored at least a temporary public relations gain thereby, but in doing so he again took a leaf from Roosevelt's book. Twelve years earlier, in November 1906, the president generated publicity for himself and for what he regarded as the great accomplishment of his administration, by traveling with Mrs. Roosevelt on the battleship *Louisiana* to Panama, and spending three days there observing progress in building the canal (characteristically, he took the opportunity to operate personally a steam shovel). The trip received all the more newspaper attention because he was the first chief executive to leave the continental limits of the United States while in office.

In the case of John Kennedy, the public relations gimmick represented almost a direct steal of an earlier idea. As part of the image of vitality associated with the New Frontier, he proposed in early 1963 that members of his administration stay in shape by embarking on fifty-mile hikes. Not many people recalled at the time that Theodore Roosevelt, who also had thoughts about the strenuous life and generating news, had tried the same thing more than half a century before. Concerned about the physical condition of senior army and navy officers, he issued an executive order late in his administration requiring that they take a fitness test by riding ninety miles on horseback in three days. The order could have been expected to cause unhappiness in military circles, but when voices in Congress and the press questioned its wisdom Roosevelt saw the chance to reap a publicity advantage. As commander-in-chief he would lead by example. With three companions he set out from the White House on horseback one morning at 3:30 A.M. and rode to Warrenton, Virginia, had lunch, and then rode back, arriving through a blizzard at 8:30 P.M. He had gone ninety-eight miles in seventeen hours, proving that what he asked of the military was not unreasonable. More to the point, at the expense of a few stiff muscles he had given another lesson in how to win favorable publicity.[57]

Of course presidents are not expected to be athletes, nor is it always necessary to do something physical to win public attention. Words are often the most effective instrument for self-dramatization. The presidents who have succeeded as publicists all used them well, and indeed, are remembered far more for things they said than for the tricks in public

relations they tried. The point holds for Theodore Roosevelt as much as
for any of the others, despite his being probably the most active person
to hold the office. He had a rare skill for finding the pungent phrase that
brought an idea to life and made him custodian of it. The list is remarkable.
"Speak softly and carry a big stick," he said of his foreign policy. The
industrialists who bilked the nation for selfish gain were "malefactors of
great wealth." He offered the American people a "square deal," the
precursor of other deals "new" and "fair." Writers like Thomas Lawson
and David Graham Phillips who abused the literature of exposure with
sensationalism and inaccuracies were "muckrakers." Roosevelt spoke of
the "trustbusters," of the "strenuous life," of "Goo-Goos," of the "lu-
natic fringe." And when he decided to run for president in 1912, he announced: "My hat is in the ring." Words like these had punch. They
probably particularly impressed reporters, who recognized the president's
skill in handling their own stock in trade.

His gift for the vivid phrase in turn had a bearing on the acceptance
during the Roosevelt years of political cartoons as a form of journalistic
expression. The genre as such was certainly not new, having a history
almost as long as the American newspaper and preceding by decades the
appearance of the first dailies. With the development of photoengraving
in the 1870s, allowing cheaper and more timely cartoons than when they
had to be hand-crafted from wooden blocks, they started to appear much
more frequently in the press. In the 1884 presidential campaign, for example, Joseph Pulitzer's *New York World* used the device to devastating
effect against James G. Blaine. The paper ran twenty-seven front page
cartoons between August 10 and Election Day, culminating on October
30 with the famous "Feast of Belshazzar" drawing that filled the entire
top half of the page with its commentary on Blaine's ill-advised dinner
the night before with New York City's moneyed elite.[58] But into the 1890s
pictures in the paper still seemed faintly disreputable, like the rouge distinguishing a painted woman from a lady. Certainly journalists agonized
over their use. According to *Harper's Weekly* in 1893, "The question of
'cuts' in the columns of the daily newspaper, if not exactly a burning one,
excites more animated comment than many of more importance."[59]

By the next decade it was no question at all. Much of the reason was
the appearance of a president whose style made him a natural subject for
cartoonists. There was something about him—the color, the frenetic quality, the sense of being larger than life—that only a cartoon could capture.
An art form that makes its statements through exaggeration is necessarily
at a disadvantage when dealing with dull public figures, because color-
lessness magnified is still colorless. But Roosevelt, in many respects a
caricature to begin with, seemed to leap out from the drawing board. All
the more because he was so easy to draw. The large, flashing teeth, the

thick-lensed glasses, the drooping mustache were ideal for caricature. So were the costumes associated with him in his various roles: the cowboy suit, the safari jacket, the Rough Riders uniform.

Above all, Roosevelt simplified the cartoonist's task by the words he used. Charles Macauley of the *New York World* was probably the first to adopt the "Big Stick" as a symbol, but literally hundreds of cartoons played on the theme.[60] "He started a house-cleaning in one government department or another," Mark Sullivan wrote, "and the press flowered with pictures of Roosevelt as the 'Old Dutch Cleanser,' his strenuous broom an adaptation of the 'big stick.' He announced his mediation between Japan and Russia, and the mace with which he conducted the peace conference was the 'big stick' not too completely concealed by festooned olive-branches—suggesting that any divagation by Roosevelt into pursuit of peace was merely a temporary departure from his native, permanent, and preferred function of hitting heads."[61] And as soon as one theme played out another came along to replace it. The hat in the ring, the muckrakers, the statement about feeling like a bull moose, all offered obvious possibilities for treatment. He was, John T. McCutcheon wrote in the *New York Evening Post* just days after Roosevelt left office, "an inexhaustible Golconda of inspiration for the cartoonist."[62]

One indication of Roosevelt's impact on political cartooning is the extent to which the top artists of the period did their best-known work in drawing him. Homer Davenport's cartoon of Uncle Sam with his hand on Roosevelt's shoulder saying, "After all is said and done, he's still Good Enough for Me," is an example.[63] During the 1904 election the Republican Party is reputed to have spent $200,000 on campaign posters of the drawing after it originally appeared in the *New York Evening Mail*.[64] Of Jay Darling's many famous cartoons, perhaps the most memorable appeared in the *Des Moines Register* in January 1919 at the time of Roosevelt's death. It showed the former president in cowboy garb turning around and waving his hat as his horse carried him off on the long trail up into the sky. The examples go on and on: Joseph Keppler's depiction in *Puck* of Roosevelt playing Miles Standish to Taft's John Alden before a demure Uncle Sam dressed as Priscilla; Clifford Berryman's humorous treatment in the *Washington Post* of Roosevelt on his Mississippi hunt refusing to shoot a bear cub; John McCutcheon's six frame account in the *Chicago Tribune* of the president "resting" at Oyster Bay.

Although Roosevelt never commented on the subject, it would be surprising if he did not recognize the unique publicity he received from cartoons. It is not simply that they reached the illiterate and semiliterate masses who could not cross the barrier of language, although that was no small consideration at a time of heavy immigration when the high school diploma was still the exception for all Americans. Pictures had an impact greater than words on the population at large, as of course they do to this day. More than keeping Roosevelt in the public eye, the generally favorable cartoon treatment he received served to humanize him. He became somebody all Americans knew because they looked at his likeness each day in their newspapers. Cause and effect in this area is tricky, but one wonders if it is altogether a coincidence that the president who inspired so many cartoons about himself was also the one to be treated with unparalleled familiarity by the people. He was the first chief executive, for example, to be known by his initials. Although family and friends addressed him as Theodore, the public commonly spoke of him as Teddy (a nickname he detested). And from that nickname came the phenomenon of the Teddy Bear, inspired by an incident on his disappointing Mississippi hunt in 1902. When a stray cub was brought into camp one day, Roosevelt ordered that the animal not be harmed and later had it turned loose. Clifford Berryman's cartoon in the *Washington Post* entitled "Drawing the Line in Mississippi" attracted wide attention to the incident.[65] The marketing of the Teddy Bear followed shortly thereafter. A big game hunter might seem an inappropriate candidate to lend his name to such a toy, but the more compelling fact was that the people felt they knew Teddy, and his fun-loving qualities somehow suited him to be associated with a stuffed animal that children could cuddle.

In a way that seems in retrospect almost unfair, Roosevelt—who enjoyed so many other advantages in generating publicity—also had a lively family working for him. Never before had the White House been occupied by so many, so young, and so untamed a set of children. There were six of them, ranging in age from Alice, the president's daughter by his first marriage, who was seventeen at the time of McKinley's assassination, to Quentin, a baby of three.[66] Their escapades kept the country enthralled and ensured that even on slow days the Roosevelt name would still be featured prominently in the press.

Roosevelt certainly did not try to exploit the news value of his children. Like other presidents who have had to contend with obsessive public curiosity about their private lives, he tried to shield them as much as possible from inquisitive newsmen. The children had strict instructions not to speak with reporters, and photographers were expected to keep their distance unless formal picture-taking sessions had been arranged. "Amazing as it may seem," Alice wrote in later years, " 'publicity' for the members of a politician's family was not considered either necessary or 'nice.' The idea of their talking for publication was beyond the wildest flight of fancy, and photographs appeared but rarely in the newspapers.[67] Roosevelt urged the press to cooperate with him by leaving the children alone. "I want to feel that there is a circle drawn about my family," he said to reporters early in his first term. "I ask you to respect their privacy."[68]

Modern journalism being what it is, he was asking for too much. As long as the country hungered for personal details about its "first family," reporters would oblige. One of the bad times for Roosevelt came in fall 1905 when his eldest son, Theodore, Jr., enrolled at Harvard as an eighteen-year-old freshman. The press hounded the young man: intruding into his social activities, observing him on the playing fields, monitoring his grades. Roosevelt wrote in despair to President Eliot asking if something could not be done to protect his son. "I have been really concerned by the . . . outrageous conduct of the newspapers in reference to Ted," he declared. "This crass, hideous vulgarity is not merely extremely distasteful, but may have a damaging effect upon poor Ted, at least in his relation to the other boys, and in the very improbable event of your having any advice to give, I should be glad to get it."[69]

Of course there was little Eliot could do, and Roosevelt had to advise his son to make the best of the situation. The letter he wrote to Theodore is an almost poignant example of parental concern, and in this instance is reminiscent of Cleveland in its resentment of prying journalism. "You have been having an infernal time through these cursed newspapers," the president said. "The thing to do is to go on just as you have evidently been doing, attract as little attention as possible, do not make a fuss about the newspapermen, camera creatures, and idiots generally, letting it be seen that you do not like them and avoid them, but not letting them betray you into any excessive irritation. I believe they will soon drop you, and it is just an unpleasant thing that you will have to live down. . . . This is just an occasion to show the stuff there is in you."[70]

It is easy to appreciate the father's concern, although in fairness the other thing to say is that the children brought much of the publicity upon themselves. Perhaps because of the crushing blow of his first wife's death, Roosevelt was a doting parent who allowed the children wide scope in amusing themselves. They responded with a level of exuberance tolerated in few youngsters their age; a level certainly not expected in the White House. Inevitably, enough tales of the high jinks filtered out to generate rich newspaper copy. Irwin "Ike" Hoover, who served for decades as major-domo in the White House, remembered the Roosevelt years as a time of misery for employees who took their responsibilities too seriously or regarded the executive mansion as hallowed ground. The children, along with other youngsters they recruited, were into every recess of the building, and no room was so ornate that it could not serve as a playground. They rollerskated and rode bicycles and walked on stilts down the long hallway on the second floor; they popped out of vases and linen closets during uproarious games of hide-and-seek; they refreshed themselves with quick dips in the White House fountain, trailing puddles of water back into the house; they deposited pet rodents and snakes in the historic furniture on the upper floors, and made darting raids in their night clothes on the hors d'oeuvres when guests were being received. A favorite pastime was crawling through the air space between the floors and ceilings, an area that in the history of the White House had been known only to rats and ferrets, and making the building echo to the howls of laughter coming through the beams. On one occasion they even brought their spotted Shetland pony, Algonquin, up two floors from the basement level on the elevator to visit in Archie's room.[71] "Nothing was too sacred to be used for their amusement," Hoover wrote somewhat acidly, "and no place too good for a playroom. The children seemed to be encouraged in these ideas by their elders, and it was a brave man indeed who would dare say no or suggest putting a stop to their escapades."[72]

Alice was easily the most prolific of the news-makers, if only because at her age it was difficult to conceal her escapades from public view. As the first teenage girl in the White House since Nellie Grant, she would have attracted attention whatever her personality. The fact that she took after her father in so many respects made the attention almost obsessive. Impulsive, unconventional, boundlessly energetic, she pursued pleasure with the same abandon Roosevelt demonstrated in his activities, and in the process kept the newspaper-reading public enthralled. "Truth compels me to state," she wrote in her autobiography, "that my major preoccupation was 'to have a good time,' and a good time meant to me consorting with people of my own age, total irresponsibility, and perpetual rushing from place to place. . . . No young person could ever be more frivolous and inane, more scattered and self-centered than I was."[73]

Certainly Alice lived by her own law. For one thing, she smoked, a most unladylike habit at that time. She also tended to get into the sort of adventures not usually associated with a president's daughter. One such occasion, which provided good press copy, was a high-speed automobile ride she and another young woman made "without chaperone" from Newport to Boston. When he read the accounts her father wrote her a letter that "scorched the paper on which it was written."[74] Not that the rebuke slowed her down perceptibly. "Why don't you look after Alice more?" a friend once asked Roosevelt. "Listen," he responded. "I can be President of the United States—or—I can attend to Alice."[75] And since he couldn't do both, she went her merry way, with reporters often in tow. "My 'publicity value' was, I fear, at times a trial to the family," Alice remarked uncontritely in her autobiography.[76]

The further fact, however, is that nothing in public reaction on reading about her happy-go-lucky romp through life would have encouraged her to be contrite. To the press she was "Princess Alice," a title that summed up the popular view. It says something about the young woman's popularity that a shade of blue was named for her, which later inspired a hit song about an "Alice Blue Gown." Publicity had elevated her into a kind of royalty. In place of "God Save the Queen," she could scarcely make a public appearance during the White House years without being serenaded to the tune, "Alice, Where Art Thou?" "It was amusing when it first happened," she recalled, "but the novelty soon wore off and I developed a pretty fair technique, that conveyed amusement, surprise, and appreciation at the combination of attention and jest. The nice people who did it were always so pleased that they had thought of it."[77]

Something extremely important in American life was happening. When public attention focuses so intently on a president's family—follows their everyday activities, soaks up gossip about them, makes judgments about what they are each like—the office ceases to be simply political and takes on symbolic characteristics as well. The concept "first family" is one of the ways the presidency is different from any other office in the land. Senators may have enormous influence, but they are after all still only politicians. A president is like a monarch, and for reasons that have at least as much to do with the way the country regards him as the power he wields. By concentrating so closely on his private life, including his family, the public makes him more than he is constitutionally. A republic is supposed to find its symbols of nationhood in inanimate objects like the flag and ritual gestures like the Pledge of Allegiance. Intense publicity elevates the presidency into a living symbol.

The importance of the Roosevelt years is not that the process began then, but that modern journalism together with a newsworthy family elevated it to a new dimension. Many reasons explain why power has flowed to the White House in the twentieth century. Among them, if not the most important then certainly worth recognizing, is the personalization and glorification of the presidency involved in this heightened concept of first family. In a sense, Roosevelt's lively brood did more than help him dominate the news; by being newsworthy they contributed in their own way to changing the nature of the office he filled.

Roosevelt, as he remarked in one of his glittering phrases, had discovered a "bully pulpit" in the White House. He stood at center stage, commanding the attention of the country and able to generate publicity at will. The headlines meant power, because they made him the dominant presence in American life. But it was not enough just to be a news-maker. Roosevelt's further insight, and a key to understanding his style of leadership, was that the way information got out—both the method of release and the timing—mattered almost as much in some cases as the information itself. Properly manipulated, news could be a means to make things happen or prevent them from happening. It could be an instrument of control: one of the unofficial tools available to a president to go along with his formal constitutional powers. Roosevelt established many of the conventions of the modern presidential-press relationship in acting on that realization.

1. Theodore Roosevelt began the practice of holding daily meetings with the press while he was governor of New York. Here he meets with Albany correspondents in May 1899, a few months into his administration. (Culver Pictures)

2

DRAWING
THE LINE
IN MISSISSIPPI

3

2. The Roosevelts at Sagamore Hill in 1903. Seated, from the left: Theodore, Archie, Edith, Quentin. Standing: Ethel, Ted, Alice, Kermit. (Wide World Photos, © Pach Bros.)

3. Clifford K. Berryman's cartoon in the *Washington Post* on November 16, 1902 introduced one of the popular symbols associated with Roosevelt and provided inspiration for the phenomenon of the Teddy Bear. (Wide World Photos)

4. Archie and Quentin Roosevelt join the 8:00 A.M. police lineup at the White House in 1902, in the sort of escapade that generated rich publicity for the Roosevelt administration. Security measures to protect the first family had been tightened considerably after McKinley's assassination. (Culver Pictures)

5

5. As the face suggests, William Loeb could be steely when it came to enforcing his chief's directives. (World's Work, December 1909)

6. Berryman welcomes Roosevelt back to Washington after the president's three-month stay in Oyster Bay during the summer of 1908. Roosevelt's lapel button attests to a political campaign in progress. Loeb is on hand to help with the luggage, while behind them the by now ubiquitous "little bear" brings up the rear. (Courtesy William Loeb)

7. Roosevelt holding forth with characteristic verve, and below him a contingent of reporters on hand to relay his words to the country. (The Bettmann Archives)

10

"GOODNESS GRACIOUS! I MUST HAVE BEEN DOZING!"

8. Archibald Butt, military attaché and friend to two presidents, tried without success to improve Taft's public image. (Library of Congress)

9. Neither girth nor adverse publicity ever kept Taft from his appointed rounds. (Culver Pictures)

10. Joseph Keppler, Jr. depicts Taft awakening from a nap to find cats labeled "The House," "The Cabinet," and "The Courts" wreaking havoc with his predecessor's "My Policies" ball of yarn. Roosevelt, who has just returned from an extended overseas tour, is clearly not pleased. (Puck, June 22, 1910)

11. Wilson addresses 1,500 supporters in August 1912 at Sea Girt, New Jersey, the official governor's residence. His speech, attacking the boss system, attracted considerable attention and provided important momentum for his campaign. Members of the press covering the event are on the platform with him, just out of view to his left. (The Bettmann Archives)

12. The Wilsons gather in 1912 for a family portrait: from left to right Margaret, Ellen, Eleanor, Jessie, and the Democratic presidential candidate. (Library of Congress)

13   14

15

13. Colonel Edward House pauses for the photographer in late December 1915 prior to departing for Europe on another of his diplomatic missions for President Wilson. (Culver Pictures)

14. A dapper Joseph Tumulty poses in September 1916 on the steps of Shadow Lawn, the rambling seaside mansion near Long Beach, New Jersey that Wilson used as his reelection campaign headquarters. Two months later the secretary would be asked to resign. (Culver Pictures)

15. The president with Edith Galt Wilson on a campaign visit to Cincinnati in October 1916. They had been married ten months at the time. (The Bettmann Archive)

16

17

16. George Creel already looked harried shortly after taking over as director of the Committee on Public Information. (World's Work, June, 1917)

17. Ray Stannard Baker parted company with one Progressive president over the matter of muckraking, and served another as press attaché at the Paris Peace Conference. (Culver Pictures)

18. Herbert Bayard Swope of the *New York World* led the American press contingent in protesting the restricted access to news at the Paris Peace Conference. (The Bettmann Archive)

18

3

The Uses of News

Theodore Roosevelt revealed more than he perhaps intended about presidential use of the news in a brief exchange he had with a reporter while appearing at the Republican National Convention in Chicago in June 1912 to contest the renomination of his former friend and now political rival, William Howard Taft. He had arranged a reception for the press, and as the correspondents filed by to shake hands Roosevelt singled one out for special attention. He grasped George E. Miller of the *Detroit News* by the shoulder and said warmly, "I never was able to fool this old fellow."[1] Everyone in the line smiled, some ruefully, at the memories he evoked. He had reminded them how the presidential-press relationship worked during the Roosevelt years. The daily quota of information from the White House was not always ladled out to the press in equal and open portions. News surfaced in different ways to serve different purposes. The trick for Roosevelt during those years was in deciding on the most effective method of release in various situations, and for reporters in getting as much information as they could without in the process being exploited by the president.

The compliment to Miller had to do with the fact that Roosevelt had found him a hard man to fool with one of his pet devices, the trial balloon. This is a disclosure about a proposed action given on a background basis, nowadays usually to columnists, to test public reaction. If the response is good the proposal becomes policy, and the reporter used to float the story gains status for his inside contacts. A negative response brings a denial. By their nature, trial balloons are difficult to identify. An advance announcement that is later confirmed by events is usually just accurate information. The story denied, and not subsequently borne out by events, is usually just misinformation. Somewhere in both categories are trial balloons successfully floated or shot down, but often the reporter himself cannot be sure when he has been used to hold the string. Still, the technique is useful as a way for a president to test the political currents without exposing himself.

The press dreaded Roosevelt's free use of the device. It was not simply that he routinely denied things he had told reporters when the resulting dispatches turned out to be inconvenient. If necessary, he would denounce the authors of the articles as liars and frauds, and consign them to the Ananias Club. About the only thing reporters could do in such cases was plead their innocence. Some newsmen made it a point never to see Roosevelt alone, but that was hardly a way to win exclusives.[2] The best protection for an enterprising journalist was to rely on experience and instinct to detect when a balloon was going up. Roosevelt seemed to regard it all as a game. If the reporter refused to be taken in, all the more credit to him. As for the others he could fool, they just had to take the consequences.

Another Roosevelt technique was blanketing the news. He understood that presidents, by being able to command publicity for themselves, can also deny it to others. If they wish to keep a rival off the front page, or at least minimize his coverage, all they have to do is give out so much news on a given day that the press is hard put to handle the flow. Since presidents always have priority, the rival is squeezed into whatever space remains.

This is what Roosevelt did to Charles Evans Hughes in 1908 when the New York governor made his move for the Republican presidential nomination. The president at one time had enjoyed a good working relationship with Hughes and might even have favored him as a successor. A cooling had occurred between them, however, and now Roosevelt was firmly committed to Taft. When Hughes announced that he would address the New York Republican Club on January 31, 1908 to outline his views on national issues, the speech was immediately recognized as launching his campaign for the White House. Obviously such an appearance by the governor of a major state and a front-running candidate for his party's presidential nomination warranted lead treatment in the press.

Roosevelt decided to steal Hughes's headlines by timing the release of a special message to Congress for the evening of the speech, and spreading word among correspondents that what he had to say would be of major news interest. It was essential that he arrange things carefully to be sure that the competing stories appeared in the same editions of newspapers. The advance copies of the message went out to the wire services under the restriction that nothing could be released until the message had been physically delivered to Congress and read in one House or the other. Reporters waiting in the Senate press gallery on the afternoon of January 31 for what they knew would be a sensation watched impatiently as the hours passed with no word from the White House. It got to be 5:00 P.M., past the deadline for all eastern afternoon papers, and still nothing had been heard. Almost another hour passed, and the midwestern papers had gone to press. Finally, shortly before 6:00 P.M., with those not privy to what was going on wondering why adjournment had not been called, the Sergeant-at-Arms announced, "A message from the President of the United States."[3]

The assembled company quickly forgot its restlessness and listened intently as the clerk read Roosevelt's words, only an hour or two before Hughes was scheduled to speak in New York City. The president called upon Congress to enact legislation he regarded as long overdue: workmen's compensation for federal employees, regulation of the abuse of the injunction in labor disputes, federal protection for union members. His bombshell, however, was a scathing, and coming from a president, all but unprecedented attack on leaders of the business community. He blamed them rather than the administration for the panic that had started the previous year, in effect saying they deserved the losses they had suffered. "The 'business' which is hurt by the movement for honesty," Roosevelt thundered, "is the kind of business which, in the long run, it pays the country to have hurt. It is the kind of business which had tended to make the very name 'high finance' a term of scandal to which all honest American men of business should join in putting an end."[4]

This was strong stuff, and left no doubts as to the competitive merits of the Roosevelt and Hughes stories. As the *New York Times* headlined its account:

MESSAGE DAZES
PARTY LEADERS

MEANT TO DWARF HUGHES[5]

And dwarf Hughes it did. On Saturday morning, February 1, the message filled the front pages of newspapers. The space devoted to the Hughes speech had to be drastically curtailed. In many cases, particularly outside New York City, the governor was driven off the front pages altogether. He had been taught what must have been a painful lesson in the art of blanketing. Roosevelt's enemies accused him of political opportunism, but as the president remarked blandly to reporters on the Sunday following, "If Hughes is going to play the game, he must learn the tricks."[6]

Roosevelt knew them all. Another of his favorite devices was the leak, a method of publicity by which the story is released to a trusted reporter on the understanding that the source's identity will not be revealed. It took a Theodore Roosevelt to recognize that under certain circumstances a technique conventionally associated with underlings trying to influence policy could also work for a president. For instance, he might have information to dispense which if made public will help him achieve an objective, but at the same time will antagonize a group he depends on for support. By leaking it he protects himself from political retribution. Or perhaps he might feel the information will seem partisan or self-serving coming from his lips. A leak can be a way to have the news appear in the papers as a disinterested statement of fact, and likely to be all the more prominently featured since journalists are not typically modest about their exclusives. Roosevelt even appreciated the nuances in choosing the recipients of leaks. All things being equal, he preferred the stories to appear in opposition newspapers because the gambit was less transparent that way.[7] When Charles Thompson, a trusted reporter, left the *New York Times* to take charge of the *New York World*'s Washington bureau, the move did not come as a complete disappointment to Roosevelt. The *World*'s opposition to him had its own uses.

A good example of Roosevelt using a leak for political gain occurred in early 1903 when he fought to push through Congress a series of antitrust measures. Most of the proposals were routine. The railroads themselves wanted a bill, which eventually became the Elkins Act, forbidding discriminatory rebates in interstate commerce. There was no reason to oppose a measure expediting circuit court action on antitrust cases. Even the idea of a Department of Commerce and Labor suited congressional conservatives, assuming that its main function would be the harmless one of collecting and distributing data on business conditions. The point of controversy was Roosevelt's further suggestion that a Bureau of Corporations be formed within the Department empowered to solicit annual reports from corporations and to conduct its own investigations. The purpose, of course, was to assist the Department of Justice in bringing suits under the Sherman Antitrust Act. Here the old guard balked. They felt Roosevelt had already gone too far with the Northern Securities and Beef Trust prosecutions of the previous year. With the proposed bill he would be altogether out of control.

Roosevelt faced a delicate political situation that January. He had committed himself to pursuing an antitrust policy of a sort, and could not afford to back down now in the face of opposition. On the other hand, neither could he afford to tear the party apart on the issue. It was a nice question whether he had the support to push the measure through against the opposition of Senator Nelson Aldrich of Rhode Island, the majority leader and chief spokesman against him. Even if he did, a close vote would represent a Pyrrhic victory at best. Roosevelt had to think ahead to his nomination in 1904. His unpopularity with the conservative wing of the party, and Hanna's availability, were already problems. A blood-letting on the Bureau of Corporations would make things many times worse. Roosevelt told reporters that he would call the Fifty-Seventh Congress back in special session if it recessed in March without acting on the bill, but it must have been the last thing he wanted to do.

He solved the problem by leaking information that he knew would break the impasse. Roosevelt learned in early February that John D. Archbold, a vice-president of Standard Oil, had sent telegrams to several senators urging them to stand fast against the bill. According to David Barry of the *New York Sun,* he heard about the lobbying when Senator Stephen Elkins of West Virginia, chairman of the Committee on Interstate Commerce, showed him the telegram he had received.[8] The president immediately recognized the opportunity that had been opened to him. Speaking individually with a few trusted reporters, he told them on a nonattribution basis that Standard Oil was working behind the scenes to block antitrust legislation. According to Roosevelt's version, Rockefeller had personally contacted six senators with a message that read in essence, "We are opposed to any anti-trust legislation. Our counsel . . . will see you. It must be stopped."[9]

The news caused a sensation. Reasonable men could disagree on the merits of a Bureau of Corporations, but the idea of Rockefeller throwing his weight around was an altogether different matter. It didn't make any difference that over the next few days no evidence to support the allegation was forthcoming. Under the circumstances Congress had to act. On February 10 the House of Representatives, anxious to demonstrate its independence of Rockefeller control, passed the measure in the form Roosevelt wanted by a vote of 251 to 10. The Senate acted just as decisively the following day. The president could not have asked for a happier resolution to the disagreement.

Almost certainly he had played a devious game. It is difficult to believe that he so misunderstood the telegram Elkins showed him as to confuse a message from a Standard Oil executive with one from Rockefeller himself. The two versions may have been the same in their final import, but at the very least he had embellished the truth for dramatic effect. Certainly it was more difficult to ask why an interested party should not have the right to communicate his views to law makers when the name was Rockefeller rather than Archbold.[10] Roosevelt's liberties were not taken seriously, however, since the leak had won public opinion solidly to his side. It didn't even matter that during the commotion his name surfaced as the source of the story. The important thing was that he had succeeded in using news as a weapon to get the law he wanted.

Backgrounders are another device to manipulate the news, and one Roosevelt used often. They come in various forms, but all involve sessions in which public officials speak with reporters on issues of the day on the understanding that their remarks will not be attributed directly to them. If the president is the source, for example, a euphemism like "White House spokesman" might be used. In some cases, as with "deep background," the understanding is that there will be no attribution at all (which makes the backgrounder much like a leak, only a collective one in that the information is released to several reporters at once). The arrangement can easily be abused by officials who say nothing so remarkable that they should not be held publicly accountable for their words. There is also something absurd about backgrounders when, as often happens, everyone knows the source of the story except the newspaper reader. In politics, as in other areas of life, a transparent veil is provocative more than discreet. Still, these sessions can be a useful way to get out information that might otherwise be awkward to impart. The point is not usually to maintain deniability; certainly not when the press is seen in a body. But being put on the record is like carving words in stone. Public figures sometimes want to be heard and still not raise their voices, and on those occasions the backgrounder is a convenience. For example, when Roosevelt decided to throw his support behind Taft to succeed him, he did not do so through formal announcement. Such a statement would have caused resentment in some quarters, and perhaps even a feeling that the president was being arrogant in thinking of the office as something for him to pass on in dynastic succession. On the other hand, he wanted his supporters to know where he stood. Roosevelt solved the problem by calling in newsmen and telling them of his preference on a background basis. Their dispatches left no further doubt on the matter, while arranging that the information got out in a discreet way.

Roosevelt's sensitivity to the uses of news, and his awareness that the management of publicity could not be handled on a hit-or-miss basis, explains why he assigned major responsibilities in this area to George Cortelyou, the secretary he inherited from McKinley, and seventeen months later to William Loeb, the secretary he had brought with him from Albany. It would not be entirely accurate to describe the two men as the first presidential press secretaries. Not until Herbert Hoover took office—an individual with a genius for demonstrating the limitations of efficiency—was one person delegated to work full time in this area and designated as press secretary. If title is the criterion, then George Akerson, Hoover's first appointee, heads the list that eventually included such figures as Stephen Early, Charles Ross, James Hagerty, Pierre Salinger, and Bill Moyers. That is a poor basis on which to judge, however, since Roosevelt's two key aides filled the same position as Akerson in all but name, and better. At a time when the White House staff had not reached today's bloated proportions they handled a host of other duties besides press relations. But news coverage of the administration always remained one of their major concerns, and in trying to shape the publicity that went out they functioned very much like modern press secretaries.

Loeb, who handled the assignment for more than six years, first joined Roosevelt shortly after the latter's inauguration as governor of New York in January, 1899. As a former stenographer for the New York State Assembly and secretary to the lieutenant governor he was a unique kind of specialist: one who in combining secretarial skills with political experience was ideally trained to serve as administrative assistant to public figures. After two years as Roosevelt's secretary he moved with his mentor to Washington to be the new vice-president's stenographer (it says something about the stature of the office that the budget did not provide for an aide so highly ranked as secretary). The assassination of McKinley in September 1901 brought Loeb to the White House, although temporarily in the subordinate role of assistant secretary to the president. In hopes of easing the transition and reassuring nervous party leaders who worried about his "radicalism," Roosevelt had invited McKinley's cabinet and other key figures in the administration to remain at their posts. The invitation specifically included the former president's popular and efficient secretary, George B. Cortelyou. For the next year and a half Loeb deferred with good grace to another as chief assistant to the president. In February 1903, with Cortelyou's appointment to head the newly established Department of Commerce and Labor, he resumed his position as Roosevelt's right hand.[11]

The post of executive secretary entailed wide responsibilities. Loeb supervised the White House staff, overseeing the smooth functioning of fifty-odd clerks, stenographers, typists, messengers, and the rest. He took the most sensitive presidential dictation himself, and used those several hours a day with Roosevelt, usually in the evening, to talk over pending matters and offer advice. He managed the president's personal finances, including household accounts. He arranged Roosevelt's appointments, and from his desk adjacent to the Oval Office screened visitors to the White House, handling as many of them on his own as he could. He served as liaison to the Congress and the executive departments, and as political fence-mender among party leaders throughout the United States. It was a full load, but precisely because he was the key figure in Roosevelt's White House another job naturally fell to him which in many ways was the most important of all. Loeb also handled the details of the administration's press relations.

At the most immediate level this meant continuing the practice started under McKinley of daily briefings for the press. The White House used such sessions to make announcements that were not worth the president's time, but still qualified for newspaper coverage. Reporters used them to tie up the loose ends of past stories and probe for new ones. Although

Roosevelt was the most accessible of presidents, there were limits to reaching him and questions always to be asked. Loeb's availability meant that the press could depend on a generous ration of news from the White House even on the slowest days.

The briefings were also occasions to cover subjects the public cared about, but would have been inappropriate to raise with the president directly. For example, Loeb was the major conduit for news about the Roosevelt children and Roosevelt family activities. He had some help in the fact that Mrs. Roosevelt employed in Isabel Hagner the first of the White House social secretaries (another indication of the concern about publicity in this administration).[12] Information about such things as dinner lists, floral decorations, the gowns Mrs. Roosevelt and Alice would wear, went out routinely to newspapers. But that still left a lot of ground for Loeb to cover. Not the least of his services to the president was that in dispensing tidbits about the family he was able to exercise some control over how far down the barrier of privacy fell.

He paid a heavy price in loss of sleep and disruption of home life to carry out the briefing function. The hard fact, as every press secretary since has learned, is that not all questions can be handled during office hours. Newsmen would routinely call Loeb in the small hours of the morning for details about stories he had gone over thoroughly the previous day with the bureau chiefs. Roused out of bed, he would patiently have to cover the same material over the phone. He could not afford to blow up if he wanted to cultivate the good will of the press. When someone once asked him why a reporter in such a situation couldn't go directly to his bureau head, the secretary replied stoicly, "He wouldn't dare call his chief at one o'clock in the morning."[13]

But personal inconvenience was perhaps the least of the pressures upon him. Much more challenging was knowing how to answer. Of course Loeb had to be responsive to the reporters' questions and accurate in the information he dispensed. On the other hand, he could not afford to be so responsive that unintended news came out of the meetings. The unique demand upon a person in this role is that he know when and how to be evasive without abusing the right not to be forthcoming. Loeb excelled at the art. According to one student of the presidency, "the kindly secretary issued statements to reporters and conducted press conferences in which he was customarily helpful, although, when necessary, he could be as bland and discreet as a polished diplomat."[14]

Above all, a presidential spokesman must know what is going on. Nothing is more likely to antagonize the press than weak or misleading answers arising out of ignorance. Here Loeb was on solid ground. Indeed, he stood so close to the center of power that reporters were more apt to worry about the source of his pronouncements than their accuracy. "When Loeb announced to the press any one of a number of items in behalf of the President," a biographer of William Loeb III wrote, "there was always an undercurrent of speculation as to which of the decisions announced in the president's name had been made by the president and which had been made by Loeb. And there wasn't a man among the whole press corps who ever had the nerve to ask. Loeb could be very gracious, but, when need be, he could be bold and forceful."[15]

The job also required a sophisticated understanding of how the newspaper business worked. When did the morning and afternoon papers go to press in each section of the country? What was the respective newsworthiness of different stories? Which papers or reporters should information be leaked to? How did the wire services' budgets shape up that day? Without a professional's knowledge on such questions his efforts would have been seriously undercut.

Oscar Davis of the *New York Times* recalled an occasion when Loeb's expertise saved him from embarrassment. Davis had been working closely with the president in December 1908 trying to round up information that would refute allegations in the *New York World* of shady dealings in the Panama Canal transaction of 1903. When Roosevelt received a packet of documents from one of the central figures in the case, Davis asked whether in view of his deep involvement in the story he could go through the material before other reporters. The president refused, explaining that he intended to transmit the documents to the Senate the very next day, along with a special message justifying his own role. Even this was an exclusive, however, since Davis knew from many conversations with Roosevelt what the message would contain. Moreover, it was an exclusive the president wanted his friend to have in payment for services rendered.

In his excitement Davis almost went careening into trouble. When he mentioned to Loeb on his way out of the White House that he intended to file the story in time to meet his evening deadline, the secretary—by now thoroughly versed in the newsman's craft—pointed out the problem to him. "Loeb warned me, earnestly, to look out," Davis wrote, "or the Associated Press would fine the *Times* heavily for premature publication of a document delivered in advance, but under confidence until released."[16] If he wanted the exclusive, Davis would have to take some precautions. Loeb counseled him to get right on the phone to Managing Editor Carr Van Anda in New York, explain the situation to him, and have him in turn call up the Associated Press to say that the presidential message would be arriving shortly but the *Times* did not want a copy. In that way the newspaper would not be bound by the release date. And so it was done, in a neat display of professionalism at the White House.

Another, and less happy, part of the secretary's job was taking the blame if possible when things went wrong. Few presidential aides have ever sacrificed themselves with more devotion. He was known in Washington as "Roosevelt's goat," and more than once saw his name in the papers under the headline, "LOEB TAKES BLAME."[17] Sometimes the confessions of guilt were so patently false as to be silly. When Roosevelt in one of his more scatterbrained moments decided to dress the White House attaches in chocolate-soldier uniforms, he brought down a predictable cry of derision. Loeb took responsibility for the idea while the president discreetly retired. The same happened on the occasion Roosevelt in one of his budgets requested $60,000 for upkeep of the White House but $90,000 to maintain and improve a nearby stable in which he kept his horses. Again Loeb stepped forward with a tortured explanation of how the responsibility was actually his.[18] Deflecting the bad publicity was as much part of the job for him as generating the good.

But the main task was always to get favorable stories into the papers. Toward that end Roosevelt picked up and expanded on a practice which began under McKinley by assigning Loeb responsibility for issuing on an almost daily basis, and in heavy volume, press releases detailing presidential actions of that day. Every bill signed, or pardon granted, or visitor seen represented a potential newspaper story (as Roosevelt discovered to his chagrin at the time of the Booker T. Washington contretemps). The releases might be simply statements of the president's position on current issues, or provide advance information—and advance publicity—about forthcoming speeches or trips. Either way they won space for him in the nation's press. And since reporters were relatively less suspicious of handouts than they would learn to be by the 1930s, and certainly no more conscientious about double-checking and reworking such material to make it their own, the information usually appeared in newspapers in the form, and often in the precise wording, the White House provided it.

A particularly effective use of the releases was in responding to critics of the administration. Loeb's duties included closely monitoring the editorials in leading journals. At strategic moments (the tactic could not be used too often) he and the president would draft a reply to criticism which they would clear with the appropriate department and then issue as a White House statement.[19] In an unequal trade, Roosevelt thus appropriated the front page to answer an argument against him buried on the editorial page.

Although the technique would be considerably refined in later administrations, some attempts were also made during the Roosevelt years to centralize the release of news about the executive branch. The president may have been remarkably candid with the press, but that did not mean he appreciated having cabinet officers or other members of the administration compete with him as a source of information. He wanted to be the one to dispense news, and to have it appear in the papers bearing his name. Roosevelt showed how seriously he felt on the matter when he upset a long-standing convention of Washington journalism by instructing the cabinet not to linger after their meetings to discuss with reporters what had gone on, and certainly not to hold forth later in their offices. He would provide such information himself, as he thought appropriate, either personally or through Loeb. It was not the easiest order to enforce in a gossipy city, where garrulousness represented almost a way of life, but to a remarkable extent Roosevelt made it stick. As part of the same effort he required at least rudimentary coordination with the White House on news out of the departments. The concern is evident in a letter he wrote from Seattle in spring 1903 to Postmaster General Henry Payne when a story involving that department threatened to get out of control. "I should advise against your issuing any further statements whatever," the president instructed. "I do not think it well to let the answers and statements go out piecemeal. When I get back . . . we can make one clear-cut definite statement issued, which shall recapitulate the whole matter, showing what has been done."[20]

As Roosevelt soon discovered, however, news cannot be engineered with absolute precision. In particular, leaks are an occupational hazard in government, and Loeb was almost constantly engaged in trying to plug them. "The President says it looks as if there is a leak in the Department," he wrote to one cabinet member, "and he would like to be advised if you know how the information got out."[21] They seldom did, or at least seldom admitted knowing. In his frustration Roosevelt even called a cabinet meeting to discuss the problem, and had Loeb follow up with a long memorandum detailing what the president expected in the future. With exquisite logic considering Roosevelt's own gabbiness with the press, the secretary conceded that those who furnished reporters with stories did not usually do so out of malice. The leaker was typically someone who out of "weakness or good nature" gives "information to some newspaperman whom he wishes to befriend or for whom he feels sorry."[22] This still did not excuse the practice in the secretary's eyes, although he never quite figured out how to stop it.

The interesting thing is that Roosevelt and Loeb cared as much as they did. Accepting that it is always an annoyance to read in the papers information presumed to be confidential, national security was not at stake. Usually the leaks did not even jeopardize the administration's political goals. They were upsetting mainly, it seems, because the White House aspired to the same efficiency in the handling of publicity that Progressivism tried to bring to all areas of government. If anything, Roosevelt regarded efficiency in this area as the fundamental priority, since everything else government did depended upon first shaping public consent through the media. The president insisted on being in control of that effort.

In an administration so attuned to the uses of news, it is not surprising that image weighs almost as heavily as substance in assessing its achievements. Indeed, what stands out in retrospect about many of Roosevelt's greatest political triumphs is the extent to which they were largely triumphs in public relations. This is not to say that he won hollow victories. It is just that his typical strategy in any situation was to play on popular emotions, with the result that people tended to credit him with more than he in fact achieved, or perhaps more accurately, with something different from what he in fact achieved.

His attack on the Northern Securities Company in 1902 is a case in point. To appreciate what Roosevelt accomplished on that occasion it is important to understand that his reputation as a trust-buster is a bit misleading. He did not aspire to restore competition by breaking up the giant industrial combines. He regarded bigness in industry as a corollary of progress, and on balance a blessing. But Roosevelt also understood that increasing numbers of people feared and resented the power of these new conglomerates, and the way they used power for selfish gain. He sympathized with the popular sentiment to the extent of feeling that lack of supervision had resulted in an unjustifiable control by the moneyed elite over the nation's affairs. The challenge as Roosevelt saw it was to encourage bigness while at the same time regulating its abuses. This could be done, he felt, by distinguishing between "good" and "bad" corporations, leaving the former alone while using the power of the government to bring the latter to account. He had the means at hand in the Sherman Antitrust Act, largely a dead letter since its passage in 1890 but still a federal law declaring combinations in restraint of trade illegal. Above all, he had public opinion on his side. The trick was to mobilize people through a dramatic gesture.

In picking the Northern Securities Company as his first target Roosevelt demonstrated again his shrewd publicity sense and appreciation for the importance of symbols in politics. He chose as adversaries men who were household names as the plutocrats of American life. He chose an area of business endeavor that probably affected people more directly than any other, and therefore stirred greatest resentment as an example of corporate abuse. And since it was essential to win in order to make his point that businessmen were not above the law, he chose a case where the opposition was particularly vulnerable, if only because of still-fresh memories of how the particular trust had been formed.

Northern Securities was a holding company incorporated in New Jersey on November 13, 1901 with a capitalization of $400,000,000 and a charter authorizing it to acquire and sell railroad securities. It emerged out of a titanic struggle in 1901 for control of railroad routes in the northwest and a connecting line to Chicago. The struggle had arrayed on one side Edward

H. Harriman and Jacob Schiff of the banking house of Kuhn, Loeb & Company, allies who already controlled the central and southern routes to the west coast, against James J. Hill and J. Pierpont Morgan, who dominated traffic in the northwest through the Northern Pacific and Great Northern lines. Both sides had vied to take over the Chicago, Burlington, and Quincy railroad, which represented Hill's connecting route to Chicago. When Hill persuaded the Burlington owners to sell out to him, Harriman and Schiff retaliated boldly by attempting to acquire control of the Northern Pacific. In the frantic scrambling for stock that ensued the adversaries drove the price up from $100 a share to $1,000 before they finally agreed to settle the matter in a more sensible way. They formed Northern Securities as a holding company to control the Northern Pacific and Great Northern lines. Harriman and Schiff received minority representation on the board of directors, and Harriman was also given a seat on the Burlington board. Peace had come to the northwest in the form of a railroad monopoly.

Roosevelt had been president barely a month when Northern Securities was incorporated, and at the time he was deeply involved in preparing his first annual message to Congress which he submitted on December 3. He had decided independently to use the occasion to warn about the trend to industrial consolidation and urge legislation to curb abuses. Northern Securities represented a stroke of luck (as the Archbold telegram had also been lucky) in enabling him to dramatize the issue through action of his own. The company was a perfect illustration of the trust problem, particularly since an estimated thirty percent of its $400,000,000 capitalization consisted of water that would require exorbitant charges on the public to return a profit. To make things even better from Roosevelt's point of view, the company had been put together by J. P. Morgan, a name that symbolized villainy in the popular mind. All of this was simply too good for a public relations-minded president to ignore. Without notifying party leaders or the business community, keeping even his own cabinet in the dark, Roosevelt instructed Attorney General Philander C. Knox to prepare a suit for dissolution. The announcement on the evening of February 19, 1902 that the government was about to file caused an explosion. The New York Stock Market opened the next day to the worst tremors since McKinley's assassination. Business leaders were predictably enraged, all the more so because of the insult in not having been consulted ahead of time. They had come to expect better treatment from the White House. But the anger on Wall Street and in Congress, something Roosevelt never fully overcame, was more than matched by public elation that he had stood up to big business. The suit was so unexpected, and involved figures of such towering significance, that it created a sensation. Many editorials castigated Roosevelt, but in the news columns he was a hero. He had taken the first step in creating the legend of the trust buster. The happy denouement came on March 14, 1904 when the Supreme Court overturned its previous interpretation of the Sherman Act in *U.S. v. E. C. Knight Co.* and ruled by a five to four majority that Northern Securities was indeed in restraint of trade and had to be dissolved.[23]

Roosevelt went on to other such victories, usually riding the crest of public opinion by picking targets familiar to ordinary people. Later in 1902 he brought suit against the "Beef Trust," an amalgamation of the Swift, Armour, and Nelson Morris companies to wipe out independent packers in the Midwest. That prosecution had obvious appeal to consumers and farmers. In 1907 (his reelection, and therefore need for campaign contributions, safely out of the way) he went after the Standard Oil company of John D. Rockefeller, a figure rivaled only by J. P. Morgan for the onus attached to his name. Suits against the American Tobacco Company, the New Haven Railroad, and DuPont followed rapidly thereafter. In all, the administration instituted proceedings against forty-four corporations, including many of the ones most visible to casual readers of newspapers.

This vigorous enforcement of the Sherman Act, while undeniably impressive when compared to the record of the three previous administrations, is nevertheless misleading as regards Roosevelt's own views about industrial amalgamation and what happened during his presidency. Between them he and McKinley presided over the period of greatest business consolidation in American history. It is not too extreme to say that the economy was restructured during their years in office. Of the 318 major corporations in the United States at the beginning of 1904, 236 with a total capitalization exceeding $6,000,000,000 had been formed since 1897. They represented seventy-four percent of all companies that might reasonably be considered as falling within the purview of the Sherman Act.[24] The Roosevelt record comes into better focus again when compared to that of his successor. Few Americans of the time were impressed that William Howard Taft—unimaginative, conservative, sadly unsuited for the presidency—initiated more suits in four years than Roosevelt did in seven; or that he dared to take on two corporations, United States Steel and International Harvester, his predecessor had carefully left alone.

The moral is not that Roosevelt consciously deceived the people or acted as the pawn of big business. On balance he probably went as far in curbing the excesses of the money men as was wise or possible in the first decade of the century. Still, the excitement he engendered by moving against companies of particular symbolic importance, and doing it noisily, made him a hero for the wrong reasons. His skill at playing the politics of the dramatic gesture explains why, despite having no animosity against bigness in industry, despite serving during the period when more mergers than ever before or since in American history occurred, and despite the counter-evidence provided in numerous histories and biographies, he was regarded in his own time and by later generations as a trust buster.

Something of the same discrepancy between Roosevelt's actual achievement, which was considerable, and the image that grew up about him, appears in the long struggle to secure a bill for government regulation of railroad rates. The passage of the Hepburn Act in 1906 represented his crowning triumph as a reform leader. Allies and enemies both conceded that without the president's involvement the victory could not have been won; certainly not in that year. And yet precisely because Roosevelt fought in a way characteristic of him, through a massive publicity campaign calculated to arouse popular emotions, he became identified as more of a militant on the issue than in fact he was and the bill he secured as more far-reaching in its provisions than in fact was the case.

The president's activity on several fronts to drum up support for a rate-regulation measure, and to combat the lobbying against it, certainly qualifies as a classic example of the uses of publicity for political purposes. He started with a widely heralded speech on January 30, 1905 before the Union League Club of Philadelphia. It was an unlikely forum to choose for the speech, and therefore a good one from the point of view of attracting attention. Philadelphia was not simply a railroad center; it served as the financial capital of a state noted for its corrupt politics and antediluvian leadership, starting with a senate delegation of Matthew Quay and Boies Penrose. The Union League Club, a bastion of old wealth and musty orthodoxies, represented as good a symbol as any of the failure of leadership in the city. Before that assemblage, in a speech the *New York Times* and *Washington Post* ran as their lead story, Roosevelt reminded his audience that industrial development demanded a more active role by government in supervising the economy, and that this meant first of all establishing an impartial public tribunal to oversee railroad rates.[25] Presumably the gentlemen he addressed were not altogether impressed by his argument (although newspaper accounts say they broke in several times with applause), but he had taken the first step in mobilizing the country.

When the Senate recessed in spring 1905 without voting on a rate-regulation bill overwhelmingly approved by the House, Roosevelt moved to a new level of activity. During 1905 and the early months of 1906 he brought into play every one of his techniques. In April and May 1905, using the occasion of a Rough Riders' reunion in San Antonio as a pretext, he took a "swing around the circle" through the Midwest and Southwest to speak on behalf of rate legislation. In October he was back on the road, this time spreading the message through the Southeast. Invoking the name of his mother as a native of Georgia, and of his two uncles as Confederate veterans, he made such legislation almost a matter of sectional loyalty. It was as if he "himself fired the last two shots for the *Alabama* instead of his uncles," a *Washington Star* correspondent wrote. "Wherever the President's visit is discussed you will hear men who believed in and fought for the Confederate cause speak of him with the affection of a comrade."[26]

As the fight heated up Roosevelt brought the press in even more directly. He arranged for a barrage of stories to appear in the papers detailing instances of railroad malfeasance and pointing to the need for government control. One of the ways he kept reporters supplied with material was by timing the release of reports on investigations initiated months before to fit in with the carefully orchestrated campaign. Another was by launching new investigations or court actions, always to a fanfare of publicity. The stories started to appear in August, 1905 with the announcement that the ICC was about to undertake an investigation of collusion between rail-roads and refrigerator car lines.[27] Thereafter the pace picked up month by month.[28] "The cannonade of head-lines took on cumulative frequency," Mark Sullivan wrote; "occasionally, indeed, two or more jostled each other on the same front page, the general saturation of the atmosphere causing *Life* to remark, plaintively, that 'there are a few solvent and respectable persons left in the country who have not yet been investigated.' "[29]

December brought two news items of particular significance. In his fifth annual message to Congress on December 5 Roosevelt praised the contributions of railroads to American development, but reiterated the need for legislation authorizing the ICC to set maximum rates subject to judicial review.[30] On December 11 came the announcement that Attorney General William H. Moody had directed all eighty-five United States Attorneys to institute proceedings wherever practicable against companies offering or receiving rebates, using the conspiracy statutes rather than the Elkins Act so that those found guilty could be sent to jail.[31] Within days federal grand juries in Philadelphia and Chicago had returned indictments against several prominent defendants, including the Great Northern line.[32]

When the Fifty-Ninth Congress reconvened in late 1905, a rate bill named after Representative William P. Hepburn of Iowa stood at the top of the agenda. As the measure moved quickly through the House of Representatives and tortuously through the Senate, Roosevelt stepped up his publicity campaign to a new intensity. Using only the *New York Times* as an index (a particularly good example since the paper was editorially opposed to federal ratemaking), eleven front-page stories appeared between mid-January and mid-March 1906 recounting examples of railroad malfeasance. They included reports on how Chicago meat packers used discriminatory rates to wipe out competition in the Midwest, on how Pennsylvania and New York Central interests cooperated "to shut out future competition from the lake ports,'' and on how Standard Oil domination of railroads threatened to drive independent oil producers out of business in Kansas.[33]

The campaign reached a climax in early May, just two weeks before the final vote on the Hepburn Act in the Senate, when the Bureau of Corporations released its report detailing Standard Oil's transgressions nationwide. "The report shows," Roosevelt said in his covering message to Congress, "that the Standard Oil Company has benefited enormously up almost to the present moment by secret rates, many of these secret rates being clearly unlawful. This benefit amounts to at least three-quarters of a million a year." The president went on to point out that other companies were also culpable. A pending investigation "as to shipments by the sugar trust over the trunk lines out of New York City tends to show that the sugar trust rarely, if ever, pays the lawful rate for transportation."[34] It is difficult to see how this storm of publicity, duplicated in newspapers throughout the country, could do anything but seal the impression of the railroad industry as shockingly unresponsive to the public interest, and of Roosevelt as champion of the people in trying to bring the industry under control.

He had considerable help in establishing that image from magazine writers, many of whom he knew personally and likely cooperated with in preparing the articles. Three periodicals in particular served the cause: *Outlook, World's Work,* and *McClure's.* Roosevelt had special ties to each that served him well on this occasion. His close friend, Lyman Abbott, published *Outlook,* a magazine Roosevelt himself joined as a contributing editor after leaving the White House. *McClure's,* the foremost of the muckraking journals, was edited by Lincoln Steffens, another close friend. And if the president did not have quite the same tie with Walter Hines Page of *World's Work* (although the two were certainly acquainted), one of the magazine's top staff writers, Harry Beach Needham, belonged to that group of journalists who because of their intimate association with the president were known as the "fair-haired boys."

The major contribution by *McClure's,* and probably the single most effective salvo in the publicity barrage, was a five-part series by Ray Stannard Baker on corruption in the railroad industry that began in the November 1905 issue. With a thoroughness of research characteristic of *McClure's* investigative reporting, Baker demonstrated how the pricing practices of railroads, which affected entire cities, were determined solely on the basis of charging what the traffic would bear.[35] He showed how companies like Armour, through private ownership of refrigerator cars, were able not only to coerce rebates from railroads, but to dominate their suppliers and competitors. "They buy transportation and fix their own price. They also buy cattle and fix their own price—for that is the usurpation of monopoly. They buy wheat and fix their own price; they buy corn and fix their own price. In some cases they buy fruit and vegetables and fix their own price. And they do these things *because*, and only because, they have that other and fundamental right of fixing the price of transportation."[36] Baker probably scored most heavily in his concluding article when he alleged that the railroad industry had mounted a massive propaganda campaign to defeat rate legislation. According to his account, the tactics included flooding the South with pamphlets at the time of Roosevelt's visit declaring that such a bill would make Jim Crow cars illegal.[37]

Roosevelt closely monitored Baker's progress during the year that went into preparing the series. He saw the reporter frequently, and according to Baker's testimony, even offered him working space at the Interstate Commerce Commission, the services of a stenographer, and access to unpublished material in the government's files.[38] Considering that Roosevelt bent the rules with his generosity, it is perhaps not surprising that the reporter responded in kind. Several weeks before the first article appeared Baker asked Roosevelt if he would like to see the proofs. The president leaped at the chance, "not because of any good I can do you, but because I have learned to look to your articles for real help." He wrote back later, "I haven't a criticism to suggest about the article. You have given me two or three thoughts for my own message."[39]

Helpful articles also appeared in virtually every issue of *Outlook* and *World's Work* between January and April, 1906. One of the most telling, by Harry Beach Needham in the January issue of *World's Work*, severely castigated the Senators who opposed the bill: "Aldrich, Hale, Frye, Spooner, Gallinger, Penrose, Elkins, Platt, Foraker, Depew and Kean— representatives of corporate business every one. . . ."[40] In a passage that suggests the White House as a source, Needham claimed that just prior to embarking on a trip to Europe the previous winter, Majority Leader Nelson Aldrich had made Senator Stephen Elkins, chairman of the Committee on Interstate and Foreign Commerce, and two other ranking members of the committee, promise that the measure passed by the House would not be reported out in his absence. "Thus a bill to regulate railroad rates failed last winter," the reporter concluded.[41] But as the magazine declared editorially in the same issue, the obstructionists would not have their way forever. "It is too early, when this paragraph is written, to make any prediction about the passage by the Senate of a bill to regulate railroad rates. But it is not hazardous to say that the President's underlying idea has very steadily gained public favor; and it is a safe prediction that some bill, which shall embody this underlying idea, will become a law—if not during this Congress then during some other."[42]

The Hepburn Act was introduced in the House of Representatives on January 4, 1906, and passed by a lopsided vote of 364 to 7 in early February. The Senate took up the measure on February 26, and after extensive parliamentary maneuvering, passed it on May 18 by almost as impressive a majority of 71 to 3. By any reasonable standard, considering the effort that went into securing the principle of rate regulation, Roosevelt had won a famous victory. The law represented the single most important step until that date in America's adjustment to being an industrial society. As long as the free marketplace no longer existed government had to assume an increasing supervisory function, and Roosevelt more than any other individual contributed with his victory to the breakthrough.

Why, then, is it also possible to speak of the act as illustrating the frequent discrepancy in the Roosevelt years between the reality of what he accomplished and the version the people accepted? The reason is similar to what happened in the case of his antitrust policy. Sheer force of publicity, which Roosevelt carefully managed, tended to obscure attention from what the quarrel was really about, and the terms on which the quarrel was resolved. The barrage in newspapers and magazines conveyed the impression of a villainous railroad industry so greedy for profit that it opposed any form of accountability, and of a heroic president so determined to bring big business under control that he would fight to the political death for the cause. The truth was more complex. By 1905 realists on both sides of the issue realized that some sort of rate legislation was inevitable, which meant that the struggle really came down to the form the legislation should take. On this subject Roosevelt, while preferring a relatively stringent measure if he could get congressional approval, found it easier than some of his contemporaries to scale down his ambitions should circumstances warrant. After working closely for a while with the militant reformers in the Senate, he abandoned them at the expedient moment and opted for a law far milder than they would have accepted.

Four questions separated the progressive and conservative camps: whether the ICC should have power to set definite or only maximum rates; whether its rulings should be subject to narrow judicial review or broad review; whether any limitations should be placed, and if so what sort, on the power of the courts to issue injunctions against ICC-imposed rates while cases were under litigation; and an issue Robert LaFollette of Wisconsin raised, whether the ICC should be authorized to evaluate the worth of railroads as a basis to fix fair rates.

When the time came to strike a final bargain Roosevelt pretty well gave way on all of these points, thus undercutting many of the themes in his own publicity campaign. In opting for ICC authority to set maximum rather than definite rates, for example, he consciously bypassed the problem of long and short haul differentials.[43] One of his major arguments had always been that authority to set rates must be delegated to an independent commission rather than thrashed out in the courts, where business would always enjoy an advantage. That is why he favored narrow judicial review, restricted mainly to such procedural questions as whether the ICC had acted within its purview and been fair in its deliberations. Although the Hepburn Act did not specifically shift final rate-making authority from the commission to the courts, it left the way clear for the judiciary to assume the responsibility on its own. Roosevelt also had been sensitive to the possibility that wide use of the injunction might cripple the ICC by delaying its decisions for years while litigation went on. He had supported various schemes to specify when suspension could occur, or to provide for the disputed amounts to be held in escrow until the courts ruled. These, too, were surrendered in the final bill. The lopsided margin by which the Hepburn Act passed the Senate is the best indication that the law was not something jammed down the throat of big business. It was the achievement of a pragmatic-minded politician who, when forced to choose, preferred partial victory in the present to the promise of total victory at some future date. In the Hepburn fight Roosevelt spoke loudly and carried a small stick.

But he still paid careful attention to image. At the climactic moment, when Roosevelt decided to accept an amendment put forward by conservatives to break the impasse in the Senate, he convoked what perhaps qualifies as the first of the presidential press conferences to make the announcement. Immediately after his cabinet meeting on Friday, May 4, the president telephoned the Capitol press gallery to say that he would receive reporters at 3:00 P.M. that afternoon.[44] Thirty-six of them gathered in the cabinet room to hear a long, and at times labored, explanation of why the so-called Allison amendment was acceptable to him, and why it represented victory in a struggle he had been waging since December, 1904. The *Washington Post* thought the conference significant enough to warrant an article just on it being called. "IVOKES AID OF PRESS," the headline declared. "PRESIDENT INVITES CORRESPONDENTS TO DISCUSS RATES WITH HIM" According to the story, "the meeting lasted more than an hour. While the President made it clear, at the outset, that he desired not to be quoted directly as to views he might express, he said he was perfectly willing that his views should be known and be stated in the language of the press who were present. . . . The President talked with frankness in the expression of his views, in answering questions which were propounded to him from all sides, and in explaining the attitude of himself and the advocates of the suggested legislation. Necessarily, the discussion was in a nature academic, but it was interesting and informative."[45] The writer might have added that it was also calculated to assure that Roosevelt's version of events would be the one to go out in the nation's newspapers.

What, then, is to be said of his reform record? If he seemed to contemporaries as something different from what he actually was, the power of publicity helps to explain why. Finally we know public figures by the images they project, wittingly or unwittingly. Roosevelt, a master of image-making, knew precisely how he wanted to appear: crusader against special privilege in the eyes of the voters, defender of sound principles in the eyes of political and business leaders. One of the reasons he is such a fascinating figure in history is that he pretty well succeeded in pulling off the sleight-of-hand.

Robert La Follette (who belonged to the progressive bloc Roosevelt abandoned when he came to terms with Senate conservatives) was one of those who thought the president talked a good fight, but at the moment of truth never quite lived up to his combative image. Although the Wisconsin senator was embittered against Roosevelt, and tended to be slanted in his own judgments, he had a point when he described the technique the president used to be all things to all people. "When Roosevelt was President, his public utterances through state papers, addresses, and the press were highly colored with rhetorical radicalism. . . . [But] one trait was always pronounced. His most savage assault upon special interests was invariably offset with an equally drastic attack upon those who were seeking to reform abuses. These were indiscriminately classed as demogogues and dangerous persons. In this way he sought to win approval, both from the radicals and the conservatives."[46] La Follette thought the trait particularly unfortunate in the case of the Hepburn Act because a strong bill could have been won—if not in the present session then in the next—had Roosevelt not substituted posturing for principles. "This cannonading, first in one direction and then in another, filled the air with noise and smoke, which confused and obscured the line of action, but when the battle cloud drifted by and quiet was restored, it was always a matter of surprise that so little had really been accomplished."[47]

The senator was not altogether fair in his assessment. Roosevelt had accomplished a good deal; perhaps all that could be accomplished at the time. But the point about sheer din of publicity serving to obscure rather than clarify issues had a certain merit. And as another of Roosevelt's antagonists ruefully recognized, the president could count on the cooperation of the press whenever he wanted to turn the volume up. "I say to you in all seriousness," Ben Tillman of South Carolina declared in the Senate on January 17, 1906, "that Theodore Roosevelt owes more of his success as a public man to the newspaper men of this country than any other one instrumentality. . . . The news is colored and sifted to suit his idea of what it ought to be to maintain the great popularity which he has won, to preserve in the imagination of the people the hold he has on them. Speaking allegorically, the actual condition at the White House has been for many, many months that of a quack doctor who has certain pills which he wishes to prescribe for the public. The newspapers have been the spoon. . . . Roosevelt's pills on Roosevelt, Roosevelt's pills on railway rate legislation, Roosevelt's pills on everything pertaining to public affairs are administered in this way. . . .''[48] Tillman didn't mean it as a compliment, but of course he described one of the foundations of presidential power.

4

The "Bully" Pulpit

In November 1912, on the eve of the election that put Woodrow Wilson in the White House and ended Theodore Roosevelt's dream of a third term, the Bull Moose candidate received the press at his home in Sagamore Hill. Except for one of the reporters, the group was well known to him and trusted. The only unfamiliar face belonged to a correspondent who had been assigned just days before to cover the candidate. Charles Thompson of the *New York Times* described what happened that afternoon. "The Colonel, as he came into the room, looked at the new man with a glance which meant nothing to the latter, but was full of meaning to the rest of us. It was an appraising look, and the first report it brought back to the Colonel's mind was unfavorable. The expression that came over his face was the one we recognized as distrustful; and when he spoke, his tone had a certain restraint in it."[1]

From that unpromising beginning the situation rapidly worsened. The newcomer made his first mistake by appearing altogether too much at home as he sat in his chair with one leg draped over the other. Then he compounded the offense by asking a bantering question about how the candidate intended to vote on Election Day. Roosevelt, bristling, demanded that he repeat what he had just said. When the reporter did so, speaking in a small voice, the Colonel snapped back that he had not agreed to see the press to answer idiotic questions. Immediately a pall descended on the room that made further conversation pointless. After a few polite exchanges, the reporters left. As they filed out of the house the distraught newcomer turned to the others and asked repeatedly, "What did I do to offend him? What did I do to offend him?" His wife was waiting for him in a taxicab outside. She had come along hoping to be introduced to the former president at the conclusion of the interview. The two of them drove away together, and neither of them ever did see Roosevelt again.

Later in the afternoon the rest of the reporters, concerned that their own access might be affected, commissioned three among them who knew Roosevelt best to go back to the house to see what they could do to patch things up. To their relief, Charles Thompson, Lucius Curtis of the Associated Press, and Jack Pratt of the *New York American* were greeted warmly. Roosevelt assured them that nothing had changed as far as the regulars were concerned. "But that new fellow won't do," he added. "I felt creepy as soon as I saw him. I knew right away he didn't have the Oyster Bay atmosphere and couldn't get it."[2] Lacking that Oyster Bay atmosphere—which Thompson described as an almost tangible thing, a combination of "mutual respect, confidence and friendliness"—the offender would have to forget about ever becoming a regular himself.[3]

The incident reveals a good deal about why Roosevelt was able to use the press as effectively as he did during his years in office. He had the enormous advantage of being able to decide which reporters would cover him, or at the very least, which ones would have access to news. It was a prerogative any modern president would envy, and one that he enjoyed by luck of historical timing. As the first president to make himself widely available to the press, he had opened marvelous new opportunities to reporters. They certainly didn't want to jeopardize what they had won. By the same token, no precedent required that he be available on equal terms to all. It made perfect sense from Roosevelt's point of view to single out for favors the people he regarded as trustworthy and cooperative. And to the extent any access is better than none, the press accepted that arrangement and even lionized Roosevelt for offering it.

Of course the newsmen on the outside bitterly resented being excluded. It is much easier to deal with an isolated presidency when everybody is treated the same way and isolation is more or less an accepted fact of life. But to see fellow journalists having free run of the Oval Office, walking around in a self-important way because of their closeness to the president, continually breaking stories which had been personally delivered to them and to know that one could not share in the same privileges, was personally and professionally galling. Yet what could the outsiders do about it? The only possible answer would have been a solid front among reporters demanding that the president see them all equally, or see none at all. If faced with such a challenge, even Roosevelt would have had to back down. But just to express the idea revealed its impracticality. No reporter was going to refuse a presidential invitation because the party was restricted to him. Nor were the coterie of favored reporters about to surrender their privileges because others were less fortunate than they.

There was no secret to the requirement for getting in Roosevelt's good graces (although not everybody willing to pay the price was accepted). The president demanded two things of the regulars, known derogatorily to outsiders as his "fair-haired boys" or "cuckoos," in return for giving them a virtual monopoly on news from the White House. First, they had to agree to print only what he wanted printed and only when he wanted it to appear. Archie Butt commented on this point in writing despairingly of the contrast between Roosevelt's firm control of publicity and the chaos that prevailed during the Taft years. "Mr. Roosevelt understood the necessity of guiding the press to suit one's own ends. . . . He saw the newspaper men freely, but they understood that they were only to print what he authorized them to use, and if they did anything else he would not allow them near the White House or office, and he has been known to have them dismissed from their papers. . . . Nothing went out from the White House except as the President wanted it."[4]

The other claim upon them, never explicitly stated but still understood, was that they support his policies and color their reporting to get his point of view across. By the lights of the time it didn't seem an altogether unreasonable requirement. Roosevelt could hardly be expected to speak candidly to men who wished ill for his programs, or even to those who didn't care one way or the other. He wanted loyalists around him, and the best way for reporters to prove their loyalty was by writing stories the president would regard as constructive. "There was always a group of news writers," Frederick Essary of the *Baltimore Sun* recalled, "whom we called the 'fair-haired,' who had his confidence and profiting by that confidence were ready to lend themselves in a large sense to any cause which he might champion."[5]

The result was a constant skewing of the news in the president's favor that went even beyond supporting his causes. On one occasion Senator Nathan B. Scott of West Virginia, a Republican who had been quarreling with Roosevelt about the allocation of patronage in his state, came heatedly out of the Oval Office and was surrounded in the west wing foyer by newsmen asking for a statement. He walked right past them, pausing only long enough to say that it was pointless to expect a fair hearing from a bunch of "praise agents" like them.[6] His reaction may have been petulant, even self-defeating, but is still understandable. Roosevelt did consistently get the benefit of the doubt from the White House press corps, and because the regulars were cronies more than detached observers, they did consistently see things from his perspective.

This close relationship with one segment of the press and freezing out of the rest had important consequences for Washington journalism. As far as the regulars were concerned, access to the president gave them much greater status than reporters had ever enjoyed before. It was not simply that they experienced the heady sensation of being on the inside and knowing what was going on. By having the president's ear they were in a position to influence him, and therefore the policies of government.

Most important, Roosevelt brought them into the governmental process when he made publicity the key to his style of leadership. Once news coverage came to be seen as critical in forming opinion and getting things done, then the people in a position to provide the coverage mattered in a way they never had previously. Roosevelt took a major step toward making journalists what they are today, part of the Washington establishment.

The further fact is that he upgraded the press corps at the price of corrupting it. By modern standards, a reporter gives up too much—indeed, he gives up everything—if he surrenders his independence to get the news. The White House regulars came dangerously close to crossing that line. Perhaps they had to take the risk in the early twentieth century to achieve the transition from being journeymen to important cogs in the way the system worked. And in fairness, the independence was soon regained, as almost any president since could testify. Still, for a time the men who occupied the highest rungs of Washington journalism carried another man's brand.[7]

A related moral of the Roosevelt years is that the president received the kind of publicity he did because he dealt with a still immature and relatively impotent press corps. Presidential-press relations in the modern sense assumes that each possesses weapons against the other. If the president has ways to manipulate the news and punish or reward individual reporters, the press is not helpless in asserting its own prerogatives. In a sense, the unique tension in their relationship arises from the countervailing power between them. This did not exist during Roosevelt's administration. Washington correspondents were just beginning to regard themselves as a group with inviolable rights and responsibilities. Roosevelt encouraged the trend by the role he assigned to the press, but at the same time he more than any president took advantage of the fact that parity had still not been won. He bullied reporters into providing the kind of publicity he wanted and got away with it. Those who felt his wrath were powerless to retaliate; the rest quaked lest the same happen to them.

Just the fact of having an institutionalized Ananias Club speaks to disproportionate presidential power in relation to the press. The term sounds rather quaint now, but was a dreaded reality during the Roosevelt years. Once inducted in the club the journalist found doors all over Washington slammed in his face. News sources he had depended on suddenly dried up. There didn't even have to be a rational reason to justify the banishment. As in the case of the hapless correspondent who lacked the Oyster Bay atmosphere, Roosevelt relied on instinct as much as evidence in choosing his victims. And once he had made up his mind, he couldn't be budged. David Barry of the *New York Sun,* a person who admired the president and enjoyed a good working relationship with him, still conceded the unfairness and ugliness in the way his press relations worked. "There was one weak spot in Mr. Roosevelt's character. . . ," the reporter wrote. "[If he] convinced himself or allowed others to convince him that a man had acted an unworthy or discreditable part, he would at once withdraw his support and friendship from that man, often without giving him an adequate opportunity to explain and justify his conduct. Mr. Roosevelt pursued this course on more than one occasion, when the victim of his censure was one who had stood by him. . . . The President's stubborness and obstinacy in these cases was the cause of chagrin to his friends and supporters who simply could not understand this peculiar weakness of the President's mind."[8]

Roosevelt even banished people he knew were innocent, such as those he used to float trial balloons. Long after he left the White House the memory of suffering arbitrary punishment at his hands remained with Washington journalists. It is indicative that when *Editor & Publisher* asked reporters on the eve of Herbert Hoover's inauguration how they hoped the new president would conduct his press operation, the only unanimous wish was that he not go back to the methods used by Theodore Roosevelt.[9] Even into the next decade the memories rankled. "There are correspondents still alive," Herbert Corey wrote in the *Saturday Evening Post* in 1932, "who are as full of umbrage as they were the day that President Roosevelt denied them."[10]

Occasionally Roosevelt took even more direct action against newsmen who offended him. He thought nothing, for example, of contacting publishers and asking them to fire a reporter, or at least transfer him. "Your man does not seem to be malicious in his inventions," the president wrote to Paul Dana of the *New York Sun* in 1902, "but he deliberately makes up stories which he thinks might have happened, but which as a matter of fact do not happen. As I say, I do not know that there is much harm in the stories, but still they have not a word of truth in them, and they lean toward the ridiculous. It seems to me that they are not proper stories to be told about the President or the members of his family. . . . I very much wish you would send instead of your present man at Oyster Bay someone who will tell the facts as they are and will not try to make up for the fact that nothing is happening here by having recourse to invention."[11] Whether the *Sun* correspondent (not David Barry) had fabricated news, and whether Dana honored the president's request that he be replaced, are not recorded. The only certainty is that Roosevelt was not one to suffer annoyance in silence.

Indeed, sometimes he screamed his rage. Such a case occurred in September 1905, and became a news item in itself. A French correspondent named Paul Lagardene had filed with his paper, *Petit Parisien*, a story based on a personal interview with the president which the Associated

Press picked up and relayed back to the United States.[12] The reason for interest was that Roosevelt had just finished serving as mediator at the Portsmouth Peace Conference which brought an end to the Russo-Japanese War. (The following year he received the Nobel Peace Prize for his efforts.) Lagardene, on the basis of his conversation with the president, was able to write an account of Roosevelt's thoughts about the respective positions of the conferees and the terms they had finally settled on. In this case Roosevelt had good reason to be livid. He had agreed to see the Frenchman because Lagardene was the grandson of a Napoleonic marshal and therefore an interesting person to meet, and also because he had just returned from the war front, covering both the Japanese and Russian armies, and might have useful information to contribute. Roosevelt never imagined that their conversation would be construed as an interview, or that he would be quoted worldwide on a matter of international delicacy.

If the president was uncharacteristically naïve in assuming that he could talk freely with a reporter (one, moreover, not susceptible to the strictures of the Ananias Club) on a subject of major news interest and see nothing in print, his response once he had been burned was typical. He decided that Lagardene would have to be branded publicly as a liar, particularly since his story was essentially accurate. Roosevelt instructed William Loeb to send a cable to the reporter, simultaneously releasing it to the press, attacking his honor and veracity. "The President directs me to say to you," the message quoted in the newspapers the next day declared, "that the alleged interview with him published in this morning's papers is not only an absolute fabrication, wholly without basis in truth, but that your conduct in obtaining permission to see him under false pretenses is thoroughly dishonorable. . . . The President had no conversation with you about the terms of peace, and your account . . . [is] without any foundation in fact."[13] As it turned out, Lagardene was among the last to learn about the president's low opinion of him. He had been sailing back to France at the time the telegram went out, and received it only on his arrival in Cherbourg. About all he could do under the circumstances was issue a statement affirming "most formally" that he had "faithfully reported the words of the President of the United States."[14] Scores of newsmen who had been used to float trial balloons never doubted it.

The story had a sequel several days later which obviously did not see print. Roosevelt, while lunching at the White House with Herman Kohlsaat, publisher of the *Chicago Record Herald,* asked him if he had read about the incident. Kohlsaat knew the president well enough to respond frankly. "Yes," he answered, "and I believe you said what the Frenchman sent to his paper, because you have said the same thing to me." The remark fazed Roosevelt not one whit. "Snapping his teeth, he replied: 'Of course I said it, but I said it as Theodore Roosevelt and not as the

President of the United States.' "[15] Lagardene's dishonor, it seems, was in confusing the two.

Perhaps the best example of Roosevelt taking after a reporter, if only because the issue was so trivial and the response so inflated, happened as a result of a holiday feature in the *Boston Herald*. On Thanksgiving Day 1904, the paper carried an article written by its Washington correspondent, Jesse Carmichael, about a turkey chase on the White House grounds. According to Carmichael's account, the Roosevelt children had amused themselves by releasing a turkey that had been donated to the first family by a Boston resident and chasing it over the South Lawn. During the merriment—the children grabbing at the bird, plucking its feathers in trying to catch it, running it to exhaustion before the game ended—the president had allegedly looked on from the South Portico roaring with laughter. Carmichael evidently saw nothing cruel in the escapade. He described the youngsters as "chips off the old block," sharing the "juvenile irrepressibleness" of their father.[16]

According to Gould Lincoln, a veteran Washington correspondent, the story originated at a social gathering of reporters, told facetiously by John Shriver of the *Baltimore American* to illustrate the frenetic style of the Roosevelt clan.[17] Whether Carmichael took seriously what was meant to be a joke, or simply appropriated the anecdote as a lively feature for the holiday issue, he enraged the president. Not only was the article the latest in what Roosevelt regarded as a series of fabrications about him; not only was it malicious in suggesting that he countenanced cruelty to animals; worst of all, this time the children had been brought in. Any president in the same situation would have been angered, and more than one would have taken the first opportunity to tear into the offending journalist. It is questionable, however, whether any other president would have dared to carry the matter to quite the extreme Roosevelt did. An order immediately went out through Loeb that henceforth Carmichael was to receive no news at the White House or any of the executive departments. This much could be expected. Eyebrows began to rise when the order further stipulated that no *Boston Herald* reporter was to receive news until the paper had printed a retraction. And to make absolutely clear that he meant business, Roosevelt instructed the U.S. Weather Bureau in Boston to withhold even the daily weather forecasts from the *Herald*. (It turned out that the president had gone a bit far with that one. The Bureau was required by law to provide them.) Roosevelt had not acted just in the heat of the moment. Weeks later, when a former editor of the *Herald* wrote to him questioning the propriety of his actions, he replied in a bristling letter that the order would stand until the paper backed down. "Dispatches such as this dispatch about the alleged cruelty to the turkey are not only false but are wilfully false," the president declared; "they are malicious inventions. . . . yet the *Herald* did not, when this fact was pointed out, either repudiate [the story] or express its regret at having admitted it to its columns. . . . So long as it takes such a position my present order . . . will remain in force.''[18]

There was much more of froth than substance to the imbroglio. The president deserved and eventually got his retraction. Meanwhile the *Herald* continued to receive the news out of Washington because other correspondents shared their material with Carmichael.[19] But to dismiss the incident as entirely a joke—who else but Roosevelt could get into a national controversy over a turkey?—is probably wrong. Buried in all the silliness are at least two important points. One is that Roosevelt would go to any lengths to get back at a reporter who crossed him. The other is that he dealt with a press not yet completely assertive about its rights. What is interesting in retrospect about the incident is not so much that Roosevelt came in for widespread editorial criticism on this occasion, which he did, as that he presumed at all to tell a newspaper it could not have access to the news and suffered no serious consequences in return.

To a large extent these quarrels can be explained just in terms of the normal tensions between presidents and reporters. As one who appreciated more than most the uses of publicity, it was natural for Roosevelt to be more than usually sensitive when things did not go his way. The abiding irony in presidential-press relations is that the incumbents who care least about what appears in newspapers, and therefore do least to cultivate the working press (Eisenhower is an obvious example), by and large seem to be most successful in avoiding flareups with reporters. Their disinterest makes them relatively immune to what is written about them. It is the Franklin Roosevelts and John Kennedys—the compulsive readers of newspapers—who get into scrapes. Theodore Roosevelt obviously belonged in the same category, and since he had less constraints on him than other twentieth-century presidents he tended to be equivalently more imperious in his responses.

A further factor contributing to ill-feeling, one which again can be said of many men who occupied the office, was his sensitivity to criticism. Considering that he was the president who theoretically cared little about opposition on the editorial page if he could get front page coverage, the trait doesn't make a great deal of sense. Roosevelt's colorful, outgoing personality and shrewd sense of publicity had his name constantly in the papers, and in ways to make him a national hero. When papers did attack him, moreover, he knew that scores more would leap to his defense. Still, the occasional criticisms rankled. ''I hate to see the president get into controversies with the newspapers,'' Archie Butt wrote to his sister-in-law late in Roosevelt's administration, ''for after all there are so few which criticize him that he ought to take it as a matter of course. One has to have the bitter with the sweet in this world and if the *Sun* abuses him and charges him with things he does not do, there are fifty others which promptly take up the cudgel in his defense. To me that is his one weakness. He cannot brook criticism, yet he will tell you that he does not mind it at all and rather invites it. Possibly he is right, for as intimately as I am thrown with him, sometimes I feel that I know but a very small side of him."[20]

It may be that we know a very small side of most presidents, because so many who exuded power and confidence, who basked in the admiration of their countrymen, still surprised by the waspish way they responded when homage was not forthcoming. Is it the pressures of the job? The isolation? The expectation of constant praise when one is raised so high? Or looking at things from the president's perspective, is it the annoyance at having to brook criticism that is ill-informed? Or malicious in its twisting of facts? Or destructive in its possible consequences? Whatever the explanation, and probably a bit of all of these are involved, Roosevelt like other presidents had thinner skin than he imagined.

In that case it is not surprising that bitter condemnations of the press crop up repeatedly in his correspondence, as they do in the letters of most presidents. "Papers like the *New York Times*," he wrote to a friend in February, 1906, "both in their editorials and in their correspondence, lie in response to the demands of the big corporations that the editors and correspondents shall lie; and lie these editors and correspondents like those of the *New York Times* do, because they make their bread and butter by so doing."[21] Or as he complained to Frank Munsey, the magazine publisher and later consolidater of newspapers, "the great mass of people . . . are obliged to get their information more or less at second hand, and largely . . . through people who make their livelihood by the practice of slanderous mendacity for hire, and whose one purpose, as far as I am concerned, is to invent falsehood and to distort truth."[22] Or again in a letter of November 1908 to Richard Watson Gilder, the editor of *Century,* when he remarked of several leading editors and publishers that they "represent a lower type than the worst and most corrupt politicians, or than the worst and most corrupt financiers, and on the whole do more evil."[23]

These harsh words would have meant relatively little, at least have been predictable, if they had expressed only the annoyance all presidents feel on occasion. Something else also lay behind them, however, which mattered a great deal. More than resenting the critical articles written about him, Roosevelt objected to a fundamental precept upon which newspapers operate. He thought the press paid altogether too much attention to wrongdoing. By the editorial conventions of American journalism, a scoundrel or thief—particularly if high-placed—automatically qualified for front page coverage, but the great majority of people who conscientiously went about their business seldom received notice. To Roosevelt, this represented twisted priorities. He wanted an upbeat view in reporting the news while crusading journalists insisted on finding malfeasance. The issue finally estranged him from some of his most ardent supporters in the press, and in an indirect way led late in his administration to a crisis in press freedoms.

Roosevelt's position was grounded in the fear that the enthusiasm for exposé in newspapers and magazines threatened social order. By concentrating so heavily on venality in high places, even when the reports were technically correct (which they often weren't), the press gave a distorted view of reality. It also misguided the public in a potentially dangerous way. If people started to think of all politicians as crooks, and all businessmen as gougers, they would become cynical about things as they are and susceptible to radical proposals for change. The result would be another free-silver craze, or worse. Roosevelt was being most true to himself when he prevailed on Israel Zangwill, the author of *The Melting Pot,* to delete lines in the play alluding to the incidence of divorce and corruption in the United States. "I am very keenly sensible of the very many evils that exist in American life," he explained; "I try to war on them, but I find that a sweeping overstatement in attacking them often does more damage than good."[24]

The problem with condemning such "sweeping overstatement" is that the criticism flew directly in the face of a tradition going back to John Peter Zenger that the highest function of the newspaper is to cast light into dark places. If the press was not to be the beacon, who would? The quarrel pitted a social conservative, a man dedicated above all to stability and to preserving institutions (if necessary by amending them), against a press nurtured in the watch-dog tradition of keeping a sharp eye on government and other centers of power (although for obvious reasons its eye was always sharper watching big government than big business).

Roosevelt revealed how strongly he felt on the matter in a speech at the Gridiron Club on March 17, 1906. His comments, later repeated at a public function, attracted wide attention, and caused something of a split in the reform movement as it had developed until that time. Even the date is revealing: at the height of the struggle to secure passage of the Hepburn Act, at a time when the president was using every resource available to him to fill newspapers and magazines with material that would sway public opinion to his side. He picked a moment when he especially depended on the literature of exposure to condemn those who did the exposing. Clearly he must have been deeply exercised about something.

The immediate provocation was a series of articles by David Graham Phillips entitled "The Treason of the Senate" that began in the March

1906 issue of *Cosmopolitan*. William Randolph Hearst had purchased the magazine the previous spring and assigned *San Francisco Examiner* editor Bailey Millard to come east and take charge of it, authorizing him to spend whatever was necessary to convert the property into a money-maker. Millard had already demonstrated his flair for popular journalism when he published Edwin Markham's "The Man With the Hoe" in the *Examiner* in 1899. Now he set about looking for fresh feature ideas to revitalize *Cosmopolitan*.

The inspiration came within a few weeks. Another Hearst editor, Charles Edward Russell, claimed that the thought of doing a series on corrupt or captive senators occurred first to him. He had been sitting in the press gallery one afternoon looking down on the "well-fed and portly gentlemen" below when he started to think about how most of them represented economic principalities rather than their states or regions. They owed their seats not to the votes of the people back home but to covert machinations in their respective legislatures, and once in Washington they quickly took their place as spokesmen for one special interest or another. "Strictly speaking we had no Senate," Russell wrote; "we had only a chamber of butlers for industrialists and financiers."[25] When he approached Hearst with the idea of developing this theme by focusing on specific cases, the publisher enthusiastically agreed.[26] A new writer had to be found, however, when Russell shortly after accepted a commission to do an article for *Everybody's*. Bailey Millard knew just who he wanted as a replacement. After several approaches he finally persuaded David Graham Phillips—a former editorial writer for the *New York World*, a frequent contributor of exposé articles to magazines, and more recently a novelist—to undertake the assignment.[27]

Cosmopolitan mounted a massive campaign to announce the series. Placards appeared on Washington streets in mid-January screaming in large type, "THE TREASON OF THE SENATE!"; Hearst papers throughout the country ran releases from the magazine's circulation department about the major revelations ahead; the February issue, which appeared on newsstands on January 15, carried a separate article reminding readers of what was to come, and assuring them that although Senator Chauncey Depew of New York, the subject of the first installment, might have resigned before the March issue appeared, it "will not affect our determination of printing this slashing review of the misdeeds of one of the most conspicuous of our undesireable statesmen."[28] The build-up more than achieved its purpose. Even Millard and Phillips were stunned at the clamorous public response that saw newsstand copies of the March issue and the April follow-up on Nelson Aldrich sold out almost before they could be delivered. By May Hearst claimed a circulation of 450,000 for *Cosmo-*

politan, about fifty percent higher than the average monthly figure for the year before.[29]

When Roosevelt received his copy of the first installment on February 17 he was appalled. He liked old Chauncey Depew. Although the senator, a former president and now chairman of the board of Vanderbilt's New York Central line, was universally acknowledged to be one of the railroad representatives in the Upper House, Roosevelt regarded him as harmless. And the two of them had always gotten along well together. It was Depew, after all, who had nominated Roosevelt for governor in a long and effusive speech at the New York Republican convention in 1898. The president said later to Lincoln Steffens that the reason he decided to declare war on the literature of exposure was because of what Phillips had done to " 'poor old Chauncey Depew. . . .' The Senator . . . was having a lot of personal troubles, and then to have himself painted as a traitor . . . 'that was too much.' "[30]

Accepting that this personal consideration was a factor, Roosevelt's motives for going on the attack went much deeper. It mattered also, for example, that he detested William Randolph Hearst. To see the publisher clambering on the bandwagon of magazine exposé, and profiting from it, was almost more than he could bear. The two men would have been enemies under the best of circumstances, but because of a quatrain that appeared in the *New York Journal* a year and a half before McKinley's assassination, their relationship resembled much more a blood feud. The author of the verse, Ambrose Bierce, later explained that he had intended only to warn that the recent shooting of Governor-elect William Goebel of Kentucky posed "a particularly perilous 'precedent' if unpunished" for the safety of the president.[31] Unfortunately for him and his employer, McKinley's assassination made it easy to interpret the warning in a different way. As the tasteless lines prophesied:

> The bullet that pierced Goebel's breast
> Can not be found in all the West;
> Good reason, it is speeding here
> To stretch McKinley on his bier.[32]

The assassination of the popular president revived memories of the poem and of the abuse Hearst papers had heaped on McKinley during the 1900 campaign. For a time it appeared that the publisher might be destroyed by what the country construed as his incitement to violence: death threats poured in on him; libraries and clubs cancelled subscriptions to his papers; in several cities mobs seized the papers from newsboys and burned them.[33]

Among those who joined the chorus of condemnation was Theodore Roosevelt. In his first message to Congress on December 3, 1901, he castigated "the reckless utterances of those who, on the stump and in the public press, appeal to the dark and evil spirits of malice and greed, envy and sullen hatred. The wind is sowed by the men who preach such doctrines, and they can not escape their share of responsibility for the whirlwind that is reaped."[34] Later the president made more explicit whom he had in mind. In November 1906, in the final days of a close race between Hearst and Charles Evans Hughes for the governorship of New York, he dispatched Secretary of State Elihu Root to speak on his behalf in Utica, and to remind the audience of that first message. "I say, by the President's authority," Root declared, "that in penning these words, with the horror of President McKinley's murder fresh before him, he had Mr. Hearst specifically in mind. And I say, by his authority, that what he thought of Mr. Hearst then he thinks of Mr. Hearst now."[35]

But not even the fact of a friend under attack and a detested enemy doing the attacking is enough to explain Roosevelt's decision to come out publicly against a literature which had done so much to create the climate for reform.[36] Much more important was his concern as a social conservative that the spate of articles that began in 1902 with Lincoln Steffens's series in *McClure's* on municipal corruption and Ida Tarbell's on Standard Oil had heated the atmosphere altogether too much. He wanted reform, but reform at a measured pace and with him leading the way rather than being dragged along. The excited reaction to the Phillips series was only one of several indications from Roosevelt's point of view that things were getting out of hand. *Everybody's* magazine, for example, had leaped from relative obscurity to being a publication news vendors could barely keep in stock when it launched a series of articles in the summer of 1904 about stock market manipulators entitled "Frenzied Finance." The series, written by an unsavory former manipulator and onetime Standard Oil cohort named Thomas Lawson, introduced the term "the system" to the vocabulary, just as David Graham Phillips in his treatment of the Senate had popularized "special interests."[37] Lawson took no fee for the articles, stipulating only that *Everybody's* spend at least $50,000 advertising them, to which he added $250,000 of his own money. This concerted effort at revenge against former associates resulted in a fivefold increase in the magazine's circulation within one year.

Roosevelt would have excited little comment if he had restricted his attack to the shrill and occasionally unreliable articles of the Phillips-Lawson type. He couldn't stop there, however, because he regarded the output of even the best magazines as potentially dangerous. "I think Steffens ought to put more sky in his landscape," the president wrote to McClure in October, 1905. "I do not have to say to you that a man may say what is absolutely true and yet give an impression so one-sided as not to represent the whole truth. . . . At the time of the French Revolution most of what was said about the oppression of the people was true; but inasmuch as the reformers dwelt only on the wrongs done by the noble and wealthy classes, and upon the wrongs suffered by the poorer people, their conduct led to the hideous calamity of the Terror, which put back the cause of liberty for over a generation."[38] Roosevelt worried about any article likely to convey the impression of widespread chicanery in the system. In some ways the better researched the article the more dangerous, because the charges leveled could less easily be refuted. It is noteworthy that in a letter labeled "Confidential," which Roosevelt wrote to William Howard Taft two days before addressing the Gridiron Club, the subject obviously on his mind, he lumped *McClure's* with *Cosmopolitan* as essentially the same in fomenting a discontent that one day might have grave consequences. "They are all building up a revolutionary feeling which will most probably take the form of a political campaign. Then we may have to do, too late or almost too late, what had to be done in the silver campaign when in one summer we had to convince a great many people that what they had been laboriously taught for several years previous was untrue."[39]

In this and other letters Roosevelt made abundantly clear what he would not say in public. However much he benefited from their writings, he regarded the Ida Tarbells and Ray Stannard Bakers and Lincoln Steffenses as only marginally better than the Lawsons and Phillipses. They all trafficked in sensationalism and half-truths. "Even of the more honest muckrakers," he wrote to the popular novelist, Winston Churchill, a few years after leaving office, "I found by lamentable experience that there were hardly any whose statements of fact I would trust."[40]

The opportunity for Roosevelt to speak his mind came when he was invited to give the address at a dinner tendered to the Gridiron Club by Speaker of the House Joseph Cannon. It was a useful forum for him in several respects. The Phillips series on the Senate had started just a few weeks before and thus still dominated conversation. The president could expect particular interest at a gathering of journalists, not least because many of the working press must have resented being upstaged by the new kind of magazine literature. He knew also that the oldtimers of the Gridiron Club felt a lingering sympathy for Chauncey Depew, a man who had addressed their first dinner in 1885 in the absence of Grover Cleveland and been the guest of the club many times since. The nicest thing about the setting, however, was that he could deliver his remarks as a kind of trial balloon. Since Gridiron speeches were rarely reported, it would be easy enough to drop the subject if he got a poor response. On the other hand, he could always find an occasion to go public if the reaction warranted.

The president turned to *Pilgrim's Progress* for his inspiration. Speaking without notes, and at the urging of Secretary Root not mentioning Phillips by name to avoid giving him even greater notoriety, he used the phrase "the man with the muckrake" to describe the newspaper and magazine writers who specialized in attacking figures in the public eye. The allusion, while not original with Roosevelt, hit home.[41] "I was a member of the club and heard the speech," Charles Thompson recalled. "It impressed the Gridironers so profoundly that they told the President—privately, after the dinner—that it was a public duty to put it in print."[42] Roosevelt hardly had to be asked. In view of the warm response at the dinner he was anxious to reach a larger audience. A few days later he told reporters that he would elaborate on the subject in a speech on April 14 dedicating the new office building of the House of Representatives.

Ray Stannard Baker described meeting a friend the day after the Gridiron dinner who greeted him jocularly, "Hello, Muckraker."[43] He didn't understand the reference at first, but as the word spread about what the president had said the previous evening he soon caught on. As the date for the dedication speech drew near, Baker became increasingly concerned about the possible ill effect it might have on the work he was involved in and regarded as important. Finally, on April 7, he wrote to the president asking that he reconsider speaking on the subject. Baker pointed out that Roosevelt had contributed more personally to the "letting in of light and air" about business practices and the exposure of "rascals" in the business community than any other individual, and that his leadership in this regard would probably go down in history as his greatest achievement. "Even admitting that some of the so-called 'exposures' have been extreme," the journalist continued, "have they not, as a whole, been honest and useful? and would not a speech, backed by all of your great authority, attacking the magazines, tend to give aid and comfort to these very rascals, besides making it more difficult in the future not only to get the truth told but to have it listened to?"[44] The appeal brought a prompt, and firm, response from Roosevelt. "I want to 'let in light and air,'" he said, "but I do not want to let in sewer gas. If a room is fetid and the windows are bolted I am perfectly contented to knock out the windows; but I would not knock a hole into the drain pipe. In other words, I feel that the man who in a yellow newspaper or in a yellow magazine . . . makes a ferocious attack on good men or even attacks bad men with exaggeration or for things they have not done, is a potent enemy of those of us who are really striving in good faith to expose bad men and drive them from power."[45]

If there was not much give in this, Lincoln Steffens for one did not expect it. He had gone over to see the president the morning after the Gridiron talk, and commented to him, "Well, you have put an end to all these journalistic investigations that have made you." Roosevelt denied that was his intention, claiming only to have been upset for Depew. "I think he may have thought that," Steffens concluded, "but I think also that he was irritated and felt the satiety of the public with muckraking."[46]

Roosevelt certainly gave the impression at the dedication ceremony of being irritated. After the appropriate prayer had been offered, and a hermetically sealed box set in place containing copies of the Constitution and the Declaration of Independence as well as assorted stamps and coins, the president looked out over the distinguished gathering—by a nice touch the Senate castigated by Phillips occupied the front row, practically within his reach—and took up the subject of crusading journalists. It was a typical Roosevelt performance in balancing "on the one hands" with "on the other hands." He deplored mendacious criticism but welcomed honest exposure; he hoped for a climate more encouraging than at present for good men to enter public life, but still wanted to see knaves punished. The major thrust of his remarks, however, was that the appetite for exposé had gotten out of hand. Invoking once more the figure in Bunyan's *Pilgrim's Progress* of the man with the muckrake, who "was offered a celestial crown for his muckrake, but who would neither look up nor regard the crown he was offered, but continued to rake to himself the filth of the floor," Roosevelt warned of the danger in having such a spirit predominate in the public prints. "There is filth on the floor," he said, "and it must be scraped up with the muckrake; and there are times and places where this service is the most needed of all the services that can be performed. But the man who never does anything else, who never thinks or speaks or writes save of his feats with the muckrake, speedily becomes, not a help to society, not an incitement to good, but one of the most potent forces of evil."[47]

Roosevelt had reason to be embarrassed (although there is no indication that he was) at reactions to the speech, which received headline treatment throughout the country. The applause came mainly from papers he habitually branded as "organs of the criminal rich." The *New York Sun,* for example, exulted that the president had turned on his former allies and showed them up for what they were. "It was a great day while it lasted," the paper crowed, "but it became too hot; the muckrakers worked merrily for a time in their own bright sunshine, and an unthinking populace applauded their performance; now there are few to do them reverence."[48] The dismay and bitterness were felt by those who had believed in him. "I met the President many times afterward," Ray Stannard Baker wrote, "and there were numerous exchanges of letters, but while I could wonder at his remarkable versatility of mind, and admire his many robust human qualities, I could never again give him my full confidence, nor follow his leadership."[49]

Of course muckraking did not disappear as an American phenomenon simply because the president disapproved. He had given the genre a name, one which some of the participants accepted proudly, but no reason to stop what they were doing. The articles kept coming through Roosevelt's administration and then through Taft's: Edwin Markham writing on child labor in *Cosmopolitan* in 1906; Ray Stannard Baker on the "color line" in *American Magazine* in 1907; Charles Edward Russell on the tenements of Trinity Church in *Everybody's* in 1908; Judge Ben Lindsey on his struggle for judicial reform in *Everybody's* in 1909. But Roosevelt in a way he perhaps did not realize had still turned a corner in denouncing one segment of American journalism and one segment of American reform. "I am so glad you like what I said," he wrote to Jacob Riis four days after appearing at the building dedication. "I felt the time had come to make . . . such a speech, and it expressed my deepest and most earnest convictions."[50] To a younger generation of reform journalists, however, those convictions represented a betrayal. As it turned out, they also provided a basis for what would be a far more serious presidential-press confrontation two and a half years later.

In retrospect such a confrontation could almost have been predicted given Roosevelt's personality and values: his activist temperament, his limited conception of the rights of the press, his disdain for crusading journalism, his high-handedness in dealing with those who opposed him, his extreme sensitivity to what was written about him, and not least important, his capacity for rage. All that remained was for the right catalyst to come along to set off the explosion, and on this score Joseph Pulitzer and the *New York World* qualified perfectly. Almost since Roosevelt entered public life the paper had hounded him. As far back as 1884, Roosevelt only four years out of Harvard College, it had mocked his pretensions as a reformer when he decided to put party loyalty first and endorse James G. Blaine's presidential candidacy.[51] The *World* clawed at him again in the mid-1890s during his tenure as president of the New York City Board of Police Commissioners because of his energetic enforcement of the city's blue laws while real criminals allegedly went free. So did the paper do most to create the major issue against Roosevelt in the 1904 presidential campaign by noting the generosity of corporate donors to a candidate they presumably should have feared, and at the same time the lack of activity by the Bureau of Corporations since its inception twenty months before. An eight-column editorial on October 1, signed personally by Pulitzer, launched the attack which continued week after week until Election Day. In 1907 the *World* returned to the theme by purchasing for $150 from a disgruntled employee of Edward Harriman a letter written by the railroad magnate describing his contribution to the president's reelection, and emblazoning its contents in a front page story under four banks of headlines.[52] But all of this was only prelude to the matter of the Panama Canal.

The trouble began on October 2, 1908, when William McMurtie Speer, a *World* editorial writer, received a tip that a group of Panamanians was in town trying to pressure prominent New York attorney William Nelson Cromwell into giving them additional payment for their part in carrying out the revolution that had separated Panama from Colombia and allowed the United States access to a canal route through the isthmus.[53] Speer passed the lead on to city editor George Carteret with the suggestion that he assign a reporter to check it out. One of the *World*'s top men spent the day trying to get verification, but when he returned empty-handed the story was shelved.

His inquiries had come to the attention of Cromwell's staff, however. At 10:00 P.M. that night Jonas Whitley, a press agent for Cromwell and former *World* reporter, stormed into the office of managing editor Caleb Van Hamm to complain about the paper investigating his employer without even bothering to consult him or allowing the lawyer to respond. Van Hamm knew nothing at the time about the aborted story, but he sensed the possibilities in Whitley's anger and soothingly invited him to lay out the facts on the spot. He claimed that the reporter's copy would be ready in about an hour, and invited Whitley to come back if he wished and check it for accuracy. Thus appeased, the press agent offered his own version of what was happening. As soon as he left Van Hamm checked with Carteret for background on the day's events, and then dictated a report for the morning paper based on what Whitley had told him. The press agent returned on schedule, and after carefully going through the copy accepted it without modification. Although it was now near midnight, he also asked and received permission to phone Cromwell, who had just returned from the opera, to get his approval as well. The lawyer accepted the story as read to him, requesting only that the *World* include his own specific denial of the charges which he dictated over the phone.[54]

The story that appeared in the *World* on October 3, supplied by Cromwell's press agent and approved by the lawyer personally, was damaging enough to cause wonder about their good sense in letting it out. It is true that the article purportedly had to do with innocent people being victimized by blackmailers. The Panama Canal transaction was so sensitive, however, so filled with rumor and innuendo, that anything written about it could only hurt. Perhaps Cromwell felt the pressure of the presidential campaign coming down to its final weeks. Charges of corruption at that moment, more than being personally embarrassing, might have grave consequences for the Republican ticket. The lawyer may have hoped to minimize the potential damage by speaking out first before his accusers could be heard. If so, he went about it in a strange and clumsy way.

According to what Whitley told Van Hamm, unnamed blackmailers had concocted a story about a syndicate of investors his client had put together to acquire for $3,500,000 the rights of French investors in the canal project, knowing at the time that because of political influence wielded by the syndicate Congress would shortly appropriate $40,000,000 for those rights. Among the people allegedly involved in the scheme were Charles P. Taft, the Republican candidate's brother, and Douglas Robinson, Roosevelt's brother-in-law. Whitley and his client insisted that the story had no basis in fact, but the blackmailers still threatened to go public with it unless Cromwell bought their silence. So seriously did the lawyer take the threat that one of his partners, William J. Curtis, had been to see District Attorney William Travers Jerome on October 1 to file a complaint. As to why Cromwell could not protect himself simply by suing for libel, Van Hamm evidently did not ask nor did Whitley explain.

The *World* hardly deserves credit for the way it handled the story. Accepting that rumors about some such chicanery had been floating about for years, and that just enough unanswered questions surrounded the Panama Canal matter to keep suspicions alive, allegations of this magnitude required more than a midnight visit from a press agent to justify appearing in print. The paper should certainly have checked with Taft and Robinson before mentioning their names. Its failure to get Curtis or Jerome to verify that a complaint had actually been filed—the reporter sent out on October 2 did ask Jerome for a statement, but was turned down—also proved to be embarrassing when the principals later denied that there had been a blackmail threat at all or that the District Attorney's office had been consulted.[55] At that point the *World* found itself out on a limb, without any independent confirmation.

About the only good thing to be said for the story was that it provided an issue for William Jennings Bryan's faltering presidential campaign. Van Hamm ordered six more articles on the Panama Canal transaction between October 3 and Election Day. The headlines reveal their slant: "CROMWELL IS A MARVEL AT PUTTING THROUGH BIG DEALS"; "PANAMA SECRETS WIPED OUT IN PARIS"; "WHO GOT CANAL MILLIONS KNOWN IN WASHINGTON"; "LIST OF SHARERS IN CANAL MILLIONS CANNOT BE FOUND"; "TAFT DISMISSED GEN. DAVIS, WHO HAD HIT AT CROMWELL"; "PANAMA AFFAIRS TO GO BEFORE CONGRESS."[56] On Sunday, October 25, the *World* turned over its entire editorial page to a review of the controversy.[57] Except for Charles Taft's denial of his involvement in the alleged syndicate (Douglas Robinson refused the paper's request for a statement), the coverage contained no new information. But it did succeed beyond expectations in raising echoes of an old refrain: Who got the money?

These articles, particularly the first, received wide replay in anti-Roosevelt journals. Among the papers to feature them was the *Indianapolis News,* a dominant voice in the state edited and universally believed to be owned by Delavan Smith. Not until his death ten years later did the truth emerge that the paper actually belonged to Vice-president Charles W. Fairbanks, who bitterly resented having been passed over for his party's 1908 presidential nomination and behind the scenes was doing everything in his power to defeat Taft's candidacy.[58] He got his revenge when Republicans in the state started to squirm at the *News*'s Panama Canal coverage. William Dudley Foulke, president of the Indiana Civil Service Association and in Roosevelt's administration a United States Civil Service Commissioner, found the stories reprinted from the *World* disturbing enough to send clippings to the president and ask him to issue a public denial that any wrongdoing had occurred. He feared that the Panama issue might yet put Indiana in the Democratic column on Election Day. Roosevelt wrote back questioning whether a statement from him would accomplish anything. "Skinning skunks is not a pleasant occupation," he said, "and tho I am glad to get rid of the skunks, it is at least an open question whether the game is worth the candle. . . . What good does it do for me to say that they lie . . .? It is a mere waste of time to correct any falsehood of theirs because they earn their livelihood by the constant, daily practice of mendacity, and it is out of the question for me to spend some part of each day reading and denying the falsehoods that they have concocted the day before."[59] To this point Roosevelt, while angry, still evidently had himself under control. He gave no indication that he contemplated a retaliatory move against his enemies in the press.

On November 2, the Monday preceding Election Day, the *News* came out with an editorial that put the challenge to the president in the sharpest terms yet. "The campaign is over," the paper declared, "and the people will have to vote tomorrow without any official knowledge concerning the Panama Canal deal. . . . Who got the money? We are not to know. The administration and Mr. Taft do not think it right that the people should know. The President's brother-in-law is involved in the scandal, but he has nothing to say. . . . For weeks this scandal has been before the people. The records are in Washington, and they are public records. But the people are not to see them—till after the election, if then."[60] Roosevelt was not the man to stand much more such baiting.

Perhaps he needed the election results to point out to him how badly he had been bloodied. Although Taft managed to carry Indiana, he did so by less than 11,000 votes. The Republicans lost the governorship, a senate seat, and twelve of fifteen congressional races. They blamed, justifiably or not, the *Indianapolis News*'s coverage of the canal issue as a major factor in the setback. On November 9, the Monday after the election, Foulke wrote to Roosevelt, enclosing a copy of the editorial, to ask again (perhaps at the president's invitation) for a public rebuttal of the charges. "If the statements of the *News* are true," Foulke advised, "our people ought to know it; if not true, they ought to have some just means of estimating what credit should be given in other matters to a journal which disseminates falsehoods."[61] The president waited several weeks before responding. Finally, in a reply dated December 1, he lashed out at Delavan Smith and journalists like him, people he said represented "one of the potent forces for evil in the community." After devoting several pages to denying the allegations made about the Panama Canal transaction, and several more to inveighing against mendacious newsmen in general, he closed by authorizing Foulke to release the letter to the press if he wished.[62] Foulke promptly turned it over to the Associated Press, and it made headlines throughout the United States on December 7, 1908.

So far the quarrel still had more to do with the sins of the press generally than with those of particular newspapers, and still involved heated words rather than an attempt to destroy a rival. Roosevelt did not even mention the *New York World* in his letter (although the *New York Sun* came in for heavy abuse). The situation changed the very next day. Part of the reason is that Delavan Smith, in an interview that accompanied the Associated Press report, pointed out that Roosevelt had singled out the wrong target. "The President's comments on the Panama editorials," he said, "are based on statements made by a prominent New York paper, not the *New York Sun,* which the *Indianapolis News* printed at the same time, with many other papers, giving full credit to the source from which they obtained it."[63]

Much more important in triggering the crisis was that the *World* chose to respond in kind to Roosevelt's attack. In a sixteen-hundred-word editorial on December 8, written by the now aroused William Speer, the newspaper accepted responsibility for the articles in the *Indianapolis News* and came back with its own broadside. Under the headline "THE PANAMA SCANDAL—LET CONGRESS INVESTIGATE," the editorial listed four lies Roosevelt had allegedly told in his letter to Foulke. He lied in claiming that not a cent of the $40,000,000 appropriated by Congress went to American citizens. He lied in saying that the money had been paid directly to the French government for distribution to French stockholders. He lied in claiming to have no knowledge of the individuals who received the payments. He lied in claiming ignorance of a syndicate of private investors who directly or indirectly had influenced government policy on the canal. "To the best of the *World*'s knowledge and belief," the editorial declared, "each and all of these statements made by Mr. Roosevelt and quoted above are untrue, and Mr. Roosevelt must have known they were untrue when he made them."[64] The statement went on to review William Nelson Cromwell's shadowy participation in the whole affair, his visits to the White House and influence on Capitol Hill, his involvement in a mysterious New Jersey-based corporation called the Panama Canal Company of America, his evasive testimony before Congress when asked to

shed light on the corporation.[65] "Whether all the profits went into William
Nelson Cromwell's hand or whatever became of them," the newspaper
concluded, "the fact that Theodore Roosevelt as President of the United
States issues a public statement about such an important matter full of
flagrant untruths, reeking with misstatements, challenging line by line the
testimony of his associate Cromwell and the official record, makes it
imperative that full publicity come at once through the authority and by
the action of Congress."[66] The lines had now been drawn.

It may be, as one of Roosevelt's biographers claims, that the president
"lost his head completely" in the face of this attack.[67] The day after the
editorial appeared he sent a brief letter to the United States attorney for
New York, Henry L. Stimson, saying that "I do not know anything about
the law of criminal libel, but I should dearly like to have it invoked against
Pulitzer, of the *World*. . . . Pulitzer is one of these creatures of the gutter
of such unspeakable degradation that to him even eminence on a dunghill
seems enviable. . . . If he can be reached by a proceeding on the part of
the Government for criminal libel in connection with his assertions about
the Panama Canal, I should like to do it. Would you have his various
utterances for the last three or four months on this subject lookt up, and
let me know?"[68]

Just how strongly Roosevelt felt on the matter became clear in a special
message he sent to Congress on December 15. In it he railed against
Joseph Pulitzer and Delavan Smith, and put forward the extraordinary
suggestion that responsibility for bringing culprits like them to account
belonged properly to government rather than to private citizens. It is
difficult to see what Roosevelt hoped to accomplish by the message since
Congress had no jurisdiction in the matter save the power to order an
investigation of the Panama Canal affair, which is precisely what the *World*
wanted.[69] Presumably the president hoped to reap a publicity benefit for
himself, although only a very angry man could have assumed the public
would take well to the suggestion that government get into the business
of prosecuting its critics. He evidently did assume the idea had appeal,
since the message contended that unjust criticism of government leaders
demeaned the country in the eyes of the world, and therefore represented
a crime against the state. "In point of encouragement of iniquity," Roosevelt thundered, "in point of infamy, of wrongdoing, there is nothing to
choose between a public servant who betrays his trust . . . and a man
guilty as Mr. Joseph Pulitzer has been guilty in this instance. . . . It is
therefore a high National duty to bring to justice this vilifier of the American people, this man who wantonly and wickedly . . . seeks to . . . convict
the Government of his own country in the eyes of the civilized world of
wrongdoing of the basest and foulest kind, when he has not one shadow
of justification of any sort of description for the charge he has made."[70]

The experience of having the president of the United States bring to bear the full power of his office to secure a criminal conviction cannot have been pleasant for Pulitzer. All the more so because he had been on the sidelines until this point, responsible for the alleged libels only by virtue of owning the newspaper. But Roosevelt aroused more of a fighting spirit than he perhaps realized when he presumed to threaten the independence of the *World*. Whatever the publisher's faults otherwise, he lived for his *St. Louis Post-Dispatch* and *New York World,* and would allow no one—president or not—to coerce those papers. Pulitzer's secretary described reading the message to him with trepidation, fearful that the publisher would blow up at the trouble his staff had caused him. He needn't have worried. Pulitzer was angry, but for a different reason. He arose in agitation from his seat, slammed his hand down, and speaking rapidly dictated the response that appeared in the *World* the following morning.[71]

> Mr. Roosevelt is mistaken. He cannot muzzle The World. . . .
> The World fully appreciates the compliment paid to it by Mr. Roosevelt in making it the subject of a special message to the Congress of the United States. In the whole history of American Government no other President has ever paid such a tribute to the power and influence of a fearless, independent newspaper. . . .
> This is the first time a President ever asserted the doctrine of lese majesty, or proposed, in the absence of specific legislation, the criminal prosecution by the Government of citizens who criticized the conduct of the Government or the conduct of individuals who may have had business dealings with the Government. . . .
> We are aware that for many years Mr. Roosevelt has been savagely displeased with the editorial conduct of The World. . . . Mr. Roosevelt's attack on The World can be explained only on the theory that he believes he can muzzle the paper, and our recent impeachment of his veracity seems to have been the last straw that broke his autocratic back.
> If The World has libeled anybody we hope it will be punished, but we do not intend to be intimidated by Mr. Roosevelt's threats, or by Mr. Roosevelt's denunciations, or by Mr. Roosevelt's power. . . .
> So far as The World is concerned its proprietor may go to jail . . . but even in jail The World will not cease to be a fearless champion of free speech, a free press and a free people.
> It cannot be muzzled.[72]

The legal maneuverings over the next several months entailed more than their share of irony. It had been Roosevelt, as a young assemblyman, who had helped defeat a proposed amendment to the New York penal code that would have allowed editors and publishers to be sued for libel anywhere in the state their newspapers circulated rather than in their own communities. "I think it is a good deal better to err a little bit on the side of having too much discussion and having too virulent language used by the press, rather than to err on the side of having them not say what they ought to say, especially with reference to public men and measures."[73] Now, in the vendetta against Pulitzer, he proceeded to do what a quarter of a century before he had warned would represent a serious encroachment on press freedom.

The government brought its first indictment in the District of Columbia. Daniel W. Baker, the United States attorney for the area working under the close supervision of Attorney General Charles J. Bonaparte, argued before a grand jury convened in early 1909 that the *New York World* and *Indianapolis News* had violated the federal statute regulating libel in the District. Although the statute (based on an English law dating to the reign of Charles II) applied only to the District of Columbia, Baker contended that the copies of the *World* and *News* circulating in the capital brought those papers within its purview, and that the offending parties could therefore be extradited to Washington, D. C. to stand trial in federal court. On February 17, 1909 the grand jury returned indictments against Joseph Pulitzer, Caleb Van Hamm, Robert Hunt Lyman (the paper's night managing editor) and the *World* publishing company on five counts of criminal libel against Theodore Roosevelt, William Nelson Cromwell, J. P. Morgan, Elihu Root, Douglas Robinson and Charles P. Taft. Delavan Smith and Charles R. Williams of the *Indianapolis News* were charged on seven counts of criminal libel. Acting on the indictments, a federal judge issued bench warrants for the arrest of the accused.

The difficulty with the District of Columbia indictments from Roosevelt's point of view was that as long as Pulitzer, his primary target, stayed out of Washington, D.C., it would take an extradition proceeding to get at him. Rather than see such a case drag on through the courts with problematical results, Roosevelt wanted to press the attack in the publisher's own territory. The problem was how to claim federal jurisdiction in a state for an offense hitherto regarded as falling under state law. Henry L. Stimson, the United States attorney for southern New York, convened his own grand jury to accomplish the task. He based the government's claim on the fact that several offenses not defined in federal statutes— including murder, rape, and burglary—had been traditionally matters for federal prosecution if the crimes occurred on federal property. In such cases the government could proceed by operating under the statutes of the state in which the federal property was located. What applied to murder and rape should apply by extension to libel. Relying on a law passed in 1898, which in turn derived from a similar bill dating to 1825 to "Protect the Harbor Defenses and Fortifications Constructed or Used by the United States from Malicious Injury, and for Other Purposes,"

Stimson argued that the *World* was liable to federal prosecution because twenty-nine copies of the newspaper had circulated at the military reservation at West Point and another within the federal building in Manhattan (the latter a free copy sent on request to postal inspectors to be checked for false advertising). According to the United States attorney, every time a publication containing libelous material appeared at a federal reservation in the continental United States or overseas it committed a separate offense, which meant that the government if it so chose could theoretically bring 2,809 suits, each with their multiple counts. By this interpretation not even the wealthiest newspaper or magazine could afford to defend itself against government prosecution. The grand jury evidently accepted his reasoning. On March 4, 1909, Theodore Roosevelt's last day as president, it returned indictments against Caleb Van Hamm and the *World* company, passing over Pulitzer only because his complicity in the alleged libel had not been demonstrated.

Roosevelt was clearly playing for heavy stakes in his attempt to curb an opposition newspaper. If *World* employees are to be believed, the harrassment took extralegal as well as legal form. Don Seitz, Pulitzer's business manager and a usually reliable source, reported that "the Administration placed an extraordinary number of secret agents upon the *World*'s trail. Its mail was opened in the post office; the portfolios of its messengers between New York and Washington were examined and the Pulitzer Building itself filled with spies."[74] But the most chilling aspects were the constitutional implications in this vendetta. If Roosevelt had prevailed First Amendment guarantees would have been eroded in at least three critical ways. A precedent would have been established for government to be the plaintiff in future such suits. In that case criminal libel would cease to be the damage done to private individuals and become the protection of public officials against criticism which of its nature cannot always be validated beyond reasonable doubt in a court of law. The administration's approach also meant that journalists could be hauled from their own communities to stand trial in a venue chosen by the prosecution. Not least, the case brought against the *World* introduced the possibility of multiple prosecutions for the same offense, enabling a vindictive administration to hound any adversary, innocent or not, into bankruptcy. "If this precedent is established," Pulitzer wrote to his staff, "it would apply to Yellowstone Park or to the twelve hundred islands in the Philippines, compelling editors to go to these places, if need be, and defend themselves. The mere threat of such a thing would stop any liberty of the press. If this precedent is established we shall have to . . . suspend publication and have a Government organ take our place. There would be no newspapers or editors. The papers would die of inanition."[75] Even in an era not as sensitive as the present to the potential for government abuse of power, these were weighty matters. Pulitzer, in defending himself, really defended the freedom of the American press.

Whatever Taft's feelings about the prosecutions, he thought it his duty to let the issues once raised be settled in the courts. His Attorney General, George W. Wickersham, vigorously pursued the cases initiated under Bonaparte. While they wended through the various stages to a decision, Pulitzer to avoid arrest remained discreetly offshore on his yacht, putting in carefully at various ports after dark to receive messages and transmit his instructions. He certainly did not appreciate the offer of District Attorney Jerome early in the struggle to favor him with a local indictment so he could remain safely in the city on bail. The two men were long-standing enemies because of *World* charges that the district attorney had failed to use the power of his office against wealthy lawbreakers. (Ironically, one of the few friendly messages Roosevelt ever sent to the publisher commended him for his editorial opposition to Jerome.[76]) With so much at stake Pulitzer preferred to trust to his own devices to remain at liberty. But he was still in exile, and bitter against Roosevelt for decreeing it. "He is drunk with success," Pulitzer wrote to his chief editorial writer, "drunk with power, drunk with popularity. . . . Roosevelt did not do anything until the *World* printed a certain editorial charging him with inveracity—an editorial perhaps too strong, let us frankly admit—still, is it not cowardly for a trustee for the nation to use the whole machine of Government for revenge?"[77]

Fortunately, the courts felt the same. One indication of the drift of opinion came when the United States attorney for Indianapolis, Joseph B. Kealing, resigned the position he had held for eight years rather than carry out extradition proceedings against Delavan Smith and Charles Williams. As he explained in a letter to the attorney general, "I am not in accord with the Government in its attempt to put a strained construction on the law, to drag the defendants from their homes to the seat of the Government, to be tried and punished, while there is a good and sufficient law in this jurisdiction in the State court. I believe the principle involved is dangerous, striking at the very foundation of our form of Government."[78]

On October 11, 1909 the adversaries in the Indianapolis proceeding finally appeared before Federal District Judge Albert B. Anderson to present their arguments. He heard the case in one day, and was ready with his decision the next. It turned out to be a stinging rebuke for the prosecution. "This indictment charges these defendants with the commission of a crime in the District of Columbia," Anderson declared. "Now the Constitution of the United States . . . provides that the case shall be tried from the State or district where the offense is committed. . . . A United States statute which would make a case triable in a district different from the district where the act was committed would be unconstitutional. . . . To my mind, that man has read the history of our institutions to very little purpose who does not look with very grave apprehension upon the possible success of a proceeding such as this."[79] Theodore Roosevelt's reaction to the decision was predictable. Speaking a year later at the Columbia Club in Indianapolis, he dismissed Anderson as a "jackass and a crook," an interesting appraisal considering that he had appointed the judge to the federal bench in the first place and later taken occasion to praise his performance.[80]

The Indianapolis decision pretty well quashed the District of Columbia indictments. Extradition proceedings had not been brought against the New York defendants pending Anderson's ruling, and once it came out there was no point in pursuing the same line in a different court. But the matter of the New York grand jury indictments still remained. A different legal issue was involved, which posed different legal problems. Pulitzer had to decide whether to base his defense on the World's justification in printing what it did, as his lawyers advised, or to challenge the very right of the federal government to bring such a case at all. He decided that the former option, even if easier to defend, would be implicitly to concede the existence of a federal libel law. The World might get off, but press freedoms would be seriously eroded. He instructed his attorneys to stake the whole defense on jurisdiction. "I think it is an act of public service," he said, "an act of special value to the entire press of the United States that these test questions should be adjudicated without any compromise whatsoever."[81]

Judge Charles M. Hough heard the arguments in the District Court of Southern New York on January 25, 1910. In a cautiously worded decision, all but inviting the government to appeal to a higher court, he dismissed the indictments the next day. "I am . . . of the opinion," Hough wrote, "that the construction of this act claimed by the prosecution is opposed to the spirit and tenor of legislation for many years on the subject of national territorial jurisdiction. It is a novelty, and the burden of upholding a novelty is upon him who alleges it."[82] In short, unless the Supreme Court ruled otherwise, if Roosevelt or the other plaintiffs wanted to sue for libel they would have to do so in the same way as everyone else, as private citizens through the state courts.

Not even these two decisions satisfied Pulitzer. He wanted for the sake of press freedom to settle the matter of jurisdiction once and for all, and although he as victor could not appeal to the Supreme Court, in a series of articles he badgered the government into taking the step for him. On January 3, 1911 the highest tribunal unanimously upheld Hough's ruling, Chief Justice Edward D. White writing the opinion.[83] "The decision . . . is so sweeping," the World exulted the next day, "that no other

President will be tempted to follow in the footsteps of Theodore Roosevelt, no matter how greedy he may be for power, no matter how resentful of opposition.''[84] It would be only a few years before the excessive optimism in that prediction became clear.

Pulitzer had won a famous victory, one which for all his other achievements belongs among his greatest contributions to American journalism. The sobering fact is that things might have turned out differently if he had lacked the financial means and the commitment to stand up to the president. The case involved a heavy drain on his resources, including legal representation in France as well as the United States. And he had to live with the realization that once he took up the fight (because he could always have avoided it with a public apology), defeat might very well entail a jail term he could not survive. Just to endure the tension of those years represented physical agony for him. It was the country's gain that he never hesitated in what had to be done.

The episode is interesting also for what it reveals about the presidential-press relationship in the era of Theodore Roosevelt. Obviously, Roosevelt was not a tyrant as the term is commonly understood. He believed in popular will, in democratic processes, even in a free press. The only thing he opposed was license, as does everybody. What, then, went wrong? The answer comes back to the respective status of president and press at a time when government by publicity was just starting to become established. Roosevelt's appreciation for the importance of news caused him to react with excessive sensitivity to the clippings that passed across his desk (he had the good sense not to subscribe directly to the papers likely to upset him). And since reporters still had not developed, at least not completely, the professional identity that in later years would protect them from presidential wrath, he was able to get away with dominating, and even bullying, the men who covered him. Circumstances allowed him to act in a high-handed way. Unfortunately, at a moment of extreme provocation they also allowed him to act in a dangerous way. The fault was in his personality, but also in the times. The next strong president would not find things so easy.

5

The Wrong Man

The reporters standing awkwardly in the west wing vestibule of the White House didn't quite know what the next move should be. It was late afternoon, March 6, 1909, and they had come as a group through streets almost paralyzed with snow to congratulate William Howard Taft on his inauguration as twenty-seventh president of the United States. Now they had just been told that Taft would not receive them. As his secretary explained, the president did not anticipate seeing the press as often as he had done while secretary of war. In the future he would summon the correspondents when he wished to make an announcement.

"For a minute or two the boys stood around," Oscar Davis of the *New York Times* recalled, "first on one foot and then on the other, and not much of anything was said. Then somebody had the inspiration to suggest that we were really not after news, but only wanted to pay our respects to the new Chief Magistrate." That explanation, while not altogether true, cleared the air. The secretary went back into an inner office with the message, and almost immediately Taft appeared, shaking hands all around and laughing heartily when one of the newsmen attempted a mild joke.[1]

Although the awkwardness lasted only a moment, the visitors still left with a nagging sense that somehow their old rapport with Taft had been lost. This was not the first time since the election he had treated them with unaccustomed coldness. Just a few weeks earlier a similar scene had occurred at the home of Mabel Boardman, where the Tafts stayed during a brief visit to Washington. Davis in company with one or two other reporters had dropped by to pay their respects, and if possible, to get from the president-elect a statement they could use in their papers the next day. "In both respects the call was a good deal of a failure," the *Times* correspondent wrote. "We did see Mr. Taft for a few moments, but there was certainly no important news in what he told us. . . . And

91

when we left the Boardman house every one of us had the same queer feeling that something had happened to 'put us in bad' with the new President. The old cordiality and friendliness which had always marked his dealings with us, in the days when he was Secretary of War and a candidate for the nomination, was wholly gone, and there was in its place a reserve that almost amounted to coldness."[2]

The surprise was in the sharp change in his manner. Obviously Taft the president could not be as easy-going and accessible as Taft the cabinet officer, but neither did it seem necessary for him to cut off abruptly a group he had worked well with in the past. During the years in the War Department he had been a particular favorite of Washington journalists. Many of them used to make it a habit in the working day to "go Tafting," as they called it. They would gather in his office about 4:00 P.M., perhaps eight to ten of them at a time, for a combination of small talk and business. "There was always a half-hour or so of very pleasant conversation which often furnished a good deal of news," Davis recalled. "Mr. Taft exerted himself to get, and keep, on good terms with the newspapermen. He talked frankly about affairs in his own department, was much more communicative, as a rule, than other Cabinet officers, and at times would even 'take assignments' for the boys. When they had struck difficulties in other departments, it was by no means unusual to appeal to Mr. Taft, and not infrequently he dug out the desired information."[3]

More than appreciating his help, the reporters liked him as a person: his geniality, his bluff honesty, his lack of pretense. The gargantuan proportions of the man if anything added to his appeal. Taft's three hundred and thirty-odd pound frame, "molded between two six foot parentheses, bulging gorgeously in the middle," was an object of fascination as well as humor to the country.[4] As most people knew, he had to have a special bathtub constructed, weighing one ton and large enough to accommodate four ordinary mortals, because he couldn't squeeze into a normal tub. A person with those dimensions, and likeable as well, was bound to inspire a legion of fat-man jokes. "Taft is the politest man in Washington," a popular line went; "the other day he gave up his seat in a street-car to three ladies."[5] While serving as president of the Philippine Commission, Taft received a concerned cable from Elihu Root, his predecessor as Secretary of War, inquiring about reports he was in ill health. He wired back that he felt fine, and as a matter of fact that he had just completed a twenty-five-mile horseback ride. "How is horse?" Root promptly replied.[6] Even Taft joined in the fun (although actually he was sensitive about his size). He enjoyed telling the story of the woman who came to see him on behalf of her son in the army, and when she received the favor she asked for, tried to think of the nicest possible words of appreciation.

"Mr. Taft," she said in parting, "you're really not near so fat as they say you are."[7]

The correspondents couldn't help but feel warmly toward such a person, and what often follows, they tended almost consciously to slant their copy to serve his interests. "No man," Oscar Davis wrote, "has ever been a candidate for the presidential nomination who had such a great body of voluntary newspaper support as Mr. Taft had. . . . Many a time, a story that might have been printed has been let alone simply because the correspondent thought it might do Taft some harm. They were just about as quick that way as they were to print the things that would do him good."[8]

Hence the perplexity, and feeling of disappointment, when he started to treat the newsmen like strangers. They thought they had a good relationship with him, and suddenly he seemed to have no time for them. Not that it immediately influenced their reporting. Every president at the beginning of his administration enjoys a honeymoon period with the press, and this president more so than most. *Literary Digest*, which ran a regular feature on press opinion about current issues, commented acerbically a few weeks after the inauguration on "the honied amiability of the newspaper comment which greeted the new administration. . . , as if the opposition press had for the moment forgotten its function of criticism."[9] The Washington correspondent of *Harper's Weekly* also remarked on the strange tranquility in the nation's capital. "The political mood. . . ," Edward Lowry wrote, "is as serene and soothing as that of the man who sits down alone in the dusk of the day to breathe softly into a flute the strains of 'The Maiden's Prayer.' All is quiet along the Potomac."[10]

It didn't take very long for the discordant notes to be heard, and soon to rise to piercing volume. Within the year Taft would become one of the most villified presidents of the twentieth century, ranking with Harry Truman in the number of attacks directed against him. And he could not even fool himself that somewhere out there a "silent majority" endorsed his leadership. He knew that the antagonism toward him in the press pretty well reflected popular attitudes. "There have been so many adverse criticisms of his administration lately," Taft's military aide wrote less than a year after the inauguration, "that he had with philosophic humor begun to accept . . . that he was extremely unpopular and had failed somehow in his duty as others might see that duty."[11]

It is easy enough to say—as both contemporaries and historians have done—that ineptness in office led to his fall from favor. But simply to cite the long list of political blunders is by itself inadequate, for they were only symptomatic of a deeper failing. Finally, Taft's tragedy was that he lacked the ability to communicate with the people: to gauge their reactions (even to predict what the reactions would be) and to reach them with his own message. The bond between official and electorate that defines national leadership was missing in this administration. And as his strained encounters with journalists in the weeks after the election foretold, nowhere did the weakness stand out more starkly than in his clumsy handling of publicity from the White House. Taft followed a president who had pioneered in the uses of news for political gain, and made his own administration almost a model of how not to use news.

Part of the problem had to do simply with personality. For all his geniality Taft did not come across as an exciting figure. He may have been like a jolly fat uncle to Americans, but that is not the same thing as presidential leadership. Even in the most conventional ways he seemed unwilling or unable to make the gestures that would stir popular enthusiasm. The faithful Archie Butt, his aide and confidant, noticed the reserve on a trip to New York City only two weeks after the inauguration. "From the minute we left Washington," he wrote, "I began to miss the excitement which always attended President Roosevelt on these trips. . . . President Taft took no notice of the crowd—it was not a large one—which had assembled at the depot. He entered his car and never came out to wave a good-bye, and I think even the depot employees missed the 'Good-bye, good-luck' of the ex-President. There was a large crowd at Baltimore, and the President never went even to the platform to wave his hand—and so it was all the way to New York." The same pattern continued when they reached the city and finished their journey by automobile. "The President did not even look out of the window to respond to the *banzai* of the people of the street. Jimmie Sloan, the secret service man, whispered to me: 'What an opportunity he is missing! For God's sake, captain, get him to lift his hat when the people yell, for if he don't they will stop yelling when he will want them most.' "[12] It was a shrewd observation; one the president would have done well to have heeded.

In fairness to him, however, personality is not something that can be willed, and he labored under the enormous handicap of following a president who had more than his share of personality. Taft was almost bound to suffer in the comparison. It may even be that his awareness of the differences between them contributed to his refusal to play to the crowd. People subjected to invidious comparisons often will lean over backward to be themselves, and Taft never lacked reminders that he was a poor substitute for the leader who had really captured the country's imagination. At the Gridiron dinner in February 1910, for example, almost one year into his administration and one year since Roosevelt's departure on an extended world tour, the skits all focused on the former president. If not exactly hurt, Taft could hardly help but be sobered by the display. "Archie," he remarked to his aide when he returned to the White House, "nothing shows what a hold Theodore has on the public mind more than the dinner this evening. Even when he is away and in no way interfering in politics, such is the personality of the man that almost the entire evening was wit and humor devoted to him, while the President with most of the Cabinet present and all the big men of the country were hardly mentioned. . . . It is a strange hold he keeps on the minds of the people."[13]

Taft reacted in an altogether human way in choosing consciously not to compete. "I have made up my mind, Archie, to one thing," he commented a few weeks later, "that I will not play a part for popularity. If the people do not approve of me or of my administration after they have had time to know me, then I shall not let it worry me, and I most certainly shall not change my methods. . . . I cannot be spectacular. . . . If I did as many of my friends want me to do, and play the role as Roosevelt played it, I would be accused in the first place of imitation and then denounced as a hypocrite, and both would be true."[14]

The same reluctance to be judged by another man's standard probably also helps to explain the president's refusal to follow his predecessor's innovations in the uses of news. His response to William Allen White in March 1909, when the Kansas editor wrote to him urging that he use the press to communicate regularly with the public, showed again the obsessive concern with comparisons, and implicitly at least, the sense that he did not measure up. "I am not constituted as Mr. Roosevelt is in being able to keep the country advised every few days . . . in reference to reforms," Taft replied. "It is a difference in temperament. He talked with correspondents a great deal. His heart was generally on his sleeve and he must communicate his feelings. I find myself unable to do so."[15] The self-evaluation doesn't ring altogether true coming from one who saw newsmen frequently while Secretary of War. But perhaps he had to discover and exaggerate differences in order to get out of the shadow of the formidible Roosevelt presence.

Even if some such psychology was involved, it only partly explains Taft's strange failure to take advantage of the publicity possibilities of the White House. His priorities as president, for example, also played a part. Once in office Taft showed a commendable, if impolitic, willingness to tackle issues the public regarded as crashing bores. He felt temperamentally most at home in areas like civil service reform, or administrative reorganization, or improved budget-making procedures. These obviously needed attending to, but just as obviously were not the fare to excite newspaper readers. "Reforms of this kind are the result of the hardest kind of work in the closet," Taft remarked on one occasion. "They cannot be exploited in the headlines. They tire the audience. Those who effect them must generally be contented with a consciousness of good service rendered, and must not look for the reward of popular approval."[16]

He had a point, although it can only be carried so far. Accepting that a president, if conscientious, must devote much of his time to technical matters of little interest to the public, not all of his business falls into that category. Not even the greater part, unless he so wills it. There was something self-righteous in the way Taft equated good public service with dull service. The fact is that he worked in the closet largely by choice.

All of which leads to the conclusion that the major reason for the publicity blackout in his administration was that he simply did not appreciate the importance of news to presidential leadership. Taft seems to have believed, an astonishing attitude for a Roosevelt protégé, that he could just go about his business, and when the people saw what he had accomplished they would applaud.[17] He had no idea that the accomplishment depended first of all on using the press to win public support for his programs. The comments about not having to worry about public opinion, about opinion taking care of itself, appear too often to be dismissed as idle chatter. "I have confidence in the sound judgment of the people based on what is done rather than what is proclaimed or what is suspected from appearances," he wrote to William Allen White; "and if I can make good in legislation, I shall rely on fair discussion to vindicate me . . ."[18] Or again in his response to a letter from the editor of *Everybody's Magazine* urging that he pay greater attention to his press operation. "I am going to do what I think is best for the country, within my jurisdiction and power, and then let the rest take care of itself. . . . I am not going to subject myself to the worry involved in establishing a publicity bureau, or attempting to set myself right before the people in any different way from that which is involved in the ordinary publication of what is done."[19]

This kind of modesty, more than being bad politics, dangerously antagonized Washington correspondents. Almost as if a sluice gate had fallen, the flow of news from the White House suddenly stopped. Archie Butt heard an early complaint from a reporter barely two weeks after the inauguration. "I lunched with Al Lewis today," he wrote to his sister-in-law on March 22, "and he tried to tell me that the press was getting very angry with President Taft for withholding news from it and its members. I told him frankly that the press, with the rest of the country, would have to readjust itself to the new conditions just as the people would have to do later. It is impossible for Mr. Taft to do as Mr. Roosevelt did and to keep the press fed with news every hour of the day. It would be unnatural for him to try to do it."[20]

Unnatural or not, the explanation hardly sufficed to placate a press corps that had become accustomed in recent years to better treatment. Rather than adjusting to the new regime, tempers rubbed increasingly raw over the months as Taft refused to an almost ludicrous extent to deal with the press. He seemed to regard every opportunity lost as a point for him in a suicidal game with the correspondents. His reaction when he botched the announcement of Charles Evans Hughes's appointment to the Supreme Court in April 1910 is revealing. After signing the appropriate document, with no advance word to reporters, he left his office to make an appearance at Howard University. "As we passed the press room," Butt wrote, "the President stopped and looked in, as if to tell old Bill Price of the *Star* and the other newspaper men who are usually there, but everyone, thinking that the day's work was over, had gone. The President said as he settled back in the big Steamer: 'Well, I think I have scooped the boys this time.' "[21]

Of course a leader who thought in terms of scooping reporters when in fact he only scooped himself was all but asking for trouble. One way or another the press would round up news from the White House. Taft's choice was whether to provide the news, and hence help pace and shape it, or whether to leave to others sole say about the coverage of his administration. In opting for the latter course he made what may have been the worst single decision of his presidency.

To get their information, reporters reverted essentially to the methods they had used in the old days. Capitol Hill, which had always been a good place to pick up items about the White House, became more important than ever. Jack Elliott of the Associated Press, for example, broke the story of Edward D. White's appointment in December 1910 as chief justice of the Supreme Court on the basis of a tip provided by his friend, Senator Nelson Aldrich.[22] Correspondents also took advantage of the four mornings a week from 10:30 A.M. to noon that Taft set aside to see senators and representatives. They would feed questions to the president through their congressional contacts, on the understanding that nothing would be said about who was actually doing the asking. Bascom Timmons, an oldtimer among Washington journalists, rather liked the system. "Although it required discreet handling," he wrote, "it was a fine arrangement for the special correspondent. He could get an exclusive answer instead of one thrown out on the public domain for everyone's use as happened in the mob press conferences of later Presidents."[23]

Above all, the press fed on leaks. The absence of controls over publicity meant that virtually anybody in the administration could use news to push his special cause or concern. And more than enough did to keep reporters well briefed on what was going on. "What surprises me more than anything else," Archie Butt wrote about the coverage of one controversy, "is the way the press has got a peep behind the scenes. I shall have more respect for its discernment in the future."[24]

The problem with this method of disseminating news, at least from Taft's point of view, was that it underscored the lack of leadership in the administration. Reporters will always get some information through leaks, but to make it the staple element in their diet meant surrendering any control over what appeared in newspapers. Publicity under such conditions had a life of its own, and like a raging wind buffeted the individual presumed to be in charge. "President Taft has no conception of the press

as an adjunct to his office. . . ," Butt wrote in dismay only weeks after
the inauguration. "Neither the President nor his secretary gives out anything of any real interest, nor do they understand the art of giving out
news. In consequence the papers seek their information from whatever
source they can find and therefore print rumors which, if printed a month
ago, would have resulted in a clean sweep of reporters from the executive
offices."[25]

Taft could not have been so unastute as not to realize himself that
something was terribly wrong with the way his publicity setup operated.
That he did not take steps to rectify the situation is partly attributable to
sheer laziness as well. After all, the things Roosevelt did to polish his
image and generate support for his programs were enormously time-con-
suming. Only someone who genuinely enjoyed the game, or regarded it
as pivotal to his presidency, would have gone to the trouble. Not only did
Taft fail to see the point, he really didn't want to be bothered. His daily
round of golf was much more important to him. As he remarked good-
humoredly in a speech at the National Press Club shortly before stepping
down as president, my "besetting sin was a disinclination for hard
work."[26]

The signs could be seen as far back as the days in the War Department,
when things were still going well for him. Even in so mundane a matter
as failing to learn the names and papers of the newsmen in his circle Taft
showed a kind of mental sloth. It didn't do much for a reporter's ego to
be anonymous, and sometimes it could be downright embarrassing. Richard Lindsay of the *Kansas City Star,* a regular participant in the afternoon
sessions with the secretary of war, discovered as much when his employer,
Colonel William R. Nelson, came to Washington on a visit. During
a routine call on Taft the publisher casually mentioned his correspondent's
name. "'Lindsay? Dick Lindsay? Who's he?'" Taft asked. "'Why,' said
Colonel Nelson, dumfounded, 'he's my Washington correspondent. I understand from him that he comes in to see you every day. Don't you know
him?' 'Never heard the name,' said Taft innocently." At a strained meeting
that evening Lindsay had to explain to Nelson that he wasn't lying down
on the job or inventing sources. Taft just tended to overlook details like
a man's name. But it was still humiliating to be showed up in that way,
as the reporter took the first opportunity to make clear. "The next day,
when we trooped into Taft's office," one of his colleagues wrote, "Lindsay
walked directly over to him, put his fists down on Taft's desk, bent over
him, and said: 'Take a good look at me, will you Mr. Secretary? I want
you to be able to remember what I look like, so that the next time you
talk to my boss you will be able to describe me. I'm Lindsay, of the
Kansas City Star!' Taft pounded his fists on the arms of his chair and
roared with joy."[27]

Taft's size may have had something to do with his lethargy. To Archie Butt's mortification (the aide did care a great deal about appearances), he would fall asleep at the most inopportune times and places. On one occasion he dozed off while Speaker of the House Joseph Cannon was actually leaning over his chair to make a point.[28] His nap at the funeral for the wife of Representative John Dalzell of Pennsylvania also came close to being low comedy. "In the midst of the services I saw the President fall asleep," Butt wrote, "and I stood horrified when I heard an incipient snore. I could not wake him up, I was not near enough to him, and just as I had about made up my mind to walk over to him to arouse him for fear he would fall into heavy snores, Justice White fell asleep also, and I let them remain so, for had either snored loudly I made up my mind to lay it to the justice when comment was made of the incident."[29]

Lack of physical energy must have been a problem for Taft, but still does not altogether excuse his propensity to put off as long as he could chores that did not interest him. When he had the choice (and even when he didn't), golf came first and business waited until later. And nothing ranked higher on his list of deferables than any chore associated with public relations. In the process he did more than squander opportunities to present himself in the best light. Taft's laziness also cut severely into the press coverage received. As he never seemed to learn, his speeches and messages had to go out well ahead of time to receive the widest play in newspapers. "President Roosevelt," Arthur Dunn of the Associated Press recalled, "would have his annual message prepared long enough in advance so that it could be mailed to every part of this country and even reach Europe before delivery. The different news organizations, in spite of the utmost urging, were never able to get President Taft's message until within a day or two of its delivery."[30] As a result hundreds of newspapers at home and abroad, those without their own Washington bureaus and utterly dependent on the wire services, were denied the option of reprinting highlights of the speeches. Constrained by limitations of time and facilities, they had to settle for running the basic news account that came over the wire.

The only consolation in this general ineptitude in handling publicity was that Taft likely would have made a mess of it had he tried harder to follow the practices of his predecessor. News management presupposes attention to technique, but also involves an artistry. It would not have been enough for Taft merely to appreciate the value of publicity; not enough even to consciously duplicate the Roosevelt method of generating it. He needed also the instincts, the special political sense, of a publicist. And here the contrast between him and his mentor was almost complete.

The indications, as one correspondent put it, that Taft's "bump of political sagacity was a dent" cropped up throughout his career.[31] (It is

probably significant that he alone among chief executives never ran for any elective office but the presidency.) During the days in the War Department, for example, reporters constantly had to protect the genial secretary from himself. Charles Thompson told of the occasion when Taft held forth at one of his afternoon sessions with the press on a disagreement between himself and Roosevelt, explaining at length why the president was wrong and hoping that he would soon see the light. The thought of how his words would appear in print obviously never occurred to him. Finally, a thoroughly concerned Arthur Wallace Dunn of the Associated Press broke in and pointed out to the secretary that "what you have just said is not said under the injunction of secrecy. Therefore, unless you do enjoin secrecy upon us, we shall most certainly print it. But we feel it our duty to warn you that if we do it will have the most unpleasant consequences to President Roosevelt and the most disastrous consequences to yourself." Taft, abashed at the lesson in political fundamentals, hurriedly agreed that his remarks were off-the-record. "Dunn, why do you hate a good story so intensely?" the disgusted Hearst representative asked after they left the room.[32]

But a public figure with this much penchant for putting foot in mouth cannot always be protected. Taft ran true to form again in January, 1908 when he appeared at Cooper Union in New York City as a declared candidate for the presidency. The effects of the 1907 panic were at a peak that winter, with hundreds of thousands unemployed and fear gripping the land. Following his speech someone in the audience asked the poignant question, "What is a man going to do who is out of work in a financial crisis and is starving?" Taft hesitated for a moment before answering. Finally, with almost a genius for saying the wrong thing, he replied: "God knows. They have my deepest sympathy if they can't work."[33] Newspapers the next day didn't make much of the exchange, but it still achieved wide currency. "God-knows Taft" they called him thereafter in laboring circles, a nickname no politician would envy.

Likely Roosevelt had incidents like these in mind when he wrote to the candidate later in the year urging him to weigh his words in the future before speaking. It must have been a difficult summer for the president watching his chosen successor waffle through the campaign. And probably the most nerve-wracking aspect was the constant possibility of another Cooper Union gaffe. "I believe you will be elected *if we can keep things as they are*," Roosevelt warned; "so be *very* careful to say nothing, not one sentence, that can be misconstrued, and that can give a handle for effective attacks. I have always had to exercise a lynx-eyed care over my own utterances!"[34]

If Taft managed more or less to follow that advice, he found other ways to demonstrate his lack of color and political instinct. His speeches, for

example, were a perennial problem. "I earnestly want your personality put into this campaign," Roosevelt urged in late August, "and I want us to choose our ground and make the fight aggressively."[35] Such prodding, in a succession of letters to the candidate, evidently achieved little. "Hit them hard, old man," Roosevelt pleaded again in mid-September. "Let them realize the truth, which is that for all your gentleness and kindliness and generous good nature, there never existed a man who was a better fighter when the need arose. . . . Now hit at them; challenge Bryan on his record. Ask that you be judged by your record, and dare Bryan to stand on his."[36]

This was rather fundamental instruction, but not nearly so fundamental as the instruction in image-making, again something beyond the candidate's ken. When photographs of Taft playing golf—a rich man's game—started to appear in the papers, Roosevelt sent word through Mark Sullivan to put a stop to them immediately. "It is true," the president acknowledged, "I myself play tennis, but that game is a little more familiar; besides you never saw a photograph of me playing tennis. I'm careful about that; photographs on horseback, yes; tennis, no. And golf is fatal."[37]

Whatever else might be said of him, the candidate who needed and benefited from this kind of advice certainly did not qualify as a political animal. Indeed, as he and Roosevelt both recognized, in many ways the experience of heading a national ticket was too much for him. When he wrote to the president early in the campaign about dreading the months ahead until Election Day, he received back a revealingly solicitous reply. "Poor old boy!" Roosevelt responded. "Of course, you are not enjoying the campaign. I wish you had some of my bad temper! It is at times a real aid to enjoyment."[38] The answer encapsulated more of the difference between them than perhaps they realized.

It only made matters worse that Taft, who so needed guidance in the handling of news, did not have at his side an assistant like Cortelyou or Loeb to provide it. To be sure, friends tried in various ways to help him. Gus Karger of the *Cincinnati Times-Star* probably rendered the most useful service. One of the handful of journalists the president genuinely felt close to—others included William Price of the *Washington Star* (whose home he visited occasionally), Oscar Davis of the *New York Times*, Richard Oulahan of the *New York Sun,* and Robert Small of the Associated Press—Karger possessed unique qualifications to act as adviser to Taft and go-between with the press. For one thing, his colleagues liked him personally and respected his professionalism. "Gus Karger was one of the most popular newspapermen who ever came to Washington," David Lawrence wrote years later, "and although he was an intimate friend of the President and naturally wanted to see the news written in the most favorable vein possible to Mr. Taft's administration, he never lost his perspective.''[39]

Nor did he ever lose the absolute trust of the president. Karger started out with an advantage in this regard because of the paper he worked for. The *Times-Star* was owned by Charles P. Taft, the president's half-brother, who had married into money and multiplied his wife's fortune through investments in such diverse enterprises as the Cincinnati baseball club, the opera house, the gas works, the leading hotel in the city, and not least, the newspaper. Charles, fourteen years older than Will, had always generously supported his brother's career, not least by settling a sum on him sufficient to assure that he would undergo no financial sacrifice in pursuing a public career. (Once when discussing the marriage of one of his wife's relatives to a European nobleman, Charles quipped, ''If they think it costs a lot to get a lord in the family, getting a president cost $800,000.''[40]) To have a Taft reporter do what he could to help the Taft in the White House seemed natural under the circumstances. And because of their own close ties going back for years, the president knew that he could count on Gus Karger never to abuse his trust.

The reporter tried hard, although never with success, to get Taft back into contact again with the press. At his urging the president agreed to meet with newsmen a few times in the cabinet room to answer their questions. Had the sessions been structured differently, or conducted on a more regular basis, they might have qualified as the first presidential press conferences—an honor that now goes to Woodrow Wilson. Instead, they petered out to a quick and unmourned end.

Part of the problem was simply the setting. The cabinet room offered accommodations for only a handful of reporters, about fifteen or so, which meant that invitations had to be doled out sparingly.[41] For every correspondent favored many others felt slighted, at least until they realized how little they had missed. It didn't take long for the word to get around. As soon became apparent, Taft did not assign high priority to these meetings, nor did he even try to use them as a forum to generate news. He demonstrated something of his attitude by keeping the press waiting until 6:00 P.M. and later for the 4:00 P.M. appointments. And when he did appear he was usually ill at ease, stiff, uncommunicative. David Lawrence, commenting on the unsuitability of the cabinet room for press briefings, remarked ''Just why a larger room was not used, I don't know.''[42] Likely the answer is no more complicated than that Taft didn't want to be bothered.

In that case Karger had to fall back on more roundabout devices to bridge the schism between president and reporters. It helped that Taft allowed him free run of the White House. Doors, including the door to the Oval Office, were routinely open to him; he even had permission to

skim the president's morning mail.[43] Allowing one person this kind of
access might easily have caused resentments among the other correspondents, thus compounding Taft's already serious problems with the press.
That it did not, that the arrangement in fact helped to ease tensions
somewhat, attests to Karger's good judgment. He never used his position
to score a beat on fellow newsmen. If he considered a matter sensitive
he sat on it; everything else became the common property of the press.
Raymond Clapper described "the thirsty correspondents waiting patiently
in Shoomaker's saloon" for Karger to drop by each day and share his
information with them.[44] They had no reason to resent him. Indeed, if
they resented anything it was that Taft didn't have the grain of sense to
bring Karger into the White House in an official capacity so he could
perform the job properly.

Archie Butt also tried to help with publicity, although in his case again
the nature of his position limited what he could do. As companion to the
president and adviser on protocol, he did not have access to inside information nor did he play a significant role in policy-making. It would
even have been inappropriate for him to have intruded in such areas,
since Taft depended on him primarily to provide escape from cares of
state. "When I am with him by myself," the aide wrote, "I never talk of
the day's business to him. I tell him of any amusing story I happen to
have heard and talk of people in whom I know he is interested. He loves
to talk about people."[45] A pleasant role, but hardly one that equipped
Butt to do much with the press. However shrewd his insights (and as a
former journalist he did have a good instinct for news), he could only deal
with the most gossamer aspects of image-making at a time when major
controversies were crippling the administration.

He nevertheless seized every opportunity to project the president as
a man of the people: down-to-earth, democratic in manner, simple in
tastes (none of which happened to be altogether true). A good example
of how he operated occurred in May 1909 during a visit by Taft to Pittsburgh. The committee in charge of arrangements had scheduled a busy
first day for the president. He was to preside in the morning at the dedication of a fountain subscribed to by society ladies, take lunch at the
baronial estate of a local magnate, move on to a reception at the country
club, and in the evening address the Yale banquet at the Pitt Hotel. The
only detail left out was opportunity for the ordinary people of Pittsburgh
to participate in the visit. At Butt's urging, Taft agreed to change the
schedule to the extent of attending the Pirates-Cubs baseball game that
afternoon. But the aide's further suggestion, that the president sit in the
grandstands so the crowd could see him, seemed to be lost when Charles
Taft persuaded his brother it would be undignified to do so. Butt persev-
ered, however. He finally managed to convince the others that nothing

would be gained if the presidential party occupied box seats high above the grandstands out of view. And once they gave in he wasted no time exploiting his victory. "I let it leak out to the press," the aide reported, "how arrangements had been made for the President to occupy the boxes and how at the last moment he refused to do so, preferring to see the game where all the lovers of sport saw it and where he could see the crowd and hear the comment of the fans. The press throughout the country made more of this ball game than the rest of the celebration combined. . . , and even the Secretary of State, who told me he thought it a great mistake for the President to go to the game, admitted to me later that it was the most popular thing he had done since his inauguration."[46]

Gestures like this clearly helped, and Butt worked hard to see that they kept happening and were adequately reported. In the long run, however, they mattered relatively little in how the country perceived the president. To have an impact the White House assistant must be close to the center of power, helping to make decisions and active in implementing them. Other people filled that role, and unfortunately for Taft, they were at least as inept in public relations as himself.

It says something about the president's failure to find his own Loeb that he went through four secretaries during his single term in office. The first, and probably the worst, was Fred Carpenter, who had been with Taft since the Philippines. Oscar Davis described him as a "shy, reserved, quiet chap," which was probably about the best that could be said for a person reporters never liked. Fairly or not, they blamed him for not doing more to put them in contact with the president; for cooperating too whole-heartedly in the decision for isolation. They also, with justification, de-nigrated his political abilities. "There had been nothing in his experience to develop any political instinct he might have had," Davis wrote, "and, if there had been, Mr. Taft was not the man to permit the same sort of relations between himself and his secretary that Mr. Roosevelt had fos-tered between himself and Mr. Loeb."[47]

Unfortunately, the problems did not disappear when Taft asked for Carpenter's resignation in May 1910 and appointed him American minister to Morocco.[48] (He did so under pressure from Charles Taft and several members of the cabinet, all of whom worried more than the president about the appalling publicity the administration was receiving.[49]) It is true that the new secretary, Charles Dyer Norton, turned out to be marginally better as regarded making Taft available to the press. "There was an immediate and distinct improvement in the relations between the President and the newspaper men," Oscar Davis recalled. "We began to get back into something of our old status with Mr. Taft, and it was no longer such a rare thing to get an appointment with him, even on very short notice."[50] Norton's background in journalism—he worked for a while as a reporter in Chicago before entering the insurance business and later serving briefly as assistant secretary of the Treasury—may have been an advantage in this respect. But the young man, ambitious to make his way in the world, something of an empire builder, also got involved in more intrigues and antagonized more people than Taft could finally afford. The president had to ask him to step down in January 1911.[51]

The last two secretaries—Charles D. Hilles, and after he resigned in summer 1912 to take over as chairman of the Republican National Committee, Carmi Thompson—were each distinct improvements over their predecessors.[52] Neither of them, however, showed particular skill or even interest in the shaping of news. In any case by the time they joined the White House staff the damage had already been done. Taft's image was indelibly etched in the public mind: as a political incompetent at best, and to many a tool of the interests. Whatever a shrewd adviser might have accomplished earlier to salvage his reputation, midway though his term it no longer mattered. The blind president served by blind aides had lost touch with the country. In the words of Edward Lowry, writing in *Harper's Weekly* in summer, 1910, "Mr. Taft . . . has no instinct for knowing what the people of the country are thinking, nor has he any sources of information: therefore he can neither guide, direct, nor control public opinion."[53]

It sounds like a harsh judgment, but at the time Lowry wrote few political observers would have disagreed with him. Too much had happened in the first year and a half of the Taft administration to believe any longer that the president would be able to carry on in the Roosevelt tradition. On issue after issue he had demonstrated his clumsiness and insensitivity to public opinion. In particular, he had demonstrated incompetence on the matter of tariff reform. Had Taft wished to leave behind a model for future presidents of the kinds of mistakes to avoid, he couldn't have done much better than his performance on the Payne-Aldrich tariff. He emerged from this first great struggle of his presidency a scarred and battered figure, reduced even in the eyes of those who wanted to believe in him.

In a way it was typical of Taft to get involved in a tariff controversy at all. No subject evoked more intense feelings throughout the country, and none more sharply divided the "stand-pat" and "insurgent" wings of the Republican party. Any president who took sides would almost certainly suffer political damage. "We know from long experience," Speaker of the House Joseph Cannon once said, "that no matter how great an improvement [a] new tariff may be, it almost always results in the party in power losing the following election. A man may do the brilliant thing in politics and personally get a lot of fun out of it, but for the sake of his party he had better do the safe thing."[54] Theodore Roosevelt, ever the astute politician, needed little persuasion. During seven tempestuous years in office he skirted the one issue likely to bloody even a gifted in-fighter like himself. "God Almighty could not pass a tariff bill and win at the next election following its passage," he answered in 1908 when a supporter suggested that he send a special message to Congress on the subject. "The only time to pass a tariff is the first year of a new admin-istration, and trust to have the effects counteracted before another Pres-idential election."[55]

But Taft, perhaps more than was wise, had made downward revision of the rate schedules a central theme during the 1908 campaign, which meant that he pretty well had to deliver once elected. It made sense, in that case, to tackle the issue right away. As Roosevelt pointed out, the sooner the better from the point of view of allowing time for party wounds to heal before the next election. Prompt action would also enable him to cement his hold on the constituency he had inherited from Roosevelt. At one stroke he would cease to be the protégé and become the qualified heir. Moreover, something scarcely mentioned in the press although of critical importance, by moving quickly he had the chance at the very outset of his administration to forge a profitable alliance with the men who controlled the outlets of opinion in the United States.

Tariff reform was a subject of special concern to the owners of news-papers and magazines. Unlike most issues in which class affiliation de-termined publisher loyalties, on this one they thought like people who bought in a protected market and sold their services in an unprotected market. Which is to say, they thought like the average consumer. Under the Dingley tariff of 1897, the most extreme measure in an era of protec-tionism dating to the Civil War, the industry paid $6.00 per ton on imported newsprint. Almost all authorities agreed that the rate far exceeded the amount necessary to protect all but the most inefficient American mills, and in view of the importance of newsprint as an overhead item and the increasing dependence on Canadian supply, represented an unfair drain on publishers' profits. The industry had been agitating for relief ever since the law's enactment. In the spring of 1909, when the issue finally came before Congress, it stepped up the pressure to a new intensity. At the annual joint meeting of the Associated Press and American Newspaper Publishers' Association, both groups passed resolutions calling for free importation of wood pulp and a reduced duty of $2.00 a ton on newsprint. "For a period of years the American newspapers have been the victims of paper combinations, mergers, corners, discriminations, and secrecy in paper quotations," the ANPA declared. "Every obligation which the pa-per maker owed to the Government as a tariff beneficiary has been vio-lated. Newspapers have been forced to bear the burden of frequent fluctuations and artificial stimulations of paper prices. The publishers ask fair treatment.''[56] Clearly, all of the chips rode on this one. Taft would make powerful friends if he delivered on his campaign pledge, and by the same token, powerful enemies if he reneged.[57]

Congress convened in special session on March 15, 1909 to consider the tariff, and the next day heard the president's message urging downward revision. What Taft had to say, or more precisely did not say, foretold many of the problems ahead, and stunned those in the audience who looked to him for leadership. The three-hundred-and-twenty-four-word message took barely two minutes for the clerk to read. Worse, in asking only for "a readjustment and revision of the import duties," it seemed guardedly neutral in tone. The president noted that in his inaugural address he had "stated in a summary way the principles upon which, in my judgment, the revision of the tariff should proceed. . . . It is not necessary for me to repeat what I then said "[58] That was it. He had an opportunity to dramatize himself and the cause, to enlist the people behind him with ringing declarations of principle and to serve notice on recalcitrant legislators that he would use all the powers of his office to redeem the pledge he had made during the campaign, and he delivered a squeal. So much for the bully pulpit of Roosevelt's day.

The disappointment in the speech cannot be ascribed entirely to Taft's refusal to play on popular emotions. A particular strategy underlay his approach, one not altogether unreasonable considering the political situation he faced. Although his party held a solid majority in both houses, with the exception of a handful of thirty or so insurgents it was not a majority enthusiastic for tariff reform. If he hoped to get a good bill through—indeed, if he hoped to get much of his program enacted at all in the years ahead—he reasoned the best chance was by working through the congressional leadership. Appeals over the head of the leadership to the public might win him popularity, but would not pay off in legislation, at least not in the short run. The president purposely lowered his voice in order not to antagonize the men whose support he needed. He called it "the policy of harmony."

The problem was that even harmony presupposes a certain parity of interest and power between those practicing it. Taft could not rely simply on soothing words and appeals to loyalty to get results from Congress. He needed a way to impress his will on others when they did not see eye-to-eye with him. Any president's greatest strength on those occasions is having the public behind him. Roosevelt, after all, worked with the congressional establishment, not against it, in shepherding through the legislation he wanted, but he and they both knew that the popular support he had built up through the press gave him bargaining leverage. In refusing to appeal for the same support Taft went into the game severely handicapped.

Perhaps his strict view of the separation of powers encouraged him to hold back. "Our President," he wrote after leaving the White House, "has no initiative in respect to legislation given him by law except that of mere recommendation, and no legal or formal method of entering into the argument and discussion of the proposed legislation while pending in Congress."[59] He took issue in particular with his predecessor's expressed pride in having enhanced the powers of the office. Roosevelt wrote in later years of his presidency that he had felt he could take any steps not specifically forbidden by the Constitution or laws if he construed such steps to be in the public interest. "Under this interpretation of executive power I did and caused to be done many things not previously done by the President and the heads of the departments. I did not usurp power but I did greatly broaden the use of executive power."[60] Taft regarded that as "an unsafe doctrine," one that "might lead, under emergencies, to results of an arbitrary character, doing irremediable injustice to private right."[61] Accepting that he did not always act on his own principles as president (on some subjects like the Philippine rate schedule and Canadian reciprocity he pushed Congress hard to get results), it still must have been easier for him to take a relatively passive role in the legislative process than it would have been for Roosevelt.

Senator Nelson Aldrich and Speaker Joseph Cannon, the party leaders in the respective houses, easily persuaded the president to leave the management of the tariff bill to them, and only come in at the end when it had reached the conference committee. Taft almost certainly erred in going along with that arrangement. For one thing it meant that he entered the fray only after the decisive battles had been fought. By tradition a conference committee on the tariff must work within fixed parameters, agreeing on a schedule somewhere between the lowest rate set by one house and the highest rate set by the other.[62] Those parameters represent the critical aspect of tariff-making, and if the president hoped to achieve a real reform bill he should have taken a hand in establishing them. Henry Cabot Lodge may have had this elementary point in mind when he remarked in a letter to Roosevelt early in the struggle, "the one thing which surprises me about Taft is that he doesn't know more about politics."[63]

The president showed innocence again in accepting a strategy that put him in the same camp with the Aldriches and Cannons. They were Roosevelt's old enemies, and the enemies of those members of his own party and of the opposition who genuinely cared about tariff reform. Taft's sincerity, or at least his good sense, was bound to come into question because of the allies he chose. He could have maintained a correct working relationship with the leadership while taking care at the same time to protect his independence. Instead, he climbed into bed with the standpatters, and as will happen, his reputation suffered. "Taft is a very large body entirely surrounded by men who know just what they want," Jonathon Dolliver of Iowa quipped, pretty well summarizing the disillusionment felt throughout the country.[64]

But the worst aspect of turning management of the bill over to others was that it meant Taft denied himself access to the press. He did so consciously, and despite the pleas of at least some of his advisers that he reconsider. The president explained his thinking in mid-July, days after the conference committee had begun to meet, while driving out to Chevy Chase with friends for another of his almost daily rounds of golf. According to Archie Butt, a passenger in the car, he said that "he was being urged to make some headlines in the papers; some wanted him to throw down the gauntlet to Congress and assert that the bill had to be this or that, or else he would veto it. . . . 'Now, boys, I will tell you frankly what I am trying to do. I realize as well as anyone else does that I could make a lot of cheap capital by adopting just such a course, but what I am anxious to do is to get the best bill possible with the least amount of friction. . . . While I would popularize myself with the masses with a declaration of hostilities toward Congress, I would greatly injure the party and possibly divide it. . . . It is only when all other efforts fail that I will resort to headlines and force the people into this fight.' "[65] Of course by then it would be too late; indeed, it was probably too late already.

Taft's refusal to go to the country is all the more striking considering that by the summer of 1909 he knew he had been duped by his titular allies. Aldrich and Cannon each packed the conference committee with men above any taint of reform sentiment; ardent protectionists who could be counted on to hold the line for orthodoxy. "I don't think that Cannon played square," the president complained to his brother Horace. "He nominated a Conference Committee that had four high-tariff men on it . . . who would not fight for the low provisions of the House bill."[66] And to his wife Helen, vacationing in Beverly, Massachusetts, where he yearned to be rather than in the sweltering Washington heat, he wrote almost poignantly of being thrown in with a breed of men he didn't quite know how to handle. "I am dealing with very acute and expert politicians, and I am trusting a great many of them and I may be deceived."[67] But still he would not attempt through publicity to strengthen his hand against them.

Despite an intensive lobbying campaign during July among members of the conference committee and congressional leaders, Taft received at the end of the month the flawed measure that could have been predicted. The proponents of the bill, who described it as a dramatic downward revision of the rate schedule, and the critics, who condemned it as even worse than the Dingley tariff, were both wrong. Essentially, the Payne-Aldrich tariff of 1909 tinkered with the rates without significantly changing them, save for the abolition of duties on hides. In the view of F. W. Taussig, a Harvard professor acknowledged as the foremost contemporary authority on the subject, the law "brought no essential change in our tariff system. It still left an extremely high scheme of rates, and still showed an extremely intolerant attitude on foreign trade." But Taussig noted something else as well that would be extremely important in the months ahead. "Though the act as a whole brought no considerable downward revision, it was less aggressively protectionist than the previous Republican measures. The increases of duty were more furtive, the reductions were more loudly proclaimed. The extreme advocates of protection were on the defensive."[68]

Taft knew, of course, that he had not won the victory he aspired to. "The bill is not a perfect tariff bill or a complete compliance with the promises made," he declared in a statement released to the press on the day he signed the measure, "but a fulfillment free from criticism in respect to a subject matter involving many schedules and thousands of articles could not be expected."[69] He described the law as a "sincere effort" at reform; one he privately felt carried so many supplemental good features that he had no choice but to sign it. The section of the rate schedules he cared most about—virtual free trade on Philippine imports except for a limitation on tobacco—had been won. The law also gave him a maximum-minimum clause to adjust duties in response to concessions from other countries. As part of the overall package Aldrich had agreed to a two-percent tax on the net income of corporations and to the introduction of what eventually became the Sixteenth Amendment, authorizing a federal income tax. Taft even received approval to establish a temporary tariff commission, which he hoped would be the first step to eventually removing the issue from politics altogether. Despite the disappointing features in the law, and despite his campaign pledge the previous fall, all of this seemed too much to throw away with a veto.

Late in the afternoon on Thursday, August 5, President Taft traveled up to Capitol Hill to sign the measure in a brief ceremony on the Senate side. He used two pens for the occasion, one for the regular bill which he gave to Representative Sereno Payne, and the other for the separate Philippine section, which he kept as a prized memento for himself. During the ceremony a violent thunderstorm hit the city, disrupting his plans for a dinner party on the south terrace that evening to celebrate the conclusion of the long struggle. But to the press the next day the storm symbolized not so much an ending as a beginning. It was the first warning of what the president could expect from the country for betraying his promise to bring the tariff down.

The fury of the attack on Taft that began immediately in newspapers and magazines raises a critical question. Is it possible, as the president and some congressional leaders believed, that the press in its frustration at failing to get the duty on newsprint it wanted created an artificial issue? In the same way that the media have been charged in recent years with manipulating events as much as chronicling them, Taft blamed journalists in his time for inciting the situation they reported as objective fact. They did so in the first instance, he felt, by their distorted coverage of the Payne-Aldrich tariff. Their stress on all of the bad features of the bill and passing over of the good made it seem far worse than it was; worse even than the Dingley tariff. And by predicting a groundswell of opinion against it they in effect caused the groundswell. The popular grievances did not exist independently; this was reporting as self-fulfilling prophecy, and all the easier to accomplish, Taft believed, because of the mood of restlessness and distrust of authority that goes along in any era of reform, and that the muckraking journalism of the past few years had done so much to encourage. The press had created an atmosphere in the United States "in which anything asserted with sufficient emphasis, without proof, will be believed about any man, no matter how disinterested or high his character."[70]

The president's indictment was not altogether invalid. It is true that publishers had a personal stake in tariff reform, and that they bitterly resented how they came out under the Payne-Aldrich act. Because of the bill passed by the House of Representatives, they had been led to expect that the duty on newsprint would drop from $6.00 a ton to $2.00. The Senate version settled on $4.00, however, and rather than splitting the difference in committee (as Taft thought fair) the final measure assessed newsprint at $3.75 a ton. To compound the disappointment, the law left the rate on wood pulp unchanged until Canada repealed its export tax, at which time the pulp would come in duty free. This was far short of what the industry wanted and thought fair, and as Taft had every justification to believe, led directly to the venomous newspaper campaign against him. "I have not been familiar myself with any situation politically," he wrote to H. H. Kohlsaat of the *Chicago Record-Herald* in March 1910, "where there has been so much hypocrisy, so much hysteria, so much misrepresentation by the press growing out of their own personal interest in legislation as within the last year, and this affects not only the newspapers but also the periodicals."[71]

Whether the press, acting out of self-interest, created a bogus issue, however, is an altogether different matter. Accepting that the organs of opinion in the country hardly deserved credit for pretending to plead the public interest when in fact they had their own profit margins in mind, the further fact is that readers in 1909 needed little prompting to be irate with the law. Resentment of trusts had been building for years (as indicated by the reaction when Theodore Roosevelt took on Northern Securities), and the public accepted almost as axiomatic that trusts flourished because of the protective tariff and exacted tribute from the country in the form of monopoly prices. Add to this that the cost of living rose on August 1, 1909 to the second highest point in American history until that time and it is clear that conditions were right for a political explosion. To ascribe discontent under such circumstances solely, or even primarily, to the machinations of disgruntled journalists was unrealistic. (For that matter it is uncertain how much the press can ever do to influence opinion if the public is not in the mood to be influenced. Probably very little.) People knew quite well on their own what they thought of the Payne-Aldrich bill, and Taft in failing to recognize it, in blaming everything on the kind of coverage the bill received, demonstrated again a certain obtuseness. To an initial blunder in failing to use publicity for political gain he now added a second in misreading the public mind.

Still, he did recognize the rumblings throughout the country, and knew that if he hoped for a Republican Congress in 1910, not to mention a second term for himself, he would have to engage in immediate fence-mending. The situation called for the kind of effort Roosevelt used to undertake so sucessfully: a swing around the circle to bring the president's case to the people. Of course when Roosevelt went on the road it was to win support for forthcoming programs rather than to limit the damage in things already done, which meant that a different spirit surrounded his trips and the prospects for success were far greater. It is always easier to be an enthusiast for new initiatives than an apologist for old ones. But Taft really didn't have much choice. The Payne-Aldrich bill had ignited a blaze in the country that had to be contained before it destroyed the administration and the party.

Typically, Taft did almost everything wrong from a public relations standpoint during the six weeks he spent relaxing with his family in Beverly before setting out. Even a neophyte should have known that this was no time to dine at the mansion of Henry Frick, the steel magnate. Taft had sensibly declined a previous invitation to luncheon, but when Frick asked him again through Secretary of State Philander Knox, a friend from days back in Pittsburgh and a fellow millionaire, "the President," in Archie Butt's words, "good-natured and complacent, yielded of course to his premier."[72] Newspapers gave the outing heavy play, and with predictable consequences. A few weeks before, Taft had signed a bill the country perceived as protecting the trusts, and within days he would embark on a tour to justify his action. Now he was portrayed hobnobbing with one of the beneficiaries in a "perfect palace hidden away among the trees" filled with Turners and Gainsboroughs and Van Dycks.[73] The publicity couldn't have been worse.

Taft added to his problems in Beverly by succumbing to the old laziness. It was essential that he make the best possible impression on the tour, and to do so required advance preparation. But he had a terrible time getting started. "If it were not for the speeches, I should look forward with the greatest pleasure to this trip," he complained to Butt. "I would give anything in the world if I had the ability to clear away work as Roosevelt did. . . . I am putting off these speeches from day to day, and the result will be that I shall have to slave the last week I am here and get no enjoyment out of life at all." The aide, while sympathetic, knew better. "I might predict that he will not have a speech written by the time he leaves Beverly," Butt wrote. "He will possibly have the outline of the one he is to deliver in Boston on the fourteenth prepared, but that will be all, and he will spend the first two or three days on the train preparing speeches; but as to preparing them cut-and-dried fashion, as President Roosevelt did, he will not."[74] Nor did he. They were written in hit-or-miss fashion, usually hours before the time for actual delivery. And for that the president known to many of his countrymen as "God-knows Taft" would pay dearly.

The approach he took in the talks was misconceived from the beginning. In view of popular hostility to the Payne-Aldrich tariff it made sense to concede to the extent necessary the bill's limitations (he obviously couldn't persuade the country to be grateful for the high duties), and then shift the debate as soon as possible into other areas. After all, he had plenty to work with. The corporation tax represented a significant gain, as Roosevelt acknowledged in a letter to Henry Cabot Lodge written just about the time the president embarked on his tour. Roosevelt described the tax as "a triumph which the west will appreciate," and suggested that it might "take the sting out of some of the inevitable grumbling about the tariff by diverting attention to what is really of far greater moment."[75] Taft could also have created diversions by holding forth on the income tax amendment as a victory, and even on the promise inherent in his temporary tariff commission (nobody knew then that it would come to nothing). He did not lack arguments to make a case.

Instead, he concentrated on the area in which he was weakest by attempting to justify the rate schedules. He also embraced the stand-patters, from whom he had every reason to distance himself, while ignoring the insurgents in the party who, on this issue at least, came closer to representing majority opinion. The pattern began in his first speech on September 14 in Boston, when he praised Nelson Aldrich of Rhode Island as one of the "ablest statesmen in financial matters in either House."[76] On the other hand, he managed later in the tour to deliver six speeches in Wisconsin without once mentioning the name of Robert La Follette. Nothing required that Taft pretend to a closeness which did not exist, but to offer no gracious comment at all about a leader who enjoyed the affection as well as respect of his constituents was stupidity.

The debacle occurred in Winona, Minnesota, where Taft appeared on September 17 to boost the reelection prospects of Representative James Tawney, chairman of the House Appropriations Committee. Tawney was in deep trouble in his district for his part in the enactment of the Payne-Aldrich bill, and because he was a popular figure in Washington and an insider in party circles, the president wanted to help him. As always, however, the help would have to be off-the-cuff. "Tomorrow Milwaukee and Winona," Taft cabled his wife from Chicago on September 16. "Hope to be able to deliver a tariff speech at Winona but it will be a close shave." A follow-up cable the next day when he reached the small community nestled on the Mississippi River in the southeast corner of the state assured Helen that he had squeezed under another deadline. "Speech hastily prepared," he reported, "but I hope it may do some good."[77]

It didn't. Not that the speech was entirely bad. Taft offered a reasoned defense of the new schedules, arguing that they incorporated many more reductions than increases. If the overall effect would not be to bring down the cost of living, he declared, that had never been his intention. He wanted to eliminate unnecessary protection, but not at the risk of jeopardizing American jobs or American industry. "I did not agree, nor did the Republican party agree," the president said, "that we would reduce rates to such a point as to reduce prices by the introduction of foreign competition. That is what the free traders desire. That is what the revenue-tariff reformers desire; but that is not what the Republican platform promised, and it is not what the Republican party wished to bring about." Taft conceded that the law did not provide "certain things in the revision of the tariff which I had hoped for." He still signed it "in order to maintain party solidarity, which I believe to be much more important than the reduction of rates in one or two schedules of the tariff."[78]

This much, while unlikely to disarm critics, could be accepted as a fair and capable exposition of what happened to be an unpopular point of view. The bombshell, which overshadowed everything else he said and seized national attention, came midway through the speech, when Taft added the further thought that "on the whole . . . I am bound to say that I think the Payne tariff bill is the best tariff bill that the Republican party ever passed. . . ."[79] The words would have been a blunder before any audience; uttered in Minnesota they represented a blunder that almost approached grandeur in its dimensions. For as Charles Thompson of the *New York World* pointed out, "the bill was not regarded with favor anywhere west of Pittsburgh, and the warmth with which it was hated in Illinois rose to heat in Iowa and to the boiling-point in Michigan and Wisconsin. Minnesota was far beyond the boiling-point; it had reached that height assigned by Holy Writ to the place where 'the worm dieth not and the fire is not quenched.' Speaking in favor of the bill was one of the few things for which a man might legally be lynched in Minnesota. So, of course, that was the place which Taft picked out as a likely place in which to eulogize it."[80]

Perhaps the president had grounds to resent the way the press handled the story. His words about "best tariff bill ever passed" fit nicely into newspaper headlines, and if the result of bannering in them in bold type across the front pages of the nation's press was to distort what he really meant, that is often the price a public figure pays for loose talk. In this case the price proved to be heavy indeed. The *Louisville Courier-Journal,* "more in sorrow than in anger," accused him of "openly endors[ing] a system of ruthless graft equally as indefensible upon moral grounds as the irregularities of the Tweed ring. . . . The exclamation made by Julius Caesar, when he beheld the dagger of Brutus stained with his blood, will come naturally to the lips of the anti-Cannon, anti-Payne, anti-Aldrich, anti-graft Republicans."[81] The *New York Times* also looked to history for a parallel to Taft's betrayal. It saw the Winona appearance as even worse than Daniel Webster's Seventh of March speech on slavery, when the senator "sought a compromise in respect to matters as to which compromise was impossible. . . . The memorandum with which President Taft accompanied his signature to the Payne bill was, in effect, a Seventh of March speech. Now he goes further than that. He no longer apologizes. He accepts, he defends, he is almost enthusiastic for 'the best tariff bill the Republican Party has ever passed,' a bill that the whole country sees is the embodiment of bad faith and broken promises."[82] To the *St. Louis Post-Dispatch,* "Mr. Taft's Winona speech puts an end to the expectation that he will lead progressive Republican sentiment to a better fulfillment of party pledges."[83]

Taft, characteristically truculent when backed into a corner, refused to admit he had made a mistake. "There are four or five free-trade newspapers of Republican tendency that are engaged in hammering me for my speech at Winona," he wrote several weeks later to his son Robert, "but my impression is that the speech is the best thing I have done."[84] On the other hand he resented the stress newspapers put upon the remark, contending that words may be literally correct and still distorted when they are blown out of proportion. "I cannot . . . see that I have done anything to call for such severe criticism," the president complained to William Dudley Foulke shortly after returning from the tour. "I meant every word of my Winona speech. . . . [It] is not properly quoted, but its purport is misrepresented and what I said is perverted."[85]

One can easily sympathize with his annoyance at newspapers for hammering away at one sentence out of a lengthy address. Anybody exposed to such treatment will sooner or later become vulnerable. The further truth, however, is that it required more than ordinary naïveté, and more than ordinary insensitivity to popular opinion, to commit Taft's particular gaffe. (Tawney, it might be mentioned, not only went down to crushing defeat in the next election, after this kind of help from the president he never held political office again.) At the very least Taft affirmed once more his right to the title "Mr. Malapropism" by the way he put a sleepy Minnesota town on the map.[86] He also affirmed that he was, and would always remain, a political innocent. "Poor Taft made a sad mess of it at Winona," Senator Jonathon Dolliver of Iowa wrote gleefully to his fellow insurgent, Robert LaFollette. "I knew he was good natured but I never dreamed he was so dull. . . . It is like taking candy from children for Aldrich to confer with Taft."[87]

Even the president eventually conceded that the speech might have been handled better. When asked by Francis Leupp in a December 1911 interview in *Outlook* whether he would repeat the Winona performance if he had it to do over, he replied "In phraseology no; in effect yes. . . . I should have changed the sentence where I proclaim the Payne Tariff Act the best ever passed. The comparative would have been a better description than the superlative. . . ." But still he could not leave well enough alone. Taft added that his troubles all traced to the fact that he had hurriedly dictated the speech to a stenographer "between two stations, and glanced through it only enough to straighten its grammar. . . . If I had prepared it two or three weeks before and revised it deliberately, as I ought to have done, I should have clarified several passages."[88] With those words he dug the hole just a little deeper. "When people remembered that he had left the golf links . . . to go to Winona," Henry Stoddard of the *New York Evening Mail* wrote, "the original mistake was immediately overshadowed by the explanation. The West was infuriated by the apparent confession that he had played golf rather than prepare carefully what he was to say to it. Everywhere there was dismay over the implication that the President of the United States gave little thought to grave public questions."[89]

If Winona represented the nadir for Taft, nothing he did on the rest of the tour helped to repair the damage. He continued to defend doggedly the rate schedules and to embrace the people who could only do him political harm. His reception of Joseph Cannon, when the speaker joined the presidential party in late October for a trip by steamboat down the Mississippi River from St. Louis to New Orleans, was particularly damaging. Taft detested the wily old Yankee: a man foul in language, foul in personal habits, foul in his political ethics. But rather than snubbing him, which would have earned the president at least a grudging respect, he did everything in his power to make the speaker feel welcome. "The President simply hates him and expresses his contempt for him whenever he can do so," Butt moaned in a letter to his sister-in-law, "yet he openly flattered him on the trip down the Mississippi, was photographed with his arms about his neck, and appeared to endorse him whenever they spoke together." To the aide it was one more indication of the contrast between the two leaders he had served and admired. "I saw how [Cannon] maneuvered to get the President in constant juxtaposition to himself and how he made use of that position to further his own ends. He gave several openings which would have afforded President Roosevelt, for instance, many opportunities to kill him politically, and which Mr. Roosevelt would have taken advantage of, too, by the way. But the President let them go by, leaving the impression that he actually endorsed the old vulgarian."[90] The country had no basis to form any other impression.

As bad as Taft's performance on the tour was from the point of view of influencing opinion, it was matched by his inability to read the indicators and recognize the political damage he had suffered. Wherever he went he received a polite reception, which he interpreted to mean the public essentially supported him. Taft, who hated to cause any unpleasantness himself (which probably accounts for his warmth to Cannon), hated just as much to hear unpleasant tidings from others.[91] And so the people lined the streets to see him as he passed by, and the sycophants told him all was well, and he believed it. "The theory that the people are discontented or are waiting to make a breach in the Republican party is in my judgment all nonsense," he assured Robert in late October.[92] Or as he explained to Secretary of State Knox, his enemies raised such a clamor because "they have become desperate . . . and their cry is heard above the quiet chant of contentment that exists everywhere in this country. . . . It is a case in my judgment where the 'shallows murmur and the deeps are dumb.' "[93]

The president would soon enough be disabused of that notion, but not before he compounded his troubles by taking the step that would make conciliation with publishers virtually impossible. The tariff issue had already caused a serious estrangement, and led to the kind of coverage in newspapers and magazines he could not long afford. If ever the time existed to soothe ruffled feathers, it was now. Instead, without any warning, he used his annual message on December 7, 1909 opening the Second Session of the Sixty-first Congress, to urge a sharp increase in postal rates on magazines. The proposal, which threatened publishers in an area of particular vulnerability, succeeded nicely in widening the breach still further.

Newspapers and periodicals, as essential instruments of public intelligence, have traditionally circulated through the mails at special rates. In 1792, for example, Congress set postage on papers at one cent within 100 miles, and one and a half cents beyond, as well as providing free delivery for printers' exchanges. The lawmakers thereby established a principle which, despite periodic adjustments in the rates, has continued to the present day. What has always remained moot, however, is how heavy the postal subsidy should be, and the related question, how much of a subsidy the industry actually needs. The third assistant postmaster general in Roosevelt's administration raised the question when he pointed out at the 1908 meeting of the National Association of Newspaper Circulation Managers that newspapers and periodicals comprised sixty-four percent of total mail tonnage and yet contributed only five percent of total mail revenue.[94] Many people, including Roosevelt, thought the disparity out of line. By the same token, most publishers pleaded that without such help it would be impossible for them to operate at a profit.

This was the issue Taft reopened at a time when the wounds of the tariff battle were still smarting. He informed Congress that the $63,000,000 loss the government incurred annually in assessing printed matter at one cent a pound which actually cost more than nine cents to deliver accounted several times over for the $17,500,000 postal deficit. "The figures are startling," Taft said, "and Congress may well consider whether radical steps should not be taken to reduce the deficit in the post office department caused by this discrepancy between the actual cost of transportation and the compensation exacted therefore. . . . I very much doubt . . . the wisdom of a policy which constitutes so large a subsidy and requires additional taxation to meet it."[95] Considering that magazines contained a higher proportion of advertising to reading matter than newspapers, and on an average circulated three and a half times greater distance through the mail, the president proposed that they be required to bear a larger share of their own overhead.

The certainty of a violent response from the industry makes doubtful whether even Taft could have been altogether oblivious to the consequences of his message; that it meant picking still another fight with a group he could ill afford to alienate further. Likely the president knew exactly what would happen, and went ahead anyway out of a desire to get back at those who had treated him badly. Arthur Dunn of the Associated Press claimed that the secretary of the Republican Congressional Campaign Committee openly expressed that motive to him in a conversation in New York. "The newspapers and magazines have been lying about us and the tariff for more than a year now," he quoted Harry Loudenslager as saying, "but we'll get even with them this winter. We'll increase their rate of postage; that's what we'll do."[96] Although Taft never put it quite so bluntly, he voiced similar enough sentiments on several occasions to lend credence to Dunn's report. "I do not care anything about them," he wrote in March 1910 to the president of the New York Trust Company. "They have shown themselves just exactly as selfish as the interests which they have attacked, and I propose to have justice done. If we wish to contribute a subsidy of fifty millions to the education of the country, I can find a good deal . . . better method of doing it than by the circulation of *Collier's Weekly* and *Everybody's Magazine*."[97]

If Taft did indeed act out of pique, it represented one more blunder on top of an array of blunders. Whatever the merits of his position, he was in a no-win situation. He had no assurance of prevailing in such a struggle. Most congressmen did not share his disregard for the importance of a good press, and on this issue were more likely to listen to the appeals of publishers than the computations of a discredited president. And even if he got the bill he wanted, it would be at best a Pyrrhic victory. Magazines and newspapers would never forgive him, and would use their considerable resources to harry him on every possible future occasion.

As it turned out, Taft ran into more of a buzz saw than he anticipated. "I never in all my knowledge of lobbies and of organized efforts to influence legislation," he complained to a member of the Senate Post Office Committee, "have seen such flagrant mis-representation and such bold defiant attempts by the payment of the heaviest advertisement bills to arouse the press of the country against the proposed legislation."[98] Worse, the effort paid off. Taft finally had to agree to withdraw the proposal for an increase in rates and as a face-saving compromise appoint a special commission to look into the matter. The panel—composed of Supreme Court Justice Charles Evans Hughes, Harvard President A. Lawrence Lowell, and Harry A. Wheeler, president of the Chicago Association of Commerce—eventually reported back in support of his position. The president had the consolation of being able to notify Congress weeks before his term ended that the commission, after exhaustive investigation, recommended doubling second-class rates to two cents a pound. But considering all the furor this was a relatively modest proposal, one which spoke itself to political realities. Even Taft seemed somewhat less the firebrand in forwarding it. "The business enterprises of the publishers of periodicals . . . have been built up on the basis of the present second-class rate," he conceded in the message to Congress, "and therefore it would be manifestly unfair to put into immediate effect a large increase in postage."[99]

Archie Butt saw the essential truth from the beginning. "The position Taft took . . . was, of course, a most impolitic thing to do," the aide wrote, "for it arrays against him practically the entire magazine world of the country. . . ."[100] In a way it didn't matter if second-class rates were unreasonably low. The president was responsible for putting through a program, and that meant sorting out his priorities. He should have realized that the potential gain in forcing publishers to pay a greater share of the postal deficit did not begin to match the potential loss to him in inciting press hostility that would hamper his ability to govern. The risk was certainly too great at a time when publishers already had reason to feel aggrieved. It may be unfair that a particular interest group must be treated with kid gloves, but that was and is a fact of life. Taft himself recognized after his humiliating defeat in 1912 that he had made a mistake in antagonizing those power brokers. "I think I might have secured a tariff on print paper at $2.00 per one hundred pounds," he wrote to Otto Bannard on November 10, 1912, "and if that had been brought about we should not have had the bitterness of spirit in reference to the Payne Bill."[101] The next day he sent a second letter to Bannard expressing another regret. "It was not necessary for me to run amuck among the magazines and attempt to curtail the profit they made in the transportation of their products at an unconscionable low rate."[102]

The destructive publicity surrounding Taft's mishandling of the Payne-Aldrich tariff, compounded by the headlines arising from such other controversies as the Ballinger-Pinchot affair, pretty well shattered confidence in his leadership within his first year in office. Well before the country went to the polls in 1910 to pass a midterm judgment on the administration, it was clear what the verdict would be. For the first time in sixteen years the Democrats took control of the House of Representatives, winning a solid majority of 228 to 160. They also picked up eight seats in the Senate. Taft by now resembled a cavalry officer drawing his dwindling force into a circle as the enemy closed in. With the election of a Democratic president and Democratic Senate in 1912 they would engulf him.

Theoretically, he might have taken stock after the early setbacks, and through new policies and new approaches to publicity have tried to retrieve his reputation in the time remaining to him. Three years, after all, provided plenty of opportunity for people to change their minds. Other presidents have made political comebacks in even shorter periods. In Taft's case, however, almost the opposite occurred. Rather than learning from his mistakes what not to do, he reacted to criticism by plodding all the more doggedly in the direction he had staked out. He reacted with the stubbornness of an essentially weak man.

In a sense the press forced such a response. Perhaps the greatest disservice it did to him, as it has done to other presidents, was to magnify his weaknesses by probing them. Unable to handle criticism, he withdrew into a shell which, as he eventually recognized himself, had the effect of denying him all perspective and all flexibility. "One of the results of my observation in the presidency," he remarked reflectively in a speech at the Lotus Club a few weeks before leaving office, "is that the position is not a place to be enjoyed by a sensitive man. . . . I don't know that this evil [of muckraking] has been any greater in this administration than in a previous administration. All I know is that it was my first experience and that it seemed to me as if I had been more greatly tried than most Presidents by such methods. The result in some respects is unfortunate in that after one or two efforts to meet the unfounded accusations, despair in the matter leads to indifference and perhaps to an indifference towards both just and unjust criticism. This condition helps the comfort of the patient, but I doubt if it makes him a better President.''[103]

It would have helped, of course, if he had not been so sensitive, but Taft again could only be himself. He was, beneath the bluff exterior, a person set in his ways, often insecure, and above all, easily hurt. The people who chuckled at the fat-man jokes, for example, and assumed the president chuckled with them, badly misunderstood him. In fact, he felt rather self-conscious about the subject (or at least grew to be self-conscious under the glare of publicity). Archie Butt noticed the sensitivity as early as the spring of 1909 when Taft refused to be seen any longer on horseback because he thought onlookers were laughing at him. "I feared he mistook the natural stare and beaming of the people on him for fun making," the aide wrote.[104] On another occasion the president worried about the country finding out that he had been put on a strict diet to alleviate his problem with gout. "He is so sensitive to ridicule by the press," Butt reported, "that he may keep [the affliction] away from his family in order to keep it away from the press. If it were known for a minute that he had an attack of gout, the press would rag him well with it, and every cartoonist in the country would take a whack at him."[105] Taft couldn't stand that.

But teasing on such matters soon became the least of his problems as political troubles mounted and newspaper commentary on the administration turned increasingly biting. In the face of the press barrage on matters petty and substantial Taft responded in a thoroughly human way, and the worst possible way for a president. He simply stopped reading what his critics had to say about him. Butt, who loved Taft as much as anything else for his sweetness of temperament, wrote in November 1909 that he could recall seeing the president visibly angry on only one or two occasions. One such time was when his secretary, Fred Carpenter, persisted in sending him clippings from the *New York Times* opposing the Payne-Aldrich tarriff.[106] He instructed Carpenter by telegram to stop it immediately. "I only read the headlines and the first sentence or two," the president said, "and then I omit the further consumption of time. . . . The articles are prompted by such wild misconceptions and such boyish desire to point the finger of scorn, that I don't think their reading will do me any particular good, and would only be provocative of that sort of anger and contemptuous feeling that does not do anybody any good."[107]

He was even more explicit—almost childishly so—on a summer evening in 1911 while on his annual vacation in Beverly. Archie Butt described the family scene:

> Last night after dinner, when he asked if the New York papers had come, Mrs. Taft handed him the *New York World*.
> "I don't want the *World*," he said. "I have stopped reading it. It only makes me angry."
> "But you used to like it very much," said Mrs. Taft.
> "That was when it agreed with me, but it abuses me now, and so I don't want it."
> "You will never know what the other side is doing if you only read the *Sun* and the *Tribune*," said this wise woman.
> "I don't care what the other side is doing," he answered with some irritation.[108]

That was the key. If a paper agreed with him he pored over it, delighted to discover the views of the press. The *New York Times*, for example, returned to favor when its editorial position changed in 1911 and it started to see things from the Taft perspective. Thereafter it ranked with the *New York Tribune*, a bastion of Republican orthodoxy, as a paper he depended on to keep him informed about opinion in the country. After the falling-out with Theodore Roosevelt he also read the *New York Sun* with delight, because it had made a specialty over the years of poking fun at his predecessor. But any journal unsympathetic to him or his policies simply ceased to exist.

Taft further shielded himself from unpleasantness by seeing reporters as infrequently as possible. Their questions were bound to be disturbing, and he didn't want to be disturbed. Better in that case just to keep his distance, whatever the price. Arthur Dunn's account of what happened when he proposed a series of articles on the president's first six months in office illustrates the intensity of this feeling and the problems it caused. By all logical standards the administration had every reason to cooperate with Dunn. As an Associated Press correspondent his stories would reach a wide audience, and considering that he had been on friendly terms with Taft for twenty years he presumably could be relied on to write with understanding and even sympathy. Dunn recalled receiving a good deal less than a warm reception, however, when he traveled up to Beverly and approached Fred Carpenter with the idea. Rather than setting up an appointment with Taft, the secretary told Dunn he would have to wait until the following Wednesday when the president planned to see the press in a body. Dunn accepted the only arrangement available to him, and on the appointed day joined several other correspondents who had showed up for the interview. When a heavy rain started to fall, Butt invited the group to take shelter on the spacious porch of the president's cottage. They waited there almost two hours while Taft, on another area of the porch, finished his business with a previous guest. From that vantage they were able to overhear the exchange after the guest left and Carpenter informed Taft that the press was waiting. "Must I see those men again!" he said loudly. "Didn't I see them just the other day!" As Dunn recalled, "it was a snarl, but it was Taft's voice. There was a murmur for a moment and then Carpenter reappeared, motioning us to go forward, and we passed around the corner to be greeted 'with the smile that wouldn't come off,' and after a quip or two, a merry 'ha! ha!' the routine questions were asked and answered. . . ." The false bonhomie did not dispel the tension everyone felt. Nor could anything of substance be accomplished in such an atmosphere. "That was the last time I saw Mr. Taft at the Beverly cottage," Dunn noted. "And that series of articles was never published."[109]

In his craving to be spared unpleasantness or controversy Taft also discouraged his closest associates from speaking their minds freely. It didn't matter who they were; if they didn't agree with him they learned to practice silence. "Mr. Horace Taft is here," Butt wrote of a visit by the president's younger brother to Beverly in the summer of 1911. "He used to argue with the President and differ from him, but one day the President turned on him and called him a theoretical pedant, and since then Mr. Horace has not expressed his real views to him again. He learned only what the rest of us have learned, that the President does not like those who differ from him and will not permit criticism. I am sorry that I dared to criticize his speech made the other afternoon, for he has spoken slightingly of my judgment once or twice since then."[110]

The chill was particularly severe if anyone outside Taft's immediate circle presumed to contradict him. So Oscar Davis learned when he filed five stories in the *New York Times* reporting on the anger at the Payne-Aldrich tariff he had found throughout the country during a seventeen-day trip covering much the same route the president took on his speaking tour. For at least two reasons Davis deserved a hearing within the White House. To begin with, he was no enemy. In an era when journalists did not worry as much as they do today about maintaining at least the appearance of objectivity, the *Times* correspondent had written the 1908 campaign biography for his old friend, William Howard Taft. Moreover, as an experienced political reporter, and one who had put more than usual research into the series, he carried professional credentials to be taken seriously. But when he returned to Washington and checked in at the White House he found that his efforts had made him an outcast.

It was the coldest reception I had ever had there. I asked to see the President, and was promptly informed that an appointment could not be arranged. It was very plain that I was no longer in even the little favor that I had enjoyed during the summer. So I went straight at the matter:

"What's the matter with you, Fred?" I said to Mr. Carpenter, the Secretary to the President. "You act as if you were in the middle of an ice house."

Carpenter fidgeted a little with a pencil on his desk, and then apparently made up his mind to be as frank in his reply as I had been in my question.

"We don't like your stuff," he said.

"Naturally," I replied. "I don't like it myself. But it's the truth, and the best thing a man in politics can do for himself is to find out the truth, if he can."

"But we don't think it's the truth," said Carpenter.

"For the love of Mike, Fred," I said, "where have you been? Who has been talking to you? Where have you got your information . . .?"

It finally came out that the information on which the President and Carpenter were relying about Mr. Taft's Western trip, and the whole situation in the country he had covered, had come chiefly from Tawney, and, of course, it was rose-colored. Tawney knew Taft, if he didn't know some other things.[111]

Taft's refusal to listen to what he did not want to hear hurt him in several respects. Obviously, no leader in a democracy can afford to lose touch with the electorate, and that is precisely what the president did in wilfully cutting himself off from tides of opinion in the country. The great challenge in the office is to receive information, from as many sources as possible and as directly as possible without going through a gate-keeper. In hiding from such information Taft really hid from the people, which is the ruin of any presidency.

He also arranged that he would not be able to use the press as an instrument of leadership. Before a president can mount any kind of publicity effort to rally support behind him he must have a sense of what the people feel and where they are willing to go. He is in no position to influence them if he doesn't know them. And a president who didn't want to see opposing viewpoints in newspapers, or to get a clue to national concerns from the questions reporters asked him, or even to be told by qualified informants of developments in the country, can hardly be said to have been making the effort to get in touch.

There was a grim symmetry to what happened in this administration. Taft's ineptness as a publicist contributed to criticism of him in the press, and the way he reacted to the criticism in turn compounded his ineptness. The result was a spiraling estrangement between the president and reporters. He started to feel they were conspiring against him.[112] He also started to question (something that can probably be said of all presidents to one degree or another) whether honest, efficient government was even possible under their constant harassment. "That is just the trouble with this whole country," Taft remarked heatedly in the summer of 1910 to Frank Kellogg, a special counsel to the attorney general who would go on to become senator from Minnesota and secretary of state under Coolidge. "It is difficult to find good men who are willing to enter politics either through the polls or by appointment, and I believe the trouble is that decent, self-respecting men are unwilling to stand for the criticism and abuse which follow one into office through the sensational press of our country."[113]

It would be foolish to dismiss Taft's complaint out of hand. One of the problems with a free press is that it does tend to be abusive on occasion. Presidents, of whom so much is expected and who come under such intense scrutiny, probably know this better than anyone else. There can't have been very many who did not find their commitment to First Amendment guarantees seriously strained while in office. Nevertheless, as Taft himself recognized on looking back from a clearer perspective after he left the White House, such a press could have been his strength as well as the gadfly holding him to account. A president, he wrote "should devote close attention to the proper methods of getting to as wide a circle of readers as possible the facts and reasons sustaining his policies and official acts. . . . I must confess that I was lacking in attention to matters of this kind and was derelict." Derelict, in particular, in shunning the reporters he needed. "They properly complained that I did not help them to help me."[114]

As a result, he stumbled along through four years of an unhappy presidency, buffeted by controversies he could not handle and often the architect of his own misfortune. That it had to end in the bitter falling-out with Theodore Roosevelt made the experience all the more painful. Simply put, he was a good man in an office unsuited to him. "If I were to sum up all the criticisms that have been made of the gentleman who is now President of the United States," the newly elected governor of New Jersey declared in November 1910, "I could express them all in this: The American people are disappointed because he has not led them. . . . They clearly long for someone to put the pressure of the opinion of all the people of the United States upon Congress."[115] The person who spoke those words, Woodrow Wilson, intended that if the opportunity to exercise national leadership ever came to him, he would be judged far differently.

6

The Clash of Personalities

Governor Woodrow Wilson of New Jersey didn't at all like the schedule of appointments his aide showed him for the days ahead. It was May 6, 1911, and he was traveling by train from Kansas City to Denver on an early leg of a speaking tour to introduce himself as a candidate for the Democratic presidential nomination in 1912. Kansas City had gone well. Several hundred of the leading citizens had heard his talk at the Knife and Fork Club and come away impressed. The newspapers had provided good coverage, and he had even managed to conceal his annoyance at the petty, personal questions asked when he met the local press. But now, looking at the schedule, it turned out that his publicity aide intended for him to give such interviews twice daily in every city he visited. Wilson saw no point to it. The message he wanted to convey was contained in his formal speeches. Nothing pertinent about his credentials to provide national leadership could come out of the kind of questions asked by local newsmen. "Do I have to go through that again?" he asked Frank Parker Stockbridge, the former newsman who had been hired a few weeks before to assist him in this critical attempt to get national exposure. "Everywhere we stop, Governor," the aide responded bluntly.

It was not the answer Wilson wanted to hear, nor did he take it well. Stockbridge had to sit with him for a while to explain the difference between a speech and the immediacy of personal presence. He pointed out that Wilson's message, no matter how uplifting, would not win him the nomination. If ideas were enough there would be no need to make the trip, since the texts of speeches could always be sent over the wires. People also wanted to know public figures as flesh and blood beings, to sense their personalities and evaluate their stature in human terms. They wanted to feel that a man was among them, not an icon. For that the local interviews were essential. Wilson eventually gave in, if reluctantly. On

126

the rest of the tour, Stockbridge wrote, he met the press with "outward grace, but with much inward protest."[1]

The candidate's introduction to the facts of presidential politics foretold a great deal about his White House years. Just by being on the tour, and accepting the demands made on him, he demonstrated his awareness that publicity was the key to success or failure for a public man. One of the reasons he would rank as a strong president is that he found his own ways, geared to his own strengths, to reach the people. But Wilson also demonstrated at this early stage a weakness that would plague him throughout his administration, and in the end have tragic consequences. He simply could not bend to the personal, democratic, sometimes trival and always urgent demands of a popular press.

The explanation for his failure is as complicated as human personality itself. In fairness to Wilson, he had been involved in politics for barely a year when he set out to win his party's presidential nomination. A lifetime spent as college professor and college president was not the best preparation for dealing with reporters whose police court origins were not that far behind them. They were a down-to-earth lot, even boisterous on occasion, who looked for the common touch in the men they covered. They admired colorfulness more than dignity, horse sense more than highflown wisdom. Wilson had never met their kind at Princeton, and didn't know quite what to make of them. Part of the reason he and the press clashed is that they were strangers to one another.

Their differences could easily have been bridged, however, but for the more serious problem of Wilson's austere personality. He was a man of enormous reserve, one who without intending it gave the impression of somehow being apart from the rest of humanity. Even at his best moments the quality of remoteness was always there. Wilson enjoyed great popularity as a teacher at Princeton, but for his ability in lecturing to large groups, not in handling the give and take of small classes. As a political leader he moved audiences with his eloquence; he rarely warmed them by his presence. The contrast between Americans calling Theodore Roosevelt "Teddy," but Woodrow Wilson seldom "Woody," conveys the difference. He was not the sort of person newsmen would naturally take to, nor the sort who would even try to win them over.

The sad part is that he was a different person in private life. For an austere figure Wilson enjoyed remarkably simple pleasures: vaudeville, popular novels, limericks, singing songs around the piano. He could be almost boyishly playful with his wife and daughters, whom he adored and depended on for company and laughter. But he simply couldn't convey the same qualities outside the family circle, however much he may have wanted to. Charles Thompson of the *New York Times* recalled an occasion

during the 1912 campaign when Wilson, in a speech, got an uncharacteristic response from the audience. Amused by a telling point he had made
someone called out, "That was a good one, Woody!" The candidate was
delighted, and showed it by delivering the rest of his remarks with more
than usual verve. "When I sat down with him at luncheon in his car,"
Thompson wrote, "his face was still glowing and his eyes still bright. 'Did
you hear, Mr. Thompson?' he asked with a happy smile. 'They called me
Woody!' "[2]

They rarely did, however. The campaign made clear, if it had ever been
in doubt, that Wilson lacked the common touch of a Roosevelt. Thompson
described having long conversations that summer with Don Martin of the
New York Herald and James Doyle of the *New York Press* about the
candidate's inability to project himself in human terms. Because the three
veteran reporters respected Wilson and wished him well, they went to
see him to discuss the problem and offer their assistance. Pointing out
how his aloofness was hurting him, they noted that other public figures,
not least Roosevelt, came across in newspapers as full-blooded personalities, and had their programs adequately explained, because they opened
up to reporters they trusted and spoke informally with them on a nonattribution basis. If Wilson would take the three into his confidence they
would try to do the same for him. According to Thompson, Wilson was
moved by the offer, but still had to reject it. "I appreciate this more than
I can tell you," he replied. "Every word you say is true, and I know it.
Don't you suppose I know my own handicaps? I'd do what you advise
if I could. . . . But it's not my nature. . . . *I can't make myself over.*"[3]

Likely the well-meaning reporters did underestimate the difficulties in
this candidate coming to terms with the press. The implication in their
advice was that his problems would disappear if he only bent a little and
treated some newsmen at least as confidants. Wilson showed greater
astuteness (although he presumably did not understand the reason why)
in recognizing that he could not do as asked, and would be a disaster at
it if he tried. The fact is that along with his aloofness went an inability
to sustain relations with people on terms other than their complete defer-
rence to him. This explains the transitoriness of his friendships, a point
that appears repeatedly in the Wilson literature.[4] He accepted few men
as intimate friends, and those without exception he sooner or later
dropped. If women fared better as objects of his affection, starting with
his first and second wives and three daughters, it was because they gave
him the love and comfort he craved without ever questioning his judgment
or imposing their will against his. Certain that what he believed was
necessarily right, and what he stood for necessarily most honorable, he
could not accept the normal give and take that goes on between friends.
To criticize or question his positions meant impeding him in his personal

mission to provide good government. The people who did not fall auto-matically into line were not simply wrong-headed; they were hateful fig-ures because they had to be acting out of spite. Even his closest associates recognized how much they risked in crossing him. As Dr. Cary T. Grayson, his physician and companion, once remarked, "if one urges Wilson to do something contrary to his own conviction, he ceases to have any liking for that person."[5]

None of this offered a viable basis for Wilson to establish a good working relationship with reporters, either collectively or by singling out a few favorites. It is true that Roosevelt also expected the "fair-haired boys" to support his policies and cooperate with his publicity arrangements. The important difference between him and Wilson, however, is that Roosevelt and the reporters in his entourage genuinely liked one another, which meant that they supported him not so much out of coercion as conviction. Moreover, as friends, they were free to stand up to him when they thought him wrong, and he respected them for it. The fair-haired boys may have worn the T.R. brand, but they were not without self-respect. Even in an era when the press did not have the independence it demonstrates today, they had to feel they were their own men. The need was even greater by the time of Wilson's presidency, and impossible to fulfill under the terms he demanded of others.

To say that Wilson did not have the personality to forge close ties with the press does not mean that he underestimated the importance of pub-licity for purposes of leadership. He had made a national reputation as governor by defying James Smith's Democratic machine and relying on public opinion to support him. His success in pushing a strong reform program through the legislature while remaining outside the system in turn inspired his strategy for winning the Democratic presidential nomi-nation. The United States would be New Jersey writ large. Wilson and his inner circle of advisers regarded his candidacy as unique in recent history in depending not on the party machinery but on a direct approach to the people. They recognized the serious concerns about him throughout the country: his regional background, his affiliation with Princeton (a rich boy's college), his alleged ties to Wall Street, and perhaps most damaging, his former occupation as a college professor, a calling which by conven-tional wisdom did not school a man in the hard realities of running a government. The way to overcome these handicaps, they decided, was to have him go out and be seen by the voters, taking care always that he appear at nonpolitical gatherings—the Knife and Fork Club in Kansas City, not the local Democratic club—in order to reinforce the image of Wilson as the people's candidate. If he made a good impression on the hustings, duly noted in the newspapers of the cities he visited, it would more than compensate for the lack of enthusiasm for him among party regulars. Frank Stockbridge, in explaining why he agreed to handle press relations on the spring tour, spoke of the novelty of the approach as the main inducement. "Nobody, in our time at least," he wrote, "had been nominated for the Presidency without the aid of a well organized political machine, backed by ample funds; nobody had ever been nominated by the force of publicity, the pressure of public opinion—not since party politics had become the highly developed and complicated affair of these later days. And yet, as I thought it over that afternoon and evening, it seemed possible."[6]

When the strategy worked, despite a formidible challenge from Speaker of the House Champ Clark, who by playing the game in a traditional way went into the convention with the greater number of committed delegates, it naturally determined how Wilson would campaign against Roosevelt and Taft, and how he would later attempt to conduct his administration. During the period between his nomination and inauguration he was almost self-consciously available to reporters. David Lawrence, one of his former students at Princeton who was now covering the candidate for the Associated Press, described how Wilson kept the door to his office in Trenton always open so that newsmen out in the hallway could see who he was in conference with or what he was doing. He also met with the correspondents virtually every day to brief them on late-breaking events.[7] Whatever other problems that arose during this period, his isolation was not one of them.

Nor did the occasional breakdowns in mechanical aspects of his press operation matter particularly, although they were annoying when they happened and disturbing reminders of Wilson's naïveté about how journalism worked. Stockbridge had constant headaches, for example, trying to pry copies of the candidate's speeches from him for advance distribution. Partly because Wilson wanted to polish his phrases until the last minute, and probably also because he didn't trust newspapers to honor the release dates, he hung on to his speeches long after they should have been fed into the publicity mill. The press agent's urgent pleas that he needed more lead time to deliver texts to the wire services, have them distributed to member papers, and set up in type, fell generally on deaf ears.

Stubbornness in an area like this annoyed reporters, but in the long run was not nearly as important as Wilson's failure to accept the press for what it was, and to use its peculiarities to his own advantage. He could not control that papers written for mass audiences were going to stress color and human interest material. However much he may have preferred a different kind of journalism, his tastes in the matter were irrelevant. The challenge facing him as a public figure was to work with the instrument at hand. Instead, he bitterly reviled American newspapers for not resembling the *Times* of London, and reviled reporters for not being so many Walter Bagehots. Of course he didn't change anything as a result. The only thing he accomplished was to turn the correspondents against him, and thereby to convert one of Roosevelt's greatest strengths into one of his greatest vulnerabilities.

Part of the reason for Wilson's attitude is that he had been burned in the past by the often frivolous reporting of the popular press. One such occasion occurred when as president of Princeton he delivered an address before a scholarly gathering in New York City on the significance of the rural-urban migration. "It is unfortunate for the purpose of society in America that we are running to big cities," he said, "because it is impossible for people to think in big cities. Thought comes from the valleys and mountains and the farms, the hills, its villages, the crossroads store where men sit around the stove and spit into a sawdust box." And then to lighten the mood he added, "whatever else may be said of the habit of chewing tobacco, this much must be admitted in its favor, that it makes men think because they must stop between words to spit." Wilson was horrified the next morning to discover that accounts of the talk in the New York papers focused solely on what he had intended as a humorous aside. "PRESIDENT OF PRINCETON SAYS CHEWING TOBACCO MAKES MEN THINK," one newspaper headlined its report.[8]

He had reason to be annoyed on that occasion, just as one can sympathize with his dismay at the first meeting he held with the press after winning the Democratic nomination. He assumed it would be a formal, almost symbolic occasion, the reporters coming by to tender their congratulations and to discuss with him in a dignified way his vision for the future. Accordingly, rather than choosing a public place for the meeting, he received them as personal guests in the study of his summer home at Sea Girt, apologizing profusely that there weren't enough chairs to go around. He didn't expect the no-nonsense, side-of-the-mouth comments from the newsmen that came as a slap in the face, immediately shattering his mood. Ray Stannard Baker described the moment:

> "Well, Governor," remarked a New York police reporter. "You've got the first page now. Hang on to it. You've got the edge on Teddy and we want a lot of good stuff from you."
> Another chimed in: "We are all on space down here, Governor, and the more we can play you up the more we can increase our checks at the end of the week."
> The Governor looked over at the first man and smiled: he thought it was a joke. He did not smile quite so broadly at the second man.[9]

The newsmen did behave boorishly, but by the same token Wilson showed something of his rigidity in the way he reacted. He could have good-naturedly assured them that news would be forthcoming without sacrificing any of his dignity. By visibly recoiling, and over the months responding increasingly to provocation with a testiness of his own, he only made things worse. He created a situation in which he and the press started to grate on each other like flint and stone. They accused him of refusing to cooperate, even hindering them, in gathering the news. He criticized them for their trivial, frivolous priorities. His concern as one who aspired to national leadership should have been to win the good will of reporters. Instead, he turned them into adversaries.

A major area where clash over news values occurred involved coverage of the Wilson family. The issue, of course, is a perennial one in American life. Presidents, like anyone else, want some privacy; at the same time public interest in the family that fills a symbolic need has the press constantly digging for more information, and when the information is not freely given, making do with speculation about what might be. The result is invariably tension between presidents and the press. In Wilson's case, however, the tension reached unprecedented heights because of the kind of man he was. His reserve and high sense of dignity would have made this aspect of public life an ordeal even if he alone had been in the spotlight. He nearly cracked upon seeing his beloved wife and daughters subjected to the treatment. Wilson, after all, was a southerner. He worshipped women in the old-fashioned way, thinking of them as innately purer and finer creatures to be shielded from the world outside. It was almost more than he could bear to have the coarse and ill-mannered denizens of the press hounding his ladies, and as if that were not enough, speculating about their personal affairs in public print.

The troubles began immediately after his nomination. A horde of reporters descended on Sea Girt looking for human interest material on the candidate's wife and daughters. Wilson had known in the abstract that this would happen, and had taken steps to prepare the family. According to his daughter Eleanor, "Father had told us to be good sports and try to be as pleasant as possible. . . ." But none of them anticipated the persistence and brazenness of the questioning. "We, who had been taught to be close-mouthed about our family affairs," she wrote, "found this prying into our lives strange and annoying. They did not hesitate to question us about any and every detail of our lives. What were our favorite colors, occupations, sports? Did we like to dance? Were we in love or engaged? Did we intend to marry and, if so, when?"[10] Despite his own advice about making the best of what had to be, Wilson fumed at the intrusions. The loyal Eleanor traced her father's troubles with the press to the trauma of those first interviews. "He resented almost fiercely the attempts to pry into family affairs and tried to protect us as much as he could. I have always believed that the first rumors of his 'aloofness' and 'unfriendliness' were the result of his annoyance at this first onslaught upon us. The newspaper people could not understand the sensitive shyness and delicacy which were an essential part of his character."[11]

Wilson seemed other than shy and delicate, to the point of almost engaging in a public brawl, when his temper finally got the better of him later in the year. The trouble flared shortly after the election when the family took off for Bermuda to rest for a month before he had to return to New Jersey to face the hard decisions in organizing his administration. On one of their first days there he and his daughter Jessie went on a bicycle ride to the local market. They returned hot and disheveled to find reporters and photographers camped on their front doorstep. Wilson walked up to them and said, "Gentlemen, you can photograph me to your heart's content. I don't care how I look. But I request you not to photograph my daughter. You know how women feel about such things, and I myself would rather not have the ladies of my family made to ——" He hadn't finished the sentence when one of the photographers snapped a picture of Jessie. It was the final straw. His face flushed and eyes blazing, Wilson advanced on the cameraman ready to pummel him. He stopped only at the last second, and in a quivering voice said, "You're no gentleman! I want to give you the worst thrashing you ever had in your life; and what's more, I'm perfectly able to do it."[12] Everyone held his breath, wide-eyed, until Wilson stalked away.

Clearly he was the aggrieved party in this instance. The fact still remains that Wilson did not know and refused to learn how to handle the news demands of the press. He could not prevent reporters from focusing on his family. The trick in that case was to volunteer information, which would have served the dual purpose of generating favorable publicity while retaining at least partial control over what appeared. Newsmen are usually willing to cooperate in keeping some things private if their basic needs are met. But Wilson tried to the extent possible to keep his wife and daughters out of the papers altogether, and succeeded thereby only in assuring that the coverage of them would be less reliable than it might have been, and considerably more offensive. In a sense, however understandable his motives, he brought much of the pain he suffered upon himself.

Wilson's misunderstanding—or perhaps it was stubbornness—about another way in which journalism works caused still more tensions between him and White House correspondents. He thought of news as the announcement of a decision made or a step taken, which it was the responsibility of the press to convey without comment or interpolation. Reporters had no business speculating about what might happen, or printing information before it had been released. Of course newspapers run on that basis would be little more than official bulletins for the administration in power. The responsibility for keeping the public informed assumes that stories will often be published which government leaders would prefer to remain under wraps. It also assumes that reporters will enter the picture while decisions are being made so that the people can have some voice in the process rather than always being presented with the fait accompli. Wilson was hardly unique among presidents in wanting the press to be little more than a conveyor belt passing along his statements as provided. But more than most, he chose to make an issue of the matter, and in the process deepened the chill in his relations with reporters.[13]

The dispute prior to his inauguration centered mainly on the attempts by newsmen to track down the names of his cabinet appointments before he was ready to announce them. Wilson regarded the structuring of his official family as a matter serious and complicated enough without the press butting in. He bitterly resented the rumors in newspapers, which made the job more difficult. In particular, he resented the people he suspected of using the media in trying to advance their cause. According to James Kerney of the *Trenton Times,* a Wilson adviser at the time, one of the reasons Democratic chairman William McComb fell from grace was that his name appeared in the papers with surprising frequency as a likely cabinet appointee.[14] It reached the point (as happened again later in the Johnson administration) that the press acquired a kind of veto power over appointments to the extent of discovering that the people it named prior to the official announcement as receiving positions ended up not getting them. When Dudley Field Malone, a deserving Democrat from across the river, saw his name in the *New York American* as the next collector of the Port of New York, he rushed to Trenton to assure Wilson that he had nothing to do with the story. And then, fearful that the prize might yet slip through his fingers, he pleaded with the reporters not to mention him again. "You fellow are all friends of mine," he said,

we've been all over the country together, and I think you like me and wouldn't like to see me lose out on anything. . . . And now, fellows, about this damn story in the *American,* will you print the following in the papers to-morrow? Just say this:

"Mr. Malone, when seen today, said there was no truth in the story. He is not a candidate for any office. Not only has none been tendered him, but no intimation has been given from any source that he is being considered. Mr. Malone has no expectations of giving up his present work."

And when you've printed that, boys, will you be kind to a poor downtrodden Irishman and leave my name out altogether?[15]

In his case it all turned out happily. Malone, the son-in-law of Senator James O'Gorman of New York and close friend of the Wilson family, received his appointment later in the year.

Wilson's sensitivity about having his intentions prematurely disclosed led to scenes of almost low comedy between him and the reporters. One such occasion was the time he warned them what he would do if they persisted in their speculations. "I have been very much embarrassed," he said, "by having the newspapers print articles under a Trenton or Princeton date line, speculating as to who will or who will not be in the Cabinet. . . . Unless this practice ceases I will be put to the necessity of publishing a card." An awkward silence came over the room, because no one had the faintest idea what he was talking about. Finally, a brave soul asked, "Just what do you mean, Governor?" "I mean," Wilson replied, "that I will publish a card in the newspapers saying that I am not responsible for anything published on this subject."[16] The thought of the president-elect resorting to a device out of Victorian melodrama must have seemed faintly ludicrous to the hardened bunch of reporters, but of course no one in the room cracked a smile.

The worst tensions, and the source also of the first suspicions among correspondents that Wilson's word could not be trusted, arose out of the newspaper reports about William Jennings Bryan's expected appointment as secretary of state. He was the obvious candidate. As three-time presidential nominee he had an important following in the party, and qualified as well as its senior statesman. He could lay further claim to the position for the part he had played in engineering Wilson's nomination. Despite the embarrassing disclosure just prior to the Jackson Day dinner in January 1912 of a letter Wilson had written in 1907 to a Princeton trustee, expressing the hope that something could be done "to knock Mr. Bryan once and for all into a cocked hat," the Nebraskan had laughed off the incident and continued to regard Wilson's candidacy with sympathy. Although he went to the convention in Baltimore that summer instructed by his state to vote for Champ Clark, he bolted to Wilson on the fourteenth ballot, taking most of the Nebraska delegation with him. The move helped to keep Wilson's hopes alive until he finally went over on the forty-sixth ballot. Even the New Jersey governor, a man not usually noted for his gratitude to fellow politicians, had to acknowledge that sort of debt.

Wilson met with Bryan on December 21, shortly after returning from Bermuda, to offer him the post as secretary of state, which the Nebraskan accepted on the spot.[17] When the president-elect saw reporters afterward, they naturally wanted to know whether the expected appointment had been made. He denied that the possibility of Bryan entering the cabinet had even come up at the meeting. Unconvinced by this answer, the reporters persisted in their questions until Wilson finally had had enough.

"You gentlemen," he said ominously, "must learn sooner or later that you must take me at my word. I have told you repeatedly that I have reached no decisions, and I object very much to questions which put my word in doubt."[18] But to Wilson's intense annoyance, the speculations in newspapers would not go away. It is difficult to understand why he kept the lid on when all he accomplished as a result, aside from deceiving the press, was to encourage continued activity by those who hoped to block Bryan's appointment. Presumably his determination not to allow reporters to pressure him into making disclosures before he was ready justified the inconvenience. When they tried again at a conference on Monday, February 13, 1913, he blew up altogether. Confronted by the same nagging questions, he slammed his hand down on his desk and exclaimed, "I'm not here to amuse the newspapers. . . . If the newspapers expect me to do [so], . . . I'll be damned if I will." Within moments he had regained his composure. "Pardon me for blowing up," he said. "These stories about Cabinet appointments are all false. I have told you men here in Trenton that I have made no selections for the Cabinet, and to keep on questioning me about it is to doubt my veracity."[19]

Of course the press doubted him, but could do nothing about it. The cabinet appointments, several of which came as surprises, were not announced until March 3, the day before his inauguration. Even then Wilson exacted a final measure of revenge. Rather than release the names to the press as a body, he let the *Newark News* and *Trenton Times* have them as exclusives for their issues of that day. Only one other paper shared the information. Joseph Tumulty, Wilson's secretary, while traveling to Washington with his family on March 3, met Frank O'Malley of the *New York Sun* on the train. He gave the reporter the names in time for a later edition of the *Evening Sun* also to run the story.[20] The rest of the press remained out in the cold on a subject that had been of prime news interest for weeks.

Perhaps the major casualty in all this rancor was Wilson's reputation for honesty. Reporters felt, and justifiably so, that he habitually deceived them. It was one thing to refuse comment on their inquiries; another altogether to answer in a misleading or untruthful way. He denied on December 21, and for weeks following, that any final decision about the cabinet had been made. They suspected at the time and learned later that he was only putting them off. Not that he typically did so with outright lies. Wilson's usual tactic when he wanted to throw up a smoke screen was to respond with the truth, but the truth expressed in such a way as to fool the unwary. "It was impossible to rely on anything said," Charles Thompson wrote. "I do not mean he lied. I mean that he took such an intellectual pleasure in stating a thing so as to give an opposite impression to the fact, though he kept strictly to the truth, that one had to be constantly on the alert to keep from being misled."[21] The problem with playing

Wilson's kind of "intellectual" game is that it made him too clever by half in the eyes of the press. Reporters then as now are likely to put up with any number of peccadillos in public figures, and perhaps even be amused by them. What they cannot accept is a politician, particularly when he is president of the United States, whose word cannot be accepted at face value. Wilson struck them as such a man.

A good example of the hard feelings caused by technical truths intended to mislead occurred in February 1913, shortly before Wilson stepped down as governor of New Jersey. The state Senate had arranged a banquet in honor of his successor, president pro tempore James F. Fielder, to be held on a Saturday night at the Hotel Astor in New York City. On the train ride into the city presumably to attend the banquet, the reporters covering Wilson asked him if he anticipated anything other than a purely social occasion that evening. They had been at more than their share of political testimonials over the years, and hoped if the dinner was not newsworthy to file brief reports on it, and then spend a few hours on their own before meeting again at midnight outside Colonel House's residence, where Wilson would be spending the night, for a late briefing. David Lawrence acted as spokesman for the reporters as they clustered around the president-elect to find out if the lid would be on for a while.

"Shall you make a speech at the dinner?" he began.

"No, I don't think I shall," said Wilson.

"Will there be any speeches at all?"

"No, it will be purely informal; just a sitting around and chatting after the dinner is over."

"Do you expect to go anywhere after the dinner is over?"

"No, I do not."

"Then there is really no reason why we should cover the dinner?"

"None at all. It has no political significance."

"And we might just as well write our stories now and turn them into the office in advance, so that we can have the rest of the day to ourselves?"

"Yes. You won't find anything that will interest your readers in anything that will happen at the dinner. It's merely social, a passing mention of it will be enough."[22]

Thus assured, the newsmen scattered throughout the city as soon as the train got in.

Charles Thompson described going off to an early dinner with William Keohan, a friend from the *New York Tribune*. Afterward, having nothing better to do, the two reporters decided to stroll over to the Astor to check things out before beginning their own evening festivities. When they got to the hotel, they found no sign of Wilson. Indeed, on calling Fielder out of the banquet hall, they were told that it was a purely Senate function which Wilson had not even been invited to attend. A reporter can commit many sins in his job, but none more serious than to lose a president or president-elect. Now Wilson was out there somewhere in a city of five million people and they didn't know where. Badly frightened, Thompson and Keohan raced in a cab to House's apartment on East 35th Street to try and find him.

To their relief it turned out that he had gone directly to the apartment from the station and never left. Nor did he intend to. The problem was that he had been involved in high level discussions about appointments to the administration ever since his arrival. Several important people were involved, including the Democratic national chairman. The dispatches filed that afternoon completely missed the significance of his trip to New York City. Thompson and Keohan discovered the truth in time to rewrite their stories for the next day's paper, but they could not track down their colleagues scattered in the bars and restaurants and theaters of midtown Manhattan to alert them. The rest of the reporters only found out what had happened when they showed up for the midnight briefing, by which time the first editions of the morning papers had long since gone to press.

It was a disgruntled group of newsmen who boarded the train the next day for the return trip to Trenton. Wilson had not actually lied to them since nobody had asked point blank whether he would be at the dinner, but he obviously knew from the tenor of the questions what the correspondents assumed and chose not to correct them. If anything, he made matters worse by his amusement at their annoyance. When two reporters passed him in the car with only a stiff nod of recognition he laughed and called out, "Come on, get off your high horse."[23] Charles Thompson claimed that the younger newsmen took it hardest; for the veterans the trick played on them was all in a day's work. But Wilson paid a price even among those who reacted calmly, because as Thompson explained, one of the things they learned from the incident was to "watch Wilson's words more carefully in future."[24]

By the time of the inauguration on March 4, president and press were thoroughly disillusioned with each other. Not yet to the extent, however, that Wilson was ready to isolate himself from reporters. For reasons philosophical as well as practical he wanted to expand on what Theodore Roosevelt had started in bringing the press into the White House. The question was how to do it in a way that suited his nature.

Perhaps the saddest part about Wilson's estrangement from newsmen was that he more than most presidents genuinely believed that the people's business should be conducted in the full glare of publicity. The man who later made "open covenants, openly arrived at" the first of his Fourteen Points had spent his career as a political scientist arguing the importance of the public knowing what its officials were up to. At age twenty-eight, only five years out of the College of New Jersey (it did not become Princeton University until 1896), his doctorate in political science and first teaching position at Bryn Mawr still in the future, he expounded on the theme in an early scholarly article. "Light is the only thing that can sweeten our political atmosphere," he wrote at that time, "light blazed full upon every feature of legislation; light that can penetrate every recess or corner in which any intrigue might hide; light that will open to view the innermost chambers of government. . . ."[25] In 1884, when the article appeared, the idealism that infused his words hardly accorded with political fashion. It turned out, of course, that Wilson was only ahead of his time. Progressivism grew largely out of this same confidence in what could be accomplished by an informed citizenry, and same concern about the dangers inherent in secrecy. "You can't be crooked in the light," Wilson declared when running for the White House in 1912.[26] As a moral man in a moral age he wanted to set an example in dispelling the dark.

He also knew, as did Roosevelt before him and the Roosevelt to follow, that the power of the presidency inheres mainly in the opportunity the office affords to influence public opinion. Presidents receive a hearing no other elected official gets, and if they use it well virtually nothing is beyond them. Long before he attempted to apply this wisdom as national leader Wilson had stressed it as a scholar. As he wrote in *Constitutional Government in the United States,* published in 1908, "that part of the Government which has the most direct access to opinion has the best chance of leadership and mastery; and at present that part is the President."[27] To be a strong president he had to rally the people behind him, explaining to them what he was trying to accomplish in order to win their support. And since the newspaper represented his primary medium of communication, it made sense to work closely with the press.

One of the questions reporters had asked him in Trenton was whether he intended to continue the "open door" policy after his inauguration. Wilson replied that he would do so as far as possible, although he didn't know how the rooms in the White House were laid out or whether the president could even be reached without going through several other offices.[28] He must have realized, however, that considerations other than the design of the building made the idea impractical. The problem with an open door policy is that it requires leaving the door always open, because the minute it shuts the sound is deafening. But any president, even one dedicated to letting the light in, has to operate occasionally in private. The symbolism of being on display simply wouldn't work in the White House.

Common sense also told him that he couldn't manage his press relations in the way Roosevelt had, by seeing reporters almost every day—either individually or in small groups—for personal chats. He had tried that system in Trenton with unhappy results. "The experience had been difficult and painful," Ray Stannard Baker wrote, "but he had considered it a part of his programme for taking the people fully into his confidence. He had found the practice expensive both in time and in strength."[29] Wilson had never been a robust individual. Now as president he would have to husband his energies for the long haul. He couldn't afford to be accessible in the old way when each reporter he favored would have scores of others clamoring for the same treatment. Aside from the physical strain, it was senseless to have to repeat his points over and over in individual conversations. Wilson might have felt differently if, like Roosevelt, he had enjoyed the company of newsmen. In that case seeing them could be a welcome break in the routine. But since he didn't like most newsmen, he needed a different way to stay in touch with them while minimizing the aggravation they caused him.

It is ironic that the presidential press conference, an institution which enhanced the status of journalists and developed into an important tool for presidents in managing the news, arose largely out of the initiator's disenchantment with the press. At the suggestion of his secretary, Joseph Tumulty, Wilson settled on a simple plan to accomplish his contradictory goals. He would let the light in, and strive to lead public opinion, by meeting regularly each week with reporters to answer their questions, which presumably were the questions on the minds of the citizenry. At the same time, he would keep reporters at least somewhat at a distance by seeing them all at once, and pretty well restricting his availability to these formal, and, he hoped, businesslike sessions. The press conferences took the place of the open door in Trenton, obviously not as personal but promising to be a good deal less wearying.

Wilson called his first conference at 12:45 P.M. on Saturday afternoon, March 15, 1913, eleven days after the inauguration. Although no transcript exists of the dialogue in the Oval Office between the president and approximately 125 reporters, it is clear the session went badly. "There was a pause," one of the participants recalled, "a cool silence, and presently some one ventured a tentative question. It was answered crisply, politely, and in the fewest possible words. A pleasant time was not had by all."[30] The correspondents struggled through a few more such exchanges and then left. They could hardly have been encouraged by what they had learned about pitiless publicity.

Whether Tumulty had anything to do with it, Wilson tried to repair the damage at his second press conference a week later. From the turnout it was apparent that the abortive first attempt had done nothing to dampen reporter interest in meeting with the president. Almost two hundred of them gathered at the appointed hour in the lobby of the executive wing, and at the signal from Patrick McKenna, the White House doorman, crowded into the East Room, nearly engulfing it. The president entered immediately after, and standing behind a desk with the correspondents clustered tightly around, spoke at length in a way that the record makes appear more than conciliatory. He apologized for the formality of the setting, explaining that "if there were any other room in which we could have met, it would have been more pleasing to me." He also apologized, at least obliquely, for their unfortunate session the previous Saturday. "I asked Mr. Tumulty to ask you gentlemen to come together this afternoon," Wilson declared, "because the other day when I saw you, just after the fatigue of the morning, I did not feel that I had anything more to say . . ." But the burden of his remarks, which he asked the reporters to keep "just between ourselves," had to do with the important role people like themselves played in the governmental process. "I feel that a large part of the success of public affairs," the president said, "depends on the newspaper men—not so much on the editorial writers, because we can live down what they say, as upon the news writers, because the news is the atmosphere of public affairs. . . . I sent for you, therefore, to ask that you go into partnership with me, that you lend me your assistance as nobody else can. . . . I did want you to feel that I was depending upon you, and from what I can learn of you, I think I have a reason to depend with confidence on you. . . , not for me, but for the United States, for the people of the United States, and so bring about a day which will be a little better than the days that have gone before us."[31]

From the transcript it is difficult to tell what went wrong. (Evidently the White House also thought the words sounded good since it released the text of these confidential remarks for publication later in the year.[32]) After all, journalists—like anybody else—appreciate being reminded of their importance, and here was a president of the United States inviting them to join hands with him in the quest for good government. By all logic Wilson and the press should have been basking in the glow of each other's warmth that Saturday afternoon. Instead, newsmen left the White House more suspicious of him than ever.

Part of the problem had to do with the human chemistry of the moment. When Wilson walked into the room he seemed to be taken aback by the sheer mass of reporters present. Rather than giving the impression that he found the turnout a happy surprise, he made the group feel awkward and unwelcome. "It was appalling," a newsman sympathetic to him remarked later in a letter. "He came into the room suspicious, reserved, a little resentful—no thought of frankness and open door and cordiality and that sort of thing. In the first place, he was embarrassed. There were about two hundred of the correspondents and it was in the East Room of the White House. It was a silly thing to do. . . . He could not be as frank as he could have been with one; and he was embarrassed and had this rankling feeling. . . . He utterly failed to get across to those men anything except that this was very distasteful to him, and they, on their part, resented it very, very seriously. They came out of that conference almost cursing, indignant."[33]

The perplexing question, considering how much he staked on the press conferences, is why he allowed such an impression to develop. There is no simple answer. Wilson's reserve, which as Ray Stannard Baker observed, "had not been diminished by his long service in a conservative university," probably contributed.[34] Reporters couldn't help but sense in their encounters with him his wish to be somewhere else. "At these conferences, so called," David Barry of the *New York Sun* recalled, "President Wilson was, as a rule, very serious in aspect and demeanor, rarely smiling or cracking a joke and plainly anxious at all times to close the meeting and get back to his den."[35] Charles Swen, a young man just turned twenty in 1913, who as Wilson's stenographic secretary sat at his right during the conferences keeping the transcript, thought this private quality far more important than shyness in explaining the president's manner. "I never saw him ill at ease—not then [referring to the March 22 conference] or any time," Swen said in an interview several decades later. "The truth is the President didn't *enjoy* the conferences, he submitted to them."[36]

Much more serious, as quickly became apparent, was the different purposes Wilson and the reporters saw the conferences filling. They regarded the sessions as opportunities to quiz the president on subjects of current interest. They were after news, and assumed—implicitly or explicitly—that the function of defining the news belonged to them. It inhered in being the ones to put questions to government officials and to expect answers. But Wilson wanted to reserve for himself the decision about which subjects the public should be enlightened on (and what the enlightenment should consist of) and which were best left alone. He felt particularly strongly on the matter in the area of foreign affairs. When a correspondent asked him at a press conference on January 29, 1914, for example, whether the country's disputes with several other nations were in any sense interrelated, the president took the opportunity to lecture the group against straying into terrain they should stay out of. "Now, I want to make this suggestion, gentlemen," he said. "The foreign policy of the government is the one field in which, if you will permit me to say so, you ought not to speculate in public, because the minute the newspapers in any large number state a certain thing to be under consideration by the administration, that is of course telegraphed all over the world and makes a certain impression upon foreign governments, and may very easily render the things that we really intend to do impossible. . . . I feel the thing very keenly. I do not think that the newspapers of the country have the right to embarrass their own country in the settlement of matters which have to be handled with delicacy and candor."[37]

Wilson obviously had a point that diplomacy cannot always be conducted in public view. It is true also that at times the press did create problems for him by raising the curtain on backstage maneuvers. One such occasion happened in the fall of 1914 when an attempt to end the war through American mediation, which was almost certainly hopeless in any case, resulted in embarrassment and ill will as soon as the newspapers got wind of it. On Sunday, September 6, Oscar S. Straus, a former cabinet member in Roosevelt's administration, appeared at the home of Secretary of State Bryan to report excitedly that the German ambassador had told him at a dinner party in New York City the night before that he thought his government might accept an offer of mediation. Bryan immediately summoned Count J. H. Bernstorff back to Washington to confirm the conversation, and asked Straus to sound out the British and French ambassadors. He also cabled the American ambassadors in London and Paris to make discreet inquiries at their posts. From all quarters came the same response: no peace was possible until the other side capitulated. It is difficult to imagine any other answer just a few weeks into the war, before the casualty lists had started to mount and patriotic slogans started to turn sour. Still, there was no harm in quietly checking out the possibilities.

The peace initiative only became an embarrassment when John O'Laughlin broke the story in the *Chicago Herald,* and other papers promptly picked it up.[38] "It 'leaked' to the press, as nearly all the so-called secret communications at that time were doing," Ray Stannard Baker wrote, "and no government would then, publicly, admit a readiness to discuss peace lest it be construed as a sign of weakness."[39] To compound the embarrassment, on September 10 Ambassador Walter Hines Page responded to Bryan's cable with a report on his conversation with Sir Edward Grey in which the British foreign secretary had taken an extremely hard line, declaring that Britain would not make peace until German militarism had been crushed. The ambassador cautioned that his communiqué must be kept "inviolably secret." It, too, was promptly leaked to the press.[40]

However annoying such breakdowns, the further fact is that Wilson was wrong, even presumptuous, in expecting a free press to print only what government authorized it to print. The right to be informed applies to foreign as well as domestic news, and whatever the inconveniences in having reporters pry into sensitive matters, they are part of the price the American democratic system imposes. Even that price can sometimes be minimized if government explains to the press why a story should not be published. But Wilson was not the man to play the game that way. The striking thing in reading through the transcripts of his conferences is how often, sometimes through entire sessions, he simply refused to respond to the questions put to him; most of the time politely, occasionally playfully, often curtly. Wilson managed, something only a complicated person could pull off, to combine sincere conviction about the importance of openness in government with equally strong conviction that reporters had no business pestering him for information. Since they didn't know how to honor the one principle without offending him on the other, the press conferences brought no joy.

By and large little news came out of them. The president told reporters what he wanted them to know, which generally wasn't much, and then clammed up. "There was always a very cool reserve," his former associate from the *Trenton Times* wrote, "and Wilson gave the impression that he was the best judge of what was good for the newspapers to have. He was saving mankind, and he would let the world know about it in his own good time. He certainly did not believe in government by newspapers, and it was his policy that the newspapers should not know of any transaction until it was an accomplished fact."[41] The efforts by correspondents to prod him into further disclosures rarely accomplished anything. According to Richard Oulahan of the *New York Times*, "the President gave the impression that he was matching his wit against ours as a sort of mental practice with the object of being able to make responses which seemed to answer the questions, but which imparted little or nothing in the way of information."[42] If they persisted in pursuing a subject, Wilson often turned testy. "How many forms are you going to ask the same question in?" he snapped at a dogged reporter in the spring of 1914. "I have answered it."[43] Or to another, inquiring whether an interview with the British ambassador to Mexico had dissipated "the impression, if it was in your mind, that he was antagonistic to the United States," Wilson asked sarcastically, "When did you discover that that was in my mind?" "I said if it was," the correspondent responded quietly.[44]

None of this endeared Wilson to the press. To their annoyance they felt like schoolboys apprehensive about being in the presence of a haughty headmaster. "Mr. Wilson did not intend, possibly, to resume the role of school-teacher," David Barry wrote, "but his attitude towards the newspaper men became what it had been towards the undergraduate. . . ."[45] Worse, they got the sense (reading Wilson correctly as it turned out) that he didn't regard them as particularly bright students. It is one thing to be treated with chill formality, and another to be cast as a dullard. Wilson had a way of doing that, to the discomfort of experienced journalists as well as those just starting out. "By and by the press conferences were abandoned," Oswald Garrison Villard wrote a few years later, "because the President could not submit to being cross-questioned by men some of whom he did not respect and by an entire group he deemed his intellectual inferiors.''[46]

The preinaugural issue of Wilson's veracity, or lack of it, also came back to haunt these sessions. His practice of throwing reporters off the track with technically correct but still misleading responses, a tactic Colonel House called "grazing the truth," went over poorly with correspondents who felt they had a professional obligation of their own to get at the truth. One such instance, widely commented on at the time and helping to set the tone of the new administration, happened in June 1913 when Attorney General James McReynolds suggested to the cabinet that a stiffly graduated internal revenue tax might be used to weaken the giant tobacco companies, enough at least to encourage competition from smaller firms. Wilson authorized the attorney general to discuss the idea with members of the Senate Finance Committee, which McReynolds did the next day. On June 5, Senator Gilbert M. Hitchcock of Nebraska introduced a rider to the Underwood Tariff embodying the proposal. It caused excited comment in newspapers, because as Hitchcock himself admitted, the same formula could easily be used to stimulate competition in other industries as well.[47]

At his press conference the following week, reporters asked Wilson for his reaction to the proposal. The exchange that followed, trivial in itself, reinforced an old suspicion about the president.

> *Reporter:* Are you willing, Mr. President, to say anything about Mr. McReynolds' tobacco trust tax plan?
> *Wilson:* He didn't have any plan that I know of.
> *Reporter:* I have been misinformed.
> *Wilson:* Yes, you certainly have.
> *Reporter:* Well, can we understand from that that there is no such plan?
> *Wilson:* There is none that I know anything about. . . .
> *Reporter:* Somebody has been mighty misleading in the last two weeks.
> *Wilson:* Yes, I have noticed that, but we are not responsible for that.
> *Reporter:* Mr. President, wasn't there some sort of agreement, understanding, that Mr. McReynolds should discuss this matter with Senator Simmons?
> *Wilson:* There was an understanding that he could discuss it with whom he pleased, yes, but he didn't propose it as a plan; and it was not thrown out except as a suggestion, to be discussed for anybody that was interested in it.[48]

From the explanation it would appear that the president responded misleadingly to the initial questions on the grounds that a "suggestion" did not qualify as as "plan" until it had been discussed at length and refined. Of course the truth is that Wilson did not want to endorse a proposal business interests would fiercely resist, and one likely to generate little support in Congress. As far as the correspondents were concerned, however, he chose a devious way to avoid taking a stand. His play on words struck them as the next thing to a lie.[49]

All in all, they didn't care for Wilson much as a person. Oliver Newman, one of the few newsmen he did get along with, a man he named in a controversial appointment to head the Board of Commissioners in the District of Columbia and who he called on frequently as a golfing companion, estimated in an interview with Ray Stannard Baker that fully nine-tenths of the Washington correspondents disliked Wilson.[50] The fact would one day come back to haunt him, because in politics, as in other areas of life, personal factors are often a key in determining success or failure. Ideally, likeability or the lack of it should have no bearing on the professional dealings between presidents and reporters. The area is too important to allow such matters to intrude. But things do not work that way, and cannot. While a personally popular president may receive rough treatment at the hands of the press (if for no other reason than to give reporters an opportunity to preen themselves on their professional rectitude), the chances of an unpopular president receiving favorable treatment are much more remote. In those cases the judgments about performance in office are colored, necessarily so, by the dislike for the sort of person he is. Something of this situation developed out of Wilson's dealings with the press.

Not that the grounds for resentment lay all on one side. If reporters faulted him for being uncommunicative, Wilson complained with some justification that the press was more interested in playing up personalities and conflict than in trying to understand how government really worked. If reporters saw him as untruthful, he rightfully disdained the banality of interests and insights many of them demonstrated in the questions they asked. Wilson occupied the highest office in the land. He expected a level of discourse higher than what might occur among city room hacks assigned to cover a local ward heeler. The reporters did not always oblige.

Nor did they always give him fair coverage. The distortion in "president of Princeton says chewing tobacco makes men think" still plagued him in the White House, only with much more serious consequences. Perhaps the cruelest treatment from Wilson's point of view came on May 10, 1915, when he appeared in Convention Hall in Philadelphia to address an overflow audience, including 4,000 newly naturalized immigrants, on the subject of citizenship. The *Lusitania* had been sunk by a German submarine three days before with a loss of 1,198 lives, including 124 Americans. Emotions of horror and vengeance gripped the country, and it waited expectantly to hear what the president would say in his first appearance since the outrage. Without mentioning the *Lusitania* by name, he used the occasion to plead for restraint, and for nobility of national purpose.

"The example of America must be a special example," Wilson declared. "The example of America must be the example not merely of peace because it will not fight, but of peace because peace is the healing and elevating influence of the world and strife is not. There is such a thing as a man being too proud to fight. There is such a thing as a nation being so right that it does not need to convince others by force that it is right."[51] In the angry mood of the moment his soaring words disappointed people more than inspired them (although the audience he addressed, many of them German and Irish immigrants, responded enthusiastically). Wilson was clearly taken aback by the reaction. At his press conference the following morning he denied that the speech had policy significance. "There was considerable surprise," the *New York Times* reported, "when President Wilson told callers today prior to the Cabinet meeting, that in his remarks at Philadelphia he was merely expressing a personal attitude, and did not really have in mind any specific thing. He did not regard the Philadelphia meeting, he said, as a proper occasion to give any intimation of policy on any special matter."[52] According to Ray Stannard Baker, Wilson regretted having used the phrase "too proud to fight," at least without elaborating on it.[53] But most of all he resented the way newspaper comment immediately following the speech, and for months afterward, took those four words out of context and made them into a slogan for cowardice.[54] The press knew better (or so Wilson thought), but in its eagerness to turn the phrase-maker's weapon against him completely distorted his meaning. He had asked Americans to keep their heads at a time of crisis; the editorial comment made it seem as if he asked them to cravenly surrender their honor.

The old issue of newspaper coverage of the Wilson family also remained a serious irritant in the dealings between president and press. Most of the attention centered on his daughters, especially on their marital plans. Jessie, the middle one, escaped with least harrassment since she married Francis Sayre early in Wilson's first term, on November 26, 1913, and thereby ceased to be of particular news interest. Eleanor's marriage to Secretary of the Treasury William G. McAdoo on May 7, 1914 spared her as well, although not without some preceding unpleasantness. She claimed that prior to the public announcement of their engagement someone intercepted a letter McAdoo had sent to her while she was staying at the Waldorf Astoria in New York City. The envelope had been opened and clumsily resealed before reaching her. Shortly after rumors about the engagement started to appear prominently in the press, and on March 13 the papers reported the story as hard fact. President and Mrs. Wilson had no choice but to issue the official announcement the same evening, weeks before they had intended.[55]

The second White House marriage in little more than four months left only Margaret to bear the brunt of the publicity, which she had done anyway as the president's oldest daughter. Her position was particularly difficult since she aspired to a career as a concert singer (she made her debut with the Chicago Symphony Orchestra in 1915), and thus had to contend with the attention of overly zealous music critics in the press as well as frustrated match-makers. By and large she seems to have carried the burden well. Louis Brownlow, at the time one of the District of Columbia commissioners, described running into her in the lobby of the Willard Hotel when he was in the company of Chief of Police Raymond Pullman. Reports had been circulating in recent weeks that she and Pullman were engaged, although in fact the two had never met. Margaret couldn't resist the opportunity this chance encounter offered. Spotting Arthur Sinnott, the Washington correspondent of the *Newark Evening News,* she called him over and said, "Mr. Sinnott, this is a wonderful occasion for me. I have just met for the first time in my life the man that the newspapers say I have been engaged to for many months. I don't think anything like that has ever happened before."[56] Sinnott sheepishly agreed, and took steps to kill the rumors. As it turned out, Margaret had the last word in another sense as well. She never did marry, becoming the disciple of a mystic in Pondicherry, India, where she died during World War II.

For Wilson, the constant pecking at his family was not so easily dealt with. He probably would have been upset even if the reports had been essentially accurate, but to have his wife and daughters paraded in the penny-dreadful press with stories fabricated out of nothing, stories touching on the most personal aspects of their lives, he found intolerable. His anger finally welled up at a notable conference on March 19, 1914. It was a time of extreme pressure for him, when everything he regarded as vile in journalism seemed to have come together. Just the week before he had announced the engagement of Eleanor after her private correspondence had allegedly been violated and its contents exposed in public print. Much worse, his beloved wife, Ellen, had taken a jarring fall in her room on March 1, and now weak and in pain was confined to bed. Wilson still did not realize the seriousness of her condition: that she suffered from tuberculosis of the kidneys and Bright's disease and would be dead by the following August. He worried deeply about her, however, and resented the speculations in newspapers about her health.

His frame of mind can be imagined when he stood before the reporters at the Thursday press conference, and gripping the back of his chair for support, gave vent to emotions long pent up within him.[57] Never before were the pain and frustration he felt at the improprieties of modern journalism so vividly on display. In a mood his secretary described as "fighting mad," he opened the conference with the following words:

> Gentlemen, I want to say something this afternoon. . . . I am a public character for the time being, but the ladies of my household are not servants of the Government and they are not public characters. I deeply resent the treatment they are receiving at the hands of the newspapers at this time. . . . It is a violation of my own impulses even to speak of these things, but my oldest daughter is constantly represented as being engaged to this, that, or the other man in different parts of the country, in some instances to men she has never even met in her life. It is a constant and intolerable annoyance. . . .
>
> Now, I feel this way, gentlemen: Ever since I can remember I have been taught that the deepest obligation that rested upon me was to defend the women of my household from annoyance. Now I intend to do it and the only way I can think of is this. It is a way which will impose the penalty in a certain sense upon those whom I believe to be innocent, but I do not see why I should permit representatives of papers who treat the ladies of my household in this way to have personal interviews with me. . . . My daughters have no brother whom they can depend upon. I am President of the United States; I cannot act altogether as an individual while I occupy this office. But I must do something. The thing is intolerable. . . .
>
> Now, if you have ever been in a position like that yourselves—and I hope to God you never will be—you know how I feel, and I must ask you gentlemen to make confidential representations to the several papers which you represent about this matter. . . .[58]

Wilson spoke off-the-record, which meant that nothing on the subject appeared in newspapers the following day. From indirect evidence, the reporters were evidently moved by his appeal, as common sense suggests they would be. Eleanor, writing from a proud daughter's perspective, remarked: "He frightened the correspondents to such an extent that for some time they left us alone."[59] But the underlying issue of privacy versus public curiosity would not go away. It remained to poison the atmosphere for the rest of Wilson's years in office.

Mutual disillusionment took its inevitable toll. Wilson met the press twice a week during his first twenty-one months in office, usually on Monday and Thursday mornings at 10:00 A.M. Starting in December 1914, he cut back to conferences each Tuesday morning. In July 1915, using the pretext of the *Lusitania* crisis as an excuse, he abandoned the experiment altogether. His next meeting with the reporters did not occur until December 1916, a few weeks after his reelection. He was in unusually good spirits, and gave the forty-odd correspondents grouped in a semicircle around his desk in the Oval Office the impression that henceforth press conferences would be resumed every Monday afternoon. The president barred questions about the last-ditch attempt being made at the time to sound out the belligerents about a possible basis for peace, instead restricting the session to banter about inconsequential matters. "If the newspaper men went away newsless," the *New York Times* reported the next day, "they carried with them from the President's office a very distinct impression that Mr. Wilson was in better health than he had been at any time since he entered the White House, and that physically he was able to cope with any problem that ordinarily might involve a tax upon his strength. In ten days President Wilson will be 60 years old. He did not look his years this afternoon. . . ."[60] The next time reporters saw him he would look his years. Following this isolated meeting Wilson retired into seclusion for an even longer period, emerging only three times late in his administration—twice in France on February 14 and June 27, 1919, and once in Washington on July 10, 1919—to urge support for the League of Nations.

Some newsmen, seemingly unwilling to face the obvious, tried elaborate theories to explain why the conferences had ended. David Lawrence, for example, speculated that Wilson grew leery of answering reporters' questions in public once American involvement in the war became a real possibility. According to Lawrence, the president feared the consequences of German and Austrian journalists relaying his comments to their respective embassies, a diplomacy by remote control easily susceptible to distortion. As a neutral he could not bar them without also barring British reporters, which he did not wish to do. The only solution was to have no press conferences at all.[61] This is a contrived theory, and fails to explain why he could not restrict the conferences to American reporters only, or at the very least, resume them on the same basis as before once America had entered the war. The truth is more simple. Wilson stopped having press conferences because he found them extremely unpleasant, and felt that little or no good came out of them. He said as much in conversation with an aide two years after abandoning the experiment. When George Creel joined the administration in 1917 as chairman of the Committee on Public Information, reporters approached him to ask his help in persuading the president to resume the old practice. Creel agreed to do what he could, because he too thought the conferences served a purpose. But Wilson refused to even consider the idea. "It is a waste of time," he told Creel. "I came to Washington with the idea that close and cordial relations with the press would prove of the greatest aid. I prepared for the conferences as carefully as for any lecture, and talked freely and fully on all large questions of the moment. Some men of brilliant ability were in the group, but I soon discovered that the interest of the majority was in the personal and trivial rather than in principles and policies''[62] And so he never went back to them.

To leave it at that, however, would be misleading, because the disappointment surrounding this experiment should not obscure how much in fact was accomplished—more, certainly, than the participants realized. For reporters, the press conference gave them a status they had lacked in Roosevelt's time, but would never relinquish again. It established the principle that presidents should be regularly available to them for interrogation, and just as important, be available on equal terms to all. The technique Roosevelt had used to garner favorable publicity, feeding the news to correspondents he could trust to puff him while freezing out the rest, simply wouldn't work any more. In the Wilson years the White House press started to emerge as an independent body whose members enjoyed certain privileges simply by virtue of being members.

Some indication of the change in status for reporters covering the president is provided by a framed charter still hanging in a downstairs room of the press quarters built during the Nixon administration. It records the founding on February 25, 1914 of the White House Correspondents' Association, established partly as a social organization but also responsible for hearing grievances by or against members and screening admissions to the presidential press conference. Until then the only self-regulation among newsmen assigned to the president had come from the Standing Committee of Correspondents, a group concerned primarily with administering the press galleries of Congress. With the initiation of regular press conferences, White House reporters needed their own governing body.[63] The need became particularly acute after Wilson, in a way uncharacteristic of him, spoke off-the-record at his July 17, 1913 press conference about the situation in Mexico, only to see his comments appear in several papers. The violation threatened for a time to end the conferences altogether. To prevent that from happening, the correspondents asked Tumulty to accredit who could attend, and to weed out the exceptional cases of people who violated the ground rules. When eleven charter members came together several months later to found an organization through which reporters would handle the responsibility themselves, the press demonstrated a new level of professional awareness. William ''Fatty'' Price of the *Washington Evening Star,* who had started it all almost twenty years before by standing outside the White House to gather news, served as founding chairman of the WHCA; David Lawrence of the Associated Press, only two years away from joining the *New York Evening Post* in a role that many regarded as making him the first of the syndicated columnists, as vice-chairman; William B. Metcalf of the *Baltimore Sun* as secretary-treasurer.

Wilson suffered too much personal tribulation to appreciate the fact, but he also benefited from the conferences. Part of the reason is that they gave him an opportunity to meet regularly with the handful of journalists he respected. Walter Lippmann recalled how he and a few other correspondents made a point of staying behind after the sessions had ended to chat informally with the president. Once the wire representatives and others concerned with spot news had scurried from the room, Wilson would sometimes sit back in his chair and talk with the remaining reporters in a more quiet, relaxed way. "The little group that stayed on," Lippmann wrote, "consisted of those who were concerned not with the raw news of announcements and statements in the formal press conference but with explaining and interpreting the news."[64] The president had enough sympathizers among the correspondents to profit from these sessions: men like Arthur Sinnott of the *Newark Evening News,* Richard Oulahan of the *New York Times* (who some editors in his home office thought was so pro-Wilson that they petitioned Adolph Ochs, unsuccessfully, to have him brought back to New York for periodic conferences), and Louis Seibold of the *New York World.* It was Seibold whom Wilson summoned after Warren Harding's nomination for two days of intensive discussion about national affairs, a meeting which resulted in an article that won the reporter the Pulitzer Prize.[65]

Although Wilson had only a primitive notion of how to structure the conferences to serve his purposes, he even made some progress in that direction. Most of the time he simply presented himself for questioning. He rarely used prepared opening statements to generate news and suggest a line of inquiry for the reporters to follow; he didn't plant questions with cooperative newsmen; by and large he didn't excel at turning questions around to hold forth on what he really wanted to discuss. His press conferences belonged mainly to the reporters to do with as they liked. But on a few occasions Wilson broke out of his self-imposed restraint, enough to demonstrate how this forum could be used as an instrument to lead public opinion. Perhaps the most impressive such demonstration (which itself says something about the downward slope of the conferences), occurred in the first weeks of his administration when he used one of the regularly scheduled meetings with the press to light a fire under the first real tariff reform measure in the United States since the Civil War.

The bill for downward revision of the tariff, a key plank in Wilson's New Freedom, had moved smartly through the House of Representatives under the leadership of Oscar Underwood of Alabama, chairman of the Ways and Means Committee. It came to a final vote on May 8, 1913, and passed by a solid margin of 281 to 139, all but five Democrats (four of them from the sugar-producing state of Louisiana) supporting the party measure. The problem lay in the Senate, a place traditionally hostile to tariff reform, where party balance was more evenly matched than in the House and where several Democrats from sugar and wool states threatened to join with the Republican minority in support of protectionism. Wilson felt he had the strength to overcome such opposition, but he worried about the lobbyists at work on wavering Democrats from the South and West. On Monday morning, May 26, he used his press conference to counterattack.

The reporters had been quizzing him about American relations with revolutionary Mexico when Wilson suddenly interrupted the flow of questions to suggest they get closer to home and talk about the lobbyists overrunning the city. "A brick couldn't be thrown without hitting one of them," the president said. "And I certainly feel like throwing some bricks."[66] He warned that the lobbyists were applying tremendous pressure to cripple a bill the people wanted, and that the only way to stop them was for the people to insist on being heard. Considering that this was the first time Wilson had used the press conference to get his message across, his words automatically attracted attention. They were all the more noteworthy in taking a page out of Roosevelt's book and calling on the public to support him against the special interests. The reporters, thoroughly alive to a big story, asked if they could quote him directly. Until then Wilson had required that the press paraphrase his remarks, but he recognized the publicity potential in their request and agreed to dictate a statement which Tumulty distributed to the reporters an hour later.[67] "I think that the public ought to know," it said, "the extraordinary exertion being made by the lobby in Washington to gain recognition for certain alterations of the tariff bill. Washington has seldom seen so numerous, so industrious, or so insidious a lobby. . . . It is thoroughly worth the while of the people of this country to take knowledge of this matter. Only public opinion can check and destroy it. . . ."[68]

Although initial reaction to the statement was not entirely favorable, papers like the *New York Times* wondering how the president distinguished between legitimate lobbying activity and the "insidious" effort of the moment, he had certainly seized national attention.[69] And then a stroke of luck came along to help him hold it. Senate Republicans, seeking to exploit what they took to be Wilson's blunder, immediately called for the appointment of a select committee to investigate the charges. The president passed word to members of his party to accept the challenge. He probably exceeded his own expectations when testimony in mid-June detailed the wide-ranging activity over the past several years of both the beet sugar and free sugar lobbies, including an attempt by the former to infiltrate the wire services.[70] Wilson had more than made his point, and he reaped the benefit. One of the reasons the Underwood Tariff finally passed the Senate on September 9 by a tight party vote of 44 to 37 (only two Louisiana Democrats bolting at the end) was his adroit management of publicity, starting at a press conference four months before.

Although such feats became less common with the passing of time, Wilson had still set in motion more than he knew with his press conferences. His successor in the White House would come back to them, and then the next president, and the president following. By the time Franklin Roosevelt had completed twelve years in office, holding to a remarkably consistent schedule of two meetings a week with reporters, the conferences had ceased to be an option available to presidents and developed into an institution in their own right. Many of the most important features in the American system of government—political parties, for example, and the paraphenalia of conventions, primaries, and caucuses that go with them—are not mentioned in the Constitution. They are rooted in custom and evolve through use. Wilson started something similar in his twenty-seven months of tense, rancorous meetings with newsmen. He added a new and unique feature to the way democracy works in the United States. A later generation of reporters would not ask whether such meetings were to be held, but how often and on what terms. And although the conferences Wilson attempted neither lasted long enough nor worked well enough to warrant comparison with the parliamentary question period in Great Britain, within a few more decades observers of government would be writing about the differences and similarities. Clearly, his experiment was not quite the failure he assumed.

It failed finally for Wilson, however, which meant that he had to fall back on other ways to get his message across in the newspapers. One of the devices he used, periodic addresses before the joint houses of Congress, turned out to have stunning impact. No president had delivered such a speech since John Adams 113 years before. Thomas Jefferson started the practice of sending copies of his messages to Congress to be read by the clerk in each chamber. He contended that presidential appearances smacked too much of the king's address from the throne, although as a gifted writer but poor public speaker the further truth is that his republican principles played nicely to his own strength. Over the decades the Jefferson practice became the norm, to the extent that many people saw separation of powers as somehow synonymous with presidents staying put at their end of Pennsylvania Avenue. The problem with republican simplicity was that a clerk droning the president's words lacked the impact of him mounting the podium to speak in person before the assembled houses. Messages from the White House declined into one of the tiresome features of Congressional routine. Except in special circumstances, they were occasions for members to leave the floor to attend to more important matters, even if that meant only an interlude of good fellowship in the cloak room. Wilson seized the country's attention in announcing his intention to follow the original precedent of Washington and Adams. The best part was that newspapers would have to give heavy and straightforward coverage to his appearances. Public fascination with the idea of the branches of government coming together in this way demanded it.

It is not clear when and how the idea occurred to him. James Kerney claimed that Walter Hines Page of *World's Work* proposed such appearances as a way to facilitate a closer working relationship with Congress.[71] More likely, if Wilson borrowed the idea from another, it came from an off-the-record interview he gave Oliver Newman at his home on Cleveland Lane in Princeton immediately after the election. Newman was presumably aware of how Wilson's thought about American government had changed over the years, largely under the influence of Theodore Roosevelt's strong presidency. As a young political scientist he had made his reputation with *Congressional Government,* published in 1885, in which he argued the supremacy of the legislative branch, and suggested for the United States a cabinet system patterned on Great Britain; in his more recent *Constitutional Government,* published in 1908, he wrote of the executive as the dominant branch because it alone was capable of leading public opinion. Newman, demonstrating the astuteness that won Wilson's respect, asked him if he had considered in that case taking a leadership role by appearing in person before Congress to speak about national concerns and priorities. The president-elect professed to be surprised by the idea. "Newman," he was quoted as saying, "that would set them by the ears." But the drawbacks also disturbed him. "I am afraid that it would be too radical," he continued. "It would be such a shock to the sensibilities of the members of Congress—to their orthodox ideas. . . . The matter of presenting the message might arouse antagonism which would tend to injure my recommendations for legislation."[72]

Assuming such an exchange occurred, the fact is that he had toyed with a similar notion prior to entering public life. "Possibly, had [Jefferson] not so closed the matter," he wrote in *The State,* a work he began while still a young faculty member at Bryn Mawr College, "[presidential addresses before the joint houses] might legitimately have been made the foundation for a much more habitual and informal, and yet at the same time much more public and responsible, interchange of opinion between the Executive and Congress."[73] On the evidence Wilson came to the idea independently, and at most was reinforced in his train of thought by conversations with journalists.

Wilson used tariff reform, the cause he would later push so effectively in a press conference, as the theme for his first visit to Capitol Hill. He had called Congress back into special session to take up the matter, and on April 8, 1913, the day after the two houses convened and scarcely a month after his own inauguration, appeared in person to urge action. The announcement on April 6 of what he proposed to do caused tremors in Washington. Some members of his own cabinet worried about the pro-

priety of breaching custom in this way, and Southern Democrats sensitive
to any usurpation of the separation of powers proclaimed their outrage.[74]
"I for one very much regret the President's course," Senator John Williams of Mississippi declared. He saw the forthcoming speech as "a cheap
and tawdry imitation of the pomposities and cavalcadings of monarchical
countries," and hoped that it would be the "only instance of the breach
of the perfectly simple, democratic and American custom of messages in
writing which Thomas Jefferson instituted."[75]

A mood of anticipation gripped the Capitol building on the Tuesday
morning of Wilson's appearance. The *New York Times* described "a clamoring crowd of fashionably dressed women and frock-coated men" clog-
ging the main entrance to the House wing as for the first time in over a
century the Senate filed in to hear a president speak, and occupied the
first two rows of seats.[76] Members of the cabinet appeared, taking their
place to the Speaker's left; diplomats and luminaries filled the galleries;
Mrs. Wilson, her daughters, and cabinet wives waited expectantly in the
executive gallery. At 12:58 P.M., promptly on schedule, Wilson entered
the chamber to standing applause, but to an atmosphere one observor
described as "distinctly tense."[77] Seemingly nervous himself as he started
speaking, his oratorical skill soon took over. "I am very glad indeed,"
Wilson said, "to have this opportunity to address the two houses directly
and to verify for myself the impression that the President of the United
States is a person, not a mere department of the government hailing
Congress from some isolated island of jealous power, sending messages,
not speaking naturally and with his own voice—that he is a human being
trying to cooperate with other human beings in a common service. After
this pleasant experience I shall feel quite normal in all our dealing with
one another."[78] Wilson thereupon launched into his plea for a tariff schedule that would confer special privilege on no group in the country. It was
a short speech, and a triumphant one. "He . . . established himself as a
result of one bold stroke," Louis Brownlow wrote, "as the leader not
only of his party but of the nation."[79] The appearance offered a further
satisfaction as well. "When Cousin Ellen and the rest of us got home
[from listening to the speech]," Helen Bones, Wilson's cousin, wrote to
her sister several days later, "we found him still looking amused. . . .
Some one said at lunch that the Bull Moosers in Congress had looked
rather surly. Cousin W. said, laughing, that probably they were mad because that was one thing their Teddy had *not* thought of doing!"[80] He
could hardly be blamed for feeling pleased with himself. "The wonder,"
the *New York Times* declared in an editorial accompanying its report,
"is that in seven years Theodore Roosevelt never thought of this way of
stamping his personality upon his age."[81]

Wilson broke another tradition, one dating to Abraham Lincoln, when he returned to Congress the next day to confer with Democratic members of the Senate Finance Committee, the body that would be responsible for the tariff bill. These were not occasions the newspapers could skimp in covering, nor could they allow personal animosities to influence the tone of their accounts. The country wanted to know every detail about his visits. It would not tolerate incompleteness, and certainly was in no mood for irreverence about the president's bold and novel leadership.

In all, Wilson averaged about three congressional addresses a year during his tenure in office. Most of the time he used the appearances to urge specific bills, but not always. On several occasions the speeches dealt in a general way with issues of contemporary concern, usually in the area of foreign affairs. The fact that he went before Congress to speak on matters having nothing to do with legislation, or for that matter with ratifying treaties, provides the best indication that his primary purpose was to mobilize public opinion behind him. He spoke over the heads of the Congress to the people, the press acting as his intermediary.

Indeed, what stands out in retrospect is the similarity between his technique and later presidential use of radio and television. The speeches were generally brief (the first one on the tariff lasted only nine minutes), which meant that Wilson could count on them being quoted in full in major newspapers, and the gist not lost even in papers that printed only selections.[82] Unlike Roosevelt's messages, and those of most previous presidents, they dealt with a single theme. He did not risk dissipating attention or impact by attempting to cover too much at once.[83] Above all, he carefully spaced the appearances to avoid overexposure while at the same time taking care to maintain the impression of ongoing presidential leadership. If he had scheduled these speeches much more often than every four months or so they would have become a bore. He avoided that, but he also made sure the country did not lose sight that he was in charge.

Another reason Wilson by and large received a good press during his first term, despite the hostility of reporters, was that he enjoyed precisely the asset William Howard Taft lacked: a secretary skilled in the ways of publicity, and able to compensate through his own personality for the problems caused by the personality of the president he served. Joseph Tumulty and Woodrow Wilson were almost complete opposites as types, which is odd considering the close bond between the two men. The secretary laughed easily, and by his wit and ebullience caused others to laugh with him. "There may be people so hardened in the grouch habit," a reporter for the *Houston Post* said of him, "that they can meet Tumulty without getting cheered up and beginning to enjoy life; but the oldest inhabitant cannot remember seeing anybody whose grouch lasted a minute

after he had been introduced.'"[84] His spirit of fun and infectious good
humor won him friends in all walks of life, including George M. Cohan,
the musical comedy star, who used to roar at Tumulty's Irish brogue
jokes. Along with the laughter went a notably generous nature. The secretary was famous in Washington for giving freely of himself and the things
in his possession to give, and in a way to make the recipients feel that
they were somehow doing the favor in accepting his offerings. Above all,
he genuinely cared about people: without pretense, without meanness of
spirit, without even an ability to hold grudges. To a legion of admirers he
summed up everything best in the stereotypical figure of the warm-hearted
Irishman. "He just has the knack of being gracious," a journalist wrote.
"And he means it; it is not affectation with him. It comes from a naturally
kindly heart. . . .'"[85]

Tumulty was the perfect candidate to assist a president whose flaw was
the absence of such qualities. It mattered also that he had the chance to
operate during the first term, when domestic reform still dominated the
agenda. By and large presidents can expect support when the country
faces international crisis, but to exercise domestic leadership they must
persuade a majority to go along. At those times skill in public relations
comes much more into play. Wilson proved his ability as a publicist in
his addresses before Congress and occasionally in the press conferences.
As the term implies, however, public relations is largely just a matter of
knowing how to respond to people. Here Wilson stumbled, and he depended more than he perhaps knew on his secretary to carry the load for
him.

Perhaps Tumulty's most important contribution, and also the one most
difficult to pin down, was simply making friends of Washington correspondents. It is not something journalists care to dwell on at length, but
their treatment of public figures often does hinge on personal considerations. An ability to engage in good-natured banter, to swap stories, to
be one of the boys, all help to influence the tone of reporting. It is disarming
also when the subject flatters newsmen by speaking pungently in their
presence, or by sharing inside information with them on a background or
off-the-record basis. This sort of manipulation (for that is what it is) was
hopelessly beyond Wilson. In Tumulty, however, he had an aide blessed
with the qualities he lacked. Although as a surrogate the secretary could
accomplish only so much, he was able to say in effect to reporters, "come
on, the old man's not so bad," and have some influence.

The difference between what might have been written and what actually
appeared is of course impossible to determine, but the newsmen themselves realized that because of Tumulty they often softened their dispatches. N. O. Messenger, writing in the (Washington) *National Tribune*,
described the combination of propriety and cordiality that applied at Tu-

multy's press briefings, and how it influenced reporters. "It is 'Mr. Secretary' this and 'Mr. Secretary' that, all quite proper and according to Hoyle," he wrote. "But when the interview is over it is 'Joe.' . . . Likewise it is 'Jim' and 'Gus' and 'Jack,' and so on. Which is as it should be. . . . For it shows the existence of a solid tie of mutual affection and trust among them which binds the official relations closer." And as Messenger also pointed out, "There is no use denying that 'Joe' puts over many a thing that 'Mr. Secretary' would find treated in a way lacking the power of the personal equation."[86]

To the extent he could, Tumulty also tried to get the president involved in this personal equation. He often prevailed on him to write letters of appreciation to newsmen for favorable articles. When Richard Oulahan's wife died, the secretary sent flowers in Wilson's name. Back came a thank you note, and Tumulty made sure the president responded with a warm letter of condolence.[87]

It wasn't only attending to the gracious gesture. The press corps knew that Tumulty was one member of the administration they could count on to stand up for them at times of trouble. Part of the reason they helped him is that he constantly helped them. Not that he tolerated being trampled on. Reporters who violated release rules, or misquoted him, or betrayed a confidence—as sometimes happened—found out just how stern he could be. The secretary did not hesitate to write to publishers demanding that the offender be punished, or if necessary, to threaten punishment himself by denying access to White House briefings or releases. Still, he did not translate annoyance with individuals into vendettas against them, or into justification for impeding the flow of news. And when others tried, Tumulty championed the press.

In early 1915, for example, a thoroughly aroused William Jennings Bryan tried to bar newsmen from the State Department on the grounds that confidential material was appearing in papers, and also because the newsmen were personally disrespectful to him. In a way Bryan had cause for complaint. His extreme reticence and attempt to restrict the flow of information from the department to official announcements had soured relations between him and the press, and some of the correspondents (the Hearst contingent evidently the worst offenders) showed their contempt by bullying him unmercifully.[88] Even the reporters who deplored the conduct of their colleagues felt humiliated by the secretary of state's inability to defend himself. On one occasion the questioning turned to his weekly appearances on the Chautauqua circuit, which he had undertaken as a way to supplement his official income. "Tell me," a reporter asked sweetly, "when is the next show going to be, and will you be performing before or after the Swiss bell ringers and Japanese tumblers?"[89] Bryan had had enough of it. When he decided that he wanted the press kept off

the premises, the reporters delegated David Lawrence and Oswald Garrison Villard (the two in their number who knew Wilson best) to see the
president and ask him to lift the banishment. Wilson felt ambivalent on
the matter. He recognized the difficulty in barring newsmen from the State
Department, but at the same time he sympathized with Bryan. To Tumulty,
on the other hand, there was no question at all. As he pointed out to the
president, however unfortunate the behavior of some reporters it would
be folly to deny the press access to news. The order had to be, and was,
countermanded.

The reservoir of good will Tumulty built up with White House correspondents served him best, and in turn was replenished, at his daily 10:00
A.M. press briefings when he met with thirty or so representatives of the
major news organizations in the country. These were the occasions he
depended on most for influencing newspaper coverage of the president.
They became particularly important after August 1915 when Wilson abandoned his own press conferences and left to the secretary sole responsibility for releasing news of the administration and fielding the interminable
questions from reporters. Unlike Wilson, Tumulty thoroughly enjoyed the
assignment. He later called the morning meetings with the press "delightful interludes on a busy day."[90] Part of the reason is that he knew he was
among friends. Even more important, he did it so well; certainly better
than the man he served. According to David Lawrence, "Woodrow Wilson little knew how artful [sic] Tumulty did handle the delicate question
of relations with the press. . . . Time and again, Secretary Tumulty revealed the President's views and articulated the administration viewpoint
with more skill than the President showed in his conferences with the
newspapermen."[91]

The foundation of Tumulty's success was in playing straight with reporters. "I found in dealing with these men that frankness and candor
paid big dividends," he wrote after leaving office.[92] Obviously the secretary operated under severe limitations in what he could disclose in the
briefings. He worked for a president who preferred to keep cards close
to the vest, and as with anyone in his capacity, Wilson's wishes came
first. From the testimony of newsmen, however, Tumulty seems to have
tried to stretch the limits, at least to the extent of steering them in the
right direction. Occasionally he would respond to questions on an off-the-
record basis, trusting his friends to respect the terms of the disclosure.
"He tells you many things in confidence," a correspondent wrote, "for
your guidance, not for publication. It is needless to say that his confidence
is strictly preserved. The man who would violate it might as well turn in
his union-card and never come back any more."[93] Above all, he never
lied to the press. "If Joseph P. Tumulty will not tell you all you want to

know," the same correspondent remarked, "he will not mislead you nor tell you what is not so."[94] That was all the newsmen asked.

Tumulty, in turn, made sure that the president's publicity needs were served at these sessions. He knew all the tricks: techniques like pacing the news, using teasers to build up forthcoming events, pushing human interest material. Experienced reporters were sometimes bemused by the secretary's antics, but of course they went along. As David Lawrence recalled, "He was able to set the stage for an address by the President or for the announcement of some other action, hinting a few days in advance that a sensation was forthcoming or revealing bit by bit, and with an air of mystery, things which appeared to the eager newspapermen to be great secrets, data which Tumulty, with all the arts known to the practiced publicity expert, divulged with an idea to headlines and conspicuous display."[95] The press also understood that some of Tumulty's remarks might be intended as trial balloons to test public reaction. What he said still represented news for them, without fear of reprisal if the balloon exploded. "There are times," a reporter wrote, "when the White House puts out tentative suggestions, by way of feelers, so to speak, to sound out public sentiment; to see how an idea will 'take' with the public. That is all right; it gives an idea of what the Administration is thinking about, at any rate."[96] The arrangement represented a *quid pro quo* in which both sides benefited. Although it is too much to say that reporters and officials can ever work together in complete harmony of purpose, Tumulty and the press came remarkably close at the daily White House briefings.

The secretary's publicity function extended to surveying as well as forming public opinion. In an era before polling, Tumulty performed one of his greatest services to the president in keeping abreast of shifting sentiment thoughout the country. In part the process involved a painstaking review of press opinion. Every day his staff clipped items from newspapers and magazines in the different regions which they arranged topically and pasted on long yellow sheets. Tumulty took them home with him each evening for his nighttime reading. If he detected trends of opinion, or issues that seemed to be causing particular concern, he would inform Wilson or the official most directly involved by memorandum. The secretary's wide circle of friends, in politics and out, provided further intelligence. He depended on letters from them (often from journalists on their travels) to supplement the paste-ups. A Mark Sullivan or David Lawrence visiting a state, a middle level functionary long resident there, were often more accurate barometers of opinion than the local press.[97] And of course he also had the chatter of official Washington. One way Tumulty tried to prevent Wilson from being an isolated president was by sharing with him the stories and gossip he heard in the corridors of the

White House and at his luncheon table at the Shoreham. Undoubtedly he did not share everything (that would have been indiscreet), but he passed on enough to become eyes and ears for Wilson outside the Oval Office.

The secretary's formal and informal soundings of opinion were not sufficient by themselves to chart the popular mood. Tumulty also had to be able to interpret his information, a challenge that depended upon instinct as much as science. His skill in assessing what the country thought, and what its likely responses would be, explains why Wilson relied on him heavily in preparing his speeches. The president explained in an interview with Ida Tarbell shortly before the 1916 election that most of the time he consulted no one. He wrote a first draft in shorthand, and revised it on his typewriter while transcribing a copy to send to the printer. But "when it seems specially important that I be understood," Wilson added, "I try it on Tumulty, who has a very extraordinary appreciation of how a thing will 'get over the foot lights.' He is the most valuable audience I have."[98] In those cases the secretary would carefully go through the manuscript, often inserting minor changes to make the meaning clearer, occasionally substituting whole passages. Tumulty's testimony that he urged Wilson not to use the "too proud to fight" phrase following the sinking of the *Lusitania* indicates that the president did not always follow his recommendations.[99] He heeded advice often enough, however, to include speechwriting under the secretary's functions.

Considering their good working relationship, both men paid a heavy price for Tumulty's fall from influence late in the first term. There had been considerable doubt about appointing him to the position in the first place, even though he had served effectively in an equivalent role during Wilson's governorship. In part the concern grew out of nativist resentment at having a Catholic so close to the center of power. Wilson, for one, scorned that attitude. "You would be surprised to know the number of letters I have been receiving telling me I must not appoint a Catholic to be my private secretary," he told David Lawrence shortly after the election. "I would like to ram that appointment down their throats!"[100] On the other hand, he did take seriously the argument of some of his advisers, notably Democratic chairman William McCombs, that Tumulty lacked the stature for a key post in the White House.[101] The dapper, rosy cheeked, good-natured Irishman somehow looked too much like what he had once been: an old-fashioned wardheeler. Moreover, even Wilson thought of him as hopelessly provincial in outlook. "The trouble with Tumulty," he said to Colonel Edward House in mid-December 1912, "is that he cannot see beyond Hudson County, his vision is so narrow."[102] Wilson initially decided that he wanted some one else. He asked Newton D. Baker, the impressive young reform mayor of Cleveland, to take the job, intending to salve Tumulty's disappointment with a plush political appointment, possibly a collectorship. Only when Baker turned him down, and House, the president-elect's closest adviser, persuaded him that the aide would fit in well in Washington, did Wilson make the appointment. At thirty-three, Tumulty was the youngest presidential secretary until that time.

But he never overcame the shaky start. For one thing, House soon had second thoughts about him, which he shared freely with Wilson. Perhaps the adviser resented the challenge Tumulty posed to his own influence with the president just by constantly being in and out of the Oval Office. Whatever the motive, House's list of grievances seemed to accumulate by the month. "Tumulty talks too much," he confided in his diary in mid-December 1913. "I find evidence of it on every hand. Stories come to me every day of his indiscretions in this direction. I feel somewhat humiliated when I think of my warm advocacy of Tumulty for Private Secretary. The President desired a man of refinement and discretion and of broad vision. He has instead just the opposite and wholly at my insistence."[103] Worse, the secretary also earned the enmity of the second Mrs. Wilson, a woman far less shy about exerting her influence in politics than the president's first wife. Tumulty had always gotten along well, almost in a mother-son way, with Ellen Wilson. When she died on August 6, 1914, he lost an ally as well as a dear friend. But from their first meeting Edith Galt Wilson thought of him as uncouth and common. Dislike turned into active hostility when she learned that the secretary, partly for political reasons and possibly also because of his feelings for Ellen, had counseled the president to put off remarrying until after the 1916 election. Although Wilson did not follow the advice, Tumulty still paid the price for offering it.

House and Edith Wilson seized the opportunity provided by the president's narrow victory in 1916, when thoughts naturally turned to restructuring the administration for the second term, to accomplish their goal. In a conversation with Wilson days after the election they pointed out that he had been hurt politically by the concern in many quarters at him having a Catholic as secretary. This was not the first time House had pressed for Tumulty's dismissal, but now in the close vote he had the evidence to support his case. He had even scouted for a replacement, coming up with the name of Daniel C. Roper, a former first assistant postmaster who more recently had run Democratic headquarters in New York City during the reelection campaign. Wilson reluctantly bowed to the urgent entreaties of his wife and adviser.

Shortly after that conversation, the president called Tumulty in and requested his resignation, offering him as consolation a better paid position on the Board of General Appraisers of the Customs. The secretary was stunned at the request. Rather than respond immediately, he equivocated for several days while the pressure mounted. Trying to nudge him, the president twice dispatched Postmaster General Burleson to speak to

Tumulty about leaving. Meanwhile Mrs. Wilson kept at her husband to force the secretary to step down, and House repeated the warning about the political consequences in having a Catholic at his right hand. Finally, on November 18, Tumulty responded to Wilson in a poignant, almost naked, letter, asking to stay if he could, offering to go if he must, but in either case wanting no other government position than the one he held.

> After deep reflection . . . I have decided that I cannot accept the appraisership; nor do I feel that I should embarrass you by accepting any other office. I had hoped with all my heart that I might remain in close association with you; that I might be permitted to continue as your Secretary, a position which gave me the fullest opportunity to serve you and the country. To think of leaving you at this time when the fruits of our long fight have been realized wounds me more deeply than I can tell you.
> I dread the misconstruction that will be placed upon my departure and its reflection upon my loyalty which hitherto had been unquestioned, for I know, as you probably do not, that rumors have been flying thick and fast in the past few months as to the imminence of my removal and even as to the identity of my successor. But despite these regrets, I feel that I can not do other wise than leave you, if you really wish it.
> You can not know what this means to me and to mine. I am grateful for having been associated so closely with so great a man. I am heartsick that the end should be like this.[104]

The day after sending the letter Tumulty spoke to a few of his friends about what had happened. One of them, a deeply shocked David Lawrence, went to see the president to try and explain the terrible mistake he was making. His account of the meeting, and of Wilson's decision to relent, suggests the intensity of emotion on all sides. "For three-quarters of an hour we talked," Lawrence wrote. "It was a dramatic conversation only because the author felt that in such a case vehemence was essential in order to impress Mr. Wilson with the ingratitude that would be his if he listened to the enemies of his private secretary and gratified their wishes. Nobody would understand, the author told the president, how one who had rendered as faithful service to him as had Secretary Tumulty could be asked to retire. None of the newspaper men who knew what had been accomplished by Secretary Tumulty for Woodrow Wilson would understand and the old taunt of New Jersey days—ingratitude—would arise once more. Mr. Wilson seemed to realize that he had wounded his faithful friend—the man who had fought his battles day and night—and he sent word through the author to his private secretary not to be disturbed."[105] Tumulty could stay on after all.

Mrs. Wilson and House found out about the decision too late to intervene. Although from the Colonel's diary entries they hoped as late as January 1917 that the secretary would resign before the inauguration in March, their maneuver had failed. But no one really won in this power struggle. If the president demonstrated his affection for Tumulty in retaining him despite even Mrs. Wilson's wishes, the further fact is that the relationship between the two men could never be the same as before. They had both surrendered too much of self-respect, and perhaps even respect for the other: Tumulty in clinging to his job when he had been asked to leave, Wilson in bowing to a conspiracy against the secretary and then not making it stick.

Tumulty continued to maintain cordial relations with reporters in the second term (his luncheon table at the Shoreham was a meeting place for Washington newsmen throughout the Wilson years), and still tried to soothe ruffled feelings between the president and the press. But with America's declaration of war on April 6, 1917, and the establishment eight days later of the Committee on Public Information, he ceased to have much to do with publicity, even giving up the daily briefings. Responsibility for publicizing the administration and its war aims passed into the hands of the CPI chairman, George Creel.

One indication of Tumulty's declining role could be seen in the new isolation that enveloped the White House. Wilson had been willing, usually at his secretary's behest, to grant occasional interviews to journalists prior to the abandonment of the press conferences, and for a while after. For example, a story in the *New York Times* in January 1914 reviewing the administration's foreign policy probably grew out of an exclusive interview with Charles Thompson.[106] Ray Stannard Baker and Ida Tarbell saw him for two almost fawning pieces in *Collier's* timed to fit in with the 1916 reelection campaign, and George Creel for another piece in *Everybody's* on what Wilson hoped to accomplish in the second term.[107] Even limited access of this sort, however, ceased to be granted during the next four years. When David Lawrence requested an interview in 1918 for an article commissioned by the *Saturday Evening Post*, the president in declining claimed to have no talent for talking about himself. "I have been thinking a great deal about your proposal of an article about my executive work," he wrote back, "and I find that I can't for the life of me think it out in any way that would be striking and effective. That is my trouble. . . . I am hopelessly useless for publicity purposes."[108] Whether he really believed that, or just didn't want to be bothered, the result was still to restore the isolated presidency of decades before. "For the major portion of his two terms in the White House," James Kerney pointed out, "he was seen less by newspaper people and confided less in them than any President since Cleveland or Harrison."[109]

During eighteen months of war it didn't really matter. The president had the CPI to glorify him, and in any case managing publicity is no problem when patriotic feelings run high. But pressures were seething under the surface, and the time of reckoning could not be put off forever.

7

The Drums of War

On April 13, 1917, one week after the United States declared war on Germany, Secretary of State Robert Lansing, Secretary of War Newton Baker, and Secretary of the Navy Josephus Daniels recommended to President Wilson that a special bureau be set up to handle censorship and publicity during wartime. In a joint letter to the president they stressed the latter need more than the former. "While there is much that is properly secret in connection with the departments of government," they wrote, "the total is small compared to the vast amount of information that it is right and proper for the people to have. . . . It is our opinion that the two functions—censorship and publicity—can be joined in honesty and with profit, and we recommend the creation of a Committee on Public Information." The cabinet members suggested that a civilian, "preferably some writer of proved courage, ability, and vision," be appointed to head the committee, and that they be included among its members.[1]

Essentially the letter represented a confirmation of decisions already made. Deliberations on the subject had been going on within the administration for weeks, starting well before Wilson's war message, and advice had also poured in from interested parties. Several of the most prominent journalists in the country—people like David Lawrence and Walter Lippmann and Arthur Bullard—wrote to the President and his advisers with their suggestions, in particular cautioning that the restrictive news policies followed in Great Britain and France simply would not work in the United States. Josephus Daniels, the cabinet member probably closest to the issue not only because of the department he headed but through his own involvement in journalism as publisher of the *Raleigh* (N.C.) *News and Observer,* agreed entirely. The most effective method of censorship, he felt, was to depend upon the press to police itself. In the long run the patriotism of reporters provided the best assurance that items damaging to the national interest would not appear in print.

Daniels's background in journalism probably contributed to his further, and more important, insight that the real challenge facing the administration was not so much to prevent the publication of military secrets as to generate publicity of a helpful sort. Considering the strong antiwar and isolationist sentiment reflected in the 1916 election, and the antagonism toward Great Britain among millions of Irish and German Americans, it was clear that a formidible task lay ahead in mobilizing the home front behind the war effort. This time the administration did not have anything like a *Maine* incident to rally the people through sudden shock. They would have to be persuaded into enthusiasm. Which is to say, the agency in charge of censorship had a much more important selling function to perform.

George Creel, a veteran journalist, saw eye-to-eye with his old friend Daniels on the respective priorities. In the first days of the war, when rumors circulated that Wilson might opt for a policy of tight news control, he wrote to the president urging a different approach. "I explained to him," Creel recalled later, "that the need was for expression not repression, and urged a campaign that would carry our war aims and peace terms not only to the United States, but to every neutral country, and also into England, France, and Italy. As for censorship, I insisted that all proper needs could be met by some voluntary methods."[2] Creel had also been in close contact with Daniels during those weeks, making the case for expression rather than repression and in the process recommending himself as a likely candidate to handle the assignment. On April 4, two days after Wilson appeared before the joint houses of Congress to ask for a declaration of war, on the same Wednesday the Senate voted for war by a majority of 82 to 6, he sent to Daniels a memorandum outlining how the work should be carried out. He called for an agency under civilian control, but with representation of the military branches and State Department. Its major function should be to publicize the activities of government, recruiting the best civilian talent available for the purpose, in order to drum up popular support for the war. Censorship (a term Creel thought best to avoid) could be handled by depending primarily on voluntary compliance with guidelines laid down by the agency.

From that point events moved rapidly. Wilson, it turned out, had never considered anyone but Creel to handle wartime publicity. On April 11, in a meeting with Daniels and Secretary of War Newton Baker, he also endorsed the proposals in the Creel memorandum. The next day the two cabinet officers drafted their joint letter to the president formally laying out the plan, this time bringing in Secretary of State Lansing as joint signatory. Wilson met briefly with Creel on April 14 to offer him the job, and immediately after issued Executive Order 2594 establishing the Committee on Public Information. The president even invoked a bit of superstition to get the enterprise off on the right foot. He predated the order to the previous day, which he regarded as lucky. The CPI started officially on Friday the thirteenth.

Creel, forty-one years old at the time Wilson appointed him, a dynamo of a man with a face some described as resembling a gargoyle's, seemed well suited in several respects to head the agency. He certainly met the criterion of being an experienced journalist. After brief stints on the *Kansas City World* and Hearst's *New York Journal,* he had founded and for a decade run his own weekly, the *Independent.* He later moved on to the *Denver Post,* although that association lasted only a short period when he found the paper too conservative for his taste. An interlude as a freelance writer for magazines followed. In 1911 he was invited back to Denver to join the *Rocky Mountain News* as editor, and played a major role in the campaign to put over the commission form of government in that city.

Nor did it hurt that the man to be in charge of censorship had the reputation of being so progressive in his politics that many people regarded him as something of a radical. Over the years he had crusaded for all the good causes, from warring on child labor, police corruption, and commercial vice, to fighting for women's suffrage and such standard devices of the era as the initiative and referendum. The record could not help but be reassuring. If the times required that accustomed rights of Americans be constrained, best then to delegate the constraining to one who had in the past shown a respect for those rights.

But Creel's greatest recommendation was his loyalty to the administration, and in particular to Thomas Woodrow Wilson. He first came under the Wilson spell even prior to the governorship, when the Princeton luminary visited Kansas City to address high school students on the meaning of democracy. Nothing in the years since had dampened Creel's ardor. In many ways it was a privilege for him to contribute a book and numerous newspaper articles to the 1916 reelection campaign, because by his reckoning he served everything noble in America in serving the president. Of course the experience of participating on the campaign staff—organizing a committee of writers to churn out pamphlets and statements on behalf of Wilson—also provided an ideal apprenticeship for his work with the CPI.

The reverse side of these virtues was less apparent. A true believer, a person not prone to qualifications or doubts, one who sees issues always with clarity and always recognizes where right and justice reside, is not necessarily the best candidate to resist the passions of wartime and present his country's case in a balanced way. Nor is a person who uncritically admires his president a likely candidate to stand against the inevitable temptation in wartime not simply to rally around the national leader, but to glorify him. America's first experience with having a ministry of propaganda would turn out to be all the more intense because of the personal qualities George Creel brought to the job.

The point is not that the CPI trafficked solely in propaganda. Creel made good immediately on his mission to disseminate hard information, virtually inundating newspapers with press releases. They came from the News Division of the CPI, the key branch in the rapidly expanding agency.[3] Under the direction of John W. McConaughy, an editorial writer for *Munsey's Magazine* and the *New York Evening Mail,* and after June 1918 of Leigh Reilly of the *Chicago Herald,* the Division functioned more like a metropolitan daily than a public relations bureau. Its offices just across from the White House (a young officer named Douglas MacArthur helped find them) remained open twenty-four hours a day, seven days a week. Wire dispatches came in around the clock from CPI correspondents overseas and throughout the country, while reporters based in Washington provided almost suffocating coverage of the federal government. All of this material flowed into the home office where a battery of rewrite men prepared the copy for release. The system introduced to government a centralization of news later administrations might envy. As Creel explained in his memoirs, informing the American people about the war could not be "left safely to . . . the haphazard business of permitting minor officials to make unchecked and unauthorized statements."[4] With his own people stationed in most of the departments he knew that professional and carefully coordinated judgments would apply in deciding what news went out and how.

A major reason for the division's success was its privileged access to information. Tumulty deferred to it, for example, in making the CPI the sole official conduit for news from the White House. Cabinet officers and other government leaders were routinely available to it for interviews. Most important, it had prior claim on announcements from the War and Navy Departments, including casualty lists and reports on military operations. These were not the kinds of items to end up in waste paper bins. And they kept coming in a torrential flow. During its lifetime the division issued 6,000 releases, an average of slightly more than ten a day. Creel estimated after the war that about 20,000 columns of CPI material appeared in the American press each week.

The figures are all the more impressive considering that the committee had to compete for newspaper space with the many executive departments that maintained their own publicity operations, including some of the newer ones like the Food Administration and the Council of National Defense. This was the era when government by "handout" came into its own (a term coined by reporters to self-mockingly cast themselves as supplicants at the back door receiving the throwaways of the household). And since newspapers in their patriotism wanted to serve, they printed more such material than sheer news value warranted. Even so, as *Editor & Publisher* pointed out, some selectivity had to be exercised in what to run.[5] The measure of the News Division's success is that its material rarely got pushed aside. Nothing required papers to print the dispatches it sent out. In fact, as Creel proudly informed the House Committee on Appropriations in 1918, the releases did not even go directly to news-papers. They were made available to Washington correspondents to do with as they wished. Only if the individual correspondent saw news value in a release would he wire it to his home office, and only if the editor agreed would it be run. On those terms the committee still managed to generate 20,000 columns of copy a week.

About the only flaw in the mechanism arose out of the secretary of state's refusal to allow the CPI to handle the news from his department. "I consid-ered," Lansing wrote in his memoirs, "that the subjects with which the De-partment of State was dealing were much too important and of too delicate a nature to be dealt with by men who were by no means expert in international affairs and who lacked the ability and knowledge to judge what was and what was not wise to publish. . . . On more than one occasion [Creel] renewed his efforts to handle the Department's publicity, but I declined to change my at-titude, so that he failed to accomplish his purpose."[6] Lansing's refusal to bend is all the more noteworthy considering that he held fast even against the president. "It has been very difficult," Wilson complained in a letter to the third assistant secretary of state, "to get one or two of the executive depart-ments, notably the Department of State, to act through Mr. Creel's committee in the matter of publicity, and the embarrassments of lack of coordination and single management have been very serious indeed."[7] Not so serious, however, that the secretary of state would change his mind.

Lansing's stubbornness obviously handicapped the CPI in its effort to establish absolute control of news about the administration and the war effort, but the agency succeeded well enough even without his cooperation to cause considerable misgivings among reporters. They realized only too well that they were not doing their jobs when stories were delivered to them by officialdom prepackaged and ready to serve. Under such an arrangement they could no longer think of themselves, at least not in the old sense, as performing an independent function. Their role differed little from that of the former journalists working for the CPI in being essentially government's messengers to the people.

The sensitivity of newsmen on this score helps to explain their rage on the few occasions the CPI misled them. And as it turned out, George Creel had the bad fortune only weeks after taking over the agency to be directly responsible for the worst such blunder, one from which his rep-utation never fully recovered. The trouble dated to June 1917, when the first contingent of American troops sailed for France, traveling in four separate groups to minimize the danger of U-boat attack. The CPI had intended to issue no announcement until all the groups arrived safely, but through mischance censors in Europe allowed an Associated Press dispatch to get through on June 27 about American troopships steaming into St. Nazaire to a tumultuous welcome. AP put the story on the wire without bothering to check with the CPI, and it made headlines throughout the United States the next day. The report would have been annoying in any case as a violation of the guidelines for voluntary censorship Creel had laid down the month before. Worse, the chairman knew what the press did not: that three other groups were still at sea, and presumably in trouble. A cable from the admiral in command of the convoy had reported two U-boat attacks already, and an engagement in which at least one submarine had been sunk. Now premature disclosure in the press only heightened the danger. Not until July 3 did the hoped-for bulletin finally arrive. The vessels had all reached France safely without suffering a single casualty.

As soon as he heard the news Creel rushed over to the office of Secretary of the Navy Daniels where they decided, as "a Fourth of July present to the nation," to announce not only the safe arrival of the ships, but on the basis of the skimpy detail in the admiral's communiqué, the story of a stirring victory at sea. Working against the pressures of deadline, undoubtedly carried away by the sheer jubilation of the moment, Creel prepared on the spot a release which in retrospect was rather more colorful than precise. It described a "force" of U-boats "gathered for what they deemed a slaughter," the terror of torpedoes whizzing by the prows of troopships, the searchlights on American escort vessels piercing the darkness as naval gunners took a deadly toll of the attackers. The *New York Times,* like virtually every other newspaper, devoted its entire front page to the story. "This is a glorious Fourth," the paper declared editorially. "The American Navy has inaugurated the war between Germany and the United States by two battles—both victories. The sea wolves that have been battening on merchant vessels were called home, and then launched in force against real foes, no longer against peaceful sailors and passengers, but against Yankee gunners who could hit back: and they went back, bleeding and beaten, without having struck one blow."[8]

Two days later Melville Stone of the Associated Press received a dispatch from a correspondent based in England which cast doubt on whether there had been a U-boat attack at all. The reporter claimed to have interviewed officers attached to the naval escort who said that the periscopes presumably sighted in fact consisted only of debris and the trail of blackfish. According to them, the heroic encounter never happened. Again AP acted without consulting the administration. Stone put the story on the wire before dispatching a reporter to get Secretary of the Navy Daniels's comment. When Daniels learned that the Associated Press had taken the word of anonymous junior officers over an official communiqué from the admiral commanding the operation, he erupted. His sulphurous comments in a telephone conversation with Stone obviously made an impression, because AP sent a follow-up message over the wire ordering member papers to kill the story. By then it was too late, however.

The damage need not have been severe but for an unfortunate conversation Creel had in his office the same day with several reporters. They asked why he didn't settle the matter by getting the Navy Department to release the exact text of the admiral's cable. He answered that it was impossible to do so because of confidential information the message contained about ship deployment, and also because the text might be used by cryptographers to break the Navy code. If he had left it at that things would have been fine. Creel added, however, that he saw nothing to be gained by releasing the cable. The technical wording in military messages tended to make such language "cryptic" to civilians. Moreover, there had been no duplicity in the way he handled the story since any fool knew that his press release on July 3 was not the official communiqué, but an "elaboration" on it. Those two words—"cryptic" and "elaboration"—came back to haunt him, much in the way Harry Truman learned to detest "red herring." "I went to Secretary Daniels' office," the *New York Times* quoted Creel the next day as saying, "where he and Admiral Benson had the report from Admiral Gleaves. It was rather cryptic. We read it over together, and then I sat down and elaborated on the text of the deciphered message."[9] As often happens, the words seemed different in print than in the saying.

The facts, when they finally sorted themselves out, neither condemned nor exonerated Creel. There had been U-boat activity in the area of the convoy, torpedoes were fired, and likely naval guns did sink one of the attackers. By the same token, the chairman almost certainly exaggerated in depicting a "force" of submarines gathered for the "slaughter." In making the heroism too great he detracted from what really happened. He also severely undermined his credibility with the press. Some indication of the reaction among journalists is provided by the *Washington Post*'s headline over the story:

CREEL WROTE "LURE" IN LURID
U-BOAT ATTACK ON U.S. SHIPS
AND SPY HYSTERIA RESULTED[10]

The *New York Times*, while more moderate in tone, was just as sweeping in its judgment. "As for Mr. George Creel," the paper declared, "it is evident that in his present position he is out of place, that his abilities, whatever they may be, are misapplied, misdirected. His long training in another field of publicity, where emotion and imagination count for much and accuracy is of minor importance, has evidently disqualified him for the service he has been called upon to perform. The Administration was ill-advised in appointing him to this responsible place. It was a blunder. The only possible and adequate corrective should be at once applied."[11] Harsh words, and Creel's first lesson that precisely because of their dependence on the CPI, journalists would not tolerate deception, intended or inadvertent.

Although flare-ups like these hurt the committee's credibility, in retrospect what is perhaps more noteworthy is that they happened as infrequently as they did. Under the monitoring of a suspicious and watchful press the Division of News maintained an impressive record of accuracy. As a double check against error, and also to protect itself against bureaucratic backbiting, it submitted all articles to the department head where the news emanated before releasing them. With this screening few dispatches ever came in for questioning. The further truth is that despite themselves, reporters came to depend on the flow of information out of the division, a flow far greater than they could have managed on their own. *Editor & Publisher* provided an indication of the division's importance to journalists when it polled editors throughout the country in spring 1918 for their reaction to the press releases descending upon them from Washington, and found overwhelming agreement that most of the material represented a waste of paper.[12] Three weeks later the trade periodical had to run a follow-up article specifically exempting the releases from the CPI. "Many of the editors who have favored us with their views as to the value of the Washington departmental and bureau press service," the periodical reported, "have taken occasion to commend the work of the Committee on Public Information, and to make it plain that their criticisms do not apply to that organization. Some of them realize that only through the efforts of the Committee is it possible to secure the release for publication of vital feature matter bearing upon the war activities. . . ."[13]

The more subtle problem of the committee's objectivity, the fact that a news story can be entirely correct in all particulars and still give a misleading impression, didn't seem to concern journalists. Unless one assumes that government, or any institution, will be as rigorous in publicizing its blunders as its triumphs, the viewpoints of its detractors as much as those of its defenders, the heavy reliance on such a source will almost certainly lead to slanted reporting. Creel denied that this happened with the CPI. "Our job," he declared, "was to present the facts without the slightest trace of color or bias, either in the selection of news or the manner in which it was presented. Thus . . . the Division of News set forth in exactly the same colorless style the remarkable success of the Browning guns, on the one hand, and on the other the existence of bad health conditions in three or four of the cantonments."[14] The chairman was a bit disingenuous in his assessment. While it is true that occasional stories about unsanitary conditions did crop up, the further fact is that the thrust of the CPI news was upbeat and patriotic. The committee didn't even have to twist the truth consciously; its reporting simply reflected the mood of the time. And if the press complacently accepted the CPI's version of events, the reason is that it was swept along by the same mood. After all, establishment newspapers are not put out by dissenters. Once the shooting begins they become routinely patriotic.

Where journalists did draw the line, but for a different reason, was when the CPI expanded its information function by publishing an official government newspaper. Wilson had long been fascinated by the idea of such a paper. In *Congressional Government* he wrote of the dilemma for American democracy in newspapers having greater power to inform and guide public opinion than government itself, and yet because of their provincialism scarcely writing about the news that mattered. It seemed to the young scholar in 1885 that the United States needed a "national organ of opinion."[15] He returned to the same theme twenty-three years later in *Constitutional Government,* this time adding the more serious indictment that newspapers failed in their responsibility because they were "owned by the special interests" and did not reflect "the general opinion of the communities in which they are printed."[16] Nothing about Wilson's experience in public life encouraged him to think better of the press, which explains why he toyed early in his administration with establishing a national publicity bureau to distribute news about government. He thought in terms of an official publication, presumably to appear daily, that would coordinate and present without bias the press releases from the various executive departments, and in so doing correct the misrepresentations he regarded as the stock in trade of commercial newspapers.

It is not difficult to understand why reporters found the concept repellent. The competition as such didn't bother them. A journal without local coverage or sports news or stock market quotations would have limited appeal to even the most serious readers. What they resented was the insult to their professional competence and integrity. Obviously the only reason for a government paper had to be that they were not doing the job. Moreover, as far as reporters were concerned, if such a paper ever became established, public enlightenment in the long run would suffer. An official version of events is inevitably self-serving, and thereby works to deceive rather than inform the people. And what assurance did the country have that once government entered this area it would not discriminate against the independent press to solidify its position by arranging for news to appear first in the official publication? By manipulating postal rates to undercut the ability of independent papers to compete? Even by imposing censorship in areas the government wanted to cover exclusively? However far-fetched such concerns, they were real enough to persuade Wilson—partly at the urging of Tumulty—to shelve the project during his first term. He far from gave up on it, however.

The president wasted no time in making his move once the CPI had been organized. He told Creel that "the government should issue a daily gazette for the purpose of assuring full and authoritative publication of all official acts and proceedings. . . ."[17] Creel saw possibilities in the venture, although in view of what he knew the press reaction would be had qualms about going ahead with it. But Wilson was determined, so the chairman quickly set about establishing a division of the CPI to put out a daily journal. The first issue of the *Official Bulletin,* edited by Edward Rochester of the *Washington Post,* appeared on Thursday, May 10, 1917, less than four weeks after the founding of the CPI. "PUBLISHED DAILY UNDER ORDER OF THE PRESIDENT BY THE COMMITTEE ON PUBLIC INFORMATION," it declared on the masthead.

Wilson finally had his outlet for presenting the news in exactly the form he wanted. The *Bulletin* served in part as a medium of communication within government and keeper of the historical record. Its major function, however, was to meet the cherished goal of being able to release information without the press interposing its own editorial judgment. No longer would important announcements be rewritten, or condensed, or perhaps ignored altogether by newspapers. In a manner reminiscent of the early years of the republic, the president now had an organ under his direct control.

In fact, aside from appearing daily (except Sunday), the *Official Bulletin* resembled a newspaper neither in style nor function. At nine by eleven inches—approximately the size of a magazine like *Time* or *Newsweek*— it was smaller even than a tabloid. The earliest issues ran to eight pages, later expanding to thirty-two pages and more by the end of the war. They contained an unremitting diet of executive announcements and regulations, including every official utterance by Wilson since the outbreak of war. In addition to paid subscriptions, copies of the *Bulletin* went without charge to public officials, newspapers, and agencies equipped to distribute information. Each of the 54,000 post offices in the country received one for public display, as did all military camps. From an initial circulation of 60,000 in May, 1917, the publication peaked at 115,000 in October, 1918 before going into rapid decline in the months preceding its demise on March 31, 1919.

The CPI tried consciously to placate the resentments and suspicions the *Official Bulletin* caused among journalists, not least by avoiding any appearance of commercial rivalry. Although the paper's annual subscription rate of $5.00 (which worked out to about 1½¢ an issue) was relatively inexpensive, Rochester's estimate at the end of 1918 that the *Bulletin* received income from only about 16,000 subscribers indicates that it made no attempt to drum up a paying readership. The publication was also careful to assure reporters that they would never be put at a competitive disadvantage. "Exclusive publication is neither the thought nor ambition," the *Bulletin* declared on May 23, 1917. "It will not interfere with the legitimate functions of the press in any manner, nor will official news be delayed or withheld in order to give the *Bulletin* any special news significance."[18] But even in keeping the promise it did little to appease journalists. The principle of government usurping their function still remained.

Something of the controversy surrounding the *Official Bulletin* is apparent from the heated reaction when the publication in its issue of March 28, 1918 compounded an earlier CPI blunder by running under a photograph of planes under construction in a factory the caption, "These airplane bodies, the acme of engineering art, are ready for shipment to France. Though hundreds have already been shipped, our factories have reached quantity production and thousands and thousands will soon follow." A similar report released by the Division of News in late February had sparked intense controversy when it turned out that only one plane had been delivered for shipment, and by the target date for full production in July no more than thirty-seven would be ready. A heated Senate debate at that time generated screaming headlines:

STORM IN SENATE
OVER WAR DELAYS

YEARS WASTED, LODGE ASSERTS,
DEMANDING FULL TRUTH BE
TOLD TO THE PEOPLE

ONLY 37 AIRCRAFT BY JULY
MEMBERS GASP AT NEWS' REVELATION[19]

George Creel and the CPI inevitably bore the brunt of criticism and distrust for having misled the country. (The fact that its source for the erroneous report was Colonel Edward Deeds, the officer in charge of aircraft production, and that Secretary of War Newton Baker had personally authorized the release, could not be made public for fear of undermining the credibility of the military.[20]) Now, incredibly, the same story had turned up in the *Bulletin*. Somehow the committee had managed to slip twice on the same banana peel.

The inflated response in Congress, however, prominently reported in the press, spoke to more than annoyance with an editorial mishap. In making the photograph the subject of a full-scale debate, one in which the speakers vied in vituperation, the Senate demonstrated that its anger went much deeper than the immediate provocation. Senator Charles Thomas of Colorado described the photograph as "primarily, secondarily, directly and indirectly, a fraud upon the press of the country." Another senator wonder whether the "misleading statements might not be the work of German propagandists. I can't imagine any propaganda of more benefit to Germany than to lull the American people into false security." To Senator James Wadsworth of New York, "it [was] time the Committee on Public Information had a censor of its own."[21]

Wilson heard the roar from the other end of Pennsylvania Avenue, and found it distressing. "My attention has been called to this release," he wrote to Creel the day after the debate. "Had it received your own personal inspection and approval? The statements about hundreds being shipped . . . are, I am afraid, very questionable as to accuracy. . . . I think it is a great mistake, as I am sure you do, to create any degree of baseless optimism about this important programme."[22] Of course Creel agreed, but he also knew by then that his critics in Congress and the press were beyond placating. They simply did not trust an executive branch that spent millions of dollars annually to publicize itself. Legislators sensed in the effort an attempt to upset the traditional balance between the branches of government; journalists sensed a challenge to their own function in keeping the public informed. For both groups the CPI and the man who presided over it were the objects of suspicion, and on more than one occasion downright hostility.

The irony is that Creel came in for criticism in the area where he least deserved it. However much the News Division and *Official Bulletin* served to trumpet the achievements of the administration, they still fell under the original mandate of the CPI to make information available. It was in the committee's other and more obtrusive activities that the distortion occurred and publicity became propaganda. From being an agency conceived to foster openness, the CPI turned into one for the manipulation of opinion. America, which has never been notably immune to enforced conformity, learned to march in step to the committee's cadence.

In a sense, the development was ordained right along. When George Creel wrote to Wilson immediately after the outbreak of war to urge a policy of expression rather than repression, he had in mind something quite different from what the terms are ordinarily construed to mean. As he explained in his autobiography, the United States suffered from too much diversity of opinion in the spring of 1917. By expression he meant persuading the country of the single truth. "During the three and a half years of our neutrality," Creel wrote, "the United States had been torn by a thousand divisive prejudices. . . . The sentiment of the West was still isolationist; the Northwest buzzed with talk of a 'rich man's war' . . . men and women of Irish stock were 'neutral,' not caring who whipped England, and in every state demagogues raved against 'warmongers.' . . . The printed word, the spoken word, motion pictures, the telegraph, the wireless, cables, posters, signboards, and every possible media [had to] be used to drive home the justice of America's cause."[23]

Of course any society at war must be united in purpose, but under the circumstances applying in 1917 the situation was right for a suffocating unity. As commander-in-chief the United States had Woodrow Wilson: humorless, rigid, convinced that absolute truths did exist and that he knew what they were. Below him it had a generation of leaders nurtured in the purity of the Progressive movement. And as its war aim it had nothing less than the resolve to make the world safe for democracy, a formidable assignment for any people. It is hardly surprising that the propagandists took over, spreading with missionary zeal a message the country was eager to hear. Hardly surprising either that in glorifying America's cause, the message also glorified its commander-in-chief.

George Creel's decision to structure the CPI's wartime propaganda largely around the name of Woodrow Wilson made sense. To mobilize the people's energies there had to be a unifying symbol, and the stars and stripes or Uncle Sam or the Constitution were altogether too restrictive in how they could be used. Almost certainly Creel intended nothing political in deciding to use the president as a symbol, although his feelings about him did in fact approach hero worship. "I find it hard always to think of you as a person," he wrote to Wilson in late December 1917, "for you stand for America so absolutely in my mind and heart and are so inseparably connected with the tremendous events of the time."[24]

The president's motives in going along with the campaign, indeed encouraging it, must also have been complicated, and to an extent unconscious. Image-building, in the narrow sense of advancing his electoral prospects, would no longer have been a consideration. He had already won all that a man of high ambition could win. Probably he recognized that the best way to unite the country, to harness its energies in common purpose, was behind himself as commander-in-chief. If he benefited politically from such a campaign, it would be in giving him greater leeway in pursuing his war policies, and more important, in negotiating a lasting peace at the end of hostilities. He had to welcome that sort of advantage.

Underlying all else, perhaps the key consideration, was Wilson's high opinion of himself. It is revealing that he could receive the letter of devotion Creel sent without evident embarrassment. The final justification in Wilson's mind for a propaganda campaign glorifying him may have been that it accorded with his own sensibilities, and, what can never be overlooked, the view he had of his place in history.

If motives are difficult to unravel, the president's deep interest in the work of the CPI is beyond question. Of the $6,850,000 allotted to the committee in its lifetime, Wilson personally supplied $5,600,000—or well over eighty percent of the total budget—from the National Security and Defense Fund. Congress, much more suspicious of government-subsidized propaganda, appropriated only $1,250,000, while an additional $2,825,000 came out of the committee's own earnings.[25] The president also scheduled frequent meetings with Creel during the war to be briefed on the CPI operations. He saw the chairman on an average of about three times a month, a figure few cabinet officers could match.[26] And when not seeing him he sent instructions by memorandum on how he wanted publicity handled.

Above all, Wilson fretted at others trespassing on the territory he had staked out for himself and the devoted Creel. Such an occasion occurred in September 1918 when Secretary of State Lansing informed him of an assignment just delegated to Walter Lippmann. The journalist had taken a leave of absence from the *New Republic* to enter government service when the United States declared war. After a stint as special assistant to Secretary of War Newton Baker during which he worked primarily on labor matters, and another on a board of experts convened by House to make preliminary plans for peace, Lippmann accepted a commission as captain in military intelligence. Wilson did not appreciate hearing that the journalist's latest mission would take him to Europe to conduct psychological warfare against Germany. "I have a high opinion of Lippmann," he wrote to Lansing, "but I am very jealous in the matter of propaganda. . . . I want to keep the matter of publicity entirely in my own hands, and I would be very much obliged to you if you would upon every proper occasion let that be known to our diplomatic and other representatives abroad."[27]

One of the advantages to Wilson in working through Creel, in addition to having everything under his own control, was that he didn't have to deal directly with reporters, something he more than ever regarded as distasteful. Most of the ideas for publicity and virtually all of their implementation came from the CPI. All Wilson had to do was provide the material for the committee to work with in his speeches and statements, and supervise how it performed. In an earlier period he had depended on Tumulty to handle the dreary details of leading public opinion. Now the CPI did the job, only much better. The scope it operated on, and the receptivity of the country during wartime to presidential image-making, offered overwhelming advantages. Creel saw to it that the opportunity was not squandered.

The CPI's drum-beating on behalf of Wilson went on in all of its divisions, but two in particular spread the message. The Division of Civil and Educational Cooperation, organized to enlist the services of scholars behind the war effort, distributed more than 75,000,000 pieces of literature during its lifetime expounding on the themes of American idealism and German guilt. The vast bulk of the material, a total approximately equal to the number of people in the United States above the age of fourteen, circulated domestically. (The National School Service, another of the division's activities, reached the rest.) Meanwhile, the Four-Minute-Men—a separate division of the CPI—carried the word to movie theaters and other places where audiences gathered, assuring that even nonreaders would be enlightened.

Days after the establishment of the CPI Creel telegraphed Guy Stanton Ford, a professor of European history and dean of the graduate school at the University of Minnesota, inviting him to come to Washington to take charge of the "scholarly" side of propaganda. The professor readily agreed. A strong-minded man who later went on to become president of his university and executive secretary of the American Historical Association, he thought that scholars, no less than other members of society, had a patriotic function to perform. That special pleading might violate what a scholar is supposed to stand for seems to have occurred to few people in that emotional time. Among the eminent academics who participated in the work of the Division of Civic and Educational Cooperation were Andrew McLaughlin of the University of Chicago, Frederic Paxson of the University of Wisconsin, Charles Beard of Columbia University, and J. Franklin Jameson, managing editor of the *American Historical Review*.

The division's major function was to prepare for general release publications ranging in size from four-page pamphlets to an elaborate three-hundred-and-twenty-one-page *War Cyclopedia* (complete with sixty-seven direct quotations from President Wilson) explaining why America had become involved in the war and what it was fighting for. In all, the division issued over a hundred titles, the most important grouped in the "War Information Series" and the "Red, White, and Blue Series." The publications were not intended to have partisan implications, or even to magnify Wilson in the eyes of the nation. It still worked out that way, however, because in interpreting American motives the authors had to start with the words of the commander-in-chief. And this in turn meant that more than giving Wilson's utterances wide circulation, by the nature of the publicity his speeches became synonymous with America speaking.

Ford's first major project illustrates the process. When he arrived in Washington in April 1917, Creel set him to work almost immediately supervising the preparation of a pamphlet entitled *The War Message and the Facts Behind It.* To that end Ford enlisted the services of historians at the University of Minnesota in putting together a document that contained the president's April 2 message to Congress, along with forty extended footnotes detailing the American case against Germany. The Government Printing Office ran off 2,500,000 copies for distribution (the CPI liked to think of it as the most widely circulated work of scholarship in human history), while scores of newspapers and magazines provided further access by reprinting passages in their pages. No other president has ever had his words enshrined in quite the same way.

Over the months the division became more sophisticated, at least more ambitious, in shining the spotlight on Wilson and the office he filled. The president's Flag Day speech on June 14, 1917 and two of his other addresses appeared as the appendix to a forty-six-page pamphlet entitled *How the War Came to America* which launched the "Red, White, and Blue" series. The CPI issued 6,230,000 copies of the document in eight languages. The committee didn't settle for just wide distribution. "As you may know," Ford wrote to all state superintendents of education in October 1917, "the Committee on Public Information published in the summer a pamphlet called *How the War Came to America* with the three great addresses of the President as a supplement. This is already being used by many schools as material in both their English and history classes. We have recently had this translated into German by one of the most competent translators and I am encouraged to suggest the possibility of this German translation being used as reading and supplementary material in high school classes in German."[28]

Evidently finding special power in the Flag Day speech, the division returned to it in September 1917 for the fourth in the "Red, White, and Blue" series. This time the speech was the focus of a thirty-page pamphlet entitled *President's Flag Day Address, With Evidence of Germany's Plans* which had a distribution of 6,800,000 copies. One reason for the impressive circulation was that the committee enlisted the Boy Scouts of America in the effort. The scouts had already been alerted in a handbook the CPI prepared for them to keep as reference during the war that they would be "summoned by President Woodrow Wilson, Commander-in-Chief of the Army and Navy, to serve as . . . dispatch bearer[s] from the Government at Washington to the American people all over the country."[29] Responding dutifully on this occasion as they did on others, they delivered about 5,000,000 copies of the Flag Day speech door-to-door in their neighborhoods.

Later in the war the Division on Civic and Educational Cooperation carried indoctrination of the young a considerable step further when it began publishing the *National School Service,* a semi-monthly sixteen-page newspaper mailed free of charge to 600,000 public school teachers to help them in curriculum planning. Eight issues went out between September 1, 1918 and the end of the year, when the CPI started to cut back on its activities. Collectively, they represented a striking departure from the federal principle. This was the first time in American history the government in Washington had tried to influence local school curriculums; and to do so, moreover, by disseminating a political message. Under normal circumstances the attempt would have been greeted with fierce opposition. The lack of comment in 1918 is the best indication of the atmosphere prevailing during the war.

National School Service endeavored to bring the crusade into the classroom (and as Creel hoped, by extension into 20,000,000 homes), by providing articles on current events, a summary of news from the battlefield (with generous use of photographs to catch the attention of the young), boxes containing snappy quotations, and most notably, ideas geared to various age groups for ways to use subjects as far afield as geography and arithmetic to get the class involved in the war.[30] As with the pamphlet program, the focus of attention was always on Woodrow Wilson, commander-in-chief. The first issue led off with a "Message from President Wilson to School Teachers of the United States," signed by the president. In the rest of the paper, and in subsequent issues, his name appeared prominently in the news columns, and many of the inspirational quotations were drawn from his speeches.[31] He symbolized America in the great national effort, which meant that he stood above politics on a plateau hitherto reserved for presidents safely dead.

Wilson's stature soared even higher as a result of the activities of the Four-Minute Men Division, an extraordinary anticipation of the opportunities for publicity soon to be opened by technology. Not until the evening of November 2, 1920, when station KDKA, located in a shack at the Westinghouse works in East Pittsburgh, went on the air to report the results of the Harding-Cox election, did radio burst upon the national attention. But in many ways the Four-Minute Men—who in fact called themselves broadcasters—provided a similar outlet for the CPI. By the time of the armistice 75,000 speakers were appearing in movie theaters and other public places throughout the country to deliver a message carefully orchestrated from Washington.

The idea, based on a scheme a group of businessmen had tried out in Chicago, was simple. Working often through Liberty Loan committees or State Councils of Defense, the division named chairmen in most cities in America to run the programs in their communities. Their job was to recruit people to give four-minute presentations during the intermission each evening in movie houses, and to distribute the bulletin sent out every week or so from the CPI headquarters as guidance in preparing the talks. The division carefully specified the kind of people it wanted in the program. "Well-known speakers," it cautioned the local chairmen, "are too accustomed to longer speeches with room for anecdotes and introduction, and should be avoided for this service in favor of young lawyers and businessmen who will present *messages* within the four-minute limit forcefully, rather than originate speeches."[32] Although the participants were allowed to put together their own talks, they operated under close constraints. The CPI announced the topic for each week. It also provided a stock of quotations and catch phrases appropriate to the theme, and for those who preferred closer guidance, a choice of model four-minute talks which the speakers could borrow in whole or in part. Later, as the operation became more sophisticated, the material included slides for patriotic sing-alongs.

The phenomenon soon spread beyond movie houses. A Woman's Division carried the work to theater matinees and women's clubs. A Junior Division did the same for the schools. By 1918 over 200,000 public schools conducted competitions for the best junior speeches, the winners receiving government certificates. Colleges, Sunday schools, churches, synagogues, labor unions, and as part of what the CPI evidently considered a morale-building program, even Army camps, all provided the audiences for these wartime heralds. "Wherever an American might be, unless he lived the life of a hermit," two students of the subject wrote, "it was impossible to escape the ubiquitous Four-Minute Men. Judging from the estimated theater and movie audience in the fall of 1918, they must have reached several million daily. In New York City alone, 1,600 speakers addressed 500,000 people each week—in English, Yiddish, or Italian."[33] George Creel estimated in his final report that the division sponsored 1,000,000 presentations during the war, reaching a total audience of about 400,000,000 people. Even allowing for exaggeration, that was not bad going at a time when the population of the country barely surpassed 100,000,000. It certainly qualified the Four-Minute Men to be regarded as the administration's preradio broadcasters.

The talks were intended simply to stimulate enthusiasm for the war and get across the importance of national unity. But this was mass communication, and as is often the case, it had unintended—and to an extent, unmeasurable—consequences. According to political scientist Elmer Cornwell, about one-quarter of all the four-minute presentations were devoted directly to conveying the president's thoughts or appeals. Another twenty percent covered themes with a high probability that he would be mentioned in the speeches. Of all the bulletins sent out by the Four-

Minute Men Division, Wilson's name or words appeared in ninety percent.[34] The problem was that in invoking his name and quoting his words,
the speakers, without being aware of it, elevated the man. They conferred
an authority on him that went beyond the authority granted in the Constitution. Any leader is exalted in wartime, but here it happened by engineering, as the result of a massive and carefully conceived publicity
campaign directed out of Washington. Perhaps the most striking example
of the committee's role in presidential aggrandisement occurred on the
Fourth of July, 1918, when the speakers were assigned to read verbatim
the words Wilson wanted addressed to the country. His audience for that
speech, in terms of proportion of total population, must have been at least
in the range later presidents achieved through radio and television.

For nineteen months of war the various activities of the CPI put Wilson
beyond press criticism. Indeed, without particular effort on his part he
probably enjoyed a more positive public image than any president until
that time. But more important than the short-term advantage to him is
what happened to the office he filled. Theodore Roosevelt expanded the
presidency by using the press to dramatize himself and make things
happen. Now wartime propaganda did the same for Wilson, only on a
much larger scale. In both cases the publicity had institutional consequences that outlasted their incumbencies. As the office grew, people
were conditioned to measure future candidates by their ability to fill the
new dimensions. The change in public perception is part of the reason
power started flowing to the White House during the Progressive era.

Of course, Congress all along resented presidential aggrandizement. In
the case of the glorification of the office under the CPI, however, it responded with downright hostility. Law-makers have never acquiesced
easily to executive dominance, and now they could sense the balance
between the branches tilting dangerously against them under the extraordinary circumstances of wartime. (The memory largely explains why Congress forbade the Office of War Information to develop its message around
the name of Franklin Roosevelt during World War II.) And if the legislators
could not directly challenge Wilson's hegemony at a time of national
emergency, they did the next best thing by hounding his chief propagandist. Creel was repeatedly hauled before congressional committees to
justify his operation, and what must have been difficult for a man of his
volatile temperament, repeatedly lambasted from the floor of the House
and Senate.

When the chairman finally lashed back at his tormentors, he succeeded
only in making the situation worse. On May 12, 1918, following a talk at
the Church of the Ascension in New York City, someone in the audience
asked him whether he thought all congressmen were loyal. The chairman
had been worn down by almost an hour of unsympathetic questioning,

and without thinking shot back, "I do not like slumming, so I won't
explore into the hearts of Congress for you." The *New York World* picked
up the answer, and as might have been predicted, it sent tremors of outrage
through both houses.[35] A clamor immediately arose for Creel's dismissal.
Not even his letter of apology to the chairman of the House Rules Committee, which he released to the press on May 17, stilled the din. Creel
offered to resign, but Wilson refused to consider the idea. When a delegation of senators called on the president to press the matter, they found
him adamant. Indeed, he risked further offending congressional sensibilities to make his position clear. "Gentlemen," Wilson declared, "when
I think of the manner in which Mr. Creel has been maligned and persecuted
I think it a very human thing for him to have said."[36] Realizing that they
were not going to get satisfaction at the White House, the miffed lawmakers did the next best thing by cutting the CPI's appropriation by
almost half in the next budget.

On the other hand—what makes sense in view of the patriotic fervor
at the time—censorship seemed far less of a problem to Congress than
Creel's propaganda activities. All the more so because of the apparent
liberality in the way the system worked. As promised, the administration
went into the war trusting primarily in the good sense and patriotism of
the press to prevent disclosures threatening to the national interest. Immediately after the declaration of war the Departments of State, War, and
Navy met with representatives of the press to work out informal guidelines
about the kinds of stories that should not be printed. George Creel simply
adopted those rules on taking over the CPI, although when it became
clear that they left many questions unanswered he issued a more thorough
statement on May 28, six weeks into the life of the agency. Reprinted in
the *Official Bulletin* on June 2, and widely circulated in pamphlet form,
it attempted to reconcile the twin goals of maximum public disclosure
with need for national security. Creel affirmed that newspapers must have
the right even in wartime to report ongoing events fully and to criticize
government leaders when criticism seemed justified. He pointed out that
the administration demonstrated its commitment to openness precisely
in publicizing the rules of censorship it laid down. Other belligerents had
issued such rules to the press under a strict injunction of secrecy. At the
same time, certain information obviously should not be published in wartime. Journalists always have to distinguish, in the slogan of the *New
York Times*, between the news "fit to print" and the rest. The responsibility weighed particularly heavily on them now.

Creel divided the news into three categories: dangerous, questionable,
and routine. The former, which he asked the press voluntarily to suppress,
included reports on military operations in progress, on troop dispositions
or movements, on fortifications, on official missions under way. The chair-

man cautioned editors that information regarded as common knowledge in some areas of the country might still fall under the interdiction nationally. He also urged them to be on the lookout for unauthorized disclosures in advertisements as well as in editorial matter. Creel provided less detail on the questionable category, citing among his few examples articles about training operations or new weapons. In these cases the chairman asked editors to submit the copy to the CPI for a quick decision. The answer would come within hours, assuring that papers which cooperated would suffer minimal inconvenience. The vast bulk of the news fell into the routine category. Creel hoped that by following his guidelines the press would actually discover more material available than it had previously believed. Some papers, in an excess of patriotism, had refrained from running stories which the administration regarded as perfectly acceptable. For them, the CPI's guidelines promised to be a liberating rather than restrictive influence.

Considering that the chairman set reasonable terms for a press eager to cooperate, it is not surprising that the system worked well. To be sure, there were a few inevitable troublemakers. The *Washington Post,* for one, caused constant headaches. On July 12, 1917, Wilson complained to the publisher of the paper, Edward B. McLean, about its coverage of Mexico. "The Mexican Ambassador," he wrote, "has called my attention to an article recently appearing in the Washington Post under the name of 'Ryley Grannon' to which he has made a protest to the Secretary of State. This is one of a series of articles of misrepresentation and distortion of fact which have recently appeared in the Post under this name. . . . I am bound in frankness to say that the character of these articles has made me feel that the Post, consciously or unconsciously, is conducting a propaganda for the embarrassment of the nation in its relations with the Allies and in the conduct of its own war against the German Government."[37] McLean responded immediately with an apology and assurance that he would try even harder in the future to avoid further mishaps.[38]

The paper never quite lived up to those good intentions. On July 26, 1918, for example, military intelligence circulated to all American newspapers through the CPI a request that they use extreme caution in printing descriptions or photographs of tanks, a weapon undergoing rapid development. A serious breach of security had recently occurred in the case of a radically improved model developed by Renault. Despite French attempts to maintain secrecy about the breakthrough, an American periodical ran a picture of the tank which duly reappeared in a French illustrated paper and presumably fell into German hands as well. The authorities wanted to prevent further such leaks. Either through obstinacy or impressive mismanagement, the *Washington Post* decided otherwise. On August 10, again under the byline of the pseudonymous "Ryley Grannon,'' it published a detailed front-page article about what it headlined the "FRENCH TANK MARVEL."[39] Military intelligence didn't even have time to get an explanation from McLean (he later claimed the article was an oversight) before the *Post* came back with another story in violation of censorship guidelines. The front-page report by Albert Fox on August 22 told of a military operation currently in progress to track down a German raider which had already sunk four fishing vessels off the coast of Nova Scotia.[40] And to make abundantly clear that the *Post* marched to its own drummer, the following month the paper ignored a special appeal from Secretary of the Navy Daniels that no mention be made of the type of artillery being used in the siege of Metz by printing another front-page story by Fox on the "American 9-inch guns, and guns of larger caliber . . . bombarding the forts around Metz."[41]

William Randolph Hearst's chain posed a different kind of problem. Like the *Post,* it occasionally ran afoul of censorship regulations. In August 1918 George Creel sent an angry telegram to the editor of the *San Francisco Examiner* complaining about an article in that paper's Sunday supplement entitled "Why the U-Boats Can't Get Our Troopships." "PLEASE WIRE AT ONCE WHERE YOU SECURED THIS MATERIAL AND PHOTOGRAPHS AND BY WHAT AUTHORITY YOU PUBLISHED INFORMATION ABSOLUTELY PROHIBITED BY LAW," the message read.[42] (Since all Hearst papers carried the same supplement, "The American Weekly," it is difficult to see why he singled out the *Examiner* for an accounting.) Much more serious than such lapses, however, was the Hearst editorial slant, in particular its rabid anglophobia. The publisher had not been helpful in his opposition to American involvement in the war, but at least he was then in the respectable company of the Scripps papers and Villard's *New York Evening Post*. Moreover, to prove his patriotism once war came he had been careful to endorse conscription and the Liberty Loan drives. The problem arose in how Hearst proposed to fight the war. Now that England was an ally he trusted it no more than he had previously. He thought it would be folly to send American troops overseas to fight beside British troops. As the *New York American* argued in late April 1917, "The painful truth is that we are being practically used as a mere reinforcement of England's warfare and England's future aggrandizement."[43] In any event, Germany was clearly winning the European phase of the struggle. An expeditionary force would face catastrophe on the high seas from U-boat attack (not until the following year did the "American Weekly" provide reassurance on this point), while those who got through would be swallowed up in the senseless carnage in Europe. It made much more sense, the publisher felt, to retire into Fortress America, challenging a Germany triumphant on the continent to attack us if it dared.

This kind of advice, coming in the late spring and early summer of 1917, when public uncertainty was likely at its peak, hardly represented a contribution to the war effort. But neither did it represent treason; at least not treason of a sort the administration was willing to challenge the Hearst empire and Hearst following by prosecuting. And in a way the publisher's excesses took care of themselves. He was a fact of life for presidents; from McKinley to Truman someone who seemed to have been put on earth to torment them. At least Wilson had the satisfaction of seeing his adversary very nearly qualify for the title of most hated man in America. Save among Irish and German groups, the primitive anglophobia that got by in normal times smacked dangerously under present circumstances of propaganda for the Kaiser. The circulation of most Hearst papers declined noticeably, while from their respective platforms rival journalists and politicans relentlessly pilloried the publisher.[44] A cartoon in the *New York Tribune,* for example, depicted him as a snake coiled in the American flag, hissing "Hears-ss-ss-t" as he prepared to strike.[45] Attacks like these didn't leave much for the president to say.

Wilson seems to have regarded the occasional editorial dissent and violations of censorship guidelines as another indication of the irresponsibility of the American press. When Breckinridge Long, the third assistant secretary of state, sent him a memorandum in November 1917 suggesting that one way to plug the leaks appearing in papers might be to establish an advisory committee of journalists, the president thanked him for the idea, but expressed doubt that it would work. "Unfortunately, personally, I believe the proper cooperation of the newspapers to be impossible," Wilson wrote back, "because of the small but powerful lawless elements among them who observe no rules, regard no understandings as binding, and act always as they please. . . . Such headings and colorings of the news as you quote from the Washington Post apparently nobody can control."[46]

The president was probably correct in recognizing that journalists are far too independent to be governed even by a committee of their own (something that had to be explained to Kennedy when he proposed a similar arrangement at the time of the Bay of Pigs crisis). On the other hand, Wilson did not give the press proper credit for its record in complying with voluntary censorship. The fact is that remarkably few violations occurred. Not only did virtually all newspapers honor the guidelines, they were probably more circumspect in editorial judgment than the code actually required. If their own patriotism didn't enforce strict standards of adherence, then community pressure did. All sorts of vigilante groups sprang up to keep the press under surveillance. In Pennsylvania, the Pittsburgh Press Club organized an intelligence bureau to supervise the newspapers in twenty-seven counties in that state. *Literary Digest* invited its readers to send in clippings of articles they regarded as seditious or treasonable.⁴⁷ A body of amateur sleuths who called themselves the American Protective League functioned nationwide under Department of Justice auspices to provide further check on possible violations of the rules laid down by Mr. Creel.⁴⁸ Something of the intolerance and hysteria of the period, a spirit the government encouraged, is indicated by an advertisement the CPI ran in the *Saturday Evening Post*. "Do not wait until you catch someone putting a bomb under a factory," it urged. "Report the man who spreads pessimistic stories, divulges—or seeks—confidential military information, cries for peace, or belittles our efforts to win the war. Send the names of such persons, even if they are in uniform, to the Department of Justice, Washington. . . . The fact that you made the report will not become public."⁴⁹ By their own inclination and the mood of the times, newspapers were not about to have their patriotism called into question.

In view of the record of compliance with voluntary censorship, and the spirit in the country demanding such compliance, Wilson's insistence on statutory censorship as well might be regarded as an example of overkill. In fact, it represented another manifestation of the intransigent mood of the period; a mood Creel, for one, worried about. His letter to Wilson during the first week of the war urging a policy of "expression not repression" had been inspired by a bill introduced in Congress only days before that provided, among other things, for censorship of the press. Edwin Yates Webb, a North Carolina Democrat and chairman of the House Judiciary Committee, submitted the so-called Espionage Act in the House of Representatives on April 2, the same day Wilson delivered his war message to Congress. An identical measure was sponsored in the upper chamber by Charles Culberson of Texas, chairman of the Senate Judiciary Committee, After ten weeks of rancorous debate, with amendments proposed and modified and discarded, Wilson finally signed the bill into law on June 15.

The controversy centered on the censorship provisions in the bill, something Wilson regarded as essential and newspapers, in a barrage of editorials, condemned as contrary to American tradition. In both the House and Senate versions the definitions of what could not be printed underwent constant revision as the lawmakers tried to reconcile libertarian concerns with the imperatives of war. What did not change was Wilson's determination to have a censorship law, and the press's resentment at any attempt to encroach on First Amendment freedoms.

Although the president likely had public opinion on his side in the controversy, to the press statutory censorship smacked of European autocracy, and was all the more abhorrent in being imposed without justification. "Does the Administration really feel," the *New York Times* asked bitterly, "that this Prussian edict would be a proper return for the services the newspapers have rendered to the authorities in Washington?"[50] Many papers expressed the same resentment, as attested by a roundup of press opinion in the *Times* on Sunday, April 22, and again on May 24. "I am convinced," the publisher of the *San Francisco Chronicle* declared, "of the impracticability of the Russian method of excision in a country as large and populous as ours." The *Los Angeles Times* warned of the "grave danger in . . . establishing a Caesarism, a Kaiserism, at home in the very era in which [the Administration] is seeking to dispossess a Caesarism abroad."[51] Perhaps the most sweeping statement came from the anti-Wilson, but pro-war *New York Tribune*. "Tyranny has always founded itself upon the press gag," the paper warned, "and the press has always prevailed to the ruin of tyranny. . . . Why, then, has Mr. Wilson adopted the chief instrument of the Czar and the Kaiser as an essential and all-essential instrument in a war for democracy and against tyranny? . . . No President in our history ever made a greater mistake than Mr. Wilson has now made. If . . . he has his way, this power will not merely wreck his Administration, but it will hereafter awaken a revolt in public opinion unknown in this country since our last King lost his American colonies by policies which Mr. Wilson would now imitate."[52]

Tumulty, on the sidelines during the controversy and unhappy about the course Wilson had taken, did his best to limit the damage. When Arthur Brisbane, the noted Hearst editor, wrote to the president in mid-April expressing concern about the Espionage Act, the secretary drafted a conciliatory reply which he persuaded Wilson to issue for public release under his own signature. The presidential letter, dated April 25, conformed almost exactly to Tumulty's wording. "I approve of this legislation," it declared, "but I need not assure you and those interested in it that, whatever action the Congress may decide upon, so far as I am personally concerned, I shall not expect or permit any part of this law to apply to me or any of my official acts, or in any way to be used as a shield against criticism. . . . In these trying times one can feel certain only of his motives . . . and await with patience for the judgment of a calmer day to vindicate the wisdom of the course he has tried conscientiously to follow."[53] The words were small consolation to journalists who still saw First Amendment rights under assault. "I know how strongly you feel on the matter of a strict censorship," a discouraged Tumulty wrote to his chief two weeks later, "but I would not be doing my full duty to you and the Administration if I did not say to you that there is gradually growing a feeling of bitter resentment against the whole business, which is daily spreading."[54]

Although the massive press campaign failed to head off censorship, it still accomplished something in bringing about a milder bill than had been contemplated. But even that bill turned out to be far-reaching in its consequences. Two passages provided the muscle the government used to eventually prosecute about 2,000 cases. Title I, section 3 defined the limits of free expression in wartime:

> Whoever, when the United States is at war, shall wilfully make or convey false reports or false statements with intent to interfere with the operation or success of the military or naval forces of the United States or to promote the success of its enemies; and whoever, when the United States is at war, shall wilfully cause or attempt to cause insubordination, disloyalty, mutiny, or refusal of duty in the military or naval forces of the United States, or shall wilfully obstruct the recruiting or enlistment services of the United States, shall be punished by a fine of not more than $10,000 or imprisonment for not more than twenty years, or both.[55]

Title XII conferred authority upon the postmaster general to bar from the mails material which in his judgment came under the law.

From the point of view of civil libertarians, even those who accepted the need for some kind of censorship in wartime, the Espionage Act raised serious concerns in at least two respects. One was the ambiguity in its wording. What did it mean, for example, to "wilfully obstruct" enlistment into the armed forces? Obviously the legislation had in mind more than picketing a recruitment office or tearing down the posters of Uncle Sam that said "I want you." Would any statement expressing doubt about the legality of the draft, or urging the immorality of human beings killing one another, represent wilfull obstruction? If so, the law slashed deeply into the right of free expression in the United States. Moreover, Congress, in failing to be specific, had left to overwrought community sentiment to determine just how deeply. Even if the higher courts eventually rectified errors in judgment, the process would take years. In the meantime freedoms would be eroded and unjust penalities meted out.[56]

Title XII posed a different problem. Unlike ordinary cases falling under the Espionage Act in which the defendants were at least entitled to trial by jury and access to counsel, this provision left the definition of wilfull obstruction up to postal authorities. Which is to say, it put newspapers and magazines completely at the mercy of the administration. It is true that publishers could sue to overturn an adverse Postal Department ruling, but the burden of proof that an injustice had been done rested on them. Aside from the perversion of normal judicial practice in having to establish innocence in a courtroom, the recourse to the law offered little comfort since the postal ban would stand until the courts ruled. By this arrangement, no matter how the case turned out, the aggrieved party always lost. Gilbert E. Roe, an attorney for the American Union Against Militarism, explained the twist in a letter to Roger Baldwin of the American Civil Liberties Union just two weeks after the passage of the bill. As he pointed out, "any Post Office official may, under this provision, forbid the use of the mails to any matter that he deems nonmailable. Before the question of the mailability of the matter can be determined by the courts the work desired will be done and [the] publisher ruined."[57]

The Espionage Act gave the president greater powers of censorship than most journalists, in their fight against an even more stringent bill, realized. But it represented only the first layer in a scaffolding of restraints put up to use, if necessary, against the press. Four months later, on October 16, 1917, Wilson signed into law the Trading With the Enemy Act, which regulated overseas news by authorizing censorship of all messages between the United States and foreign countries. A Censorship Board established by executive order administered the controls. Section 19 of the law also required foreign language newspapers and magazines to file with their local postmasters sworn translations of all editorial content "respecting the government of the United States or of any nation engaged in the present war, its policies, international relations, the state or conduct of the war, or any matter relating thereto," before being accepted in the mails. If rejected by the Postal Department, the publications could not be distributed through any other outlet.

As with the Espionage Act, the Trading With the Enemy Act used flawed and potentially dangerous means to pursue reasonable goals. It made sense in wartime that the government should be concerned about monitoring communications in and out of the country. A Censorship Board to supervise the task was also easily justified. In appointing George Creel to the board, however, Wilson almost went out of his way to antagonize the press. He made explicit what previously had been discreetly veiled: that the country's chief information officer was also one of its chief censors. It was no secret that Creel already wielded unofficial punitive power. Through liaison with the Justice and Postal Departments he could easily have initiated proceedings under the Espionage Act, or had he wished to punish newspapers in a different way, have arranged with the War Trade Board to cut off their supply of newsprint. But the chairman always played down this aspect of his position, as he had to for one whose avowed goal was expression rather than repression. The idealism in relying on the self-restraint of a free press during wartime is tarnished if the club held behind the back starts to become visible. In putting Creel on the Censorship Board Wilson brandished the club. He mixed two roles that didn't really jibe, and in doing so subordinated the more sensitive one based on trust to the harsher one based on power.

The administration was also heavy-handed in its curbs on the foreign language press, which of course meant primarily German newspapers.

Assuming that immigrant expressions of sympathy for a homeland which are permissible in peacetime cannot always be tolerated when that country is the enemy, some judgment is still required to determine when the line has been crossed. In assigning the responsibility for deciding to Postmaster General Albert Burleson, again without effective means of appeal, the Trading With the Enemy Act reaffirmed the narrow view of permissible dissent during World War I. Oswald Garrison Villard, for one, worried about this point. Although he accepted the principle of controls on the foreign language press, he pleaded with Wilson in the final days before passage of the bill to hold public hearings on how best to impose them. Burleson, he argued, simply could not be trusted with such power. The president wrote back through Tumulty that a hearing would be "practically out of the question."[58]

The concerns extended beyond who was to administer the law. As the administration made clear, it regarded the requirement for sworn translations as essentially a bargaining chip. Understaffed and underfinanced papers having to honor that provision would be inconvenienced at best, and in some cases seriously hurt. There was a way out, however. The president had authority to issue revocable permits to foreign language publications excusing them from the requirement as long as they remained on good behavior. But let them print something the administration deemed uncooperative and they would be back in custody. Was it proper, journalists asked, to blackmail the press into submission? By authorizing the president to confer or revoke a special privilege, the law brought great pressure on one segment of the press to do nothing that might antagonize the men in power. Under such circumstances it was almost impossible for newspapers to speak with an independent voice.

The weapon involved raised still another question. If government had the right to impose prior restraint on foreign language publications (which of course is what the sworn translations entailed), why could it not do the same with other publications? They all came under the same First Amendment guarantees. In that case censorship ceased to threaten newspapers with punishment for violating the law and went all the way to threatening their very right to publish. The rules changed in an ominous way.[59]

And still the administration wasn't finished. Seven months later, with the country by now barely paying attention, a third censorship bill became law.[60] The Sedition Act signed by Wilson on May 21, 1918 was originally intended to clear up ambiguities in the Espionage Act; to underline that any attempt to interfere with recruitment, whether successful or not, or any expression against the Liberty Loan drives, whether heeded or not, were prohibited under the law. In a fit of enthusiasm, however, Congress tacked on nine new offenses which Wilson evidently accepted without hesitation. They included writing or speaking in "disloyal, profane, scurrilous or abusive language" about the form of government in the United States, the Constitution, the flag, the armed forces, and even the uniform worn by the armed forces. Writings or statements intended to bring the form of government, the Constitution, the flag, and the uniform into "contempt, scorn, contumely, or disrepute" were similarly enjoined. Offenders faced imprisonment for up to twenty years and/or fines up to $10,000.

Although these all represented criminal matters to be handled by the Department of Justice, Postmaster General Burleson also saw his authority expanded under the Sedition Act. He interpreted the bill, and justifiably so, as essentially an extension of the Espionage Act, which meant that he now had much wider grounds to refuse mailing privileges to publications he regarded as objectionable. The decision rested entirely with him. If the courts came in at all it would be when aggrieved parties sought an injunction or writ of mandamus to overturn his ruling, and then they had to prove their innocence. Burleson's hand was further strengthened by the Sedition Act's amendment to the original Title XII which now authorized him not only to bar offending publications from the mail, but to return undelivered any mail sent to such offenders. Again, it was his decision to make.[61] Even Woodrow Wilson must have felt by the spring of 1918 that he had the statutory authority to cover any contingency.

Burleson, a longtime congressman from Texas, responded to the powers made available to him like a man who had found his calling. On June 16, 1917, the day after the passage of the Espionage Act, he addressed a secret communication to all postmasters directing them to keep a "close watch on unsealed matter, newspapers, etc., containing matter which is calculated to interfere with the success of any Federal loan . . . or to cause insubordination, disloyalty, mutiny, or refusal of duty in the military or naval service, or to obstruct the recruiting, draft or enlistment services . . . or otherwise to embarrass or hamper the Government in conducting the war."[62] He instructed them to intercept such material and forward it directly to Washington.

The Postmaster General had a much more potent weapon to use against dissenting journals, however, than simply barring particular issues from the mails. His real power lay in the ability to revoke their second class mailing privileges, a key to survival for publications that drew only a small part of total circulation from newsstand sales and home delivery. Under the Classification Act of 1879, in order to qualify for postal rates of one cent per pound newspapers and periodicals had to contain a certain proportion of editorial matter to advertising, and what would prove to be critical, had to appear regularly at stated intervals. The latter requirement gave Burleson and the solicitor for the Post Office, William H. Lamar, their opening to deliver the crippling blow. After withholding one issue from the mails for violation of the Espionage Act, they would revoke the publication's second class permit on the grounds that by failing to appear regularly it no longer qualified as a newspaper under the law. By a Kafkaesque logic, dissenters were thus held responsible for not coming out with issues the government itself suppressed.

The flood of intercepted newspapers and periodicals that descended on Washington for clearance spoke almost to a national paranoia. In an America fighting to make the world safe for democracy, disloyalty came in strange forms. "It became criminal to advocate heavier taxation instead of bond issues," Zechariah Chafee of the Harvard Law School wrote, "to state that conscription was unconstitutional though the Supreme Court had not yet held it valid, to say that the sinking of merchant vessels was legal, to urge that a referendum should have preceded our declaration of war, to say that war was contrary to the teachings of Christ."[63] Most of the attention centered on German language and socialist publications, both of which suffered crippling blows within the first two or three months of the Espionage Act. In all, the number and circulation of German papers in the United States declined by about half during the war.[64] Often their political stance had nothing to do with the suppression. Language was itself sufficient justification, as part of the larger campaign to wipe out German influence in American life (a cause which also saw sauerkraut renamed "liberty cabbage" during the war, and German measles "liberty measles").[65] The socialist press fared even worse, if only because of its opposition to what it regarded as a war by and for capitalists. About forty-five socialist publications were interdicted by the Postal Department during 1917, including Victor Berger's respected *Milwaukee Leader,* Eugene Debs's *Appeal to Reason,* the *New York Age,* and the *American Socialist.*[66]

The suppression that probably caused most controversy, and provided a good illustration of how the Postal Department operated, came against the *Masses* just a couple of weeks after the passage of the Espionage Act. This was not a case of moving against an obscure periodical put out in a garret and known only to a handful of sympathizers. Although the magazine's circulation rarely exceeded 25,000, it had played a large role in the cultural ferment of the late Progressive period. The staff included Max Eastman as editor, Floyd Dell writing on literary matters, John Reed as roving reporter, and Art Young supervising graphics. Among those who supported the magazine were Amos Pinchot, younger brother of Gifford and a staunch defender of liberal causes, Mrs. O. H. P. Belmont, the suffragist, and E. W. Scripps, the newspaper publisher. The socialist ideology of the *Masses* was obviously offensive to an Albert Burleson, but even on this score the magazine had toned down considerably from its ardor of earlier days. During 1915 and 1916, influenced in part by the disillusionment at seeing socialist parties in Europe put patriotism before doctrine, and in part by the sobering reality of what violence actually entailed, it had shifted from supporting class struggle to a militant pacifism. Eastman, to the disgust of orthodox socialists, publicly endorsed Wilson's reelection in 1916 on the grounds that he had kept us out of the war, while John Reed, of all people, was persuaded to join a writers committee for the president organized by George Creel. Even Floyd Dell admitted to voting for Wilson.

The break came with the declaration of war in April 1917. More than ever doctrinaire in its pacifism, and now feeling betrayed by the administration, the *Masses* shouted defiance at Washington. "Woodrow Wilson knew, or ought to have known," John Reed wrote in the June issue, "that the great silent mass of this people were not interested in going to war on mock-idealistic pretexts. . . . And he must know, too, that the masses of America will not enlist, and that that is why conscription must be used. This is Woodrow Wilson's and Wall Street's war."[67] Max Eastman rejoiced that the socialists "were able to stand up against the patriotic stampede" at their St. Louis convention by overwhelmingly endorsing a resolution against the war and the participation of workers in fighting the war.[68] A George Bellows cartoon in the July issue depicted Christ in prison stripes with ball and chain around his leg. According to the caption, "THE prisoner used language tending to discourage men from enlisting in the United States army. It is proven and admitted that among his incendiary statements were—THOU shalt not kill and BLESSED are the peace-makers."[69] And from Eastman came a manifesto: "For my part I do not recognize the right of a government to draft me to a war whose purposes I do not believe in. But to draft me to a war whose purposes it will not so much as communicate to my ear, seems an act of tyranny, discordant with the memory even of the decent kings."[70]

To postal authorities this was all obviously inflammatory stuff, but they could do nothing about it in the absence of Congressional authorization. As soon as Wilson signed the Espionage Act on June 15, however, they went into action. When the August issue was presented for mailing on Tuesday, July 3, the postmaster of New York held up the magazine and sent copies to Washington for examination. Two days later he informed Eastman that the issue was in violation of the Espionage Act and could not go through the mails. When asked the following day, Solicitor Lamar refused to specify what he found objectionable in it, citing only "the entire tone and spirit."[71] The answer was a chilling introduction to the era of censorship in American life. "I spent the whole winter," Eastman declared in a speech two weeks later, "trying to think of the worst possible consequences of our going to war, and advertise them in the public press, but I never succeeded in thinking up anything half so bad as this."[72]

The *Masses* had too much influence, however, to die the quiet death Burleson and Lamar would have preferred. On July 13, at a luncheon meeting of the Civil Liberties Committee presided over by Amos Pinchot and attended by Dudley Field Malone and Commissioner of Immigration Frederic Howe, the group decided to send four lawyers to Washington, including Clarence Darrow, to consult with the administration on its censorship policy. When they arrived in the capital Wilson refused to see them, and Burleson to explain the reasons for the suppression of the magazine, or to say anything about his future plans, other than to insist that he was acting within his legal mandate.

A previous direct appeal to Wilson had proved just as fruitless. Within days of the Postal Department's action Amos Pinchot, Max Eastman and John Reed sent a joint letter to the president asking him to intervene in the case. Wilson responded immediately in a friendly note addressed to Pinchot, agreeing to look into the matter. The same day he wrote to the postmaster general to inquire why the publication had been suppressed. Burleson responded on July 16 that he had no wish to suppress the *Masses* or any other periodical, but that it had published material obstructive to the war effort and therefore was in violation of the law. He suggested that since the *Masses* had filed a bill in equity on July 12 to overturn his ruling, the courts should be allowed to resolve the case. Wilson accepted this position.[73]

The magazine's plea for a court order enjoining the Postal Department from banning the August issue came before Judge Learned Hand on July 21. In preparation the government had finally specified its complaints: four cartoons (one by H. J. Glintenkamp, for example, showing a shattered Liberty Bell) and four editorial passages (such as the one by Eastman praising the courage of Emma Goldman and Alexander Berkman, who were currently under indictment for advising young men opposed to the war to refuse to register for the draft). On July 23 Judge Hand granted the injunction on the grounds that "none of the language and none of the cartoons in this paper can be thought directly to counsel or advise insubordination or mutiny without a violation of their meaning quite beyond any tolerable understanding." He rejected the government's contention that the "remote bad tendency" of words, their possible indirect consequences, constituted a basis to suppress newspapers.[74] The same day the government obtained an order setting aside the injunction until the case could be heard in higher court the following November.

By that time the magazine would be all but dead. In early August the September issue was presented for mailing and again held back pending advice from Washington. When the decision came ten days later it brought a new jolt. The letter from Solicitor Hunt ordered the magazine, in view of the fact that it had ceased regular publication, to show cause why its second class permit should not be revoked. This was a legal formality to announce a decision already made in the Postal Department. Eastman tried desperately for a few more weeks to keep the *Masses* alive. In September he turned one more time to Wilson, hopeful that the president's recent statement in response to a peace appeal from the pope against "punitive damages, the dismemberment of empires, the establishment of selfish and exclusive economic leagues" might yet indicate sympathy for a publication with similar ideals. Wilson's answer, released by Eastman to the *New York Times* and printed on the front page, was polite but unencouraging. "I think that a time of war must be regarded as wholly exceptional," the president declared, "and that it is legitimate to regard things which would in ordinary circumstances be innocent as very dangerous to the public welfare. . . . The line is manifestly exceedingly hard to draw and I cannot say that I have any confidence that I know how to draw it. I can only say that a line must be drawn and that we are trying, it may be clumsily but genuinely, to draw it without fear or favor or prejudice."[75]

Eastman fared no better when he wrote to Burleson in October asking for the restoration of his second class privileges. Although in briefing reporters on the letter Eastman told them that the editors of the *Masses* were "perfectly willing to abide by the regulations" laid down by the Postal Department, this time he received no reply at all from Washington.[76] On November 2 Circuit Court Judge C. H. Hough ruled that the determination by the government of a publication's mailability must stand in the absence of overwhelming evidence that an error had been made.[77] The *Masses* had lost its suit, its second class permit, and its ability to survive. It passed out of existence that month, another casualty in the administration's war against dissenting journalism.[78]

Burleson, given his head by a president whose own tolerance of the press was limited, emerged rapidly as the administration's authority on First Amendment issues. It is true that Wilson tried occasionally to curb his enthusiasm. When Burleson gave a particularly unyielding interview to the press after the passage of the Trading With the Enemy Act, for example, the president wrote to him counseling restraint.[79] "I am sure you will agree with me," he said, "that we must act with the utmost caution and liberality in all our censorship. . . ."[80] A week later he sent a second memorandum expressing doubt about the suppression of the *Milwaukee Ledger,* even though the courts would uphold the government. "I am afraid you will be shocked," Wilson wrote, "but I must say that I do not find this hearing very convincing. [Although] some of the things quoted probably cross the line. . . , I do not think that most of what is quoted ought to be regarded as unmailable. . . . There is a wide margin of judgment here and I think that doubt ought always to be resolved in favor of the utmost freedom of speech."[81]

The important point about these exchanges, however, is that Wilson almost invariably accepted Burleson's justifications for pursuing a hard line. Not only did he rarely overrule his cabinet officer, when others complained about the Postal Department's policies he came strongly to Burleson's defense. One such occasion was when Herbert Croly, editor of the *New Republic,* wrote to him to express deep unease about the Burleson interview that had also caught the president's eye. "I can assure you," Wilson replied, "that the matter of the censorship has given me as much concern as it has you and after frequent conferences with the Postmaster General I have become convinced that not only have his statements been misunderstood but that he is inclined to be most conservative in the exercise of these great and dangerous powers and that in the one or two instances to which my attention has been called he has sought to act in a very just and conciliatory manner."[82]

The president revealed a good deal about his own limited perception of the press and press freedoms in describing Burleson as "inclined to be most conservative" in the way he used power. The truth is that the postmaster general, abetted by his solicitor, William H. Lamar, took advantage of wartime hysteria not so much to curb disloyal utterances as to suppress political points of view they happened to disagree with. "You know," Lamar once declared, "I am not working in the dark on this censorship thing. I know exactly what I am after. I am after three things and only three things—pro-Germanism, pacifism, and 'high-browism.' "[83] Wilson certainly cannot be characterized as a yahoo in that sense, but in failing to step in he did passively accede to the mentality. The result was a serious erosion of press freedoms during his second term. Lamar caught the spirit as well as anyone when he wrote in *Forum* in early 1918: "For us to permit an exaggerated sentimentalism, a misapplied reverence for legal axioms which our courts have held have no true application to the questions involved to restrain us, would be criminal not only to our soldiers, sailors, and ourselves, but to posterity"[84]

In some ways the repression was all the more insidious because of the selectivity in the choice of targets. The administration never moved against mainstream dailies. Part of the reason, of course, was that such papers supported the war and subscribed to the broad consensus on social issues that linked the two major parties. But even when they strayed from the reservation they suffered no retribution. The *New York Evening Post,* for example, hardly endeared itself to the administration in January 1918 when it published the secret treaties between the allies, something Wilson later claimed not to have been aware of until he arrived in Paris a year later.[85] Nor did the *New York Times* cause joy when it proposed in September 1918 that the time might be right to initiate preliminary peace negotiations.[86] Burleson and Attorney General Gregory overlooked those transgressions because the *Evening Post* and *Times,* or for that matter the Hearst papers, were in a position to fight back. It made much more sense to concentrate on publications outside the mainstream, the kind protected neither by political orthodoxy, nor social respectability, nor economic clout. "The record soon showed," Villard wrote in his autobiography, "that the Post Office Department was concerned only with arresting small-town editors, suppressing foreign-language publications or little far-Western newspapers, in other words terrifying helpless fry who could not strike back"[87]

The editor of the *Nation* spoke from experience, because finally connections and respectability had spared him from the treatment suffered by the helpless fry. On Friday, September 13, 1918, he was informed that the issue of the *Nation* dated for the next day had been judged unmailable. Seizing copies of the magazine, he rushed to the office of New York Postmaster T. G. Patten for an explanation, honestly bewildered at what could have caused offense. It was true that the lead article, an unsigned piece presumably written by Villard himself and entitled "Civil Liberty Dead," scathingly denounced Attorney General Thomas Gregory for having ordered the arrest of 75,000 young men in the New York City area in an attempt to round up draft dodgers, less than three percent of whom later turned out to be guilty. But since the *Nation* based its information on an article in the conservative, pro-war *New York Tribune,* and quoted the outraged remarks of several senators, and since President Wilson had himself ordered an inquiry, it was difficult to believe that this could be the cause of trouble. The rest of the issue consisted of relatively tame fare. Albert Nock had contributed a piece entitled "The One Thing Needful" which criticized Samuel Gompers's recent appointment to go on a fact-finding mission to study labor conditions in Europe. "When Mr. Gompers drops the sample case and mounts the tripod. . . ," Nock wrote, "the public will get from him at his best merely the kind of information that a sturdy partisan drummer, traveling continually in an atmosphere of sheer bagmanism is able to furnish; and with all that the people can do nothing."[88] An article by Stuart Sherman on "Carlyle and Kaiser Worship" certainly wouldn't upset the administration, nor would the one praising a pending revenue bill.

Patten admitted to Villard that he didn't know himself why the issue had been seized; he was only following orders from Washington. Not until the publisher reached the capital the next day did he discover the truth. In a conference with Solicitor Lamar the offending piece turned out to be the Nock article. As the solicitor explained sternly, "Mr. Gompers has rendered inestimable services to this government during this war in holding union labor in line and while this war is on we are not going to allow any newspaper in this country to attack him."[89] He offered a compromise, however. The government would release the issue if Villard agreed before it went in the mail to have the offending page ripped out.

Of course the publisher rejected that absurd proposal, but unlike many other victims of arbitrary authority he had a way to fight back. Villard had been fairly close to the president in the first term (before his pacifism got in the way), and enjoyed a continuing friendship with Joe Tumulty. He knew that the secretary, who had been fuming for over a year at the high-handedness of the Postal Department and the "boll weevil from Texas" who ran it, would particularly want to help. A plea to the White House acomplished its purpose. Wilson raised the matter at his cabinet meeting on September 17, and after hearing Burleson's explanation, ordered the *Nation* released.[90] It went in the mail the following day.[91]

The selective nature of wartime censorship had two consequences for the American press which made this a less than distinguished era in its history. One was to encourage an even deeper conformity than might otherwise have been the case. Almost as if trying to demonstrate their respectability, newspapers and magazines responded to the climate of suppression not so much with defiance as with earnest professions of patriotism. The reaction of the *Nation* after receiving a presidential reprieve was typical. Despite a continuing angry exchange of messages between Lamar and Villard, the magazine assured its readers in the September 21 issue that it had "no desire to overstep the bounds of reasonable and legal criticism and had no suspicion that it had done so."[92]

Whether journals caved in to pressure is more difficult to prove, but even that probably happened on occasion. The Civil Liberties Bureau thought so, for example, in explaining the *New Republic*'s refusal to run an ad on behalf of 113 International Workers of the World leaders charged with obstructing the war effort. When the Chicago postmaster held back three hundred sacks of third class mail soliciting contributions to their defense fund, and postal authorities also started to tamper with the organization's first class mail, a group of liberals decided to intervene. An ad appeared in the *New Republic* on June 22, 1918, signed by Thorstein Veblen, John Dewey, and Helen Keller among others, urging contributions to the I.W.W. General Defense Committee on the grounds that the defendants were "at least entitled to a fair trial and an open-minded public hearing."[93] But when the group tried to run the ad in subsequent issues, the magazine refused. After conducting an investigation, the Civil Liberties Bureau alleged that the *New Republic* had bowed to pressure from the Postal Department, which threatened to revoke its second class mailing privileges if the ad continued to appear. A telegram of protest from the bureau to President Wilson on September 27, 1918 accomplished nothing.[94] All in all, the *Nation* summed up the journalism of the period when it declared shortly after the armistice that "during the past two years we have seen what is practically an unofficial control of the press, not merely by Messrs. Burleson and Gregory, but by the logic of events and the patriotic desire of the press to support the Government to the best of its ability."[95]

The same influences also help to explain the remarkable passivity of journalists in the face of the crackdown on dissenting publications. There were exceptions, to be sure, but by and large newsmen demonstrated little understanding that First Amendment rights cannot be selectively defended; that when any paper is suppressed all are threatened. Or if they did protest the treatment of dissenters, it was in the mildest terms. The record is not altogether surprising considering that reporters are like any other group in tending to subscribe to the dominant values and attitudes of their time, and many of them—caught up in the passions of the moment—probably believed the victims of suppression were disloyal. Historical timing is also a factor. Only in recent decades, influenced by experiences like the McCarthy phenomenon and the Nixon presidency, have newsmen become truly sensitive to what the First Amendment is about. In the early decades of the twentieth century they had not yet learned to fear governmental abuse of power. And so the Wilson administration, by sensibly confining its attack to journals least able to defend themselves, pretty well had its way. That the rest of the press turned a blind eye only compounded the pity.

How well, then, did the administration deliver on its early promise of expression rather than repression? To the extent it never attempted to prosecute an establishment paper, censorship of that segment of the press during World War I can be described as self-enforcing. Of course to the extent the administration quickly enacted legislation giving it power to prosecute, one might say it encouraged newspapers to do the right thing by holding a gun to their heads. Whether such a system is voluntary or coercive is largely a matter of perspective. The only certainty is that nonestablishment newspapers and magazines, the truly vulnerable ones, were the victims of policies at least as harsh as any going back to the Alien and Sedition Laws.

Although Wilson ordered an end to censorship on November 27, 1918, sixteen days after the armistice, not much changed during his last two and a half years in office. Partly because the United States remained in a technical state of war with Germany until a joint resolution by Congress in 1921 terminated hostilities, but more importantly because of the red scare that gripped the country immediately following the cease fire, Burleson and Lamar ran their operation more or less as before. Postmasters continued to relay suspected publications to Washington, and papers like the *Milwaukee Leader* and *New York Call* which petitioned to have their second class privileges restored continued under interdiction. When a United States District Court sustained the *Leader*'s suit in August 1920, Burleson persuaded the president that the case must be taken to the Supreme Court. Not, as the postmaster general pointed out, because the newspaper was doing anything illegal, but because of the radical ideology it espoused. "There is an insidious attempt to keep within the letter of the law," he wrote to Wilson, "but in effect to inculcate in the minds of their readers a belief that this Government should be overthrown by force, to encourage a belief in modern communism, to hold up as an ideal Government the Soviet System in vogue in Russia."[96] It is tempting to speculate that the president's stroke had something to do with his accepting this argument. In any event, Burleson won his final victory. On March 7, 1921, three days after Harding's inauguration, the Supreme Court ruled that a publication which had lost its second class mailing privileges for violating the law lacked legal grounds to have the privileges restored.[97]

It was left to the unlikeliest of presidents, Warren Harding, to take the first steps to restore the right of dissent in American life. His postmaster general, Will Hays, moved quickly to grant second class permits to the radical publications seen as threats to national security in the previous administration. The strange juxtaposition of roles itself speaks to the blind side of Woodrow Wilson: a president who could never quite find room in his visionary world for what a free press truly is.

8

The Peace Conference

On Sunday, January 12, 1919, a day raw and overcast, crowds massed along the Quai d'Orsay opposite the French Foreign Office to watch the dignitaries arrive for a mid-afternoon meeting of the Supreme War Council.[1] It was a momentous occasion: a coming together of the world leaders to make arrangements for the formal opening in a few days of the Paris Peace Conference. Marshal Foch, strolling over from his apartment on the rue de l'Université, was among the first to arrive. In his heavy field coat, the braid on his cap the only indication of rank, he did not look like the commanding general of the Allied forces. Soon Secretary of State Lansing drove up in an army limousine, his tall silk hat and regal manner very much identifying him as a gentleman of rank. President Wilson arrived shortly after, accompanied on the drive by his wife and Admiral Grayson, followed a few minutes later by a serious-looking Premier Clemenceau. Just before the appointed hour another automobile brought the leaders of the British delegation: the ruddy-faced prime minister Lloyd George, and towering over him, a soft felt hat pushed back on his head, Foreign Secretary Balfour.

Following the meeting, which lasted about an hour, a secretary in the Foreign Office delivered to the press attachés of the four powers a communiqué about what had happened. In two terse sentences the world leaders announced only that they had discussed "questions necessary to be settled in connection with the extension of the armistice" and "the method of procedure of the council by which preliminary matters must be carried on."[2] They volunteered no further details. Ray Stannard Baker, the liaison to the American correspondents, knew immediately how his group would respond when he showed up at the Press Bureau with the release. "I shall never forget," he wrote three years later, "the disappointment, exasperation, disgust, when that first communiqué was put out."[3]

The reaction had to do with far more than the lack of news content in the release, although that struck the reporters as suspicious enough. Some of them speculated that the failure to provide details about the meeting might indicate a falling-out among the Allies even before the conference got underway; others that it more likely meant a major decision had been reached, perhaps to undertake a joint expedition against the Bolshevik regime in Russia. (In fact, nothing of interest happened at the meeting.) What really angered the correspondents, however, was the indication in the release of a deepening news blackout in Paris. They had already discovered that the phrase "open covenants openly arrived at" did not mean, as many of them had originally assumed, that they would have free access to the working sessions of the conference. They had also found their contacts with the American delegation less than satisfactory ever since President Wilson and his party had arrived in Europe on December 13. To have reason to suspect now that they would not even be briefed fully on what went on behind the closed doors at the Quai d'Orsay came as a final blow.

The simmering discontent among newsmen had already sufficiently colored their dispatches back to the United States to attract the attention of Joseph Tumulty. He had been left behind in Washington to handle the routine chores of the administration and keep the president abreast of reactions at home to the work of the Peace Conference. By the Monday, January 13, he saw a serious situation developing. "In past two weeks the trend of newspaper dispatches from Paris has indicated a misunderstanding of your general attitude towards problems pending at peace conference," the secretary warned. "Situation could easily be remedied if you would occasionally call in the three press association correspondents who crossed on *George Washington* with you, merely giving them an understanding of the developments as they occur and asking them not to use information as coming from you, but merely for their own guidance. It would show wisdom of various compromises as well as circumstances of such compromises."[4]

The advice made sense, and if acted on might even have altered the course of events in coming months and years. But Wilson looked at things from an entirely different perspective. Particularly in the area of foreign affairs, he tended to be much more impressed by the potential harm journalists could do than the potential benefits in working with them. He regarded publicity as something to be tightly controlled; ideally, as something that would virtually not exist until the conferees had reached a final agreement. And compared to Lloyd George and Clemenceau, he stood forth as an apostle of openness. They were all obsessed by the power of the press to do mischief, and all determined to put a lid on what appeared in print even if it meant muzzling the 500 or so correspondents who had gathered in Paris from around the world to cover the conference.

The news blackout that American reporters sensed on Sunday became reality the following Wednesday, January 15, when the Council of Ten convened at 10:30 A.M. in Foreign Minister Stephan Pichon's office—an elegant room with rich tapestries decorating the walls and windows overlooking a private garden—for another in a series of discussions to lay the groundwork for the conference. Prime Minister Lloyd George opened the session by complaining vigorously about two stories that had appeared recently in French newspapers: one on the council's decision to keep German gold reserves in a safe place, and another on its tentative decision about the number of delegates to be apportioned to the British dominions and smaller nations. The understanding had been that nothing would be released to the press on either matter for the time being. Pichon did little to clear the air with his explanation that the information had only been made available to French papers because American and British reporters already had it. Considering that no such stories had turned up in the Anglo-American press, the excuse seemed a bit lame. More important, if the Allies started to play the game that way, leaking news to reporters of their own country lest another country's reporters secure a competitive advantage, it would soon become impossible to keep any secrets at all among them. The somewhat chastened French conceded the point. In order to prevent further disclosures, the conferees agreed on the spot to restrict news about their deliberations to brief daily bulletins issued through the press attachés, who would provide follow-ups the next day on business already completed. Everything else would be regarded as subject to strict censorship.[5]

With secrecy enshrined in the only place that mattered, Wilson proposed to make at least a gesture of openness where it didn't matter. He asked whether there would be any objection to having reporters present at the opening session of the conference on Saturday, and at subsequent plenary sessions attended by all the nations represented in Paris. As the president pointed out, the major powers would be serving their own purposes as much as those of the press in providing such access. Any time the full conference convened word would inevitably leak out about what had happened. It made sense in that case to let the correspondents witness the proceedings for themselves rather than receive garbled accounts coming from self-serving sources. Moreover, in making the concession the major powers would be giving up relatively little since they controlled the agenda for those sessions. "In these large Conferences nothing of an embarrassing nature would be discussed," Wilson argued. "Important and delicate questions would have been discussed beforehand and only such questions as had been digested in various ways would be placed before these Conferences.''[6]

Although the president's logic hardly accorded with what reporters understood as open diplomacy, even his limited suggestion evoked spirited opposition from the other leaders. Foreign Secretary Balfour objected that the plenary sessions did not necessarily have to be the formalities Wilson assumed. He saw them as a potentially useful forum to settle disagreements among the smaller nations. If the president's proposal were accepted, however, the meetings would have to be turned into formalities, thus vastly complicating the work of the Council of Ten. The result would be to require that the council consult individually with the parties to all petty disputes so that solutions could be worked out ahead of time before going to the full conference for ratification.

Lloyd George raised a different concern. He worried that offering an audience of reporters to the smaller nations would encourage them to speak interminably for the benefit of constituents back home, and perhaps even lead to outbreaks of invective that would make the search for a settlement all the more difficult. Pichon pitched in with a warning about the danger in advertising to Germany the inevitable disagreements among the Allies. But the most emotional response came from Clemenceau. He reminded Wilson that the Big Five had agreed to arrive at their decisions unanimously. The French premier intended to honor that obligation. He would give way when necessary in the deliberations, and would remain silent in dissent when the decisions he disapproved of came up for ratification at the plenary sessions. If reporters were present to record those debates, however, he would have no choice but to speak his mind, and the result would only be to sow confusion.

Wilson retreated in the face of this barrage. Without surrendering his proposal, he said that ''he had merely raised the point for discussion and he did not wish to press the question. . . .''[7] The conferees agreed to put off the decision for the present.

The president had more success at the afternoon meeting when Pichon suggested, as a way to further assure the confidentiality of their discussions, that the other powers appoint representatives to join the French in censoring cable messages out of the country. Although one of the terms for agreeing to Paris as the site of the conference had been that cables to American and British newspapers would not be interfered with, Wilson did not remind his hosts of their promise in speaking against the proposal. Instead, he pointed out that he would be personally embarrassed by such a step, since when his government took over the cable two months earlier charges had been heard that the reason was to intercept unfavorable dispatches about him sent from Europe. To impose censorship now would seem to lend substance to such charges. In any event, the best way to control leaks was to prevent reporters from getting information they should not have in the first place. The conferees could at least afford to put the press on trial for a while since nothing of a particularly sensitive nature was due to come up in the immediate future.[8] Clemenceau and Lloyd George, while unconvinced, reluctantly gave way.

All of which meant that after a day of deliberations devoted mainly to press matters, the Allied leaders had reached agreement on only one point. Whatever other privileges might be granted to reporters, they would not be briefed on the progress of negotiations in the Council of Ten. The daily communiqués would tell them of decisions already made that were safe to reveal. The leaders would not pass on further information, nor would they be available to newsmen to discuss the work of the conference.[9]

The announcement caused an explosion. "ADOPT SECRECY FOR PEACE CONCLAVE," the *New York Times* blared in a four-column headline the next day. Richard Oulahan, his article dripping bitterness, contrasted the stringent procedures with the noble sentiments of a few months before. "After all that has been promised concerning open discussion in the making of a peace," he wrote as his lead, "steps were taken at today's session of the Inter-allied Conference which show that the whole intent is to keep the people of the world in the dark as to what is going on behind the closed doors of the Quai d'Orsay. . . . The whole spirit of this action taken is contrary in every respect to the assurances given to the American people, and already a feeling of discouragement and indignation is displayed among newspaper representatives from the Allied countries."[10]

For an America conditioned since its involvement in the war to believe that international affairs were to be conducted in the future with a new openness, the reports of the decision taken in Paris hit with jarring impact. Tumulty sounded almost a note of panic in the cable he sent to Admiral Grayson when the news broke. "American newspapers," he declared, "filled with stories this morning of critical character about rule of secrecy adopted for Peace Conference, claiming that the first of the fourteen points has been violated. In my opinion, if President has consented to this, it will be fatal. The matter is so important to the people of the world that he could have afforded to go any length even to leaving the conference than to submit to this ruling. His attitude in this matter will lose a great deal of the confidence and support of the people of the world which he has had up to this time."[11] The secretary could not have been reassured by the response to his Monday telegram which came back from Wilson the same day. "Your cable about misunderstandings concerning my attitude toward problems created by the newspaper cablegrams concerns a matter which I admit I do not know how to handle. Every one of the things you mention is a fable. I have not only yielded nothing but have been asked to yield nothing. . . . I cannot check [the inaccurate reports] from this end because the men who sent them insist on having something to talk about whether they know what the facts are or not. I will do my best with the three press associations."[12]

Most disturbing in Wilson's message was the indication of the distrust, even contempt, he felt for the newspaper representatives from his country. He was about to be embroiled with them in a dispute involving not so much policy as principle, and the two sides could barely communicate. The president considered that he had fought for and would continue to fight to get everything reporters had a right to expect. For the correspondents, the decision for secrecy in the Council of Ten mocked the meaning of a war fought to make the world safe for democracy. And Wilson had arrayed against him some of the foremost journalistic talent of the time; men and women embarked, incidentally, on what they assumed would be the crowning assignment of their careers. They included, in addition to correspondents for daily newspapers, people like Ida Tarbell of *Red Cross Magazine,* Oswald Garrison Villard of the *Nation,* Will Irwin of the *Saturday Evening Post,* W. E. B. DuBois of the *Crisis,* Norman Angell of the *New Republic,* Lincoln Steffens on assignment for *Everybody's,* Mark Sullivan writing for *Collier's,* and William Allen White doing features for the Wheeler syndicate.[13] "In many ways," Ray Stannard Baker wrote later, "the most powerful and least considered group of men at Paris were the newspaper correspondents—we had one hundred and fifty of them from America alone. I heard them called 'ambassadors of public opinion.' Here they were with rich and powerful news associations or newspapers or magazines behind them, and with instant communication available to every part of the world."[14]

The decision for secrecy had thoroughly aroused these ambassadors of opinion. So much so that their angry dispatches back to the United States on January 15 represented only the beginning of a response. It was early evening before they got the word from Ray Stannard Baker. He had been working in his office at the American Press Bureau on the Place de la Concorde, only a few doors from the American delegation's headquarters in the Hôtel Crillon, when a telephone call from the British Press Bureau relayed the information, and told him that British reporters were drawing up a petition of protest to Lloyd George. Thoroughly concerned, Baker rushed to an outer room crowded with correspondents preparing their stories for the day to fill them in on what he had heard.

In the ensuing outcry Herbert Bayard Swope of the *New York World,* who on the trip over to Europe had been elected by his colleagues president of the United States Press Delegation, stepped forward as the leader.[15] Working in collaboration with several other newsmen, he prepared on behalf of the American press contingent a petition of protest to Wilson to match that sent by British reporters to Lloyd George. "Mr. President," it declared: "We direct your attention to the fact that this method, if followed, will limit our information to things accomplished. . . . The public will be denied the opportunity to be informed of the positions assumed by the various elements within the conference, and public opinion will thus have no chance to function in the way that you have always advocated and that you defined in the Fourteen Points. Wherefore, we vigorously protest, on behalf of the American press representatives, against what we have ever reason to regard as gag-rule; and in common with the action of our British colleagues, who have laid their case before the Prime Minister, we appeal to you for relief from this intolerable condition." Swope personally added the final paragraph: "We stand where you stand. 'Open covenants of peace, openly arrived at.' "[16] Ten journalists representing the wire services and major American dailies signed the document.[17]

With the press in virtual rebellion, news policy all but had to dominate the discussion a second time when the Council of Ten convened in Pichon's office on Thursday morning. The lines between the countries were by now firmly drawn. France, supported by Italy, urged the most stringent measures to guarantee secrecy. Wilson spoke for openness, at least to the extent of admitting reporters to the plenary sessions of the conference and allowing cable messages to go on the wire uncensored. Great Britain hovered between the two sides, on some questions sympathetic to the French position and at other times supportive of Wilson. But on the fundamental issue, despite all the hours of talk and clash of principles, the powers essentially agreed. The important decisions would be made in the Council of Ten, and there absolute confidentiality must be maintained.[18]

The problem remained how to get that point across to the press. Wilson, obviously concerned by the petition the reporters had sent him and by Tumulty's cables describing reactions at home, noted at the Thursday meeting that the American people expected more publicity than was so far being provided. He had to be assured by Lloyd George that the complaints addressed to both of them about a gag-rule did in fact apply to the council's meetings as well as those of the full conference. The president finally suggested that Ray Stannard Baker and his counterparts from the other Allied countries bring the correspondents together that afternoon to explain why the council had to conduct its business in private, and to solicit suggestions about what might be done within reason to better serve the needs of the press.[19]

The gathering at 5:00 P.M. at the Interallied Press Club accomplished nothing, and may even have worsened the situation. One difficulty was that the reporters discovered their own lack of unity; a circumstance all the more awkward because the divisions broke down more or less along lines of nationality. Earlier in the afternoon the American and British press contingents had each held preliminary meetings among themselves to agree on the positions they would take. Predictably, the Americans came away with the most adamant stand on press rights. They demanded that reporters be admitted to all working sessions of the conference, or at the very least, that a pool of reporters be allowed to cover the Council of Ten and verbatim minutes be provided for those not in the pool. The British contingent, while more moderate in its demands, also refused to accept the rationale for absolute secrecy. Why, the Britons asked, couldn't the press attachés sit in on the meetings of the Allied leaders, and at the end of each day hold briefings to supplement the official communiqués? The attachés could always be asked to leave if particularly sensitive subjects came up.

Only the French correspondents accepted the terms as offered with equanimity. Part of the reason was that they had been conditioned over the years to put up with much stricter rules of censorship than applied in the other two countries. Likely they had also been conditioned to bow when necessary to government pressure, and on this question no one doubted how their government expected them to respond. But the telling factor was that the most prestigious French journals—papers like *Le Temps, Le Petit Parisien, Le Echo de Paris, Le Petit Journal, Le Matin*—enjoyed a semiofficial status which assured them access to news whatever the rules of silence laid down. In a real sense, they could afford to be realistic about how diplomacy worked because the price of realism did not apply to them.

When it became apparent at the 5:00 P.M. meeting that nothing could be accomplished in a roomful of excited people all trying to speak at once, the reporters agreed to turn the matter over to a subcommittee consisting of three delegates from each of the major powers and two representing the smaller nations. Sir George Riddell, president of the British Newspaper Proprietors' Association and press officer for the British delegation, served as ex officio chairman. After an amicable dinner with Riddell at the Hotel Ritz, the fourteen member committee got down to business. From that moment all amity disappeared. The stormy session, which lasted into the small hours of the morning, only confirmed what had already become clear: that French journalists would not stand in common cause with journalists from other countries. Harsh words filled the elegant room at the Ritz. At one point Arthur Krock of the *Lousiville Courier-Journal* found himself in deeper trouble than he bargained for when he remarked that French newspapers were notorious for being dominated by their Foreign Office. The Marquis de St. Brice of *Le Journal*, resenting the slur on himself and his countrymen, challenged the Kentuckian to a duel. Only with difficulty did the thoroughly alarmed Krock get out of the scrape.[20]

At the end of hours of squabbling—the American representatives finally breaking the impasse by threatening to walk out—the reporters had to settle for two separate resolutions. One, joined in by the French, set forth the minimum recommendations: as complete communiqués as possible, full summaries of each day's proceedings to supplement the communiqués, the continuation of contacts between reporters and delegates, equal treatment for the press by abolishing censorship in all Allied countries, and permission for journalists to attend the formal opening ceremony on Saturday without implying their right to be present at future plenary sessions. The document specified that French journalists dissented from the opinion of their colleagues in refusing to claim such a right.[21] A second resolution, agreed to by reporters from the United States, Great Britain, Italy, and the smaller nations, petitioned for the press to be admitted to all "the sittings of the Peace Conference."[22] Arthur Krock, Herbert Bayard Swope and John Nevin of the Hearst chain signed for the United States.

The Council of Ten's attempt to work out an accord with the press by explaining the reasons for secrecy had failed in its purpose. When the Allied leaders convened in Pichon's office on Friday morning, January 17, they weren't even sure what the reporters had proposed in their resolutions. Lloyd George wondered, for example, whether the request for full summaries to supplement the communiqués meant that the press wanted an account of individual speeches. If so he would not tolerate it, because negotiations could not be conducted under such conditions. Statesmen must have the freedom to change their minds, something that would be impossible if every word they uttered was to be broadcast immediately throughout the world. "The Conference would tend to resemble the Council of Trent," the prime minister declared, "whose labours were terminated in forty-three years after the death of all the original members."[23] Similarly, Wilson queried whether he was correct in assuming that when the reporters asked for admission to the "sittings" of the conference they referred only to the plenary sessions. The Council's interpreter, Professor Paul Mantoux, who had also served as interpreter the night before at the stormy gathering of journalists, informed the president that they seemed to have in mind access to all meetings.[24]

After extended discussion the leaders decided to stick essentially to the arrangement they had worked out on Wednesday. They accepted Wilson's suggestion in agreeing that the press could attend Saturday's opening ceremony and plenary sessions to follow, with the proviso—insisted on by Lloyd George—that the Allies still reserved the right to hold such

meetings in camera. Publicity about the deliberations of the council, however, would be restricted to the daily communiqués.

In view of their firm stand, Wilson suggested that it might be wise to
issue a statement explaining one more time why the privileges requested
by the press could not be granted. Since Lloyd George had spoken most
eloquently on the subject, he was asked to prepare a draft which the other
leaders could go over and ratify at their afternoon meeting. The document
the prime minister submitted, with minor modifications by Wilson, represented the most thorough exposition so far of one point of view in a
controversy already starting to poison the conference.[25]

Lloyd George cited several reasons why diplomatic negotiations, particularly when as complex as those in Paris, must be conducted in private.
Premature publicity might spark prejudices or emotions making it almost
impossible for the thirty-two nations gathered at the conference to resolve
their differences. An arrangement requiring every issue to be debated in
the public prints would slow the negotiations immeasurably at a time
when the world situation demanded speed. Nations would be less able to
trade concessions if the public at home read of the bargain before it had
been completed. Above all, the press, in asserting its right to publicize
everything, misunderstood how democratic processes actually worked.
Any system, no matter how open, must allow opportunity for confidential
exchanges of opinion. "The essence of democratic method," Lloyd
George wrote, "is not that deliberations of a Government should be conducted in public, but that its conclusions should be subject to the consideration of a popular Chamber, and to free and open discussion on the
platform and in the Press."[26] The conferees would certainly be held to
such accountability.

These were all telling arguments, but they were also arguments for a
traditional diplomacy at a time when the press, and many Americans, had
been led to expect something different. In a sense, the troubles in Paris
really began on January 18, 1918, a full year before the conference, when
Wilson appeared before the joint houses of Congress to present his Fourteen Points. As the first of the fourteen, and presumably the most important, he promised "open convenants of peace, openly arrived at, after
which there shall be no private international understandings of any kind
but diplomacy shall proceed always frankly and in the public view." The
words sounded straightforward enough. By any conventional reading they
repudiated the spirit exemplified by Congress of Vienna, when the Tal-
leyrands and Castlereaughs settled the affairs of Europe without concern
for public opinion and certainly without having a pack of reporters baying
at their heels. The president seemed to be saying that not only were
treaties under the new diplomacy to be subject to popular ratification, the
negotiations leading up to them were also to be conducted in public so

the peoples of the world could influence their representatives at each stage along the way. Or so American journalists interpreted the message as they embarked for Paris.

Of course Wilson didn't meant that at all, and in fairness to him, diplomacy attempted under such conditions would probably have been impossible. It is not clear why he even allowed the confusion. Perhaps, as happened at other times in his career, his fondness for how words sounded caused him to pay inadequate attention to what they said. The misfortune in that case is that he didn't choose a different style of eloquence. "If his rhetorical taste had been for paradox rather than for parallelism," Arthur Schlesinger, Jr., noted, "he would have written 'open covenants, secretly arrived at'—and would have been more accurate."[27]

More likely Wilson knew just what he was saying, and had good political reasons in January 1918 for phrasing point one in the way he did. Only a few weeks prior to the speech the Bolsheviks had seized power in Russia, and in taking over the Foreign Office had come across copies of the secret treaties concluded between the Allies earlier in the war. Leon Trotsky, the commissar for foreign affairs, promptly released the documents to the world. The *New York Times* published some on November 25, 1917, and less than three weeks later, on December 13, they showed up also in the *Manchester Guardian*.[28] Although public reaction was much milder than might have been expected (only Villard's *New York Evening Post* bothered to print the full text, and depending on one's source, six or nine other American papers printed portions), the disclosure still came as an embarrassment.[29] At the very least it tarnished the image of this as a war fought for the noblest of ideals. Wilson had good reason at the time he addressed Congress to seize the moral high ground, in particular by drawing a sharp distinction between the revelation of secret treaties and diplomacy as it would be conducted in the future. A phrase like "open covenants of peace, openly arrived at" served the purpose nicely.

In the process he also sent a signal to Europe that he would not be bound by the arrangements worked out before the United States entered the war. If every one of the Fourteen Points represented a challenge to the secret treaties, it made sense to start with one challenging the concept of secret treaties at all. The Allies didn't have to assume he meant diplomacy in a fish bowl to get the message. And once they accepted his principles as the basis for negotiations they conceded at the very least that old concessions would have to be rewon.[30]

But to go from the political expediency in the phrase to a literal interpretation of it was an altogether different matter. Certainly as far as Wilson, an essentially secretive man, was concerned. Far more than Colonel House, for example, he deplored the idea of the press intruding in the diplomatic process. "I try my best to keep him from being so secretive,"

House recorded in his diary in December 1917. "It would be much better to take the public into his confidence whenever it can be done without injury to the public welfare. I should inaugurate an entirely new policy if I were President. I should do away, as far as possible, with secret diplomacy. In most instances it could be done with entire safety."[31] Wilson did not agree. Indeed, he evidently needed reassurance just to accept point one at all. "I urged, and made a strong argument for, open diplomacy," the colonel wrote. "I said there was nothing he could do that would better please the American people and the democracies of the world, and that it was right and must be the diplomacy of the future. I asked him to lay deep stress upon it and to place it first."[32]

The difficulty in accepting House's advice was that Wilson would be guilty of betrayal if he failed to follow through on the promise. Harold Nicholson, a normally astute observor, probably oversimplified when he argued that the recriminations that weighed so heavily in Paris could have been avoided if the press had simply been told to stay home because no news would be made available.[33] Wilson never really had that option, not in a society that took First Amendment guarantees reasonably seriously. In holding out more than he was prepared to give, however, the president almost guaranteed that he would turn reporters against him.

It seems extraordinary in retrospect that Wilson never tried in the year between the Fourteen Points speech and the opening of the Peace Conference to clear up the ambiguity, or to prepare correspondents in some way for what they would encounter in Paris. The closest he came to an explanation was in a memorandum interpreting the Fourteen Points which Frank Cobb of the *New York World* and Walter Lippmann of the *New Republic,* two journalists serving on House's staff during the war, drew up in October 1918 for the guidance of the Allied leaders. Although the document, which Wilson endorsed as accurately reflecting his thought, still left unclear why a simple statement about "open covenants of peace" would not have sufficed, at least the journalists established that the several words following those first four did not mean what they said. "The phrase 'openly arrived at' need not cause difficulty," Cobb and Lippmann wrote. "In fact, the President explained to the Senate last winter that the phrase was not meant to exclude confidential diplomatic negotiations involving delicate matters. The intention is that nothing which occurs in the course of such confidential negotiations shall be binding unless it appears in the final covenant made public to the world.

The matter may perhaps be put this way: It is proposed that in the future every treaty be part of the public law of the world; and that every nation assume a certain obligation in regard to its enforcement. Obviously, nations cannot assume obligations in matters of which they are ignorant; and therefore any secret tends to undermine the solidity of the whole structure of international covenants which it is proposed to erect.[34]

The problem with the explanation is that it appeared in a confidential state paper, and therefore was useless as regards enlightening the press or the public. If reporters were naïve in taking literally a promise impossible to keep, the president deserves criticism for not doing more to disabuse them. All he accomplished by his reticence was to instill in newsmen a sense of double-cross that may have mattered as much in poisoning the atmosphere in Paris as the publicity policy actually adopted.

Both sides deserve criticism also for not trying to find a middle ground between impractical openness and self-defeating secrecy. The reporters were unreasonable in assuming that they should be part of the circle every time the Allied leaders put their heads together. Wilson was equally unreasonable in expecting the peoples of the world to be satisfied with bland generalities, month after month, while statesmen settled their nations' destinies. It should have been possible to inform the press about the issues in contention, the positions of the various nations, the progress toward solutions, without violating the necessary confidentiality between negotiators. For all the justification in barring reporters from the meetings of the Council of Ten, and what eventually became the Council of Four, Wilson still had a responsibility to find other ways to keep the press at least reasonably well informed. And the blame rests particularly heavy with him, since once the newsmen realized they would not have the access they wanted they had no choice but to accept the access they could get. The president failed in that responsibility, with ultimately tragic consequences for himself.

Most reporters recognized right away how little they had won in being admitted to the plenary sessions of the conference; indeed, that they had been almost insulted by the paltriness of the prize. In the five months of the conference, from January 18 to June 28, the delegates met in plenary session a total of six times, one of them in camera. Newsmen were barred from the meeting on May 6 when Wilson, Lloyd George and Clemenceau outlined to the smaller nations the peace that had been formulated on their behalf before presenting it the following day to Germany. Otherwise virtually nothing of substance happened at those gatherings in the Clock Room of the Quai d'Orsay. They were occasions to ratify decisions already made, or perhaps more to the point, to placate the sensitivities of the smaller nations by giving them an occasional sense of participation.

The daily communiqués from the Council of Ten (and eventually the meetings of the special commissions) also turned out to be useless as a source of information. If anything, they had a grim humor about them in demonstrating the unflappability of diplomats determined to reveal nothing. On February 12, for example, two days before Wilson was scheduled to depart for the United States on a brief visit, he and Clemenceau engaged in a particularly emotional exchange over terms for renewing the armistice with Germany. The premier wanted a temporary renewal for a month, with stiff new conditions imposed; the president an indefinite extension under the old arrangement until the time came to submit the final treaty. To the Frenchman it was essential that Germany accede to the territorial demands that would be laid down before the Allied armies demobilized; to the American (not so much disagreeing as stressing a different point) it was much more essential that the conferees move forward quickly in their deliberations without allowing minor issues to sidetrack them.[35] At the end of hours of heated discussion the official communiqué announced simply that "the Supreme War Council met this morning from eleven to one o'clock, and resumed its session that afternoon from three to five-thirty. The conditions of the renewal of the armistice were drawn up."[36]

It would be wrong to call bulletins like this incomplete, or bland, or even misleading. They had nothing to do with providing information to the press. Appearances required that a statement be issued, and appearances were served. In every other way the bulletins mocked their presumed purpose. A reporter for Le Figaro put the situation in perhaps the most generous light when he wrote that "the peace communiqués give us daily, along with the names of the ten sitting members, excellent time-tables: the hour of opening and closing, and sometimes, also, the date of the next sitting, all written with the elegant discretion so pleasing to diplomats who are conscious of the gravity of words."[37]

Under the circumstances not much was lost when the Allied leaders stopped meeting in the Council of Ten on March 24 and retired into even deeper seclusion as the Council of Four. Thereafter, with two fleeting exceptions, the communiqués ceased altogether.[38] In some ways the silence was cleaner than the previous arrangement because it was more honest; in other ways it represented a naked, and therefore infuriating, reminder of how things worked.

Ray Stannard Baker, the press attaché, could do little to fill the news void, if for no other reason than that he didn't know much himself about what was going on. He had set as one of the conditions for taking the job that he be kept fully informed by Wilson and other members of the American delegation of developments at the conference. "This was not because it was necessary to pass on all this information at once to the correspondents," he explained in his autobiography, "but because I felt that I myself must know in order to be an intelligent servant."[39] The problem was that he asked for something easier promised than given. He worked for a president who preferred to keep his own counsel, and for a delegation itself largely uninformed. He worked also in an environment where secrecy and rumor had been elevated into weapons of diplomacy. The press attaché never had a chance.

Even if Baker had known more, the need to operate under the constraints imposed by the president would have been crippling. Baker's first responsibility, after all, was to serve a man who had set strict limits on what he wished publicized. "It is highly important that the right news be given out," Wilson's wife quoted him as saying shortly after he arrived in Europe, "so I am going to ask Baker to accept this position, and come to see me every night at seven o'clock, when I will go over with him everything that has transpired during the day, telling him what is finished and what is unfinished business, and suggesting that the completed business be furnished all the papers, but that questions still under discussion be omitted."[40] As it turned out, they only started to hold such evening meetings late in the conference, and then largely because Wilson needed someone to whom he could unburden himself. (By April he was no longer on good terms with House.) The key point, however, is that because the president regarded all major questions as unsettled until the entire treaty had been drafted, he rarely authorized Baker to pass on to reporters any of the information he divulged. His distinction between finished and unfinished business really represented a formula for saying that Baker could deal in matters removed from controversy and on everything else had to clam up; hardly a basis for informative briefings.

Little wonder that the aide's sessions with the press turned out to be dreary and, in the main, useless affairs. The only major service Baker performed for reporters—early in the conference when news was particularly scarce—was in making available to them position papers from experts in the American delegation explaining the historical and political background of questions to be discussed at the conference. It took some effort to pry the documents loose, since several of the authors worried about having their findings appear in public print and their conclusions attributed to the American commission. But however much the correspondents needed such help, it still represented a poor substitute for the news that comprised their stock in trade.

Nor could Baker do much to ease the perennial problem of communications back to the United States. Only eight of the seventeen Atlantic cables were still functioning after the war, and they had to carry a particularly heavy traffic in official messages as well as the overload from the one cable still operating to Japan and the Far East. The 6,000 words at Baker's disposal to divide daily among the American correspondents did not begin to fill the need (he pointed out that they sent up to 70,000 or 80,000 additional words at their own expense when space allowed).[41] He made do as best he could by assigning 1,000 words to each of the three wire services, and apportioning the other 3,000 among representatives of major publications and chains. The CPI helped also by cabling each day 3,000 words of the texts of documents and speeches, thus avoiding duplication in what the correspondents sent out. But the official quota, supplemented whenever possible by what reporters could get through on their own, still meant that many stories remained stranded in telegraph offices until they had lost all news value. And even if the press officer could not be held responsible for the situation, he had to live with the unpleasantness that followed.

Whether anyone else would have had more success in filling Baker's position is at best problematical. George Creel, whose service with the CPI had thoroughly tarnished him in the eyes of the press, was out of the question. It is true that Wilson originally offered him the job, but he realized almost immediately the impracticality of the idea. Indeed, the major reason he took the aide with him to France was as a gesture of support after Creel became the target of outcries against censorship when the administration, against Creel's advice, seized control of the cable. "I went to the President at once," the chairman recalled, "and released him from his offer, pointing out that any service I might be able to render would be more than offset by the harm of my presence at his side. . . . 'But sir,' I added, 'since it has been published that I am to be a member of your party on the *George Washington,* I've got to go. These last two years have been pretty hard for me, and if it is made to appear that I have lost your confidence. I'm sunk. All I want is a chance to save my face.' "[42] Wilson agreed not to leave the aide in the lurch.

What the consequences would have been had Creel tried to fill the press liaison's role became apparent when he had no sooner set foot in Paris than he ran into a buzz saw of controversy. He had been asked to take charge of the cable situation, dividing space as fairly as possible and supervising its use. But on a touchy matter like this, and one involving old adversaries, the result was bound to be unhappy. The reporters screamed that Creel's quotas constituted censorship, and however much he tried to explain that he could not make available facilities that did not exist, they did not trust him enough to listen. The embattled chairman, not noted for patience himself, did the sensible thing by withdrawing under fire. Thereafter he stayed away from the press.

Aside from Creel, the only other obvious candidate to handle publicity was Joseph Tumulty. He certainly would have welcomed the assignment. Indeed, not being included in the American delegation had bitterly disappointed him. But Wilson had his own reasons, and good ones, to keep the secretary in Washington. Save for Theodore Roosevelt's brief trip to the Panama Canal Zone, no previous president had left the continental United States while in office. Not only was Wilson shattering tradition, he would be gone for months, largely out of touch with the day-by-day running of the White House. It was essential that he find a qualified person to fill in for him. And who more appropriate than the man who had served as factotum for him since the days in Trenton? All the more because he needed Tumulty's special skill in reading public opinion to keep him informed about reactions at home to the work of the conference.

As to whether the secretary would have made a difference in opening channels of communication had he filled Baker's position, it seems unlikely. In image-making, yes. The stream of cables Tumulty sent to Admiral Grayson with ideas about what might be done to project Wilson in warm and human terms attests to the importance he attached to that kind of publicity, and to his shrewdness in orchestrating it. "If the President visits hospitals have press representatives with him to get human interest story," he wired on December 16, 1918. "Do not let his visits be perfunctory. Let him sit beside bed of common soldiers. Keep President in touch with Lawrence, Seibold, Swope, press associations, Hills and Gilbert. Don't forget movie men." Or again on January 16, 1919, when publicity at the conference was just starting to become a problem. "Stories . . . only show . . . President as an official living in a palace and guarded by soldiery. . . . Try to get newspapermen Probert, Bender and Levin to inject some emotion in stories. Can't President meet poilus and American soldiers face to face. . . ? President's smile is wonderful. Get this over in some way. . . ."[43] Techniques like these clearly served a purpose, and although Grayson tried to act on the suggestions as best he could, common sense suggests that the work would have been done better had Tumulty been on hand to supervise it. But persuading Wilson to open up to newsmen about the progress of negotiations would have been an entirely different matter. The secretary did not have the clout, nor the president the inclination. Whoever served as liaison to the press was probably fated to suffer the abuse that follows from having little to say.

If the sessions with Baker accomplished little, reporters fared scarcely better in their daily briefings with the heads of the American delegation. On December 17, 1918, four days after arriving in Europe, Wilson wrote to his fellow commissioners—Secretary of State Lansing, Colonel House, General Tasker Bliss, and Henry White, a career diplomat and the only Republican in the group—asking them to meet regularly with reporters "for such interchange of information or suggestion as may be thought necessary."[44] The briefings began four days later and continued into March.

They were impressive enough occasions from the point of view of pomp. Each morning at 10:30 A.M. twenty to fifty reporters would gather in the drawing room of Lansing's ornate suite at the Hôtel de Crillon to await the commissioners. The room was decorated in white enamel, and liberally adorned with mirrors and gold-leaf molding. On the ceiling high above figures of angels and cherubs and assorted unidentifiable creatures, together with garlands and implements of war, stood out in bold relief.[45] Certainly the reporters had not known such elegance back home, and when the peace commissioners appeared through the mirrored doors they only added to the effect. Lansing, in particular, cut an impressive figure. "The Secretary always was in formal garb," William Allen White recalled, "a tailcoat with silk binding, a double-breasted watch chain, dark gray striped trousers, gray spats, and shiny patent leather shoes."[46]

All the sessions lacked was news content. In Lansing's case the reason stemmed in part from the fact that he shared, and in some ways even exceeded, the reticence of the president he served. The secretary had little use for the press. A priggish individual, self-important in manner, quick to detect slights, trained in a diplomatic career dating to 1892 to believe the less said for public consumption the better, he was hardly the ideal candidate to keep correspondents abreast of developments in Paris. Ray Stannard Baker thought him "one of the most difficult men to approach, and, in connection with the commissions in which he was himself directly engaged. . . , the least communicative of any of the Commissioners."[47]

It should be said on Lansing's behalf that an incident in mid-January, unfortunately timed at the very moment news policy was dominating discussion in the Council of Ten, did little to encourage greater candor on his part. Wilson had been coming under extreme pressure from the French government, from Marshal Foch in particular, to commit American troops to a military expedition against the Bolsheviks in Poland. As part of the campaign the semiofficial newspaper *Le Temps,* almost certainly at the instigation of the Quai d'Orsay, ran articles on three successive days claiming that the United States had agreed to contribute an army corps to the venture. Although Lansing immediately denied the reports, no mention of his disclaimer appeared in the French press. On the contrary, dispatches based on the *Le Temps* story started to be cabled back to the United States.

At his meeting with the American correspondents on Monday morning, January 13, the secretary of state—by now livid—undertook to squelch the rumor once and for all. These briefings were intended to be completely on a background basis, solely for the guidance of the reporters. It was understood that the commissioners would not be quoted directly, nor their remarks attributed to them. With that protection Lansing dealt with the *Le Temps* articles in language rather less than diplomatic. He called them "lies" (seconded by General Bliss, who called them "damned lies"). To his embarrassment a story appeared in the socialist newspaper *L'Humanité* the next day accurately reporting what he had said, putting the words in quotation marks, and attributing them to him.[48]

Much more serious than the violation of the ground rules laid down for the briefings was that the secretary of state now found himself up to his neck in an internal dispute of the host country. The French left bitterly opposed Foch's plan to move against Bolshevism in Eastern Europe. In being able to print Lansing's acid denial that the United States endorsed the proposal, L'Humanité in effect recruited him as an ally against its own government. The secretary had wanted only to bring an end to a campaign carefully orchestrated by the Quai d'Orsay to pressure Wilson into acting against his own better judgment. He certainly did not intend to side publicly against Clemenceau and Foch on an issue of heated controversy in France. The story in L'Humanité accomplished precisely that, placing him in a position no diplomat cares to occupy.

Lansing sensibly ignored the article when it appeared on January 14, but when the next day's issue of L'Humanité followed up with a reminder of the Le Temps allegation and the secretary's reply, something had to be done. General Bliss summoned the executive committee of the U.S. press delegation, including Herbert Bayard Swope, Arthur Krock as proxy for Richard Oulahan, Laurence Hills of the New York Sun, and Arthur Evans of the Chicago Tribune, and told them that the group must take responsibility for policing itself. There would be no more briefings, the angry commissioner declared, until the correspondents exposed the guilty party and provided assurance that similar violations would not happen in the future.

The detective work turned out to be easy. Lewis Gannett, covering the conference for Survey Magazine, came forward voluntarily as the source of the story. A recent graduate of Harvard, with only a year or two prior experience in journalism on the New York World (he had a distinguished career later as book review editor for the New York Herald Tribune), Gannett apologized for the incident, claiming the problems he caused were largely inadvertent. He said that he had not known about the nonattribution rule because he joined the briefings after they began, and also because he had noticed items appearing several times in the Paris edition of the New York Herald attributed to Lansing without apparent protest. His motive in supplying the information to his friend and fellow socialist, Marcel Cachin of L'Humanité, was to correct the distortions about American policy in the French press, and to reassure the newspaper, which probably represented Wilson's single strongest supporter in Paris. But L'Humanité did not handle the story in the way he intended. "To my surprise," Gannett explained in a letter to his employer, "instead of being worked into an article, the statement [I provided] was printed almost intact, and very curtly. Of course that was unfortunate and undiplomatic. . . .

Regardless of knowing or not knowing the no-quotation rule, I knew that.''[49] The commissioners agreed to drop the matter, however, when they received the press committee's report, and its recommendation that Gannett's apology be accepted on the understanding that he would lose his privileges if any further violations occurred.

If reporters exaggerated the importance of the incident, a quirk of timing explains why. January 15, when Gannett acknowledged his responsibility for the story, was also the day the Council of Ten announced that news about its deliberations would henceforth be limited to the barren daily communiqués. Many of the excited dispatches cabled back to the United States that evening drew a connection between the two developments. Raymond Carroll of the *Philadelphia Public Ledger,* whose syndicated articles also appeared in papers like the *Washington Post, New York Sun,* and *Boston Transcript,* put the case most directly. He identified Gannett as the trouble-maker, and pointed out that following the flare-up "almost the first business of Wednesday's peace conference was to pass the gag rule."[50] The Associated Press, while more circumspect, made the same connection.[51] However logical cause and effect seemed in the circumstances, the truth is that the Allied leaders arrived at the decision on news policy independently of the report in *L'Humanité* (it did not even come up in their discussions). Moreover, although the incident would hardly have encouraged Lansing to change his ways, he had been closed-mouthed with the press long before an errant reporter embarrassed him.

But the problem with the briefings had to do with much more than official reticence. The major reason they failed was that Wilson kept the commissioners, with the exception of House, almost as much in the dark as everyone else. "There was none of the frankness that should have existed between the Chief Executive and his chosen agents and advisers," Lansing complained in his memoirs.[52] It could not have helped to salve the secretary's wounded feelings that he had to put up with constant reminders of how little he mattered. As Ray Stannard Baker noted, a large circle of correspondents invariably gathered around House for conversation after the briefings had ended. Fewer sought out Lansing, and fewer still White and Bliss.[53] Indeed, the latter two seemed to be there mainly in an ornamental role. Bliss, who did not feel comfortable in the presence of reporters, said virtually nothing at the briefings. White, on the other hand, was like a superannuated professor who very much wanted to share what he knew with the press, but knew nothing they wanted to hear. Occasionally he would reminisce about his younger days in the diplomatic corps, telling stories "about the Empress Eugenie, and the last Napoleon, and the barricades," and as he rambled along tempers already sorely strained would fray just a bit more.

Not surprisingly, the daily briefings became something of a joke among reporters. "The President is so utterly the controlling factor," Arthur Krock wrote in the *Louisville Courier-Journal* in early February, "that his associates cannot speak with authority and therefore naturally do not speak at all."[54] And when they tried, the result as likely as not was embarrassment. William Allen White told of the occasion that Henry White, with evident pleasure, passed along a decision made in one of his committees the previous evening. "When he had gone," the editor of the *Emporia Gazette* recalled, "several of the reporters who had been on the job early that morning revealed to us . . . that the President had overruled Henry White and that the news he gave us was utterly useless. The President had not thought it worth while to notify him what had been done. His humiliation when he found the truth was . . . painful and unnecessary."[55]

The meetings, which even Ray Stannard Baker described as "farcical," eventually wound down of their own accord.[56] First House dropped out, and later Bliss, leaving Lansing and White to carry out a presidential directive beyond their ability to fulfill. It was almost a relief when the four Allied leaders, reaching a climactic point in the deliberations, gave orders in mid-March to abandon the briefings. The experience had been painful for all concerned.[57]

The reporters did better in one-on-one meetings with members of the American delegation. As often happens, sources would occasionally make available to individual correspondents information they would not release in open conferences. Much depended, of course, on the prestige or usefulness of the journal the correspondent represented, or on the personal relationship that might have developed between him and the official. General Bliss, for example, provided the confirmation for Herbert Bayard Swope's report in the *New York World* in March 1919 that the Kaiser probably would not be brought to trial.[58] Admiral William Benson fed several items on naval matters to Charles Thompson of the Associated Press. William Bullitt, another useful source, maintained close ties with Oswald Garrison Villard.[59] Herbert Hoover and Bernard Baruch also proved to be helpful on occasion.

Far and away the most useful source of news in Paris, however, both for the quality of the information he had to offer and his accessibility to newsmen, was Colonel Edward House. Each evening at 6:00 P.M. he would meet with a group of reporters in his suite at the Hôtel Carillon for an informal conversation about the day's events. To Frederick Essary of the *Baltimore Sun,* those sessions represented "the one satisfactory source of news of American activities at the Conference. . . . He went very far in these informal conversations to enlighten us regarding what was happening behind the scenes."[60] House also managed to squeeze in appointments, sometimes for as brief a period as five minutes, with individual correspondents. Charles Thompson, for instance, recorded in his diary meeting with the commissioner almost every morning to gather material for his afternoon dispatches.[61] For particularly favored journalists, the access might be even more extensive. "Every day," William Allen White wrote in his autobiography, "I walked with [House] late afternoons along the banks of the Seine and we discussed the passing show in the various secret conferences. I am sure that he was candid with me. I am certain that he had no guile. So far as he knew what was pending and why it was important, he told me. Much that he told me was in confidence. If he knew something about the undercurrents of the great peace conference I would have known it."[62]

Some of the major news beats to come out of the conference can be traced to these meetings with the cooperative commissioner. Herbert Bayard Swope's report on the amended text of the League of Nations covenant, which appeared in the *New York World* on April 2 and 3, is the shining example. The correspondent went to House and pointed out that garbled or inaccurate versions of what the covenant contained would only provide ammunition for Senate opponents of the League. If he could get accurate information he would be able to write a story laying to rest many of the groundless fears circulating back home. Obviously impressed by this argument, House put a copy of the secret document on the corner of his desk and left the room, staying away long enough for Swope to take detailed notes. When the reporter filed the dispatch, he in turn protected his source by claiming that it was "based upon information received from various members of the special committee and may be depended on as authoritative."[63] Even his colleagues conceded that Swope had scored the single most impressive triumph in covering the conference.

House, who right along had been much more the champion of open diplomacy than Wilson, acted as he did out of his own firm convictions. He thought the news blackout in Paris a major blunder. "I do not understand the President's position," he wrote in his diary on May 31. "It is doing him irreparable injury. What news our press obtains is largely from me at our afternoon meetings. They believe, I take it, that I give them this information with the President's sanction, but as a matter of fact, I give it in spite of his disapproval."[64]

It might seem that House's candor with the press should have gone far to compensate for the lack of information from other quarters, and thus have helped to ease the bad feelings in Paris. Several reasons explain why things did not work out that way. To begin with, he could only be available to a relatively small number of journalists, and they by and large the celebrities in the group. The majority of the one hundred and fifty-odd American reporters in Paris operated completely in the cold. Moreover, although he knew a great deal, even House's information was limited. Nobody, not even his closest adviser, shared the president's full confidence. For most of the developments at the conference the press remained at the mercy of a communications system designed not to communicate.

The major problem, however, was that House's policy of openness to reporters had a self-destruct component built in. Various reasons have been assigned for the estrangement between him and the president, two men who for years had maintained an extraordinarily close relationship. Almost certainly Wilson resented the concessions House made in his absence during the president's visit to the United States. Shortly after returning to France Wilson—at the urgent prodding of Tumulty—had to deal with news reports that the principle won the previous January about incorporating the League covenant in the treaty had since been surrendered. On March 15 he issued to the press through Ray Stannard Baker a stiff denial of those reports which was widely interpreted as a rebuke to House.

The president is also said to have bridled at his aide's new assertiveness in Paris. House seemed to be taking advantage of the closer ties he had with the Allied leaders, arising out of his many diplomatic trips (as well as his more likable personality), to assume a role more like that of a presidential associate than subordinate. The colonel showed obvious lack of tact, for example, on the day that Clemenceau dropped by unexpectedly for a visit while House was entertaining Wilson in his suite. He ushered the premier into another room for what he called "one of our heart to heart talks," leaving Wilson to cool his heels in the parlor.[65]

However much it weighed in the final reckoning, House created additional problems for himself by serving as the conduit of information to the press. Two things happened almost inevitably as a result: he became a favorite of the reporters, someone who appeared in their dispatches as wise and knowing and skilled in negotiations (which may have been part of his motive, consciously or unconsciously, all along), and he won the enmity of others less fortunate than he in the publicity they received. Lansing, for one, resented the colonel's frequent meetings with journalists, accusing him of leaking news without presidential authorization.

Much more serious was that the formidable Mrs. Wilson started to suspect House of trying to upstage her husband. Matters came to a head in early April because of an article in the London *Times* by H. Wickham Steed, the foreign editor of the paper, and soon to replace Geoffrey Dawson as editor-in-chief. The *Times*, of course, was no ordinary newspaper and Steed no ordinary journalist. His position made him a member of the ruling establishment in Great Britain, and a person who hobnobbed on terms of familiarity with the leaders of the various delegations in Paris. What he wrote mattered, in the same way that decades later government officials would learn to pay close heed to the pronouncements of a Walter

Lippmann or a James Reston. Steed vastly admired the diplomatic skill of Colonel House, a close friend, and almost equally disapproved of what he regarded as Wilson's obstructionist attitude (he had little use for Lloyd George either).[66] Provoked, perhaps, by the president's failure to accept his solution for the Saar impasse by giving France a League of Nations mandate for fifteen years, the *Times* editor finally lashed out in print. "In so far as there is a real improvement in the prospects of the Conference," he wrote, "it is believed to be attributed chiefly to the practical statesmanship of Colonel House, who, in view of President Wilson's indisposition, has once again placed his *savoir faire* and conciliatory temperament at the disposal of the chief peacemakers. Colonel House is one of the very few Delegates who have 'made good' during the Conference. It is, indeed, probable that peace would have been made successfully weeks ago but for the unfortunate illness which overtook him at the very outset of the Conference. When he recovered the Council of Ten had already got into bad habits. . . . The delay that has occurred since the return of President Wilson and Mr. Lloyd George has been due chiefly to the upsetting of the good work [he accomplished] during their absence."[67]

On the day the article appeared House showed up at the Wilson residence to keep an appointment with the president. As he often did, the colonel stopped for a while to chat with Mrs. Wilson until the president was ready to see him. She immediately confronted him with Steed's column and in a cold fury demanded an explanation.[68] Accounts differ about what happened next. Mrs. Wilson claimed that the flustered House sprang up, grabbed his coat, and fled from the building "as though pursued."[69] She had a flair for melodrama, however, and her version of events is seldom reliable. More likely, as David Lawrence reported, the president called his aide in at that point, and nothing more was said on the subject.[70] The only certainty is that accumulated grievances took their toll. Relations between Wilson and House became increasingly chilled and formal, and eventually broke off altogether. They never saw each other again after the conference ended, nor was the colonel invited to join the mourners at Wilson's home when his former chief died. For the press, the consequences of the estrangement were even more immediate. It meant that by early April, midway through the conference, their major source of news had less and less to offer.

Wilson, of course, was not the man to take up the slack. Part of the reason, aside from his feelings about reporters, was that the business of the conference almost totally occupied his attention. The president did not delegate authority well, which meant that he had to steep himself in details on a bewildering variety of subjects in order to establish an Amer-

ican position, argue for it, and ratify the agreements made by his sub-
ordinates. The task was further complicated by the fact that the other
Allied leaders did not share his commitment to the Fourteen Points. Every
day brought a confrontation with three determined and powerful adversaries in which he fought more or less alone. It was natural, at least to
Wilson, to worry first about securing the best possible treaty, and to put
off until later the matter of using the press to win public support for it.
This explains his curt response when David Lawrence suggested that he
might be creating political problems for himself at home by not doing
more to publicize his efforts. "I don't give a damn about the politics of
it," the president shot back; "if this thing is a success we will get the
benefit of it, and if it isn't, we will be attacked anyhow."[71]

The enormous drain on Wilson's energies in Paris also contributed to
his choice for isolation. During those months he asked far too much of
his frail system. As the pressure mounted his skin took on a grayish hue
and a tic developed in his face, perhaps the first warning of the stroke
that in a few months would cripple him. He simply couldn't manage
sessions with reporters on top of everything else. "Often at the close of
the day, when I went up to see him," Ray Stannard Baker wrote, "he
seemed utterly beaten down, worn out. It seemed cruelty to ask him to
do another thing, say another word. . . . Contacts with the correspondents
took physical and nervous energy, and therefore he reserved his strength
for what he considered more important matters."[72]

The decision, while understandable, still resulted in Wilson's being the
only head of state not to meet periodically with the press of his country,
a distinction that hardly endeared him to American correspondents.[73] He
scheduled only two conferences with reporters: one on February 14, just
prior to his visit home, and the second on June 27, the day before the
treaty was to be signed. The first one in particular turned out badly, and
must have confirmed his assumption that very little good came out of
such meetings. It had been made clear at the beginning that the interview
would be a backgrounder: the newsmen were not to quote the president
or attribute remarks to him.[74] On that basis Wilson spoke candidly, and
even with good spirits, on a variety of subjects.

The report in the Paris edition of the *New York Herald* the next morning,
written by its chief correspondent, Truman H. Talley, broke all the rules.
Throughout the article Talley consistently cited the president as his
source. Worse, he quoted Wilson on a subject of particular sensitivity—
the apparent surrender to the British on the second of the Fourteen Points
about freedom of the seas—and in words inappropriately jocular in view
of the principle at stake. According to the story:

    After he had finished with the League proposals he was asked whether
the freedom of the seas had entered into the negotiations.
    "I am glad you asked me that," he said laughingly,"for I want to tell
you a good joke on myself. I didn't see the joke until I came over here.
Under the League of Nations there will be no neutrals. They will all
be in the League, subject to the League decisions on the matter of
exertion of armed forces. If there are no neutrals there will be no issue
over sea rights, for the freedom of the seas puzzle arose over the
relations of belligerents and neutrals. The League now will settle all
matters of naval policy and regulation, such as codes and armaments.
So it might be said, 'there ain't no such thing' as the issue of the freedom
of the seas."

When Laurence Hills of the *New York Sun* asked Wilson if he had gotten
that argument from the British, Talley again put the response directly.
"No, I arrived at that conclusion in the privacy of my own soul," he
quoted the president as saying with a hearty laugh.[75]
Wilson had already sailed when the embarrassing and potentially destructive article appeared, but a committee of the American Peace Committee, comprised of Lansing, White, Bliss and John Foster Dulles,
immediately contacted the Correspondents' Executive Committee demanding an explanation. The response on February 18 attempted to put
the best possible light on a violation impossible to defend. The reporters
conceded Talley's breach of ethics, suggested that it "was committed less
in a spirit of deliberation, and more, perhaps, because of carelessness and
ignorance of the proper methods to be employed," and recommended that
his press privileges be revoked for ten days. It was probably just as well
that neither the committee nor commissioners knew that the offending
article had also run as a front page lead in the New York edition of the
Herald, under a headline that read in part, "'FREEDOM OF THE SEAS' ISSUE
IS DEAD, HE [Wilson] TELLS AMERICAN CORRESPONDENTS.'"[76] Nor
did they know that Herbert Bayard Swope, who sat in judgment of Talley
as a member of the Correspondents' Executive Committee, had himself
identified Wilson as the source of the story in his dispatch to the *New
York World,* and had also directly quoted the president's freedom of the
seas response.[77] The commissioners accepted the recommendation by
revoking Talley's privileges for two weeks. Six days later, again at the
recommendation of the committee, they lifted the punishment altogether
so as not "to make the matter in any sense one of personal persecution."[78]
The correspondents were obviously foolish to justify Wilson's refusing
to see them. By the same token, almost certainly the president did not
need an incident like this to persuade him to remain in seclusion. He
adopted the course suited to his nature and beliefs. In the process he
antagonized men who, ironically, started out more prepared to support

him than they had been for years. The point was not so much that old grievances had been forgotten as that the correspondents tended to be patriots first, and wanted to stand up for their country when a clash of national wills developed in Paris. Wilson never gave them the chance. "The newspaper men," William Allen White wrote, "for the most part eager to support the American position, were not permitted to know even semi-officially what the American position was. It is not surprising that under this state of facts they began to lose confidence in American leadership."[79]

Nor did it help to ease frustrations that reporters perceived, in a probably exaggerated way, their rights being violated by French and British censors. This was something they had been guaranteed would not happen, and for it to occur at all represented to them a betrayal on top of betrayals. "It was like having someone over your shoulder all the time," David Lawrence recalled.[80] They resented the feeling, and reminded each other in endless talk of the indignities they suffered.[81]

The actual cases of censors interfering with correspondents' cables back to the United States did not altogether justify the unhappiness. In a few instances, it is true, authorities intercepted messages on military, as opposed to political, grounds. For example, Oswald Garrison Villard failed, first in England and then in France, to slip past the censors a story about British troops mutinying in Folkstone and Dover. But only two incidents qualified clearly as political suppression, and both times the dispatches went through a few days later. That the incidents mattered as much as they did speaks to one of two possibilities. It may be that the correspondents had become such purists on the First Amendment that, like old fashioned moralists, they saw even one violation as representing ruin. More likely, the sour mood arising out of secretiveness at the conference caused the press to overreact to relatively minor provocations.

The first case to stir controversy involved a report from Frederick Moore to the *New York Tribune* about rumors in the Chamber of Deputies that Wilson had threatened to withdraw American troops from Europe, and to leave the conference himself, unless the Allies gave in to his demands. Moore filed the dispatch on January 15. Rather than put it on the wire, French officials intercepted the message and relayed it all the way to Clemenceau, who raised the matter at the meeting of the Council of Ten on January 16.[82] Not until the premier received Wilson's denial of the rumor as "an abominable falsehood," which he announced publicly the next day in the Chamber of Deputies, did he allow the dispatch to go through. It reached the *Tribune* on January 18.

An incident like this could be evaluated in various ways. To the French it demonstrated the harm to be done by trafficking in hearsay or speculation, and thus justified the strict controls on publicity that had been laid down for the conference. But the American press, and for that matter American public opinion generally, saw things differently. Correspondents were not free to report the news from Paris if the French could exercise control over what went out on the wires and when. Even if used selectively, a gag-rule was still a gag-rule. A worried message to Ray Stannard Baker from the Committee on Public Information warned of the negative reaction at home, and urged that he secure from "highest possible authority" a public denial that the conference intended to censor correspondents' dispatches.[83]

The other incident aroused even more controversy because it directly involved the president. Herbert Bayard Swope had been kept closely informed during late March and early April about the disagreement among the Allied leaders in assessing the reparations to be demanded of Germany. While the United States held out for a figure based on estimated capacity to pay, France insisted on compensation for all of its suffering (without ever settling on what the final amount should be). Even Lloyd George, responding to political pressure at home, demanded that the Germans pay dearly for their perfidy. After many days spent in a futile effort to settle their differences, the leaders finally agreed to shelve the decision for the time being and let specific reparations be worked out at a post-conference meeting. Swope's source, who he never identified, gave him a copy of the appropriate clauses soon afterward.

On Thursday, April 10, the reporter wired the story at urgent rate to a *World* representative in London for immediate relay to New York. Later in the day, after allowing himself eight hour lead time, he tracked down Laurence Hills of the *New York Sun,* with whom he had an arrangement to share information, and gave the story to him. Assuming that the dispatch had already reached the *New York World,* the *Sun* correspondent filed his report from France at ordinary rates.

In fact, several days elapsed before the *World* received Swope's cable. British authorities, alarmed at the possible repercussions of a report that stiff reparations had not yet been fixed, intercepted the message and relayed it on April 12 to Lord Riddell in Paris for advice on how to proceed. The press attaché showed the cable to Lloyd George and Balfour, and they—"much perturbed and surprised"—agreed that it must not be sent.[84] Lloyd George went immediately to Wilson and asked his help in delaying the message at least through the following Tuesday, April 15, when he was scheduled to appear before the House of Commons. He feared that the terms might appear to be a violation of his campaign pledge to make Germany pay, and as such would generate angry questions in Parliament and perhaps even force a vote of confidence.

The president, himself thoroughly alarmed at the possibility of the British government falling just when a treaty seemed within reach, summoned

Swope and asked him as a matter of patriotism to contact his paper immediately with a request that it hold up on printing the dispatch. Swope readily agreed. He still assumed when speaking with the president that the cable had gone through, and likely also felt he could afford to be cooperative since the story was already on the streets. That afternoon he and Hills wired their respective papers with the request for a delay in publication.

Not until the next day, Sunday, April 13, did the truth come out. Swope's contact in London notified him that the British had intercepted his cable, and the same day he received a return message from the *World* informing him that the paper had never received the dispatch he described. Hills, meanwhile, heard from the *Sun* that it could not cooperate since his report had arrived on Friday, April 11, and been run routinely the following day. Beaten on his own story, now aware that Lloyd George had taken matters into his own hands to suppress the report even prior to consulting with the president, Swope hit the roof. He demanded that the British release his cable immediately. Demonstrating at the very least a certain insouciance in the face of an American correspondent's outrage, they in turn suggested to him that he authorize them to kill it. On the Monday Riddell proposed a compromise: the British would send the second part of the cable containing Swope's copy in return for holding back temporarily on the first part which consisted of the text of the reparations clauses. Swope refused to accede to any censorship at all, so the British just went ahead and did things their own way. His dispatch started to dribble in to the *World* late Monday night, and arrived bit by bit over the two days following. The headlines in the Thursday edition, when the entire report had finally cleared censorship, were hardly calculated to garner public support behind the treaty:

BRITAIN SUPPRESSED
NEWS FOR AMERICA
DESPITE HER PLEDGE

The World's Readers Deprived of Text of
Reparations Section of Peace Treaty Until
Lloyd George Could Speak in Commons—
Premier Asked President to Stop Publication—
His Censors Held It for Five Days—The
World Now Prints It.[85]

Considering the much stricter controls on the press in France and Great Britain, even isolated incidents like these are not enough to say that censors bullied the American correspondents covering the conference. Until as late as January 10, for example, French newspapers could not so much as announce the names of their country's delegates to the conference. During the week of April 25, 1919, authorities seized *Bonsoir* on three separate occasions, the second time for mentioning the first seizure. They suspended *Information* for eight days in March for publishing an item about alleged new armistice terms that had already appeared in the English press.[86] The few cases of censors delaying the transmission of cables back to the United States (and some of the presumed such cases probably resulted from nothing more sinister than overclogged lines) were clearly insignificant by comparison. But perception is often as important as reality, and the fact is that American reporters perceived censorship as a major problem in Paris. It was an easy judgment to make in the atmosphere of secrecy and suspicion. And as a result the correspondents had still another reason to feel betrayed. Many of them even gave up on trying to cover the conference. "An exodus home promptly began," Oswald Garrison Villard recalled, "some actually cabling for permission to return; a considerable group left on February 5, quite disgusted."[87]

An even more serious consequence of the news policy in Paris, one that hit American reporters particularly hard, was that it compounded their inexperience in writing about foreign affairs. No matter how many years had passed since their cub reporter days, these were men who had been schooled in a different kind of journalism. They knew the ins and outs of party politics, the sources of power in Congress, the difference between the substance and froth at national conventions. But an international conference posed a completely different challenge. Many of them had never been to Europe before; few could speak a foreign language; hardly any could claim a background in the history or politics of countries other than their own. They came from a nation newly emerged from isolation, and now were expected to write perceptively about it assuming a role of world leadership. It was an impossible assignment.

The result told in their dispatches, as the correspondents realized themselves. "I cannot imagine a worse punishment for some of the clan than to compel them to reread today their dispatches from Paris," Oswald Garrison Villard wrote years later.[88] William Allen White also looked back with regret. "We did not ask the right questions apparently. We did not comprehend the significance of the conference even if we sensed its importance. And some way, with all the thousands and hundreds of thousands of dollars spent by the American press in cable charges and in reporters' salaries, the American people got only the facts and not the truth."[89]

The danger with superficial reporting was that it sacrificed substance for color, and much worse, raised hopes unwarranted by the actual state of affairs in Europe and the world. Baker thought the damage particularly severe in the weeks preceding the conference. "Too much emphasis was . . . given at first to the superficial, spectacular, and optimistic," he wrote, "and too little to the grave fundamental issues at stake. There was too much political drama, too little attention to deep-seated economic and financial problems. Everything was made to look too easy. The gathering conference was even written about as a kind of international circus staged for the amusement of the world, not as an assemblage—even a tragic assemblage—faced with problems too vast for it or any other group of men to solve, and yet forced to act, act, act, with every act affecting the destinies of mankind."[90] The reality would come as a shock to the American public because of the lack of preparation in their newspapers. They would feel personally cheated by the complexities of international issues and the inability of fallible men to propose more than imperfect solutions. And for that an administration which failed in its mission to educate by working through the press was largely to blame.

The publicity blackout in Paris also made reporters more susceptible than they should have been to manipulation by special interest groups. News was where one found it, and if conventional sources dried up then correspondents turned in a major way to the people anxious to reach them. Notably, the lesser powers fell into that category. "For the most part ruled out of court by the Conference itself," H. Wilson Harris of the *London News* wrote, "they applied themselves as an alternative to impressing public opinion outside. . . . Invitations to educative lunches and propaganda dinners poured in from every side on the Allied journalists and anyone else whose influence on the public was of any account."[91] The problem with this kind of pressure was that it militated against well-rounded reporting about the conference. Obviously, the smaller nations should have been heard. They had all the more right to air their case in the press when the Allied leaders pretty well excluded them from the decision-making process. But a cacophony of individual voices, with those able to scream the loudest the ones heard most clearly, accomplishes little in putting complex questions into perspective.

To make matters worse from Wilson's point of view, some of the nations most active in wooing the press—Italy and Poland, for example—were also those with the most sizeable constituencies in the United States. "The Poles had developed their propaganda into almost a *tour de force* of efficiency," H. Wilson Harris remarked.[92] And even their effort paled next to Italy's on the Fiume question. Everything went to win the Adriatic port, including the outright purchase of editorial support in French newspapers.[93] Whether the publicity effort affected coverage of the dispute in American papers is difficult to say; perhaps it had no affect at all. Still, accepting that nothing Wilson did short of surrendering his principles would have appeased Italian-American voters on the issue, and that the rest of the country more or less understood his position already, he might have benefited by working closely with reporters to impress upon readers back home why Orlando's territorial demands had to be resisted. This he failed to do.

Another consequence of the dearth of official news in Paris was that leaks weighed proportionately heavier than they would have otherwise as an alternative source of news, and they of their nature heightened the mood of suspicion and mutual recriminations at the conference. Nations used the device not so much to inform the public as to secure a selective advantage over their rivals, a tactic that brought retaliations and counter-retaliations until finally the peace-makers were awash in intrigue. Lloyd George's complaint on January 15 about unauthorized material appearing in French newspapers, a complaint that resulted directly in the decision to restrict information to the daily communiqués, certainly did nothing to stem the tide. Only two days later Wilson pointed out at a Council of Ten meeting that his suggestion made to the other heads of state in the privacy of his own home about a possible solution to the Adriatic question had turned up promptly and accurately in the *London Daily Mail*.[94] Worse, the leaks almost always highlighted disagreements and acrimony among the negotiators, generally to the prejudice of one of them. They were virtually designed to instill bad feeling.

Wilson's resentment of back-stabbing journalism—for that is what it was—surfaced at the Council of Ten meeting on Thursday, January 30, when he observed that English newspapers had been carrying a lot more information lately about the Council's deliberations than appeared in the daily communiqués. The president particularly resented the disparagement of his "idealistic views" in the reports. He reminded the group that so far he had honored the injunction of secrecy, speaking only to people in that room and to members of the American delegation. If the articles continued to appear, however, he would be compelled to tell his side of the story. "A public discussion would become inevitable," Wilson warned, "and such a public discussion would be fatal."[95]

Lloyd George agreed entirely with the president, in part perhaps out of embarrassment in realizing that someone in his delegation had to be the source of the leaks. (Indeed, he ordered an immediate investigation, and several weeks later reported to the Council of Ten that "the person concerned [had been] dealt with as far as possible" and "the newspaper correspondent responsible . . . sent away from Paris.")[96] At the afternoon session on January 30 Lloyd George seconded Wilson's complaint by noting that a recent dispatch in the *Daily Mail* was "accurate enough to have been supplied by somebody who either directly or indirectly had inside knowledge."[97] He did not see how the heads of state could continue to deliberate under such conditions.

Matters came to a head in mid-March when the prime minister felt the knife usually wielded against Wilson in his own back. He had argued at the council meeting on Tuesday, March 18 against a proposal supported by France to put Danzig, and with it two million Germans, under Polish sovereignty.[98] The next day several Paris papers with close ties to the government—*Le Temps, Le Petit Journal, L'Echo de Paris*—printed detailed accounts of the discussion, complete with hitherto secret maps.[99] Obviously seething, Lloyd George raised the breach of security at an evening session of the council on March 21. "The account contained actual quotations of the words used by [me] between quotation marks," he complained. "Had a verbatim report been given, [I] would not have objected so strongly. But the report gave a very wrong impression of what [I] had said, and the distortion permitted an opportunity for violent attacks against [me]."[100]

This time conventional words of apology would not suffice. The prime minister warned that "if similar disclosures were to be repeated, [I] would prefer not to take any further part in the discussions, and to put off expressing [my] views until the final Conference took place." He reminded his colleagues that he had hesitated about having the conference in Paris in the first place out of concern that "the local press would take an undue part in the proceedings. . . ." Now his worst fears seemed to be realized; the negotiations threatened to become "absolutely futile." He condemned as "doubly mischievous" that the leak appeared in *Le Temps,* a paper "in close touch with the government." Surely some way could be found "to prevent responsible officials from giving away such information, especially when the information so given was deliberately altered in order to make it the ground for a violent attack on one of the Allied countries."[101]

Clemenceau, who undoubtedly appreciated that the spring of 1919 was no time for a British public figure to be depicted in the press as standing up for Germany, conceded the prime minister's right to be upset. He volunteered to file a complaint with the directors of *Le Temps* (in other words, to rebuke the paper for printing news his own government had leaked), although cautioning at the same time that he dared not enforce the French censorship laws too strictly. The leaders further agreed that France would launch an investigation to discover "if possible" the source of the leak, and that the Secretariat would issue a circular to members of the various delegations reminding them of "the necessity for strict reticence in regard to the proceedings of the Conference."[102]

This discussion occurred at a Friday session. It is probably more than a coincidence that the last meeting of the Council of Ten, and with it the last daily communiqué, took place the following Monday, March 24. Thereafter the Allied leaders met as a Council of Four, without aides in attendance and without statements to the press at the end of the day. They had first tried such sessions in early March when House sat in for Wilson during the president's visit to the United States. Wilson participated in similar meetings when he returned on March 14. Now on March 25, four days after a leak to the press had set off a major explosion, the Council of Ten disappeared altogether.

The point is not that leaked news is blameworthy in itself. The press will always depend upon information obtained in this way, and the more so as it is cut off from ordinary channels of news. But in Paris the leaks had characteristics that made them poisonous. For one thing, they came predominantly from a single source—the French. For another, they leaned heavily toward half-truths and distortions. For still another, they played on popular emotions (in a city where emotions already ran high enough) by portraying the other negotiators as insensitive or callous to the needs of the host country.[103] By the rules of the game in Paris the publicity advantage went entirely to one side; the home team called balls and strikes.

Clemenceau's great advantage—something that would not have been available to Wilson in Washington or Lloyd George in London—was that he could lay down guidelines for the press of his country on how he wanted certain stories handled and which ones he wanted suppressed. Since French newspapers lacked the tradition of independence not to cooperate, the briefings at the rue François-Premier were occasions to give reporters not so much information as marching orders. Indeed, a favored minority of journalists went straight to the Quai d'Orsay for their instructions. Men like Andre Géraud of *L'Echo de Paris,* Jules Sauerwein of *Le Matin,* Jean Herbette of *Le Temps* and Leon Bassée of Havas operated at the very center of power, often dealing directly with Foreign Minister Pichon. Their writings resembled government position papers more than newspaper reports.

As advocate of the Fourteen Points, the naysayer to virtually all of France's demands for security and revenge, Wilson inevitably became the prime target of this guided journalism. Leaks portraying him as naïve and imperious cropped up repeatedly in Paris papers, and editorials by the score castigated his obstructionist attitude. Perhaps the most impressive aspect of the publicity effort was the way the government could turn the flow on or off at will, almost like using a faucet. It demonstrated how easily at the time Wilson came under particularly savage attack for attempting to apply the principle of self-determination to the Saar. When Colonel House went to see Clemenceau on April 15 to report that the president had finally relented, agreeing to French occupation for fifteen years, he asked if the premier would reciprocate by calling off his minions in the press.[104] Clemenceau, in an understandably expansive mood, acted immediately. He summoned his secretary and told him "that all attacks of every description on President Wilson and the United States must cease; that our relations were of the very best and that there was no disagreement between our two countries on the questions before the Peace Conference."[105] French newspapers the next day almost purred.

To an extent the French even succeeded in infiltrating the American press. They worked hard to win the good will of newsmen from foreign countries, particularly those from the United States. The lavish Interallied Press Club at 80 avenue Champs Elysées, for example, located in a mansion the government rented from a wealthy furniture dealer named Dufayel, demonstrated that expense was no factor when it came to pleasing journalists. William Allen White described the $2,500,000 structure as "a gorgeous palace of a rather vulgarly rich man—a palace he had adorned in the decorations with naked women spreading over fireplaces, or standing on the newel posts, or bending over doorways and windows. It was a forest of obtrusive nudity, and it became known to the American press delegation as 'The House of a Thousand Teats.' "[106] There the hosts gave dinner parties, arranged lectures and free entertainments, held lavish receptions. Correspondents were always welcome to drop by to dine in the well-appointed restaurant where food sold for about one-third the price of ordinary establishments, or to meet celebrities who might interest them. To attend further to the comfort of their guests, the French kept the club well-stocked with handouts. Nobody needed to worry about deadlines if worn down by too much work, or more likely, too much pleasure.

By and large American reporters resisted such blandishments. They regarded information coming from French sources as distorted and self-serving, and the more they aspired to objectivity the less likely they were to use it. On the other hand, the press contingent from the United States also included men who for their own reasons could be influenced. The foremost example, because of his own prestige and the prestige of the paper he represented, was Laurence Hills of the *New York Sun*. He, more than most of his colleagues, distrusted the League concept and for that matter the whole baggage of Wilsonian idealism. He also had close ties to Wilson's political enemies in the United States. The circumstances made him an obvious candidate to drift into the French orbit.

Hill recalled forming "very friendly relations" with Andre Géraud, the editor of the right-wing *Echo de Paris* who wrote under the pen name "Pertinax." The Frenchman, a spokesman for the military establishment, outdid even Clemenceau in setting national security as the first priority for France. "We constantly exchanged views," the *Sun* reporter wrote. Géraud fed him tidbits of information with a Gaullic flavor while Hills in turn impressed on his friend that Wilson "had really been repudiated at the polls just before he sailed, something the French had entirely forgotten, or overlooked."[107] The result of their alliance, of course, was to influence the way major newspapers in both countries covered the conference.

Wilson could do relatively little to counter the publicity barrage. He tried on occasion to best the French at their own tactic, but never with notable success. One such occasion happened in early February when he received from a friendly French editor, one whose word he regarded as unimpeachable, a copy of a memorandum from the Maison de la Presse to Paris newspapers instructing them to push hard on three themes: (1) to magnify Republican opposition in the United States to the president and his administration; (2) to emphasize chaotic conditions in Russia; and (3) to show that Germany was willing and able to renew the struggle. "If this keeps on I shall suggest moving the Conference to Geneva, or somewhere out of Paris," the president said to Ray Stannard Baker at the time.[108]

The opportunity to use the threat as his weapon in the war of leaks came a few days later. On Monday morning, February 10, *Le Figaro* appeared on the newsstands with an article by Alfred Capus, the editor of the paper and a noted academician, which warned Wilson against taking too much upon himself. "President Wilson has lightly assumed a responsibility such as few men have ever borne," Capus wrote. "Success in his idealistic efforts will surely place him among the greatest characters of history. But failure will plunge the world into chaos and will make the responsible author of this chaos one of the most pitiful figures that history has ever presented."[109] Considering the paper's reputation as a personal organ for Clemenceau, the warning was difficult to ignore. Moreover, *Le Figaro* carried in the same issue (as did other Paris papers) an Associated Press interview with the premier, the first he had granted since the conference began, in which he rebuked those who would sacrifice France to high, but fuzzy, ideals. Reporters already had a lot to buzz about when Admiral Grayson, acting on the president's instructions, appeared at the Press Bureau around noon with the information that Wilson thought the conference might have to be moved out of Paris.

It is difficult to believe that the president seriously intended to follow through on the threat, one likely to wreck the negotiations. But he did throw a scare into Clemenceau. The premier rushed over to House's suite at the Hôtel Crillon that afternoon to get reassurance about American intentions. As regards what Wilson really hoped to accomplish, however, a muting of the press campaign against him, nothing much changed. If anything, the strategy may have backfired. French newspapers, whether spontaneously or by direction, responded defiantly that their country would not be blackmailed. And the campaign of abuse went on as before.

Wilson tried a much bolder maneuver in early April when the impasse among the Allied leaders brought the conference to what is sometimes called its "Dark Period." As the meetings of the Council of Four dragged on day after day with no sign of progress—indeed, no official word at all about what was happening behind the closed doors—a mounting restiveness gripped Europe and the United States. French newspapers, of course, blamed Wilson for the delay. Suspicions deepened even among American reporters, and from Tumulty came concerned reports about the uneasiness building up at home. "There is great danger to you in the present situation," he cabled the president on March 25. "I can see signs that our enemies here and abroad would try to make it appear that you are responsible for delay in peace settlement and that delay has increased momentum of bolshevism and anarchy in Hungary and Balkans. Can responsibility for delay be fixed by you in some way?"[110]

Wilson responded to this appeal by authorizing Baker to issue a press release on March 27 denying that the League of Nations was holding things up. As to the actual problem—exorbitant French demands for security and compensation—he preferred to remain silent lest anything he say heighten the host country's intransigence. But Baker prevailed on him for permission to leak the truth to at least a few reporters in order to counter the negative publicity at home. The dispatches that people like Swope and Oulahan sent out helped to ease the pressure somewhat, although they did nothing to budge the French.

So matters stood when on April 3, not so much tired as ravaged, every ounce of strength exhausted, Woodrow Wilson collapsed. "The attack was very sudden," Admiral Grayson wrote to Tumulty a week later. "At three o'clock, he was apparently all right; at six he was seized with violent paroxysms of coughing which were so severe and frequent that it interfered with his breathing. He had a fever of 103. . . . I was at first suspicious that his food had been tampered with, but it turned out to be the beginning of an attack of influenza. . . . His condition looked very serious."[111] Wilson had obviously pushed himself beyond the limit of endurance. The strain had finally caught up with him.

With the United States and France at an impasse, Europe virtually in anarchy, the press in the Allied countries clamoring for a settlement, and at this critical juncture Wilson suddenly incapacitated, catastrophe seemed imminent. "The President must in some dramatic way clear the air of doubts and misunderstandings and despair which now pervade the whole world situation," Tumulty cabled frantically on April 5. "Only a bold stroke by the President will save Europe and perhaps the world. . . . He has tried to settle the issue in secret; only publicity of a dramatic kind now can save the situation. This occasion calls for that audacity which has helped him win in every fight."[112]

Wilson, although still seriously ill, attempted the bold stroke on the Saturday evening Tumulty's cable arrived. He authorized Admiral Grayson to leak to Richard Oulahan of the *New York Times* that he had summoned the *George Washington* to take him home. Grayson asked only that the reporter delay a day before filing his story, presumably to allow time for the order to go out.[113]

Wilson had flirted often enough in the past with leaving the conference to suggest that the summons of the liner was not entirely a bluff. On at least one occasion after the February threat to move the conference out of Paris, for example, he spoke to Ray Stannard Baker about possibly pulling out himself.[114] But the way Wilson handled the announcement indicates that his immediate purpose was to break the impasse of the past few weeks through a dramatic gesture. Although he would sail for home if he must, likely he hoped that the leak would make the trip unnecessary. Even Oulahan recognized the underlying strategy. "Now far be it from me," the *Times* reporter wrote several years later, "to say President Wilson and Admiral Grayson knew that . . . a translation of my dispatch would be quickly communicated to the French Government. And further still be it far from me to say that President Wilson had a shrewd conviction that my dispatch would create the impression in the minds of the other members of the Big Four that he meant business in sending for the *George Washington*. But as things turned out there was modification of the proposed terms of peace to which he objected and President Wilson remained to sign the Versailles Peace Treaty in behalf of the United States."[115]

The story broke in the *New York Times* on Monday under a six-column headline: "WILSON SUMMONS HIS SHIP, THE GEORGE WASHINGTON."[116] By evening every paper in the United States had the bulletin splashed across its front page. Viewed as an attempt to use news to influence policy, it received interestingly different treatment in the American and French press. Newspapers in the United States pulled out all stops. The *Times*, for example, followed up on its Monday report with a banner headline in the Tuesday edition: "PEACE CONFERENCE AT CRISIS, EARLY RESULTS EXPECTED; WILSON'S PLANS FOR RETURN INTERPRETED AS WARNING." For the rest of the week the story dominated the paper's front page. Most major American dailies responded the same way. The *New York World* also went with a banner headline on Tuesday: "WILSON WARNS HE WILL MAKE NO MORE CONCESSIONS . . . TENSIONS GROWING IN PARIS."[117] Although more restrained in its treatment, the three-column headline in the *Washington Post*—"WILSON DETERMINED TO CONCEDE NO FURTHER: SENDS FOR SHIP"—left no doubt that a major development had occurred.[118] "WILSON READY TO WITHDRAW IF SELFISH AIMS PRE-

VAIL," the *St. Louis Post-Dispatch* added. "FIGHTING SPIRIT SAID TO BE AROUSED, AND HE WILL INSIST ON STICKING TO 14 POINTS—LIKELY HIS VIEW WILL WIN."[119]

By contrast, the news barely qualified as filler material in the French press. An item buried on page four of *Le Temps* on the afternoon of April 8, that "President Wilson has telegraphed for the *George Washington,* now in the United States, to leave for Brest," constituted the entire report.[120] The paper offered no editorial comment. In subsequent issues it published only brief allusions, without explanation, to Wilson's possible departure before the completion of the conference. Nothing in the reports suggested a crisis in the negotiations. *Petit Parisien* carried a terse statement on April 8 that Wilson had cabled for the *George Washington,* and another on April 9 quoting Joseph Tumulty and Assistant Secretary of the Navy Franklin Roosevelt as denying the report. *L'Echo de Paris* and *Le Petit Journal* each made do with one minor blurb. None at all appeared in *Le Journal. Le Matin* referred fleetingly to the story in its issues of April 8, 9, and 10, but mainly to deride the "ridiculous rumors" it saw as emanating from the Hearst press.[121]

Who, then, won the battle of the news leak? Clearly, Wilson, in playing against a stacked deck, accomplished little in influencing French opinion. The message he hoped to convey—that Clemenceau's refusal to moderate his demands threatened to destroy the conference—simply didn't get across.[122] The president remained, as he had been right along, the impractical one standing in the way of realistic solutions. Moreover, as *Le Temps* reminded its readers on April 12, he was a man who had been politically repudiated in his own country. It may even be that the intense coverage of the story in the United States also worked against him. Assuming Tumulty still knew how to read public opinion, people at home evidently were not responding well to the threatened departure. "The ordering of the *George Washington* to return to France," he cabled on Wednesday, April 9, "looked upon here as an act of impatience and petulance on the President's part and not accepted here in good grace by either friends or foes. . . . Withdrawal most unwise and fraught with most dangerous possibilities here and abroad. . . . The President should not put himself in the position of being the first to withdraw. . . . Rather he should put himself in the position of being one who remained at the Conference until the very last, demanding the acceptance of his 14 principles. . . . A withdrawal at this time would be a desertion."[123]

The other part of the equation, however, is that the *George Washington* story may have contributed—as Ray Stannard Baker and Henry Dexter White both argued—to the breaking of the logjam at the conference in the days immediately following.[124] It is noteworthy that the same Paris newspapers that ignored Wilson's threat to leave were at the same time uncharacteristically conciliatory on the issues dividing the heads of state. On April 8, for example, *Le Temps* denied French annexationist designs on the Saar in a statement almost certainly inspired by the Foreign Office. "We say so all the more willingly," the paper declared, "because the political policy of *Le Temps* has always been to discourage annexationist ambitions."[125] Perhaps the leak did cause sober second thoughts among the negotiators about what would happen if they failed to reach an agreement. The only certainty is that during the second and third weeks of April Wilson and Clemenceau managed to work out compromises—true neither to the Fourteen Points nor to French aspirations—on the thorny issues between them.

But by that time months of negative publicity had already done the damage. The irony of the news system adopted in Paris—official secrecy, with rumors and leaks filling the void—is that the heads of state responsible for the secrecy were probably the big losers in the long run. Public opinion might have been more patient with them, even sympathetic, if it had been instructed in the complexities of the peace-making. A policy of openness might also have put greater pressure on the negotiators to compromise their differences. And even if this is asking too much of what an informed citizenry can accomplish, almost certainly the results of candor would not have been worse than the sullen spirit that secrecy bred. The sad part is that Woodrow Wilson, who went into the conference with loftier ideals than the other leaders, ended up paying the heaviest price for the betrayal of those ideals.

The dispatches back to the United States were almost uniformly negative. Reporting that had first turned sour when newsmen saw their hopes for a new kind of diplomacy dashed (people who pride themselves on being cynics often do take the heavier fall when their innocence is exposed) grew all the more mean-spirited as details of the agreements started to become public, few of them having much to do with the Fourteen Points. Americans did not read about nations coming together to advance democratic goals. The conference described in their newspapers stood for politics as usual, played by the old rules for the old selfish ends. Tumulty repeatedly urged the president to act on the problem by granting interviews to influential journalists and acknowledging helpful articles, but always to no avail. The secretary "was pessimistic about the reports from Paris," his biographer wrote. "He realized that the fault was not Creel's or Baker's; it lay with Wilson."[126] Which is to say, it lay with a president who despite the rhetoric throughout his career had never learned to work with a free press. This time the weakness mattered, as even Ray Stannard Baker admitted. "In the afterlook," the aide wrote, "such failure as Wilson suffered at Paris was largely a failure of intelligent and determined publicity."[127]

As if the president had not created difficulties enough for himself in his approach to the press, he managed with the last decision for secrecy also to antagonize the United States Senate. The body charged with ratifying the treaty obviously wanted to know at first opportunity what the document contained. Certainly it would not respond well to being among the last to find out. Considering the strained feelings caused by Wilson's failure to include any senators in the American peace delegation, the sensitivities of lawmakers on the subject were worth taking seriously. This is why several of the president's advisers urged on him the wisdom of early publication of the treaty in order to undercut any talk of secrecy and to forestall the possibility of a leak. But Wilson agreed with the Allied leaders that a treaty should not be made public until the time came to submit it for ratification. Prior to formal presentation of the document to the Senate, he felt, it remained only a draft subject to further revision by the negotiators. A state paper at that stage did not belong in the public domain. Hence his anger at discovering that a copy of the treaty had been sent to the State Department in April, which seemed almost a way of asking for premature release. The president sternly instructed Lansing to assume personal responsibility for seeing that not a word about it leaked out of the department.

On Wednesday, May 7, the conference met in plenary session to present the treaty to Germany. The same day the American, British, and French press bureaus released to reporters a 12,000 word summary they had prepared jointly (the treaty itself ran to 75,000 words) covering the high points of what the document contained. There was much to say for this attempt to satisfy public curiosity until the actual ratification process could begin two months later. It represented a rare example of Allied cooperation, and had the further virtue of being a thoroughly professional job as regards accuracy.

But the strategy of using a summary to forestall publication of the real thing proved almost immediately to be a blunder. Too many people were involved in the arrangement who had no reason to cooperate. The Germans, shocked at the harsh terms imposed upon them, promptly leaked the treaty to the press, and by late May copies were routinely available on European newsstands. It was only a matter of time before the document surfaced in the United States as well, thus assuring that the Senate would indeed be the last to receive it.

The inevitable happened on June 8 when the *Chicago Tribune* ran extensive extracts from a version even more complete than that provided by Germany, which its Paris bureau chief had cajoled out of a minor functionary in the Chinese delegation by persuading him that the newspaper wished to help publicize the inequities of the Shantung settlement. Frazier Hunt, a *Tribune* war correspondent passing through Paris on his way back to the United States, was delegated to take the document with him, and he received the byline credit for one of the major news breaks in covering the conference.[128] His story, which also appeared syndicated the next day in the *New York Times,* could not have done much to soothe the ruffled feelings of the lawmakers. "While the Senate is fuming at its inability to get a copy of the treaty of peace with the Central Powers," Hunt wrote as his lead, "and the whole country is amazed at the refusal of the administration to . . . make known to the people of America the treaty terms, which are already known to the people of the conquered countries, I am able to present one of the original copies of the document."[129]

To make matters worse, the Senate learned at the same time that copies of the treaty were also circulating on Wall Street. Assuming that somebody in the American commission must be the source, and wanting to embarrass the president, the Foreign Relations Committee subpoenaed six financiers—including J. Pierpont Morgan, Jacob Schiff and Thomas Lamont—to appear in Washington to explain how they were obtained. Wilson had no choice but to endorse the subpoenas. "I am heartily glad that you have demanded an investigation with regard to the possession of texts of the treaty by unauthorized persons," he cabled Senate Minority Leader Gilbert Hitchcock from Paris. "I hope the investigation will be most thoroughly prosecuted." But the president refused to budge on releasing the treaty to the Senate, despite its already wide circulation. As he explained, "I have felt in honor bound to act in the same spirit and in the same way as the representatives of the other great powers in this matter, and am confident that my fellow-countrymen will not expect me to break faith with them."[130]

Whether that confidence was warranted, by the time he sent the cable the matter had already been taken out of his hands. On June 8, the same day his story appeared in the *Chicago Tribune,* Frazier Hunt traveled to Washington and turned the treaty over to Senator William Borah of Idaho, who started to read from it the next afternoon in the Senate chamber. Immediately a heated debate broke out lasting almost five hours as Wilson loyalists tried to block his maneuver. In the angry mood of the moment to no avail, however. By a vote of 47 to 24 the Senate beat back a motion to interpose. A treaty not yet officially received thereupon became part of the official record.[131]

At that point everything that could possibly go wrong in the handling of news about the peace-making had gone wrong. For months the reporting from Paris had stressed broken promises and flawed idealism. Not even a start had been made toward educating the country about the issues at stake in the postwar world and about America's new global responsibilities. Senators whose support the president vitally needed had been offended by what they construed as cavalier treatment. Although the impact of bungled publicity is impossible to measure, most likely the foundation for future rejection of the treaty had already been laid by the time Wilson returned to the United States in mid-summer for the great struggle of his presidency.

9

The Final Defeat

America gave Woodrow Wilson a hero's reception on Tuesday morning, July 8, when the *George Washington* steamed into New York harbor bringing him home. Tumulty had arranged for a flotilla of battleships and other naval vessels, with aircraft and blimps hovering overhead, to meet the liner and escort it in. The rest of the day consisted of nonstop celebration. Cheering crowds lined the route Wilson's motorcade took to Carnegie Hall for a brief appearance by the president, and there a densely packed throng of 4,000 applauded for minutes before allowing him to speak. Later in the evening another 10,000 partisans showed up at Washington's Union Station to welcome him, and still more waited at the White House grounds. The outpouring of enthusiasm that day, reminiscent of the spirit displayed when Wilson first arrived in Europe, gave every indication that he had come home to a country prepared to support him on the treaty, and above all, on the League of Nations.

Wilson may have been misled by the crowd reaction and by what seemed at the time to be solid pro-League sentiment throughout the country. Despite the negative dispatches from Paris, majority opinion in the summer of 1919 probably still endorsed the concept of an international organization to prevent future world wars. But the fact of popular approval did not answer all questions. For example, how deep was the commitment? How strong would it be when other matters vied for attention? How much did the people really know about the League of Nations? Most important, did they support Wilson's League or just the idea of a League subject to certain conditions? The battle would hinge on questions like these, and in July 1919 no one really knew the answers.

Opinion in the nation's press illustrated the complexity. A poll taken by *Literary Digest* in April 1919, to which 1,377 editors responded, seemed to indicate overwhelming editorial support. Of the newspapers surveyed, fifty-two percent endorsed the League as proposed, thirty-five percent endorsed it conditionally, and only thirteen percent were opposed. In no section of the country did more than sixteen percent of the editors come out against; in some it was as few as seven percent.[1] Better yet, Wilson had the most prestigious dailies on his side: in New York City the *Times* and *World* and *Evening Post;* in Boston the *Globe* and *Christian Science Monitor;* in Philadelphia the *Inquirer* and *Public Ledger;* in Baltimore the *Sun;* in the South the *Atlanta Constitution* and *Louisville Courier-Journal;* in the Midwest the *St. Louis Post Dispatch* and *Des Moines Register;* in the Far West the *Rocky Mountain News* and *San Francisco Bulletin.*[2]

But looked at another way, the poll also suggested troubles ahead for Wilson. He wanted the League covenant in exactly the form he had written it. When the French ambassador, for example, suggested certain minor changes that would placate Senate critics and yet be acceptable to his government and the British government, the president bridled: "Mr. Ambassador," he said sternly, "I shall consent to nothing. The Senate must take its medicine."[3]

If he felt that way, the interesting finding in the *Literary Digest* survey was not how many newspapers were for the League, for with reservations, or against, but the combined strength of those against and those setting conditions for their approval. Wilson made both groups his enemies. And when considered as a bloc a very different picture of press attitudes emerged. Suddenly only in the South did the president enjoy majority support, largely for partisan reasons. In New England fifty-eight percent of newspapers opposed him; in New York, New Jersey and Pennsylvania fifty-four percent; in Indiana, Illinois, Ohio, Michigan and Wisconsin fifty-two percent; in the Plains States fifty-four percent; in the Mountain States fifty-three percent; on the West Coast fifty-two percent. These hardly represented lopsided majorities against him, but were worth taking seriously on an issue where he needed a two-thirds vote in his favor.

Wilson also would have done well to consider the important audiences some of his adversaries in the press reached. William Randolph Hearst's opposition, predicated on a primitive anglophobia, could have been predicted, but still mattered in fanning the already heated resentments of millions of Irish- and German- and Italian-American voters. The same applied to the *Chicago Tribune,* a paper with enormous influence in the Midwest. At the opposite end of the spectrum the defection of liberal publications like the *Nation* and *New Republic* also posed problems. In their case opposition to the treaty (and by extension the League it encompassed) arose from disillusionment with its punitive spirit and failure to pay more than lip service to the Fourteen Points. Although the journals involved did not circulate among a vast number of people, they reached the very ones Wilson could least afford to lose. Oswald Garrison Villard of the *Nation* and Herbert Croly of the *New Republic* spoke to the well educated, to opinion makers, above all, to men and women of liberal temperament who ordinarily would be the staunchest supporters of a League of Nations. Any erosion among that group would hurt badly.[4]

In short, Wilson had to overcome more of a publicity disadvantage than he perhaps realized. And he did not start out well. His appearance before the Senate on Thursday afternoon, July 10, to present the treaty turned out to be an opportunity lost as regards stirring the country through oratory. The president may have been handicapped by the special circumstances of this appearance. For the first time he addressed a Republican Senate, one he had urged the country the previous October not to elect. Moreover, it was a Senate more than a bit miffed at being among the last to receive the treaty. Whether the strained mood in the upper chamber had anything to do with the outcome, or whether Wilson was simply tired, he did not perform particularly well on this occasion. Only at the very end of the speech, when he dramatically set aside his script and turned to the Republican side of the chamber, did the president approach the lyricism which had so often sustained him in the past. "The stage is set," he declared, "the destiny disclosed. It has come about by no plan of our conceiving, but by the hand of God, Who led us into this way. We cannot turn back. We can only go forward, with lifted eyes and freshened spirit to follow the vision. It was of this that we dreamed at our birth. America shall in truth show the way. The light streams upon the path ahead and nowhere else."[5]

Many members of his party were deeply moved, or professed to be. "I think that in breadth of vision," Senator John Williams of Mississippi said later to reporters, "the address is the greatest thing that the President has ever uttered, and when I say that, that means the greatest thing ever uttered by any President of the United States since Lincoln died." But by and large Republicans found the talk uninformative and fuzzy. "Soap bubbles of oratory and souffle of praises," Senator Frank Brandegee of Connecticut remarked. Senator George Norris of Nebraska detected only "a fine lot of glittering generalities." To Senator Medill McCormick of Illinois, the president had been "soothing, mellifluous, and uninformative."[6]

More revealing than these partisan reactions was the agreement among spectators in the gallery that somehow Wilson's appearance had not come off. "The President's address was heard with the keenest interest by his splendid audience," the pro-League *New York Times* reported, "but it was heard in silence. He was not at his best in the delivery of his speech. . . . Several times during the first half of his address he dropped a word in reading the typewritten copy, on small cardboards, which he held in his hand, and then reread these sentences."[7] It had not turned out to be the kind of personal triumph that would generate momentum for ratification.

Nor did Wilson come out ahead when he agreed to meet with the Senate Foreign Relations Committee at the White House on August 19 to answer questions, on the record, about the treaty. It was understood that although the press would not be present in the East Room during the grilling, verbatim transcripts would be released pages at a time as quickly as stenographers could prepare them. Almost one hundred correspondents overflowed the West Wing lobby to record the great confrontation. The three-and-a-half hour meeting, followed by what must have been a strained lunch, ended more or less in a draw. Wilson proved to be patient, and often candid, in fielding the senators' queries.[8] "Never before did the President show himself more tactful or more brilliant in repartee," the adoring Tumulty wrote.[9] But even if he did hold his own, the further fact is that nobody emerged from the session with opinions changed. Nor were press accounts of the interrogation, difficult in any case to wade through, likely to sway opinion. Wilson may even have been a net loser in dissembling on the secret treaties, denying knowledge of them until he arrived in Europe. The claim was far-fetched, and if true hardly reflected credit on him. The president is either an incompetent or a liar, the *New Republic* snarled, stating the two unfortunate possibilities.[10]

Wilson clearly had to take the initiative in rallying public support to his side. One way would have been to work closely with the press, feeding it a daily dosage of stories on the importance of the League of Nations. The many concerns about American involvement in an international organization could easily have been addressed through this forum: Was the method of representation fair? How much of sovereignty would the United States surrender? How great an obligation assume? A major function of the presidency is to explain in what direction the country must go, why it must do so, and at what cost. A major instrument for such instruction is the daily newspaper. Theodore Roosevelt had already demonstrated that much.

But Wilson was not the man to work closely with reporters, and in any event too much had probably happened between them by the summer of 1919 to make the collaboration feasible. He had his own method for leading public opinion, one that had served him well on numerous occasions in the past. This president would arouse the people through oratory. The press had no choice but to report his speeches, so in a way the whole country would hear him. And hearing, the country would respond.

Although Wilson first started to think of a speaking tour across the United States months before he returned from Europe, the discouraging failure to build momentum behind the treaty during July and August—the sense that support might even be slipping away—finally decided the matter. Certainly it was not a trip he wanted to make. His always fragile health had been ravaged by the work load and tensions and recriminations in Paris. Most likely he never fully recovered from the illness in April, and coming home had provided no respite. While struggling with the Senate over the treaty he also had to expend precious time and energy to avert a threatened railroad strike, all in the suffocating heat of a Washington summer. He started to suffer severe headaches; at one point in late July an attack of dysentery felled him. Visitors to the White House were shocked to notice the gray pallor to his skin and twitching of his face muscles. "I know that I am at the end of my tether," he said one day to Tumulty.[11] And he was. Wilson at sixty-three had suddenly become very old and very infirm. But the failure to use publicity over the past eight months to rally support for the treaty meant that the task would now have to be accomplished through a single, dramatic stroke. He probably had already made up his mind about what had to be done when a delegation of Democratic senators visited him in the White House in late August and urged a speaking tour through the West as the only way to save the League.

Whether the strategy was wise is another matter. Even if he did make converts on the trip, the impact upon senators elected for six years would not have been immediate. And the possibility of instant conversion among the electorate was itself problematical. Presidential use of publicity, whatever form it takes, must be a cumulative process, both in winning public support and in translating the support into political power. Wilson hoped to accomplish too much too quickly through personal appearances. It is not even clear, as some historians have speculated, that things would have turned out much differently had radio been available to him.[12] Minds are simply not changed overnight. Moreover, by late summer, 1919 the signs all indicated that the president would have to make some concessions—if only minor ones—to put together a two-thirds coalition of senators behind the treaty. He belonged in Washington, bargaining as closely as he ever bargained in Paris to round up the votes. The decision to leave the city served only to remove him from the center of action.

At 7:00 P.M. on Wednesday, September 3, President and Mrs. Wilson embarked from Union Station on a 10,000-mile trip scheduled to last twenty-seven days and to include forty major addresses. With the South already solid and the East in firm Republican control, the president intended to visit the areas where gains might be made: the Midwest (save for Chicago, where the *Tribune* and Hearst press held sway) and the Far West, which had provided the essential support against Charles Evans Hughes in 1916. A special train of seven cars—their red Pennsylvania Railroad colors looking out of place beyond the Mississippi—had been put together for the tour. Wilson and his wife traveled at the rear of the train in a dark blue private coach named the "Mayflower" after the presidential yacht.

Things went reasonably well at the beginning. The reception he received traveling through Ohio, Illinois, Indiana, and Missouri was warm if not fervent, about as good as could be expected in an area populated largely by German-Americans with strong Republican ties. During those early days Wilson also made himself available to newsmen more than he had for years. A group of about thirty correspondents accompanied him, including some of the best-known names in the business. James Hagerty, whose son would become press secretary to Dwight Eisenhower and president of ABC News, drew the assignment for the *New York Times*. The *New York World* was represented by Louis Siebold and the *New York Evening Post* by David Lawrence, both among the president's strongest sympathizers in the press. Two men who later rose to high administrative positions in their agencies, Byron Price of the Associated Press and Hugh Baillie of United Press, provided wire coverage, as did Jack Neville of International News Service and J. Jerome Williams of Universal. In all, they comprised a promising group for the president as regarded the level of reporting he could expect.

Wilson demonstrated his new affability early in the trip. Following the first of his rear platform talks at Richmond, Indiana, the president strolled to the press car to greet the correspondents he knew and introduce himself to the rest. He positively exuded good will. "What are you writing, Baillie?" the United Press representative recalled Wilson saying to him when they had been introduced. "'Mr. President,' I replied, 'I am writing the story of your speech back there at Richmond, Indiana.' 'Aha!' said he, grinning widely. 'I'm glad to see you writing it after, not before!' And, chuckling, he went down the aisle, kidding the other reporters."[13] The first lady's generosity in sharing with them the overflow of foodstuffs presented to the president at almost every stop provided another nice personal touch. "Mrs. Wilson always sent the surplus back to the diner where we ate," Baillie wrote, "and the usual opening gambit when we sat down to a meal was, 'What is Mrs. Wilson offering today?' "[14] Tumulty, meanwhile, helped to keep the press in good humor by attending to routine details with the old efficiency. Twenty-four hours before each stop, for example, the reporters received a "maneuver sheet" prepared by advance men in the different cities outlining the president's itinerary minute by minute.

But the greatest boon was that from the beginning, before absolute exhaustion set in, the president met several times with them in the club car for off-the-record conversations of a sort highly uncharacteristic for him. As Baillie described those encounters, "they were surely the most informal of their kind ever held—more like bull sessions than press con-

ferences. Wilson would sit somewhere around the middle of the car, with
the reporters about him, and we would all gab and argue together—as
though the President were one of the reporters himself. We'd ask him the
questions that were most agitating the opposition. . . . [He] would answer
without palavering or hemming and hawing. He'd reach over and tap you
on the knee and say, 'Now, look here,' and argue nose-to-nose with any
member of the press corps."[15] For a few days in those conversations
Wilson came as close as he ever had to enlisting reporters into his camp.

The troubles started in the second week of the tour; by which time the
president had reached Idaho, the home of one of his most implacable foes,
William Borah. On September 12 William Bullitt, a former member of the
American Peace Delegation, testified before the Senate Foreign Relations
Committee about a conversation he had with Secretary of State Lansing
the previous May subsequent to resigning his commission out of disillusionment with the treaty. He said that Lansing agreed with him that many
of the provisions were "thoroughly bad." According to Bullitt, the secretary also thought the League of Nations "useless," and declared that
"if the Senate could only understand what this treaty means and if the
American people could really understand it would unquestionably be defeated."[16]

The testimony caused a sensation, relegating even Woodrow Wilson to
secondary space on the front pages of the nation's press. Bullitt could
not have picked a worse time to reminisce; just when the tour seemed to
be developing momentum. The real horror was that his account turned
out to be essentially accurate. A nervous telegram from Lansing on September 16 acknowledged that such a conversation had taken place, which
meant that any attempt to issue a public clarification would only compound
the embarrassment. "My God!" the distraught president said to Tumulty.
"I did not think it was possible for Lansing to act in this way."[17]

As an immediate consequence of the bombshell the mood between
Wilson and the press started to change. He refused to answer their questions about Bullitt's testimony. "Tensions on the train grew noticeably,"
Baillie recalled; "Wilson, suspicious and much on his guard, looked grave
indeed."[18]

By the time he reached the West Coast—ironically, where the cheers
turned out to be loudest—his physical condition had also deteriorated to
an alarming extent. The agonizing headaches were back; he suffered constant pain from neuritis of the shoulder; he barely picked at his food. And
in Portland, Oregon, a tragic accident occurred that only added to the
strain. On the afternoon of Monday, September 15, Wilson went on a
fifty-mile automobile outing along the Columbia River highway hoping to
refresh himself prior to his appearance that evening at the fully-booked
Civic Auditorium. While moving along at high speed one of the cars in

the presidential motorcade went out of control, killing a reporter and seriously injuring another. The dead man, Ben Allen, had been an active participant in the club car bull sessions of just a few days before. The incident obviously did nothing to soothe the president's nerves, and somehow seemed to symbolize the ugly cloud hanging over this attempt to appeal to the idealism of the American people.

Wilson had ceased by now to be open with the press. Only two days before Allen's death, in Seattle, the correspondents received an indication of just how much things were returning to normal. While waiting outside the president's suite in the Hotel Washington to interview local leaders in conference with him about the League, they were surprised when a Secret Service agent threw open the double doors and ushered them in. Wilson invited them to sit along one side of the room during the meeting, and to take notes if they wished. The reporters scribbled furiously during the frank exchange that followed. When it ended, Wilson turned to them and announced in a firm voice, "Of course, everything that has been said here is in confidence. And . . . I will expect my friends of the press, who have been my guests here, to observe that confidence." The information they could have gotten by interviewing participants after the meeting was thus put nicely beyond their reach. "By letting us in," Hugh Baillie commented, "the President had locked us out of the story."[19]

Despite his physical decline and greater distance from reporters, Wilson enjoyed a personal triumph on the West Coast. Buoyed by crowd enthusiasm, he came closer than he had earlier in the tour to recapturing the eloquence of a better time. It made for a good press to be preaching to the already committed, inspired by their adulation to soaring words. The only problem, as he must have realized himself, was that none of the senators back East seemed to be paying attention.

By now, moreover, the strain was starting to tell on him. His appearance in San Diego on September 18 had been particularly grueling. He addressed the largest audience to date in that city: 50,000 people jammed into Balboa Stadium. The setting required that he use a public address system, something no president had ever tried before and which seemed in some ways to unsettle Wilson. He had to stand within a glass cage at an exact distance from the microphone chalked out for him on the platform. His lips compressed in a tight, white line betrayed the annoyance he felt as technicians fussed over him and fiddled with their equipment. Finally, with the introductions completed and the audience quieted down after a prolonged ovation, the president stood alone in the hushed stadium ready to speak. At that moment the dah-dee-dah-dah of the telegraph in the press area cut through the silence. The enraged Wilson wheeled on the culprit, pointed his finger, and exclaimed, "STOP–THAT–ELECTRICAL–INSTRUMENT!"[20] Unfortunately, his positioning turned out to be too good. Those were the first presidential words ever to come booming over a loudspeaker.

He completed the speech without further incident, and moved on immediately to keep the next appointment. But this time, at Admiral Grayson's insistence, the train stopped between San Diego and Los Angeles to allow Wilson to spend one night at least in the quiet of a hotel. If the therapy was pathetically inadequate to the need, it represented the best that could be arranged in view of the president's tight schedule. And even that brief rest evidently did him good. The reporters traveling with him agreed that his two speeches the next day before enthusiastic crowds in Los Angeles were the most effective he had delivered so far. After a slow start Wilson seemed to be hitting his stride.

The train then turned eastward on the last leg of the journey, through Utah and Wyoming into Colorado. Wilson's final speech, at Pueblo on September 25, may have been the most moving on the tour. He had intended to say only a few words, but as had happened several times before, crowd enthusiasm pumped life into his ravaged body. Drawing on the last reserve of strength, the president delivered a long and eloquent address on his dream that nations would henceforth settle their disputes through law rather than battle. He spoke of the graves of American soldiers he had visited in France, and pleaded that future presidents not be required to send young men across the ocean to be buried beside them. "I believe . . . we will see the truth, eye to eye and face to face," Wilson declared. "There is one thing that the American people always rise to and extend their hand to, and that is the truth of justice and of liberty and of peace. We have accepted that truth and we are going to be led by it, and it is going to lead us, and through us the world, out into pastures of quietness and peace such as the world never dreamed of before."[21] Few who heard the words could have come away unimpressed.

The presidential train moved on that afternoon, headed for the next scheduled stop at Wichita. Only three miles out of Pueblo, however, it pulled into a siding at a place called Baxter, little more than a dot on the map. Tumulty announced to the reporters that President and Mrs. Wilson, accompanied by Admiral Grayson (and of course the ubiquitous Edmund Starling of the Secret Service), had decided to take a walk. They wanted quiet, which meant that the press would not be allowed to tag along. If anything newsworthy happened on the stroll, Grayson would report back to the correspondents. Unhappy at being excluded, but unable to do anything about it, the newsmen sprawled on the grass beside the train and watched as the Wilsons debarked from their car and disappeared up a country road. They stayed away longer than expected—almost two hours. And when they neared the train Wilson and Grayson broke into a trot, the president grinning as he mounted the rear platform. It seemed that he would be all right after all. The press had no way of knowing that Grayson had suggested the walk as a last desperate measure to pull his patient back from the abyss.

The next morning the train stopped on the outskirts of Wichita to meet the welcoming committee for the usual triumphal procession into the city. To the reporters everything seemed to be normal. A line of cars was parked along the road to carry the presidential party in. Flags and banners floated everywhere. Little girls in starched dresses waited patiently to present the president with flowers, and local dignitaries to shake his hand. Friday, September 26, shaped up as just another hectic day on the tour.

But this time Wilson did not appear. During the night his fragile system had at last given out. He had called for his wife, complaining of an unbearable headache, and asked her to summon Grayson. When the doctor arrived he recognized that something was terribly wrong. Nothing he tried seemed to alleviate Wilson's distress. Eventually, unable to find comfort in his cramped sleeping quarters, the president moved to the compartment he used as an office where his wife and physician propped him in a sitting position with pillows. He finally fell into a fitful sleep around dawn. A couple of hours later, when Grayson checked back, the seriousness of the situation became evident. Wilson, again awake, showed signs of loss of motor control, and as well as a perceptible drooping of the left lip. The rest of the tour had to be canceled.

Twenty-three days before, already virtually invalided by the pressures of the previous months and years, the president had embarked on a campaign that would have strained the heartiest constitution. He had traveled 8,000 miles by rail through twenty states, experienced in rapid succession extremes of climate and altitude, spent only one night away from the roar and confinement of the train, delivered thirty-six major addresses averaging about an hour in length, spoken several other times from the rear platform of his car, conferred with local leaders in almost every city he visited, and on the side participated in a numbing sequence of well-meant but exhausting parades and receptions. He finally could go no further. Now, although only his closest associates knew it, he was near death.

Grayson enlisted the help of Tumulty to convince the reluctant president that the tour was over. As soon as Wilson acknowledged the inescapable, the secretary rushed out to inform the newsmen, who were standing outside their car wondering about the delay. "Gentlemen," he said, "we are not going to Wichita. The President is very ill. It will be necessary for us to start back for Washington as soon as the railroad arrangements are completed, and we will go through with no stops other than those that are imperative."[22]

At 11:00 A.M., after reporters had frantically scoured the area for telephones to call in their stories (one had to persuade a watchman to let him into a factory that had been closed for the great day), the train pulled out for the seventeen-hundred-mile trip back to Washington. As it hurtled cross country at full throttle, barely stopping long enough to change overheated engines, blinds drawn in the president's car at every junction to provide privacy from oglers trying to peer in, newsmen kept a round-the-clock vigil for any change in Wilson's condition. The releases Grayson issued to the press through Tumulty hardly told the full truth of the situation. "The President has exerted himself so constantly and has been under such a strain during the last year," an early bulletin declared, "and has so spent himself without reserve on this trip that it has brought on a serious reaction in his digestive organs."[23] A few hours later came a second statement which at least inched closer to the facts. "President Wilson's condition is due to overwork," it reported. "The trouble dates back to an attack of influenza last April, in Paris, from which he has never entirely recovered. The President's activities on this trip have overtaxed his strength, and he is suffering from nervous exhaustion. His condition is not alarming, but it will be necessary for his recovery that he have rest and quiet for a considerable time."[24] Reporters still did not know that even such optimism was unwarranted. Indeed, some of them—no admirers of Wilson—privately questioned the fact of an illness at all, wondering whether he had canceled the tour out of disappointment at its results.

Now was the time for newsmen to break out the whiskey bottles (something that had been discouraged previously), and pass the hours with marathon card games and off-key singing. And as will happen, tension and fatigue encouraged its own silliness. At one point they convened a mock trial in the club car to decide who qualified as "king of the boll weevils," Tumulty's term for people who got on his nerves. They chose—in good spirits—the aide responsible for filing their copy along the route, and roused him from a deep sleep to do a war dance around him. Tumulty climaxed the ceremony by setting on the bewildered victim's head a crown made of baling wire.[25] In the atmosphere of uncertainty even such larks provided a kind of release.

The train reached Union Station at 11:00 A.M. on Sunday, September 28. Gritty to the end, Wilson spurned a wheel chair and walked with his daughter Margaret to the car waiting to take him to the White House. He looked wan and stooped, but not so feeble that bystanders could tell at a glance the seriousness of his condition. Watching the president make his way at a steady pace to the car, even lift his hat to acknowledge the cheers of the crowd at the station to greet him, it was still possible to speculate about his real motives in returning.

The next day ten of the correspondents who had accompanied Wilson on the trip went to the White House by invitation to join the president and his wife for tea. They found only Mrs. Wilson waiting to receive them. She apologized for her husband's absence, explaining that he was still resting from the rigors of the previous few weeks. The first lady did not mention what the previous afternoon had been like when they got back to the White House. "All the rest of that day," she wrote years later, "my husband wandered like a ghost between the study at one end of the hall and my room at the other. The awful pain in his head that drove him restlessly back and forth was too acute to permit work, or even reading. Late in the afternoon we went for a short motor ride; but still the demon of pain pursued him."[26]

The final and crippling stroke came at about 8:00 A.M. on Thursday, October 2, four days after the president's return to Washington. Mrs. Wilson peeked into her husband's room, as she had been doing throughout the night, and found him sitting up in bed trying to reach a water bottle on the table beside him. His left arm hung down limply at his side. At his request she helped him to the bathroom and then rushed off to summon Grayson. While on the telephone Mrs. Wilson heard a slight noise coming from the president's room. She found him slumped unconscious on the bathroom floor. He had suffered a massive cerebral thrombosis, a blood clot in the brain, which had paralyzed the entire left side of his body.

Wilson hovered close to death for the next several weeks. Indigestion, and then a swelling of the prostate gland that caused an obstruction of the urethra and threatened to poison his system, vastly complicated a situation already dangerous enough. At one point physicians warned Mrs. Wilson that unless she gave them permission to operate to remove the obstruction he would be dead within hours. Fearful that he could not survive the surgery, fearful of the consequences of avoiding it, she delayed, and the condition cleared up on its own.

None of this information was released to the press. According to newspaper reports the president had suffered a nervous breakdown, complicated by digestive and prostatic problems. All he needed was a spell of complete rest to be his old self again. "It has been positively stated at the White House," the *New York Times* reported the day following the paralyzing stroke, "that no alarming symptoms have developed, but rather that the President is simply 'worn out' after the tension of the last year. The statement is made that although it will require time and a rest for him to build up, his vitality is by no means exhausted."[27] The next day's paper repeated that "he is mentally keen and active and asks many questions."[28] By the Sunday he was described as positively jocular. "When the President awoke today he joked with Dr. Grayson. The latter, in taking the President's temperature, told him that it was normal. 'My temperature may be normal, but my temper will not continue so if you keep me in bed much longer,' replied Mr. Wilson."[29] And by the Monday they practically had to use force to keep him from returning to work. According to an Associated Press dispatch, "After the best night's sleep he has had since he was taken ill ten days ago, the President was in such good spirits that Rear Admiral Cary T. Grayson, his personal physician, had difficulty in persuading him to remain in bed. The physician insisted on this point, however, and indicated he had no intention of permitting the patient to get on his feet until the change in his condition was more decisive."[30]

Secretary of the Navy Josephus Daniels claimed that Wilson, when he first recovered consciousness, made his wife and Grayson promise that if he should prove to be seriously ill the facts would not be made public.[31] Presumably the president worried about further unsettling the country at a time of labor unrest and rocky transition into the postwar era. He must have had in mind also the possibility of political enemies invoking the disability clause in the Constitution to demand his removal from office. In any event, as Wilson never seemed to learn, secrecy turned out to be a double-edged sword. He could prevent the truth from emerging, but could not prevent wild stories—far more destructive in their impact— from taking the place of truth. "The air of mystery surrounding Wilson's disappearance within the White House was so thick," Hugh Baillie recalled, "that all sorts of rumors were abroad—he was dead, insane, comatose."[32] A widely heard account, for example, alleged that, to prevent him from committing suicide, the president was being confined to the room Theodore Roosevelt had used as a nursery, and for the safety of the children equipped with window bars. What could have been predicted as well, in the atmosphere of uncertainty endless speculation went on as to who was really running the country.

One of the difficulties during those tense weeks was that Tumulty didn't know himself the details of Wilson's condition. He knew about the stroke, of course, and evidently shared the information with friends among the White House correspondents, swearing them to secrecy. "Many of us were informed in strict confidence . . . of the president's sickness," Frederick Essary of the *Baltimore Sun* wrote. "We knew that he had suffered a mild 'stroke' while on the train approaching Wichita, Kansas. We knew that he had suffered a still more alarming stroke a few days after he returned, and we knew that his physicians and his family feared that any moment he might be stricken a third time and that such a development in all probability would be fatal. This information, given to us in the most confidential manner, only increased our uneasiness."[33]

Essary had even been brought in to the extent of being asked to carry out a delicate political mission. Feeling that Vice-president Thomas Marshall must be informed of the seriousness of the situation, but reluctant to have a member of the president's official family perform the task lest it seem that death or resignation was imminent, Tumulty enlisted the reporter—an old friend of his and Marshall's—to deliver the message for him. The unprepared and unqualified vice-president nearly buckled under the shock.[34]

But beyond the broad facts Tumulty remained as much in the dark as everyone else. Mrs. Wilson, who had never softened to the secretary, refused to allow him (or, for that matter, any member of the administration) direct access to her husband. Even on matters of state Tumulty had to operate largely on his own. Memoranda he sent through to the president often never got answered, or if replies did come back they were over Mrs. Wilson's signature. In some cases circumstances required that he take personal responsibility for administration policy. Thus, Tumulty wrote and issued the presidential statement on October 25 declaring a threatened strike by half a million coal miners to be "not only unjustifiable; it is unlawful."[35] With the sick-room closed to all but Wilson's wife, doctors, and nurses, the secretary was in no position to brief the press even off-the-record on the president's progress or lack of it. He had no basis to judge. The only information the country received were vague statements about continued improvement, which as the reporters realized only too well may or may not have had much to do with the facts.[36]

Not until February 10, 1920, more than four months after the stroke, did the full story appear in the press. Dr. Hugh H. Young of Johns Hopkins, one of the consulting physicians, released a detailed statement to the *Baltimore Sun*—which the *New York Times* picked up the next day—about what had happened and the prognosis for the president's recovery. Young acted with the approval of the Wilsons, and likely even at their instruction. "The family had realized, after some weeks had passed," Frederick Essary wrote later, "the importance of giving to the public an authoritative account of the President's disability, but did not wish to broadcast it, so to speak. That is why one paper was selected to carry the statement, all others being at liberty to follow it if they chose."[37] The explanation was certainly kind, if a bit tortured. About all it left out was why almost nineteen weeks elapsed before "the importance of giving to the public an authoritative account" occurred to the president.

Even before the public disclosure of the stroke Wilson had lost the first and probably key battle in the struggle for ratification. (Which gives rise to an intriguing thought. He nearly died in fighting for the League; had he actually died on October 2 the possibilities are that a grieving nation would have accepted the treaty as a memorial to him.) The president's enemies had been busy during the summer and fall of 1919. Henry Cabot Lodge, for example, performed a critical function as chairman of the Foreign Relations Committee in dragging out the hearings on the treaty to an almost farcical extent to allow time for opposition to coalesce. The Massachusetts senator devoted two full weeks just to reading aloud the

268 page document, a pace that must have enabled him to enunciate each phrase clearly (although he often spoke to an empty chamber). Six more weeks went into taking almost 1,300 pages of testimony from about sixty witnesses. On September 10, feeling it had covered the ground sufficiently, the committee issued a majority report signed by Lodge and eight fellow Republicans which recommended forty-five amendments to the treaty and four reservations.

By the time the showdown debate began in October, Wilson—now crippled and for all practical purposes out of the fray—had long since dissipated his early advantage. When he first returned to the United States in July majority sentiment still favored the treaty; perhaps as written, at worst with minor revisions. Three months later the situation had changed dramatically. To get ratification at all he would have to make significant concessions to the reservationists. And concessions were beyond the president's ability to contemplate.

In pressing their advantage League opponents could count also on the help of a small group of correspondents who leaped at the chance to translate dislike of Wilson into partisan activity against him. It was not one of the happier moments in the history of American journalism. Not only did these newsmen supply material to the Borahs and Johnsons, they accepted in return handouts from the irreconcilables which they wove into their own copy and even managed to insinuate into the copy of colleagues trying to report the story objectively. The technique was simple enough. At the time (the practice is less common now), reporters often cooperated with each other by sharing carbon copies of their articles, a practice known as black-sheeting. All the anti-Wilson newsmen had to do was generously black-sheet the material made available by League opponents to give it wider and more convincing distribution than would otherwise have been possible.[38] Ray Tucker, the columnist, thought their contribution crucial to the way things finally turned out. He wrote of reporters who "conspired hourly with the 'irreconcilables' and performed service far beyond the call of newspaper duty."

> They tipped off most of the Congressmen to Wilsonian statements and maneuvers, and started Congressional counterattacks before the War President could unlimber his orators. They wrote phillipics for the Borahs, Johnsons, and Reeds, cooked up interviews . . . , carried on research into the League's implications, dug up secret material. Their dispatches bristled with personal hostility to the League, and carbon copies which they distributed to pro-Wilson writers affected even the latter's supposedly favorable articles. The convenant was defeated by the Senate press gallery long before it was finally rejected by the Senate.[39]

While Tucker perhaps exaggerated the power of the press, he certainly had a point that it had ceased to be the docile instrument of Theodore Roosevelt's time.

November 17 was a special day in Wilson's road back from near-death. He had managed in the previous weeks to look over a few papers, occasionally to sign his name to documents (although in a pathetically shaky scrawl), even to receive briefly the king and queen of Belgium. Now for the first time since the stroke he was strong enough to be wheeled out of the White House and spend an hour or so all bundled up on the South Lawn. But Wilson could not have been in a relaxed frame of mind during the excursion, because he knew that the enemies of the League were closing in. The next day he would address a letter to his supporters in the Senate urging them to reject the resolution of ratification Lodge had submitted on November 6 containing fourteen reservations to the treaty. On Wednesday, November 19, the upper chamber would vote. Wilson must have realized as he reclined in his wheel chair looking up at the clear sky how grim things looked.

The vote, coming late in the afternoon after hours of debate, marked the first step toward the president's final defeat. Acting on his instructions, Democratic loyalists joined with the irreconcilables to reject the Lodge reservations 55 to 39. Senator Gilbert Hitchcock of Nebraska, the minority leader and Wilson's field commander in a hopeless cause, moved next for reconsideration of the treaty with five minor reservations, four of which unknown to the Senate had actually been authored by the president before he embarked on the western tour. This time the vote against was 51 to 42. Finally, Senator Oscar Underwood of Alabama moved for ratification of the treaty without any reservations at all. By a decisive majority of 58 to 38, more or less along party lines, the Senate again said no.

Not until March 19, 1920, when the Senate voted one last time on ratification with the Lodge reservations, was the issue finally resolved. Wilson, almost suicidal in his refusal to compromise, still insisted on his version of the treaty or none at all. By now, however, he commanded a restive army. Twenty-one Democrats crossed party lines to accept the best terms left to them. But their defection still wasn't enough. On the final tally the treaty received 49 ayes to 35 nays, seven votes short of the necessary two-thirds majority for ratification. It never came up again.

No single reason explains Wilson's defeat. Perhaps it had been a mistake to leave the country for so many months, however much he wanted to take personal charge of the negotiations. He certainly blundered in not including an eminent Republican, or even a senator, in the American peace delegation. The speaking tour turned out to be wrong in strategy and tragic in its consequences. He should have been in Washington winning support among wavering senators rather than thousands of miles away exhorting the already committed. His rigidity in refusing to accept any compromise, a trait only heightened after the stroke, was also central to the story. But underlying all else may have been a larger failure. Finally, hope turned to ashes for the president because of his inability to work with and through journalists. Overwhelming sentiment built up over the months on behalf of the League would have been difficult to resist in the Senate, if it could have been resisted at all. The mood of the country was essentially sympathetic all along. It remained for Wilson to arouse and channel public opinion until it became a force working for him. The task could only have been accomplished through the press, and had to begin from the first days in Paris and before. Instead, Wilson ignored the publicity function of his office during the critical months, hoping to retrieve everything through last-minute rhetoric. He waited too long.

The last years before his death in February 1924 were spent in bitter isolation at his home on S Street. The election of 1920, a "solemn referendum" on the League issue, had put Warren Gamaliel Harding in the White House, thereby sealing the doom of the noble experiment in internationalism. "In the existing League of Nations," Harding declared on April 12, 1921 in a speech before the joint houses of Congress, "this Republic will have no part."[40] Wilson did not believe that, but he knew that his dream would have to wait for another day.

Just three months before the end, in November 1923, the crippled ex-president spoke to the country for the last time of the faith no political defeat could shake. Bernard Baruch's daughter, Belle, an ardent League advocate, asked him if he would be willing to go on the radio on November 10, the eve of Armistice Day, to renew the appeal for a peace based on international law. Wilson disliked the new medium and had no prior experience using it, but this request he could not turn down. By now only a shell of his former self, he labored for days to prepare remarks scheduled to last less than ten minutes. The speech went badly. His effort to commit the words to memory did not succeed, so he had to read from a typed script which he had trouble seeing. Barely intelligible at the outset, he stumbled along with long pauses, Edith Wilson's prompting audible in the background. At the end, thinking he was off the air, came the almost pathetic words: "That is all, isn't it?" They went out clearly over a network of stations reaching as far north as Providence and Schenectady.[41]

The address probably had a good deal to do with the moving scene outside Wilson's home the next afternoon, when the country celebrated the fifth anniversary since the signing of the armistice. He had spoken the previous day to what at the time was the largest audience in the history of radio, an estimated three million people. And now, as if reminded of his existence, more than 20,000 of the faithful clogged the area around S Street to pay him homage. Pilgrimages to the Wilson residence had become something of a custom on Armistice Day, but never on this scale. At one point the crowd spilled over five city blocks, the chrysanthemums and American flags many of them carried creating a splash of color in the nippy fall weather. Wilson showed the effects of his illness when he emerged from the house in morning coat and top hat to greet the multitude. Only with difficulty did he get through the door, leaning heavily on a thick cane. His hair had turned completely white, and hung down to his neck in a fringe. After the cheers had died down, he thanked them briefly for their support. Toward the end of the two-minute talk his voice choked and he apologized for showing emotion. When he had finished and turned to go back in a band broke into the hymn, *How Firm a Foundation*. Suddenly Wilson stopped, asked for quiet, and in a tone one reporter described as like that of "an implacable prophet out of the Old Testament," delivered a final comment.[42] "Just one word more," he said:

> I cannot refrain from saying it: I am not one of those that have the least anxiety about the triumph of the principles I have stood for. I have seen fools resist Providence before and I have seen their destruction, as will come upon these again—utter destruction and contempt. That we shall prevail is as sure as that God reigns.[43]

Those were the last words he ever uttered in public. They received wide coverage in the press, but another story overshadowed them. According to the three-column headline in the *New York Times* the next day, "HITLER FORCES RALLYING NEAR MUNICH."

10

Conclusion

From George Washington raging at the leak of the Jay Treaty in the late eighteenth century to Richard Nixon staggering under disclosures about his administration in the late twentieth century, much of American political history has hinged on the often stormy relationship between presidents and the press. They are like old antagonists who by mischance find themselves trapped in the same room; they don't get along, but neither can they avoid each other. The squabbling has been going on for almost two hundred years now.

One of the critical phases in this relationship took place during the Progressive era. It was then that both parties experienced great internal changes which in turn changed their dealings with each other. On the one hand, the modern presidency emerged during those years. As power flowed to the office it made the chief executive the focus of national attention in a way he had never been before, save in times of extreme emergency. He became a symbolic as much as political leader: a figure expected to be above petty partisan concerns, and by his presence to instill in the people a sense of unity and confidence and purpose.

But as the office changed so did the status of those who covered the office. A kind of professionalization occurred among Washington newsmen, which involved a heightened awareness of the responsibilities they filled and the standards incumbent upon them to uphold. It is true that much about the press still smacked of police court days, when men entered the calling with scant education and scant prospects for much more than careers as roustabouts. With each year this was less the case, however, just as with each year journalists were less willing to surrender their prerogatives in the face of presidential challenge. The progression could be measured from one administration to the next. Theodore Roosevelt got away with bullying newsmen who displeased him in the first decade of the century; by the second decade newsmen who perceived themselves

266

as being bullied reacted by causing Woodrow Wilson some of his greatest problems at the Paris Peace Conference.

Roosevelt and Wilson, the two men who did most to hasten the transformation of the presidency, had in common perhaps only one thing. Both actively courted power, and both recognized that power in the first instance meant generating the right kind of publicity for themselves. They were the first presidents to base their leadership on direct appeals to the public, and to do so, moreover, using newspapers and magazines as their sole instruments of communication. The game changed with the advent of radio after World War I and television after World War II. What made Roosevelt and Wilson unique were the remarkably sophisticated and modern campaigns of publicity they carried out while working with essentially traditional tools.

Their achievement is all the more impressive considering the special kind of communication involved when a president goes to the people. He must try to reach an audience which is likely to be inattentive unless he can convince his listeners that their own interests are at stake. It is an audience largely unsophisticated about affairs of state, and easily distracted by other concerns. And the president must not only reach the minds of these people, he must reach their hearts. The point of presidential publicity, after all, is only secondarily to spread intelligence. Its real concern is to win converts. Both Theodore Roosevelt and Woodrow Wilson excelled at the art.

Roosevelt started out with an enormous advantage just in being himself: colorful, exuberant, unrestrained in his likes and dislikes, eternally controversial. The word is often abused, but he certainly belongs on the small list of charismatic presidents. Indeed, he was so much the natural newsmaker that contemporaries sometimes overlooked how much artifice went into polishing the Roosevelt image. Not only did he work hard to keep his name and causes in the papers, he used techniques that later generations of journalists came to realize exploited some of the vulnerabilities of their craft.

Reporters were vulnerable simply in having a president go out of his way to cultivate them. The perennial and unanswerable question in journalism is, How close can newsmen get to their source without sacrificing independence? Obviously they want to be as much as possible on the inside, but they also know that in gaining access they are likely to be inhibited both by the personal relationships that develop and by the recognition that they risk losing their privileged position if they print stories the source does not appreciate. The line that must not be crossed is always difficult to draw, and never more so than when covering the White House. No journalist wants to be a lap dog of the administration. On the other hand, few journalists are so blasé that they would shrug at the chance for easy access to the president, sharing his confidences and basking in the glow of his company. Nor should they lightly spurn such an opportunity, since it pays off in the kinds of news reporters most covet.

The temptations to go along were particularly great in Theodore Roosevelt's time, in part because of the novelty in being taken into a president's confidence, and in part also because the press had not yet developed the concern about independence that later took root. And so Roosevelt, by befriending reporters, was able at the same time to manipulate them. They wrote what he wanted, when he wanted, with the form of attribution he wanted. They did so, moreover, with no discernible sense of being used (of course the reporters who did not share their privileges probably thought differently on the matter). It was compensation enough just to belong to the team, to be able to help a man they regarded as a genuinely great president, and in the process to enjoy the not inconsiderable fringe benefit of being made to feel important themselves.

Roosevelt understood something else about modern journalism that also contributed to his success as a publicist. Whatever the sympathies of publishers or reporters, there are certain mechanical aspects to how newspapers are put out that an enterprising president can turn to his own advantage. If he does, the initiative about what appears in the press will rest largely with him. Obviously, the convention that any presidential act or utterance is front page news gives him enormous leverage (not least in enabling him to blanket news coming from other sources). So does the convention that the story must be reported objectively, without interpretive comment. It means that he does not have to worry about backtalk on the front page. He can often influence the amount of space his story receives by releasing it on a slow news day, or alternatively he can bury the story by slipping it out with many other announcements on a busy day. He can prevent reporters from writing follow-ups on the story, or from eliciting comments from political opponents, by timing the release close to the hour papers go to press. He can generally arrange prominent treatment for a story by making it available to one paper as an exclusive, a tribal trophy in the competitive world of journalism that few editors will allow to go unnoticed, The examples go on and on. What they all demonstrate is that the press to a certain extent is locked in by its own rules and conventions. Roosevelt played on those rules brilliantly to convey the image of himself he wanted the country to have.

Wilson went at things somewhat differently, and in a way that made him at once a throwback to presidents who preceded him and a harbinger of what the presidency would become. Often stiff in dealing with people, especially in dealing with the press, he compensated by reviving rhetoric as an instrument of public persuasion. "Eloquence and greatness are by no means the same," a reporter wrote in the Kennedy era, "but in politics the former is almost always the indispensable tool of the latter."[1] One can question whether the aphorism applies as well in the twentieth century as it did in the nineteenth, when speech-making represented a kind of art form and public figures were judged by their mastery of the art. It certainly applied to Wilson, however. With the possible exception of Franklin Roosevelt, he more than any modern president relied on the power of the spoken word to move people. And however old-fashioned the device, they responded to him.

But in another sense the Wilson style can be seen as strikingly modern in its implications. Although he may not consciously have intended it, the leadership he provided leaned heavily on maintaining a distance between the leader and the led. The impact of his appearances before the joint houses of Congress, after all, derived largely from the ceremonial aspect of those occasions. For that matter, all of his formal addresses—the words inspirational rather than home-spun, the setting usually a vast hall with him behind a distant podium—were a barrier to intimacy. When Wilson arranged to see reporters he did so appropriately in another structured setting: the presidential press conference, with established rules and a charged atmosphere arising out of the chief executive's fulfilling an almost constitutional function in appearing before the Washington correspondents. And after the press conferences ended he retired into even greater seclusion by channeling publicity through the CPI. If there was banter and good fellowship in this administration, the president did not participate. He left that side to Joseph Tumulty. But what he did do worked well enough, and in such a way, as to take on some of the characteristics of what later came to be called the imperial presidency.

By that time, however, Wilson in turn had to contend with a corps of capital reporters imbued with their own ideas about the power of the press. It is not surprising that the purveyors of news started to assert themselves. They could hardly be expected to underestimate their own importance when presidents attached so much importance to what they did. Nor is it surprising that they thought in terms of having a function to perform independent of the presidency. If government by publicity was to be the norm, than the role of the press in bringing the full truth to the people, as opposed simply to passing on what the politicians wanted told, mattered more than ever.

Washington correspondents were well situated in several respects to take such responsibility upon themselves. To begin with, they comprised an elite group among journalists. Turner Catledge, who rose to become managing editor of the *New York Times,* described in his autobiography how the men on the copy desk occupied a higher rung on the ladder than news-writers when he first joined the paper. "They made more money and worked more regular hours than reporters, and were more highly valued by most executives. The shift in status came with the proliferation of bylines in the late thirties. The byline gave the reporter increased prestige."[2] That change happened earlier, more or less during the Progressive period, for the correspondents who reported the news from Washington. (Even the bylines started to creep in during the Wilson years.) To be a Richard Oulahan covering the capital for the *Times* meant something; it conferred status not only in the eyes of fellow journalists, but among the people one wrote about.

As influence and visibility came to Washington reporters, they were also in a position to undertake roles arising out of the American form of government that enhanced their stature all the more. One was in serving as a kind of central switchboard for the sprawling federal network. In a parliamentary system, the prime minister is chief legislator and chief executive at once; he brings with him to the legislature full information about affairs of state, and even if he chooses on occasion to be less than forthcoming, he is still answerable to an opposition which is in a position to grill him, and, because it has taken its own turn at running the government, knows from first-hand experience what questions to ask. The chamber he appears in, moreover, is the single embodiment of the nation in a way that is impossible when power is divided among three branches. Because the United States lacks an equivalent focus of authority, journalists are called on to play a somewhat more direct role than required elsewhere, almost a quasi-official role, in informing the branches of government what the other branches are up to. The importance of the function may help to explain why the country has been relatively more tolerant than other societies of unauthorized disclosures in the press. The need for unofficial channels of communication within government to supplement the formal channels almost requires such disclosure.

Another consequence of separation of powers and lack of party discipline is that the enactment of legislation tends to be a more drawn-out process than under a parliamentary system, and to entail a more overt appeal to public opinion. Only rarely in the United States can the majority party automatically deliver votes for a program. As seen in the great legislative victories in the Roosevelt and Wilson administrations, and the disastrous setbacks in the Taft administration, campaigns to put through important measures tend to be fought out over months (sometimes even longer), and all along press coverage is a critical element in the maneuvering. Again, reporters of the Progressive era had every reason to feel they mattered.[3]

They responded in a predictable way as prominence came to them. The idea of being just middle men in the transfer of information from officials to the public, a role that entailed little more than a mechanical function, grew increasingly less acceptable. Rather, they started to see themselves as spokesmen for the public; the ones to ask the questions of government leaders the people could not ask directly themselves, and to impress upon the leaders by their questions what the people were concerned about. It followed that failure by officials to make themselves available represented a sin far worse than merely making journalists' work more difficult. As the rancor at the Paris Peace Conference attested, such failure infringed on the "people's right to know."

Journalists also took it upon themselves to be watchdogs against governmental abuse of power. The tradition, of course, is as old as the American newspaper itself: in Jefferson's words, to provide that check on government which no other institution can provide. What changed in the first decades of the twentieth century was that the responsibility became specifically a reporter's responsibility. No longer did it involve simply, or even primarily, writing editorials in opposition to wrongdoing. The challenge now was to ferret out the facts which those who had abused the public trust would prefer to remain hidden. It was in this spirit that the muckrakers went about their work, as did the *New York World* when it tangled with Theodore Roosevelt on the circumstances surrounding the Panama Canal.

With presidents increasingly sophisticated in the uses of publicity as an instrument of leadership, and journalists increasingly alive to their own responsibilities independent of the president, the logic of events put the two on a collision course. Fundamentally different concepts of news motivated them, and to this day neither has yielded an inch to the other. Presidents resent journalists harping on every instance they can find of corruption or incompetence, on the grounds that to devote constant attention to such matters, while taking for granted the many more things done well, is to give a distorted version of the truth. To journalists, on the other hand, stories exposing malfeasance are innately the most newsworthy. Presidents, whose role entails finding ways to accommodate opposing points of view, are offended by what they see as excessive attention to conflict in political reporting. Journalists see such conflict as the key to how decisions are made in a democracy. Presidents who are elected to carry out a program regard the setting of the agenda for national action as their prerogative. Journalists who can bring issues to prominence just by writing about them challenge that prerogative.

Above all, they are antagonists on the matter of access to news. By the nature of the office presidents are always sensitive to the need to hold back information potentially damaging to the national interest (and of course to their own political interest). For reporters, higher priority attaches to the right of the citizenry to know what their leaders are doing with the mandate they have been given, and the right also to influence the leadership before final decisions are made. How many times has free disclosure really jeopardized the national interest, newsmen ask? The cases of secrecy causing harm are legion.

It would be foolish to claim that either side is right or wrong when issues like these are at stake. Not only do presidents and the press come at the debate from entirely different perspectives, they have entirely different interests to defend. About all that can be said is that the debate deals with questions central to the nature of American democracy, and is not the kind that can be resolved by one side proving the other wrong. A great deal depends, as a result, on the debate continuing. The only way to end it would be for one of the parties to silence the other, which of course would mean government silencing the press. If that happened everybody would be the loser.

Notes

CHAPTER ONE

1. An account of the walk, and of Roosevelt's reactions, appears in Lincoln Steffens, *Autobiography*, pp. 502–3. It should perhaps be mentioned that the book is not altogether reliable, and that William Allen White does not mention the episode in his autobiography.

2. *Times* (London), September 16, 1901.

3. Lincoln made the statement in the first debate at Ottawa, Illinois on August 21, 1858. See John G. Nicolay and John Hay, eds., *Abraham Lincoln: Complete Works* 1, p. 298.

4. "The Advance of Fifty Years," *Editor & Publisher* 1 (October 5, 1901):4.

5. J. Lincoln Steffens, "The Business of a Newspaper," *Scribner's Magazine* 22 (October 1897):447.

6. Charles H. George, "New York's Newspapers," *Journalist* 13 (March 21, 1891):5.

7. The figures are drawn from tables in Alfred McClung Lee, *The Daily Newspaper in America*, pp. 748–49.

8. Ibid., pp. 725–26, 728–29.

9. On this point see Daniel Boorstin, "Selling the President to the People," *Commentary* 20 (November 1955):422.

10. The account of the wedding appeared in the *New York Times* on June 3, 1886. For a good example of the honeymoon coverage see the *New York World* for the five or six days following.

11. Joseph B. Bishop, "Newspaper Espionage," *Forum* 1 (August 1886):535.

12. James Parton, "The *New York Herald,* from 1835 to 1866," *North American Review* 102 (April 1866):375–76.

13. David Barry, *Forty Years in Washington*, p. 270.

14. Ralph McKenzie, *Washington Correspondents Past and Present*, pp. 12–13.

15. His comments appear in Charles Wingate, ed., *Views and Interviews on Journalism*, p. 30.

16. See *Historical Statistics of the United States*, p. 207.

17. For a widely discussed article by Joseph Pulitzer arguing the importance of such training, see "The College of Journalism," *North American Review* 178 (May 1904):641–80.

18. Quoted in William Rivers, *The Adversaries*, p. 20. Another comment by Roosevelt on the importance of the working press appears in *An Autobiography*, p. 354.

CHAPTER TWO

1. See, for example, Delbert Clark, *Washington Dateline*, pp. 53–54.

2. The best account of Price's resourcefulness was provided by Harry Godwin's son in a publication put out by the National Press Club. See Earl Godwin, "White Housekeeping," *Goldfish Bowl* 4 (July 1937):1. At the time he write the article Earl Godwin covered the White House for the *Washington Times*. For another account see the obituary on Price in *Editor & Publisher* 64 (October 1931):38.

3. The assignment ended unhappily for Price when he and Frederick Essary, a correspondent for the *Baltimore Sun*, were implicated in a scandal in 1917. A congressional investigation revealed that they had accepted payment from a New York brokerage house for advance information on a note Wilson sent to Germany just prior to America's involvement in World War I. Price was fired by the *Star*, although he signed on shortly after as chief editorial writer for the *Washington Times*. See *Editor & Publisher* 49 (January 13 and February 10, 1917).

4. An account of White House press arrangements in the McKinley administration appears in Ida Tarbell, "President McKinley in War Times," *McClure's* 11 (July 1898):214.

5. The building of the west wing is described in Charles Hurd, *The White House: A Biography,* pp. 225–44. The work was carried out with remarkable speed, but so carelessly that the mansion had to be rebuilt again within a relatively short time. See Louis Brownlow, *A Passion for Politics,* p. 35.

6. During the Spanish American War, however, the Associated Press did have a direct telegraph wire from the White House to its office in the Star Building. See F. B. Marbut, *News from the Capital,* p. 169. Frederick Essary comments on the advantages in having telephones available in *Covering Washington,* pp. 87–88.

7. This is still the case, and an important factor in explaining the pack mentality of modern journalism. For an example from the 1972 election, see Timothy Crouse, *The Boys on the Bus,* pp. 20–23.

8. Quoted in William Rivers, *The Adversaries,* p. 18.

9. The meeting is described in David Barry, *Forty Years in Washington,* pp. 266–68.

10. Louis Brownlow, *Passion for Politics,* p. 399. Lincoln Steffens also wrote of these "barber chair" conferences in his *Autobiography,* pp. 509–10.

11. Oscar Davis described his evening meetings with Roosevelt in *Released for Publication,* p. 128.

12. Brownlow, *Passion for Politics,* pp. 352–53. The quotation appears on page 352.

13. Isaac Marcosson, *Adventures in Interviewing,* pp. 87–88.

14. William Allen White, *Masks in a Pageant,* p. 307.

15. Marcosson, *Adventures in Interviewing,* p. 87.

16. Lincoln Steffens, *Autobiography,* p. 509.

17. Charles Thompson, *Presidents I've Known,* pp. 118–19.

18. Davis, *Released for Publication,* p. 124.

19. Ibid.

20. Essary, *Covering Washington,* p. 121.

21. He was the first president to ride by automobile, starting with his visit to Hartford, Connecticut on August 22, 1902. So was he the first, in 1905, to descend in a submarine, and in 1910, after leaving office, the first to ascend in an airplane.

22. Roosevelt embarked on several such tours, and took in all sections of the country. In the summer of 1902, for example, he visited New England and the Midwest; in spring 1903, the West Coast; in fall 1905, the South.

23. Thompson described Roosevelt's thoughtfulness in *Presidents I've Known,* pp. 142–43. The quotation appears on p. 142.

24. Ibid., p. 146. Jack Pratt was with the *New York American,* Hearst's morning paper, and Lucius Curtis with the Associated Press.

25. See Clark, *Washington Dateline,* pp. 46–47, and Essary, *Covering Washington,* pp. 97–98. John Callan O'Laughlin of the *Chicago Tribune* was another one the president listened

to with respect. In 1907, at the height of the controversy over Japanese immigration into the United States, he appointed the newsman assistant secretary of state in charge of Far Eastern affairs to help work out a solution. See Arthur Krock, *The Consent of the Governed*, p. 225.

26. Oscar Davis acted as intermediary from his managing editor, Carr Van Anda, with a proposal for Roosevelt during his last days in office about joining a newspaper combine in New York City. A group had already been formed to purchase the *New York Sun*, and Van Anda thought that the *Press* might also be available, which if consolidated with the *Sun* would have given that paper complete wire service coverage. Van Anda wanted Roosevelt to come in as editor. Although the president turned the idea down, it clearly fascinated him. He brought it up several times in conversation in later years. Davis believed that the major factor in Roosevelt's decision was that he had already promised his friend, Lyman Abbott, that he would join *Outlook* as a contributing editor after returning from his African safari, and did not want to renege. See Davis, *Released for Publication*, pp. 135–39.

27. Thompson, *Presidents I've Known*, pp. 122–23.

28. Marcosson, *Adventures in Interviewing*, pp. 86–87.

29. Mark Sullivan, *Our Times*, vol. 3, *Pre-War America*, pp. 80–81.

30. Ibid., pp. 72–73. The sentence appeared in J. W. Bennett, *Roosevelt and the Republic*.

31. White, *Masks in Pageant*, pp. 284–85.

32. Steffens, *Autobiography*, pp. 511–12.

33. Butt recounted the conversation in a letter to his mother dated July 26, 1908. See Lawrence Abbott, ed., *The Letters of Archie Butt*, pp. 73–74. Butt was himself a former newspaperman. He covered Washington for the *Louisville Evening Post* and *Nashville Banner* until the outbreak of the Spanish-American War, when he secured an army commission. Rather than return to journalism after the war, he elected to remain in the military and ended with the plush assignment of serving as aide to Roosevelt and later William Howard Taft. He died in April 1912 in the *Titanic* catastrophe, and is now commemorated with a memorial on the south grounds of the White House. Reporters didn't altogether know what to make of their former colleague. Much about him invited ridicule: his short, squat body, his extreme courtliness, his sycophantic attachment to power (or so it sometimes seemed), even his name. Newsmen used to joke that Archibald Willingham de Graffenreid Butt was the only man in the world with a name that sounded like a trunk falling down a flight of stairs. But he was really an extraordinary individual: insightful, kind, loyal. Roosevelt and Taft both relied on him heavily. More than trusting his good judgment and discretion, they valued having him as a friend. It says something about Butt's qualities that he retained the friendship of both men even when they were bitterly feuding with each other. His clear-headedness and lack of malice explain why his letters, particularly to his mother and sister-in-law, Clara, are a major source of information on the Roosevelt and Taft administrations.

34. Barry described the conversation in *Forty Years*, pp. 277–78.

35. The libelous article appeared on October 12, 1912 in *Iron Ore*, a weekly published in Ishpeming on the Upper Peninsula of Michigan. For an excerpt see Henry Pringle, *Theodore Roosevelt*, p. 401. George H. Newett, the paper's editor and defendant in the suit, came to trial on May 26, 1913 in the nearby community of Marquette. Roosevelt brought a parade of character witnesses into court to testify to his sobriety. Some of the reporters covering the trial, who had previously accompanied him on one or more of his campaign trips, also came forward. Two of them have written at length about the trial: see Davis, *Released for Publication*, pp. 417–21, and Thompson, *Presidents I've Known*, pp. 193–97.

36. Sullivan described their meeting in *Our Times* 3, pp. 146–47.

37. An account of the urgent summons to the White House appears in Essary, *Covering Washington*, pp. 95–96.

38. Sullivan, *OurTimes* 3, pp. 71–72.

39. *New York Times,* October 15, 1912.

40. Ibid.

41. *New York Times,* October 17, 1912.

42. Willis J. Abbot, a long-time Hearst employee who in 1921 assumed the editorship of the *Christian Science Monitor* and raised the paper to its present eminence, wrote of Roosevelt's shrewdness on this point in *Watching the World Go By,* p. 244.

43. Arthur Wallace Dunn, *From Harrison to Harding* 2, pp. 24–25.

44. Roosevelt to Major John Pitcher, March 2, 1903; in Elting E. Morison, ed., *The Letters of Theodore Roosevelt* 3, p. 437.

45. Quoted in Pringle, *Theodore Roosevelt,* p. 243.

46. Roosevelt may have had a personal as well as political motive for the policy. His mother had been from Georgia, and despite his lack of sympathy for the Confederate cause, he did feel a tie to the region.

47. The only other guest to join Washington and the Roosevelt family at the dinner was Philip Bathell Stewart, a mining and utilities executive and frequent hunting companion of the president's. For extended accounts of the controversy see Louis R. Harlan, *Booker T. Washington: The Making of a Black Leader, 1856–1901,* and Dewey W. Grantham, "Dinner at the White House: Theodore Roosevelt, Booker T. Washington, and the South," *Tennessee Historical Quarterly* 18 (June 1958):112–30.

48. The item appeared at the bottom of column eight on page 3 of the October 17 issue of the *Washington Post,* just below an announcement of similar length that the first assistant postmaster general had returned to work after a long illness. The two notices were presumably regarded as of equivalent importance.

49. *Richmond Times,* October 18, 1901; quoted in *Washington Post,* October 19, 1901.

50. Quoted in Sullivan, *Our Times* 3, p. 136.

51. Roosevelt to Lucius Nathan Littauer, October 24, 1901; in Morison, ed., *Letters of Roosevelt* 3, p. 181.

52. Roosevelt to Curtis Guild, Jr., October 28, 1901; ibid. 3, p. 184. The reference is to Charles W. Eliot, president of Harvard University, and Arthur Twining Hadley, president of Yale University.

53. *New York World,* October 20, 1901.

54. Sullivan, *Our Times* 3, pp. 145–47.

55. Arthur Wallace Dunn, for example, who based his version on a conversation with the president, quoted Roosevelt as saying: "I'll tell you how it happened. The man was here talking with me when luncheon was announced, and I told him to come in and have lunch with me while we continued our talk. That was all there was to it." See *Harrison to Harding* 1, pp. 358–59. A similar account is provided by Harry Thurston Peck, who described Roosevelt as saying to a friend: "When luncheon-time came around, my first thought was to invite him to stay and lunch with me. Immediately it flashed across my mind that this would make no end of trouble. But I asked myself: 'Are you afraid to do it?' and I answered 'No!' And so I invited him to come in to luncheon." See *Twenty Years of the Republic,* p. 676. The self-conscious lack of fear rings true as something Roosevelt might have said. Interestingly, a black servant who helped serve the meal also described it as a luncheon. See James E. Amos, *Roosevelt, Hero to His Valet,* pp. 50–55. On the other hand, Roosevelt's official biographer described being a guest at the White House during this time, and the president inviting him to stay over an extra night so he could join Washington for dinner. See Joseph Bucklin Bishop, *Theodore Roosevelt and His Time* 1, p. 165. Willard B. Gatewood discusses the conflicting accounts of what happened, and the possibility that Roosevelt may have contributed to the confusion with his own varying testimony, in *Theodore Roosevelt and the Art of Controversy,* pp. 32–61.

56. Roosevelt to Hermann Speck Von Sternberg, September 6, 1905; in Morison, ed., *Letters of Roosevelt* 5, p. 15.

57. Roosevelt described the ride in a letter to his son, Kermit. See Roosevelt to Kermit Roosevelt, January 14, 1909; ibid. 6, p. 1475.

58. According to Walt McDougall, who drew the cartoon together with another *World* staffer, Valerian Gribayedoff, Blaine thought it lost him the election. "He . . . informed me," the cartoonist wrote of a conversation with Blaine several years after, "that he believed there were good reasons for the *World's* claim that the celebrated Belshazzar's Feast cartoon, which the Democratic State Committee enlarged to enormous size and placarded all over the city, had of itself influenced the election of 1884 sufficiently to account for the eleven-hundred-odd votes that lost him the State of New York." "Pictures in the Papers," *American Mercury* 6 (September 1925):68. The claim is by no means far-fetched, since New York State spelled the difference in the electoral vote, and Blaine lost it by only 1,149 votes.

59. "Things Talked of," *Harper's Weekly* 37 (April 22, 1893):367.

60. Stephen Hess and Milton Kaplan credit Macauley with introducing the symbol in *The Ungentlemanly Art*, p. 132.

61. Sullivan, *Our Times* 3, p. 78.

62. John T. McCutcheon, "Roosevelt as Cartoon Material," *New York Evening Post*, March 13, 1901.

63. Davenport started out as a staunch Democrat. As ace cartoonist for William Randolph Hearst's *New York Journal* he introduced the brutish figure labeled "The Trusts," and got at Mark Hanna by decorating his suit with dollar signs. Impressed by Roosevelt's record, he moved over to the *New York Evening Mail* in 1904 to support the president's candidacy. "He's Still Good Enough For Me" was one of the results. See W. L. Capple, "Cartoons that Made and Unmade Presidents," *Editor & Publisher* 73 (July 27, 1940):5.

64. See Hess and Kaplan, *Ungentlemanly Art*, p. 132.

65. Clifford K. Berryman, "Drawing the Line in Mississippi," detail from "The Passing Show," *Washington Post*, November 16, 1902.

66. The others, in descending order, were Theodore, 14; Kermit, 12; Ethel, 10; and Archibald, 7.

67. Alice Roosevelt Longworth, *Crowded Hours*, p. 34.

68. Quoted in Mary Randolph, *Presidents and First Ladies*, p. 179. Randolph was a Roosevelt family friend.

69. Roosevelt to Charles W. Eliot, September 29, 1905; In Morison, ed., *Letters of Roosevelt* 5, p. 52.

70. Roosevelt to Theodore Roosevelt, Jr., October 2, 1905; ibid. 5, pp. 52–53.

71. Alice Longworth mentioned that few, if any, constraints were placed on the children. The only rules imposed were that they avoid the downstairs rooms open to sightseers and try not to cause damage. Longworth, *Crowded Hours*, p. 45.

72. Irwin "Ike" Hoover, *Forty-Two Years in the White House*, p. 28.

73. Longworth, *Crowded Hours*, pp. 46–47.

74. Ibid., pp. 60–61.

75. Quoted in Owen Wister, *Roosevelt: The Story of a Friendship*, p. 87.

76. Longworth, *Crowded Hours*, p. 59.

77. Ibid., p. 77.

CHAPTER THREE

1. The anecdote is related in Arthur Krock, *The Consent of the Governed*, p. 228.

2. See Willis Abbot, *Watching the World Go By*, p. 244.

3. Oscar Davis described the suspenseful wait in the press gallery in *Released for Publication*, pp. 69–71.

4. *New York Times*, February 1, 1908.

5. Ibid.

6. Quoted in William Harbaugh, *Power and Responsibility,* p. 336.

7. Veteran journalist David Lawrence commented on this point in "Shop Talk at Thirty," *Editor & Publisher* 77 (May 27, 1944):64.

8. David Barry, *Forty Years in Washington,* p. 271. According to Barry, Roosevelt not only leaked the story to selected White House reporters, he dictated the wording he wanted used. But Barry is not an altogether reliable source since he is inaccurate in other particulars. Most notably, he associates the leak with the fight for the Hepburn Act in 1906.

9. Quoted in Henry Pringle, *Theodore Roosevelt,* p. 241.

10. Ironically, Roosevelt did not realilze at the time the bombshell he in fact had. Not until the fall of 1908, at the height of the presidential campaign, did William Randolph Hearst release damaging correspondence he had bribed an Archbold employee to steal for him three years before. It showed that the Standard Oil executive had worked closely with several senators—including Foraker, Hanna, Penrose, Quay, and Bailey—to influence legislation, and that one at least, Senator Joseph Foraker of Ohio, had received $50,000 "in accordance with our understanding." See W. A. Swanberg, *Citizen Hearst,* pp. 271–72 and passim.

11. Loeb had close personal as well as professional ties to the president and his family. The Roosevelt children were not being polite when they called him "Uncle Bill." They looked upon him as almost a member of the family, somebody to take their problems to and whose word they trusted. His marriage in 1903 widened the circle. The Roosevelt and Loeb couples became close friends, often spending time together at Oyster Bay and at informal White House functions. And when William and Katherine Loeb had their own child, a son born on December 26, 1905, Roosevelt acted as godfather at the christening at Christ Episcopal Church in Oyster Bay.

12. See Ishbel Ross, *Ladies of the Press,* p. 311.

13. The story and quotation appear in Louis Koenig, *The Invisible Presidency,* p. 175. This is an excellent treatment of Loeb, and one I have relied on heavily.

14. Ibid., p. 173.

15. Kevin Cash, *Who the Hell is William Loeb?,* p. 45.

16. Davis, *Released for Publication,* p. 123.

17. Merriman Smith, *A President is Many Men,* p. 82.

18. Koenig, *Invisible Presidency,* p. 162.

19. Ibid., p. 176.

20. Roosevelt to Henry Payne, May 23, 1903; in Elting E. Morison, ed., *The Letters of Theodore Roosevelt* 3, p. 479.

21. Quoted in Koenig, *Invisible Presidency,* p. 177.

22. Ibid.

23. The Knight case (156 U.S. 1), decided in 1895, was the first judicial interpretation of the Sherman Act, and pretty well gutted the law at its outset. The court ruled by an eight to one majority that the government could not proceed against a near monopoly in sugar refining because the Constitution only authorizes regulation of interstate commerce, and manufacturing is distinct from commerce.

24. See Arthur Link, *American Epoch* 1, p. 49.

25. The *New York Times* ran the story as its second lead on January 31, 1905, filling the entire left-hand column on page one. The lead story was an account of a hunger-crazed mob in Warsaw firing on government troops. The *Washington Post* also used it as a second lead, but devoted two entire columns on page one to the account. Its lead story reported on the failure of a Russian military operation against the Japanese.

26. Quoted in Harbaugh, *Power and Responsibility,* p. 242.

27. *New York Times,* August 16, 1905.

28. This is not to say that all, or even most, of the stories were orchestrated from the White House. Once Roosevelt launched the campaign it kept going under its own momentum,

needing only the occasional encouragement of a new investigation or trial to maintain interest. During the week of September 24–30, 1905, for example, the *Washington Post* ran four front-page stories and three on inside pages dealing with the subject, and as far as one can tell no more than one was White House inspired.

29. Mark Sullivan, *Our Times*, vol. 3, *Pre-War America*, p. 235.

30. Theodore Roosevelt, *Presidential Addresses and State Papers* 4, pp. 560–658. The portion of his address dealing with rate legislation appears on pp. 567–77.

31. *New York Times*, December 12, 1905.

32. The report that the Chicago grand jury was ready to hand down indictments appeared in the same issue as Moody's directive. For an account of the eight indictments issued by the grand jury in Philadelphia, including one against the Great Northern line, see the *New York Times*, December 15, 1905.

33. See the *New York Times*, January 10–13, 27, 30, February 2, 14, March 9, 13, 1906.

34. Ibid., May 5, 1906.

35. Ray Stannard Baker, "The Railroad Rate: A Study in Commercial Autocracy," *McClure's Magazine* 26 (November 1905):47–59. See also his second article in the series, "Railroad Rebates," 26 (December 1905):179–94.

36. Ray Stannard Baker, "Railroads on Trial III, The Private Car and the Beef Trust," 26 (January 1906):327. He developed the theme further in "Railroads on Trial IV, Private Cars and the Fruit Industry," 26 (February 1906):398–411.

37. Ray Stannard Baker, "Railroads on Trial V, How Railroads Make Public Opinion," 26 (March 1906):535–49. *Collier's* magazine returned to this subject the following year in "Tainted News," 39 (May 4, 1907):13–15. The article was taken up and elaborated on by William Z. Ripley in *Railroads: Rates and Regulation*, long the standard work on the subject. By now the railroad propaganda campaign is a staple in the literature on the Hepburn Act. William Harbaugh, for example, cites Ripley in writing of a "powerful propaganda barrage" which "yet failed of its target, mainly because the public recognized it for what it was even as it was born" (*Power and Responsibility*, p. 242). It may be that the campaign has been overdrawn. Gabriel Kolko makes this case in arguing that the Baker and *Collier's* articles rested on thin evidence, and that the railroads had no reason to propagandize in the way alleged since they did not oppose government regulation as such. Their quarrel was with the kind of rate legislation encompassed in the original House bill. See Gabriel Kolko, *Railroads and Regulation 1877–1916*, pp. 118–19, n.41, and pp. 128–29, n.6. But even conceding Kolko's point, the fact remains that allegations of railroad attempts to manipulate opinion served the president's purpose in making the public all the more receptive to a strong reform measure.

38. So Baker reported in a letter to his father dated January 29, 1905. Cited in Harold S. Wilson, *McClure's Magazine and the Muckrakers*, p. 275.

39. Ray Stannard Baker, *American Chronicle*, p. 194. Roosevelt evidently meant what he said. On October 16 he sent Baker galley proofs of the annual message he was to deliver to Congress in December for the reporter's comments.

40. Harry Beach Needham, "The Senate—of 'Special Interests,' " *The World's Work* 11 (January 1906):7065.

41. Ibid., p. 7060.

42. "The Freight Rate Question—A Simple Proposition," *The World's Work* 11 (January 1906):7028.

43. In fairness to Roosevelt, he had been advised that the courts would likely declare ICC authorization to set definite rates an unconstitutional delegation of power. The last thing in the world the president wanted was to have the entire bill go down the drain because a key provision was flawed. As a result, he had argued throughout for maximum rather than definite rate-making authority for the ICC. He got what he wanted in this respect from the Hepburn Act.

44. The episode is described in Sullivan, *Our Times* 3, p. 256.

45. *Washington Post,* May 5, 1906. Roosevelt summoned the entire press corps again to announce the Conservation Conference held at the White House on May 13, 1908. Between forty and fifty reporters showed up on the latter occasion.

46. Robert M. La Follette, *La Follette's Autobiography,* pp. 478–79.

47. Ibid., p. 479.

48. *Congressional Record,* 59th Congress, 1st Session, vol. 40, part 2, January 17, 1906, p. 1181. The point of Tillman's long speech was to rebuke the president for treating so badly a press corps which served him so well. The subject came up because of a petty controversy in the newspapers over the previous few days. A woman named Mrs. Minor Morris had appeared at the White House demanding an audience with Roosevelt. She wanted him to intercede on behalf of her husband, who had been fired from his job in the War Department. When she was told that the president could not see her on such business, she refused to leave. Accounts differ whether she became hysterical and had to be forcibly evicted, or whether the screaming started only after a White House clerk tried to push her out. Either way, William Loeb was not happy with the coverage of the incident in the *Washington Evening Star,* and so informed the paper. The *Star* responded with an editorial declaiming on freedom of the press and its refusal to be muzzled. That was all the inspiration Tillman needed to get in his few thousand words.

CHAPTER FOUR

1. Charles Thompson, *Presidents I've Known,* p. 120.

2. Ibid., p. 121.

3. Ibid., p. 119.

4. *Taft and Roosevelt: The Intimate Letters of Archie Butt* 1, p. 30. The evaluation appears in a letter to his sister-in-law, Mrs. Lewis F. B. Butt, dated March 28, 1909.

5. J. Frederick Essary, *Covering Washington,* p. 88.

6. The anecdote is related in H. H. Kohlsaat, *From McKinley to Harding,* p. 149.

7. Oswald Garrison Villard commented on this point a few years after Roosevelt's death when he wrote, "Curiously, [he] made the position of the Washington correspondent more important while also undermining the integrity and independence of the writers." See "The Press and the President," *Century* 111 (December 1925):198. Villard was the son of Henry Villard, the financier and publisher of the *New York Evening Post,* and grandson on his mother's side of William Lloyd Garrison, the abolitionist. He took over the *Evening Post* from his father, and after selling it in 1918, retained its weekly edition, the *Nation,* which he built into a leading journal of liberal opinion.

8. David Barry, *Forty Years in Washington,* pp. 282–83.

9. See George H. Manning, "Liberalizing of President's Contacts with Press Hoped for from Hoover," *Editor & Publisher* 61 (January 12, 1929):5.

10. Herbert Corey, "The Presidents and the Press," *Saturday Evening Post* 204 (January 9, 1932):100.

11. Roosevelt to Paul Dana, July 30, 1902; in Elting E. Morison, ed., *The Letters of Theodore Roosevelt* 3, p. 303.

12. The AP account appeared in American newspapers on September 13, 1905.

13. *Washington Post,* September 14, 1905.

14. Ibid., September 19, 1905.

15. Kohlsaat, *McKinley to Harding,* pp. 150–51. Willis Abbot of the *Christian Science Monitor* described the same conversation, only had it occurring between Roosevelt and Archie Butt. See *Watching the World Go By,* p. 224.

16. *Boston Herald,* November 24, 1904.

17. Gould Lincoln, "The President Looks at the Press," manuscript in Oral History Collection, Gould Lincoln AC 75–52, Lyndon Baines Johnson Library, Austin, Texas.

18. Roosevelt to Edwin Bradbury Haskell, December 10, 1904; in Morison, ed., *Letters of Roosevelt* 4, p. 1063. Haskell had stepped down as editor of the *Herald* in 1887 after serving in that post for twenty-five years.

19. Two journalists writing about the incident both mention the black-sheeting that went on. See Essary, *Covering Washington*, p. 94, and Delbert Clark, *Washington Dateline*, p. 56. "The order," Essary wrote, "was intended to destroy Carmichael's value as a newspaper man. . . , but it did nothing of the sort. Carmichael's friends went to his rescue. . . . They volunteered by the score to protect him on all news of the executive end of the Government. The result was that he had laid down on his desk each night an armful of copy, enough to overwhelm him."

20. Butt to Mrs. Lewis F. B. Butt, December 7, 1908; in Lawrence F. Abbott, ed., *The Letters of Archie Butt*, p. 223.

21. Roosevelt to John Albert Sleicher, February 25, 1906; in Morison, ed., *Letters of Roosevelt* 5, p. 167.

22. Roosevelt to Frank Andrew Munsey, January 16, 1912; ibid. 7, p. 481.

23. Roosevelt to Richard Watson Gilder, November 16, 1908; ibid. 6, p. 1364.

24. Roosevelt to Israel Zangwill, October 15, 1908; ibid., p. 1288. Zangwill, an Englishman and prominent Zionist, had requested permission to dedicate the play to Roosevelt when it came out in book form.

25. Charles E. Russell, *Bare Hands and Stone Walls*, pp. 142–43.

26. The idea fit in nicely with Hearst's own political ambitions. Right along one of his key planks in running for public office had been direct election of senators. Hearst papers started drum-beating for the cause as early as February 1899. The publisher pledged to work toward that goal in accepting the Democratic nomination for Congress in October 1902, and in 1903 introduced an appropriate resolution in the House of Representatives. He returned to the theme in his unsuccessful try for the Democratic presidential nomination in 1904. By the time Russell approached him in 1905 he must already have had the following year's gubernatorial race in mind.

27. Phillips was reluctant to accept the commission because he wanted to concentrate on his fiction. He suggested that William Allen White could do a better job. When it turned out that White was not available, Millard appealed to the author's public-spiritedness to win him over, promising also that the magazine would foot the bill to hire Phillips's brother, Harrison, and Gustavus Myers as research assistants.

28. "The Treason of the Senate: An Editorial Foreword," *Cosmopolitan* 40 (February 1906):480.

29. See the introduction by George E. Mowry and Judson A. Grenier to the Quadrangle edition of *The Treason of the Senate*, p. 28. It provides an excellent background to the Phillips series.

30. Lincoln Steffens, *Autobiography*, p. 581.

31. Quoted in Walter Neale, *Life of Ambrose Bierce*, p. 93. Bierce was already highly regarded as a short story writer. Perhaps his most famous work, *The Monk and the Hangman's Daughter*, appeared in 1892. But there was a mordancy to his writing which this time got him and his employer into trouble.

32. *New York Journal*, February 4, 1900.

33. For an account of public hostility to Hearst, see W. A. Swanberg, *Citizen Hearst*, pp. 230–31.

34. Willis Fletcher Johnson, ed., *Addresses and Papers of Theodore Roosevelt*, p. 10.

35. *New York Times*, November 2, 1906. The Bierce poem must have been a factor in Hearst's losing the election, but to his credit he never held the author responsible. "I have never mentioned the matter to him," Bierce wrote, "nor . . . has he ever mentioned it to

me. I fancy there must be a human side to a man like that. . . ." Quoted in Neale, *Life of Bierce*, p. 94.

36. It may be that Phillips's series, if not up to the caliber of the earlier efforts in *McClure's*, made its own contribution to the reform impulse. At least a Senate suddenly subjected to public scrutiny proved remarkably willing while the articles appeared to swallow previously unpalatable fare. In May 1906 it passed the Hepburn Act; in June the Pure Food and Drug law; also in June the Meat Inspection Act. On this point see Mowry and Grenier, eds., *Treason of Senate*, p. 44.

37. Lawson claimed to be taking issue not with individuals, but with a moral climate. The guilty financiers were simply creatures of the environment which had produced them. "If not one of them had ever been born the same good and evil would to-day exist. Others would have done what they did, and would have to answer for what has been done, as they must. So I say the men are merely individuals; the 'system' is the thing at fault, and it is the 'system' that must be rectified." Thomas W. Lawson, "Frenzied Finance: The Story of Amalgamated," *Everybody's* 11 (July 1904):1–2.

38. Roosevelt to Samuel Sydney McClure, October 4, 1905; in Morison, ed., *Letters of Roosevelt* 5, p. 45.

39. Roosevelt to William Howard Taft, March 15, 1906; ibid., pp. 183–84.

40. Roosevelt to Winston Churchill, August 4, 1915; ibid. 8, p. 959. Churchill enjoyed an enormous readership during the late nineteenth and early twentieth centuries, so much so that the future prime minister had to add the middle initial "S" to his name to distinguish himself from his better-known contemporary.

41. In fact Roosevelt misused the muckrake allegory. It is supposed to describe a person obsessed by the desire for wealth, not one who traffics in scandal.

42. Thompson, *Presidents I've Known*, p. 160.

43. Ray Stannard Baker, *American Chronicle*, p. 201.

44. Ibid., pp. 202–3.

45. Ibid., p. 203.

46. Steffens, *Autobiography*, p. 581.

47. *New York Tribune*, April 15, 1906.

48. Quoted in Mark Sullivan, *Our Times*, vol. 3, *Pre-War America*, p. 97.

49. Baker, *American Chronicle*, p. 204.

50. Roosevelt to Jacob August Riis, April 18, 1906; in Morison, ed., *Letters of Roosevelt* 5, p. 212.

51. *New York World*, August 26, 1884.

52. Ibid., April 2, 1907.

53. The best source on the events in the *World* office that day is provided by Pulitzer's business manager, Don C. Seitz, in *Joseph Pulitzer: His Life and Letters*, pp. 352–54. For an account by another *World* employee see John L. Heaton, *The Story of a Page*, pp. 268–69.

54. "We may expect during a heated political contest all kinds of stories which are not worthy of notice," Cromwell said in his disclaimer, "but this one I wish to denounce in the strongest terms as a lying fabrication without a shadow of truth in it. Neither myself or any one allied with me, either directly or indirectly, at any time or in any place in America or abroad, either bought, sold, dealt in or ever made a penny of profit out of any stocks, bonds or other securities of either the old Panama Canal Company or the new Panama Canal Company, or ever received for the same a single dollar of the forty millions paid by the United States. I make this the most sweeping statement that language can convey" (*New York World*, October 3, 1908).

55. Heaton writes of the attempt to get a statement in *Story of a Page*, p. 268.

56. In order, the stories appeared on October 4, October 14, October 16, October 19, October 20, and October 23.

57. The lead editorial, entitled "William Nelson Cromwell—Who? What? Why?" filled two and a half columns.

58. See Seitz, *Pulitzer: Life and Letters*, p. 354. Although no one picked it up at the time, Fairbanks gave a clue to his involvement with the *Indianapolis News* on the day Roosevelt sent a special message to Congress denouncing the paper. He was sitting in the presiding officer's chair when the clerk started to read the message. As the *New York Times* described his reaction, "Apparently only one man in the Senate Chamber took the matter seriously, and that was Vice President Fairbanks. The reference to the *Indianapolis News* and Delavan Smith in the first paragraph caught the Vice President's attention at once, and immediately he summoned Senator Dixon to the chair and left the chamber. He did not return to his place until all the personalities in the message had been passed" (*New York Times*, December 16, 1908).

59. Roosevelt to William Dudley Foulke, October 30, 1908; in Morison, ed., *Letters of Roosevelt* 6, pp. 1322–23.

60. *Indianapolis News*, November 2, 1908.

61. See ibid., December 7, 1908.

62. Roosevelt to William Dudley Foulke, December 1, 1908; in Morison, ed., *Letters of Roosevelt* 6, pp. 1393–97.

63. *Indianapolis News*, December 7, 1908.

64. *New York World*, December 8, 1908.

65. For Congressional attempts to prod him on the corporation, see U.S. Congress, Senate, Committee on Interoceanic Canals, *Investigation of Panama Canal Matters*, Hearings, 59th Congress, 2nd session, Document 401, Serial Set 5098, pp. 1150–55.

66. *New York World*, December 8, 1908.

67. Henry Pringle, *Theodore Roosevelt*, p. 235.

68. Roosevelt to Henry Lewis Stimson, December 9, 1908; in Morison, ed., *Letters of Roosevelt* 6, pp. 1415–17.

69. If anything, the senators showed vast amusement at being consulted. According to the report in the *New York Times* the next day, "President Roosevelt's special message on the purchase of the Panama Canal got an extraordinary reception from Congress today. In the Senate it was not read for an hour or so after it came in, and then it was greeted with smiles and laughter. The Senators were immensely amused by the violence of the President's language in denunciation of the newspapers which have offended him by their insinuations of impropriety on his part in the canal purchase. Every assertion that this or that statement was 'false' or 'false in every particular,' and every similar denunciatory declaration provoked renewed merriment" (*New York Times*, December 16, 1908).

70. Ibid.

71. See Norman Thwaites, *Velvet and Vinegar*, pp. 57–58.

72. *New York World*, December 16, 1908. The allusion to a possible prison sentence was not melodramatics. Pulitzer genuinely feared the prospect, and even had his agents investigate the accommodations in places he might be sent. He had good reason to worry because his blindness and nervous collapse made life an agony under the best of circumstances. A term behind bars probably would have killed him.

73. Quoted in Joseph Bucklin Bishop, *Theodore Roosevelt and his Time* 1, p. 22.

74. Seitz, *Pulitzer: Life and Letters*, p. 373.

75. Quoted in ibid.

76. Pulitzer occasionally sent one of his editors or top staff people to chat with Roosevelt on an off-the-record basis so he could get reports back on the president's thinking. Samuel Williams, a *World* correspondent, had two such meetings in the spring of 1906. On May 24 he wrote a long letter to his employer describing the president's warm, and obviously insincere, feelings for the paper. Included in the report were extensive quotes of statements Roosevelt wanted relayed verbatim to Pulitzer. "The *World* and I stand on the same ground,"

the president said at one point. "Your paper is magnificent and strong. . . . You are against fakirs; so am I. Your showing up of Jerome, for example, was magnificent" (quoted in W. A. Swanberg, *Pulitzer*, p. 332). Considering Roosevelt's true feelings about the paper, he was being uncharacteristically devious in these remarks. The moral, presumably, is that even a relatively forthright president has to smile through clenched teeth on occasion to placate his press critics.

77. Quoted in Seitz, *Pulitzer: Life and Letters*, pp. 371–72. The letter is undated.

78. Quoted in Heaton, *Story of a Page*, p. 276.

79. *New York World*, October 13, 1909.

80. The remark in Indianapolis is mentioned in Heaton, *Story of a Page*, pp. 280–81. Roosevelt's earlier high opinion of Anderson was expressed in a letter to Mark Sullivan, May 13, 1907; in Morison, ed., *Letters of Roosevelt* 5, p. 667.

81. Quoted in Seitz, *Pulitzer: Life and Letters*, p. 381.

82. *New York World*, January 27, 1910.

83. *U.S. v. Press Publishing Co.*, 219 U.S. I, 31 SCT 212, 55 LEd 65.

84. *New York World*, January 4, 1911.

CHAPTER FIVE

1. Oscar Davis, *Released for Publication*, p. 157. Davis recalled that the meeting with the new president occurred in late afternoon on Inauguration Day, March 4. He may be right, but no mention of such an encounter appears in the press. Nor does it seem likely that reporters would have picked a day when Taft's schedule was particularly crowded to make a courtesy call on him. He did see newsmen briefly two days later, however, at which time he laid down a no-quotation rule, saying that his formal statements would be addressed to Congress or delivered in speeches. *New York Times*, March 7, 1909. This was probably the meeting Davis remembered.

2. Davis, *Released for Publication*, p. 127.

3. Ibid., p. 94.

4. William Allen White used the phrase in *Masks in a Pageant*, p. 329.

5. The line is credited to Supreme Court Justice Davis Brewster. It is quoted in Mark Sullivan, *Our Times*, vol. 3, *Pre-War America*, pp. 14–15.

6. Quoted in ibid., p. 14.

7. Quoted in ibid., p. 15.

8. Davis, *Released for Publication*, p. 95.

9. "Picking Flaws in the New Administration," *Literary Digest* 38 (March 20, 1909):452.

10. Edward Lowry, "The White House Now," *Harper's Weekly* 53 (May 15, 1909):8.

11. Archie Butt to Mrs. Lewis Butt, February 24, 1910; in Archie Butt, *Taft and Roosevelt: The Intimate Letters of Archie Butt* 1, p. 289. All of the Butt correspondence cited in this chapter is addressed to Mrs. Lewis Butt, his sister-in-law whom he addressed as Clara. Hereafter only the dates of the letters will be given, following the page citation.

12. Ibid., pp. 18–19; March 21, 1909.

13. Ibid., p. 278; February 9, 1910.

14. Ibid., pp. 298–99; March 5, 1910.

15. Taft to William Allen White, March 20, 1909; quoted in *The Autobiography of William Allen White*, p. 451. The next day Taft said almost exactly the same to Roosevelt in a letter hand-delivered at the pier by Archie Butt when the former president sailed on his world tour. "I have not the facility for educating the public as you had through talks with correspondents," he declared, "and so I fear that a large part of the public will feel as if I had fallen away from your ideals; but you know me better and will understand that I am still working away on the same old plan and hope to realize in some measure the results that

we both hold valuable and worth striving for" (quoted in Henry Pringle, *The Life and Times of William Howard Taft* 1, p. 401).

16. Quoted in Donald Anderson, *William Howard Taft: A Conservative's View of the Presidency,* p. 92.

17. As a sympathetic journalist put it, "He moves forward slowly, trying with all his might and main to do what is best, leaving to the people to find out as best they can what he has done. He won't advertise himself, and he succeeds one of the greatest advertisers the world has ever known" (Edward Lowry, "Mr. Taft and His Critics," *Harper's Weekly* 54 [August 6, 1910]:15).

18. Taft to William Allen White, March 20, 1909; quoted in *Autobiography of William Allen White,* p. 451. The president said the same in an interview midway through his term in office. See George Kibbe Turner, "How Taft Views His Own Administration," *McClure's Magazine* 35 (June 1910):221.

19. Taft to J. H. Cosgrave, February 23, 1910; quoted in Anderson, *William Howard Taft,* p. 217.

20. Butt, *Taft and Roosevelt* 1, p. 26; March 22, 1909.

21. Ibid., p. 336; April 25, 1910. This was far from an isolated case. The following year, at the time of Henry Stimson's appointment as secretary of war, the president still derived pleasure from the game. According to Butt, "what he enjoyed more than anything else, I believe, was the way he scooped the newspaper boys, who think they know in advance everything that goes on" (ibid. 2, p. 655; May 14, 1911).

22. See David Lawrence, "Shop Talk at Thirty," *Editor & Publisher* 77 (May 27, 1944):64.

23. Bascom Timmons, "This is How It Used to Be," in Cabell Phillips et al., *Dateline: Washington,* pp. 50–51.

24. Butt, *Taft and Roosevelt* 2, p. 491; August 20, 1910.

25. Ibid. 1, pp. 30–31; March 28, 1909.

26. Arthur Dunn of the Associated Press quoted the remark in *From Harrison to Harding* 2, p. 206. Although an observation like this made in a semihumorous talk before reporters should not be taken altogether seriously, the evidence does tend to support Taft's self-assessment. Certainly contemporaries arrived at the same judgment independently. Senator Joseph Foraker, for example, commenting on the president's "well-known fondness for golf and his almost constant traveling about over the country in attendance upon all kinds of public occasions," concluded that one reason his administration failed, using Taft's own words, was that he had "too much love of personal ease" (Joseph Foraker, *Notes of a Busy Life* 2, pp. 398–99).

27. Charles Thompson, *Presidents I've Known,* pp. 228–29. Thompson, still the Washington correspondent of the *New York Times* when the incident occurred, went on to describe how he feared his turn might come next. About a week after the Lindsay embarrassment a friend on the *Pittsburgh Dispatch* told him that the secretary of war had inquired casually about the identity of the *Times* man. Thompson made sure Taft found out. "That afternoon, when we entered his office, I said: 'Mr. Secretary, Mr. Heiss tells me that you asked him yesterday who *The New York Times* man was, and that he replied, "He is a short man with a fragmentary mustache and a catarrhal voice." I don't impugn the accuracy of the description. On the contrary, I hope you'll commit it to memory, so that you can recite it if Mr. Adolph Ochs ever asks you, as Colonel Nelson did, if you know his Washington correspondent.' It took Taft probably two minutes to stop laughing" (ibid., pp. 229–30).

28. See Butt, *Taft and Roosevelt* 1, p. 18; March 21, 1909.

29. Ibid., p. 85; May 12, 1909.

30. Dunn, *From Harrison to Harding* 2, p. 207.

31. Walter White, who quoted the phrase, credited it to Oscar Davis. See *Masks in a Pageant,* pp. 328–29.

32. Thompson, *Presidents I've Known,* p. 230.

33. *Washington Post,* January 11, 1908.

34. Roosevelt to William Howard Taft, July 17, 1908; in Elting E. Morison, ed., *The Letters of Theodore Roosevelt* 6, p. 1133. Roosevelt himself italicized the passage in a handwritten postscript to the letter.

35. Roosevelt to William Howard Taft, August 29, 1908; ibid., p. 1202.

36. Roosevelt to William Howard Taft, September 11, 1908; ibid., p. 1231.

37. Quoted in Sullivan, *Our Times* 3, p. 306. Again, the advice doesn't seem to have registered. "It would seem incredible that anyone would care one way or the other about your playing golf," Roosevelt wrote to the candidate on September 14, "but do you know I have received literally hundreds of letters from the West protesting about it. . . . I don't suppose you will have the chance to play until after election, and whether you have the chance or not, I hope you won't." In Morison, ed., *Letters of Theodore Roosevelt* 6, p. 1234.

38. Roosevelt to William Howard Taft, July 15, 1908; quoted in Pringle, *Life and Times of Taft* 1, p. 358.

39. Lawrence, "Shop Talk at Thirty," p. 64. The best indication of Karger's status among fellow journalists is that in the course of his career they elected him president of the National Press Club and chairman of the standing committee in charge of the press galleries of Congress.

40. Quoted in William Manners, *TR and Will: A Friendship That Split the Republican Party,* p. 66.

41. J. Frederick Essary of the *Baltimore Sun* reported that fifteen correspondents attended the president's first meeting with the press. See "The Presidency and the Press," *Scribner's* 97 (May 1935):306.

42. Lawrence, "Shop Talk at Thirty," p. 64.

43. One reason the president allowed Karger such liberties was that he intended the reporter to be his official biographer some day. Even after leaving office Taft continued to turn over to him copies of his speeches and letters. See Oswald Garrison Villard, "The Press and the President," *Century* 111 (December 1925):199. The plan came to nothing because of Karger's premature death on November 16, 1924.

44. Raymond Clapper, "White House Spokesman Mystery Stirs Senate Curiosity at Last," *Editor & Publisher* 59 (January 15, 1927):15.

45. Butt, *Taft and Roosevelt* 1, p. 43; April 8, 1909.

46. Ibid., p. 107; June 1, 1909.

47. Davis, *Released for Publication,* p. 178.

48. According to the official announcement, Carpenter stepped down because "the duties of secretary to the President . . . had been so heavy upon him as to threaten his health," and Taft thought the "delightful climate" of Morocco would be just the right kind of therapy. In his story in the *New York Times* Oscar Davis punctured that excuse, pointing out that Carpenter had been "sacrificed" to the mounting criticism of the administration. "President Roosevelt and Mr. Loeb, his secretary, were past masters in the fine art of publicity," the reporter wrote, "and again and again employed it to the great advantage of their Administration. But from the day he took the oath of office as President, Mr. Taft has had the soft pedal jammed down on everything connected with his Administration that he could possibly keep under cover. . . . The question which is interesting friends of the Administration here to-night is whether or not the change of secretaries is going to be followed by a change on the part of the President to correspondents. . . . It will be easy, undeniably, to find men more skilled in the arts of publicity than Mr. Carpenter, and men to whom such work is more congenial, but the best of them will be of limited service with the conditions remaining what they have been inside of the office" (*New York Times,* May 28, 1910).

49. The major impetus from within the cabinet to remove Carpenter came from Attorney General George Wickersham and Postmaster General Frank Hitchcock.

50. Davis, *Released for Publication,* pp. 184–85.

51. He can hardly be said to have departed with accolades ringing in his ears. "Politicians have watched with close interest the work of Mr. Norton ever since he took up the White House post," the *New York Times* commented. "His office is one of the most important political posts in the Government. Its importance in that respect had been developed very greatly under Secretaries Cortelyou and Loeb, and Mr. Loeb especially showed an extraordinary talent in that place. Both of Mr. Taft's Secretaries have been obliged to stand comparison with the work of Mr. Loeb, and it is not unfair to either to say that both have suffered by it. Mr. Carpenter made no pretense of being a politician. Mr. Norton has been more ambitous in that respect, but his efforts have not been an unmixed success" (*New York Times,* January 22, 1911).

52. Hilles did not join the staff until February 26, 1911, after one or two others had turned down the position. Thompson, who succeeded him on July 17, 1912, made a great hit with reporters on his first day in office (of course much too late to do Taft any good). "At the close of the day," the *New York Times* reported, "he gave a 'seance' to the newspaper men, and in a brief speech announced that he desired to adopt a new deal by which the White House offices would be less exclusive, and the newspaper men might feel that they could get at him any time during the day to get the news. 'I'm for the reciprocal square deal,' said Carmi. 'I will treat you fairly, and you must treat me fairly. I realize that what you want is the news. Any one can come in here any time and get it, but it will not always be an exclusive. We must tote fair with all. How's that?' Inasmuch as during the last three years the correspondents have never heard such encouraging talk about their work at the White House they replied in concert: 'That sure is the square deal' " (*New York Times,* July 18, 1912). Shortly after the election Thompson resigned to accept an appointment as treasurer of the United States. Charles Hilles returned to the post for Taft's remaining weeks in office. See the *New York Times,* November 21, 1912.

53. Lowry, "Mr. Taft and His Critics," p. 15.

54. Quoted in L. White Busbey, *Uncle Joe Cannon,* p. 211.

55. Butt, *Taft and Roosevelt* 1, p. 334; April 22, 1910. Roosevelt made the comment to Frank Kellogg, a special counsel for the United States in the Standard Oil case, who repeated it two years later in conversation with Taft and Butt.

56. *New York Times,* April 23, 1909. The text of the Associated Press resolution appeared in the newspaper on April 21, 1909.

57. Arthur Dunn saw one difference between newspaper and magazine publishers. He argued that the former wanted lower duties on newsprint and wood pulp out of self-interest alone; the latter in part at least because they tended on principle to be free traders. See *From Harrison to Harding* 2, p. 115.

58. William Howard Taft, *Presidential Addresses and State Papers* 1, pp. 69–70.

59. William Howard Taft, *The Presidency,* pp. 7–8.

60. Theodore Roosevelt, *Notes for a Possible Autobiography;* quoted in ibid., p. 126.

61. Ibid.

62. Champ Clark, who would be speaker of the house in the next Congress, addressed this point in his memoirs. "[The stand-pat chiefs] did not tell [Taft] . . . that there was a practice in the House, as old as the government itself—so old that it amounted to having the effect of law—that where the House proposed one rate on an item in the tariff bill and the Senate proposed another, the conferees could not go below the lower rate and could not go above the higher rate. In betwixt the House rate and Senate rate they could do as they pleased. . . . Consequently, when the bill got into conference [Taft] found that he was sewed up; that there were only six items in which he was interested on which he could secure a reduction" (Champ Clark, *My Quarter Century of American Politics* 2, p. 5).

63. Lodge to Theodore Roosevelt, April 29, 1909; in Henry Cabot Lodge and Charles Redmond, eds., *Selections From the Correspondence of Theodore Roosevelt and Henry Cabot Lodge* 2, p. 334.

64. Quoted in James Watson, *As I Knew Them*, p. 140.

65. Butt, *Taft and Roosevelt* 1, pp. 143–44; July 16, 1909.

66. Taft to Horace D. Taft, August 11, 1909; quoted in Pringle, *Life and Times of Taft* 1, p. 436.

67. Taft to Helen H. Taft, July 18, 1909; quoted in ibid., p. 429.

68. F. W. Taussig, *The Tariff History of the United States*, pp. 407–8.

69. *New York Times*, August 6, 1909.

70. Taft to Guild A. Copeland, February 9, 1910; quoted in Anderson, *William Howard Taft*, p. 213.

71. Taft to H. H. Kohlsaat, March 14, 1910; quoted in ibid., pp. 213–14.

72. Butt, *Taft and Roosevelt* 1, p. 190; September 3, 1909.

73. So Butt described the Frick mansion (ibid.).

74. Ibid. 1, p. 185; August 24, 1909.

75. Roosevelt to Henry Cabot Lodge, September 10, 1909; in Lodge and Redmond eds., *Selections from Correspondence of Roosevelt and Lodge* 2, p. 346.

76. *New York Times*, September 15, 1909.

77. Taft to Helen H. Taft, September 16 and 17, 1909; quoted in Pringle, *Life and Times of Taft* 1, p. 453.

78. Taft, *Presidential Addresses and State Papers* 1, pp. 217, 225.

79. Ibid. 1, p. 222.

80. Thompson, *Presidents I've Known*, p. 218.

81. *Louisville Courier-Journal*, September 19, 1909.

82. *New York Times*, September 19, 1909. The parallel the *Times* chose itself indicates intensity of feeling. On March 7, 1850 Daniel Webster spoke in the Senate on behalf of the compromise resolutions of that year intended to avert a Civil War. They included organization of the territories acquired from Mexico without restriction on slavery and strict enforcement throughout the North of the fugitive slave act. "I wish to speak today, not as a Massachusetts man, nor as a Northern man, but as an American," he began in words later generations of school children committed to memory. "I speak today for the preservation of the Union. 'Hear me for my cause.' " In 1850, however, his position shocked antislavery opinion in the country and destroyed whatever chance he still had for the presidency.

83. *St. Louis Post-Dispatch*, September 19, 1909.

84. Taft to Robert A. Taft, October 28, 1909; quoted in Pringle, *Life and Times of Taft* 1, p. 456.

85. Taft to William Dudley Foulke, November 18, 1909; ibid.

86. Taft's penchant for saying the wrong thing plagued him throughout his presidency. In a speech defending the tariff at Lowell, Massachusetts on April 29, 1912, for example, he spoke of himself as having been "a man of straw long enough" (*New York Times*, April 30, 1912). Less than a week later he topped even that one by telling an audience at Hyattsville, Maryland: "I am a man of peace and I don't want to fight. But when I do fight I want to hit hard. Even a rat in a corner will fight" (*New York Times*, May 5, 1912). The words do not appear in the official transcript, so conceivably he did not utter them (See Pringle, *Life of William Howard Taft* 2, p. 783). But more important, by this time the country just assumed the worst. "The sentence even took the spirit out of his sincerest supporters," Henry Stoddard of the *New York Evening Mail* wrote. "One may put some heart into fighting for a lion, but not for a desperate rat" (Henry Stoddard, *As I Knew Them*, p. 376).

87. Quoted in Belle Case La Follette and Fola La Follette, *Robert M. La Follette, June 14, 1885–June 18, 1925* 1, p. 282.

88. Francis E. Leupp, "President Taft's Own View: An Authorized Interview," *Outlook* 99 (December 2, 1911):812.

89. Stoddard, *As I Knew Them*, p. 375.

90. Butt, *Taft and Roosevelt* 1, p. 201; November 14, 1909.

91. Oscar Davis spoke of this as one of the president's greatest weaknesses. "Mr. Roosevelt," he wrote, "wanted always to know what the opposition was, and what it was doing. Mr. Taft liked to be told that everything was well. But that is absolutely fatal in politics, as it is in war" (*Released for Publication*, p. 176).

92. Taft to Robert A. Taft, October 28, 1909; quoted in Anderson, *William Howard Taft*, p. 207.

93. Taft to Philander Knox, October 24, 1909; ibid.

94. See *Editor & Publisher* 7 (June 20, 1908):6.

95. Taft, *Presidential Addresses and State Papers* 1, pp. 480–81.

96. Dunn, *From Harrison to Harding* 2, pp. 136–37.

97. Taft to Otto Bannard, March 2, 1910; quoted in Anderson, *William Howard Taft*, p. 210. The phrasing doesn't do justice to the intensity of Taft's feeling. He detested both of the journals mentioned for their muckraking style and *Collier's* in particular because of its role in the Ballinger-Pinchot controversy, which before it ended generated almost as many destructive headlines as the Payne-Aldrich tariff. Secretary of the Interior Richard Ballinger and Chief of the Forest Service Gifford Pinchot had been at odds almost from the first days of the administration over the Interior Department's policy of restoring to the private domain land which had been previously withdrawn as a conservation measure. Ballinger acted with the approval of Taft, both of whom questioned the legality of using for conservation purposes a 1902 statute which only authorized the government to set aside areas for water power sites. When Louis Glavis, an obscure official in the General Land Office, charged the secretary of the interior with conspiring to turn over to Morgan-Guggenheim interests vast tracts of federal coal land in Alaska, Pinchot seized on the allegation to go public with the dispute. Taft did not want a showdown with Pinchot, a Roosevelt protégé and hero to Roosevelt followers, but neither did he want the bickering in his official family to continue. He ordered Attorney General Wickersham to look into the Alaskan matter. When no proof of wrongdoing was turned up, the president, after consulting with the cabinet, gave Ballinger a bill of health and ordered Glavis dismissed. So matters stood, tense and unresolved, when the November 13, 1909 issue of *Collier's* appeared with an article by Glavis repeating the charges against Ballinger in lurid terms. "ARE THE GUGGENHEIMS IN CHARGE OF THE DEPARTMENT OF INTERIOR?" a headline on the cover of the magazine asked, the question mark curling over the page against a backdrop of Alaskan mountains until it collided with a sinister, shadowy hand reaching down for the grab (see L. R. Glavis, "The Whitewashing of Ballinger," *Collier's* 44 [November 13, 1909]: 15–17, 27). In the resulting outcry everything fell apart for Taft. He alienated the Roosevelt wing of the party by having to ask for Pinchot's resignation on January 7, 1910, and hurt himself further by allowing Ballinger to stay on— an albatross around his neck—well into 1911. *Collier's*, meanwhile, informed by a presumably reliable source that a joint congressional committee which had been appointed to look into the charges would by prearrangement find Ballinger innocent, after which the secretary would file a million-dollar libel suit against Glavis and the magazine, retained Louis Brandeis as special counsel in December 1909. The lawyer's brilliant work at the hearings added to Taft's embarrassment, and undermined whatever scheme for a libel suit may have been afoot. See Norman Hapgood, *The Changing Years*, pp. 182–90. In the midst of all this turmoil the president certainly could think of better ways to spend public funds than to subsidize a *Collier's* weekly.

98. Taft to Senator Frank Flint, February 15, 1911; quoted in Anderson, *William Howard Taft*, p. 210.

99. *Congressional Record*, 62d Congress, 2d Session, vol. 48, part 3, February 22, 1912, p. 2318.

100. Butt, *Taft and Roosevelt* 1, p. 268; January 29, 1910.

101. Taft to Otto Bannard, November 10, 1912; quoted in Anderson, *William Howard Taft*, p. 206. Taft erred, of course, in speaking of a tariff "at $2.00 per one hundred pounds." He meant $2.00 per ton.

102. Taft to Otto Bannard, November 11, 1912; ibid., p. 211.

103. *New York Times*, November 17, 1912.

104. Butt, *Taft and Roosevelt* 1, p. 68; April 27, 1909.

105. Ibid. 2, p. 544; October 6, 1910.

106. Ibid. 1, p. 206; November 14, 1909.

107. Taft to Fred Carpenter, October 24, 1909; quoted in Anderson, *William Howard Taft*, p. 227.

108. Butt, *Taft and Roosevelt* 2, p. 749; August 29, 1911.

109. Dunn, *From Harrison to Harding* 2, pp. 110–12.

110. Butt, *Taft and Roosevelt* 2, p. 749; August 29, 1911.

111. Davis, *Released for Publication*, pp. 177–79.

112. "I am beginning to think," Archie Butt wrote in the summer of 1910, "that the President really does not think that he conspired with [Vice-President James] Sherman and [New York politician Timothy] Woodruff to rebuff his predecessor, that he encouraged [Representative] Nick Longworth to strike at the Speaker, or that he sent Senator [Murray] Crane snooping around the West to secure Ballinger's resignation, or that he was a party to a sneer at Senator Aldrich. He has worked himself into a belief that the press has conspired to harass him with charges of this character" (*Taft and Roosevelt* 2, p. 491; August 20, 1910).

113. Ibid., p. 459; August 1, 1910.

114. Quoted in Anderson, *William Howard Taft*, pp. 234–35.

115. Ray Stannard Baker, *Woodrow Wilson: Life and Letters* 3, p. 181.

CHAPTER SIX

1. Frank Parker Stockbridge, "How Woodrow Wilson Won His Nomination," *Current History* 20 (July 1924):564.

2. Charles Thompson, *Presidents I've Known*, p. 288.

3. Ibid., p. 274. The italics are Thompson's.

4. Arthur Link touched on this aspect of his personality in *Wilson: The New Freedom*, pp. 67–70. See also Alexander L. George and Juliette L. George, *Woodrow Wilson and Colonel House*, passim. Contemporaries noticed the trait as well. "If you will look over the Wilson friendships," Henry Stoddard of the *New York Evening Mail* wrote, "you will find that they were everchanging. . . . The separations were his choice; not the choice of his early supporters. . . . In his view, friendship meant service to him and not by him; friendships were bridges burned behind as he himself moved on, a solitary traveller" (*As I Knew Them*, pp. 484–85; see also David Barry, *Forty Years in Washington*, p. 308).

5. Quoted in Link, *New Freedom*, p. 69.

6. Quoted in David Lawrence, *The True Story of Woodrow Wilson*, p. 47.

7. David Lawrence, "Shop Talk at Thirty," *Editor & Publisher* 77 (May 27, 1944):64, 60.

8. David Lawrence mentioned the incident in *True Story of Wilson*, pp. 340–41. Wilson himself alluded to it in one of his campaign speeches in 1912, a clear indication that the memory still rankled. See Woodrow Wilson, *The New Freedom*, pp. 101–2.

9. Ray Stannard Baker, *Woodrow Wilson: Life and Letters* 3, p. 367.

10. Eleanor McAdoo, *The Woodrow Wilsons*, p. 166.

11. Ibid., p. 168.

12. Thompson, *Presidents I've Known*, p. 295.

13. David Lawrence regarded this disagreement about the nature of news as the most serious point of contention between Wilson and the press. "The growing tendency in recent years in America to anticipate news and to discuss future events or the processes by which conclusions are reached, were deeply resented by Mr. Wilson. His theory was that nothing is news until it was completed . . . that only conclusions or decisions were of interest to the public . . ." (*True Story of Wilson*, p. 340).

14. James Kerney, *The Political Education of Woodrow Wilson*, p. 262.

15. Quoted in Link, *New Freedom*, p. 7.

16. The exchange is mentioned in Lawrence, *True Story of Wilson*, p. 344.

17. See William J. and Mary B. Bryan, *The Memoirs of William Jennings Bryan*, pp. 187–88.

18. *New York World*, December 22, 1912.

19. Quoted in Link, *New Freedom*, p. 6.

20. Kerney, *Political Education of Wilson*, p. 265.

21. Thompson, *Presidents I've Known*, p. 297.

22. Ibid., p. 298.

23. Lawrence, *True Story of Wilson*, p. 346.

24. Thompson, *Presidents I've Known*, p. 301.

25. Woodrow Wilson, "Committee or Cabinet Government?" in Ray Stannard Baker and William E. Dodd, eds., *The Public Papers of Woodrow Wilson* 1, p. 115. The article appeared originally in *Overland Monthly* 3 (January 1884):17–33.

26. Wilson, *New Freedom*, p. 116.

27. Woodrow Wilson, *Constitutional Government in the United States*, p. 70.

28. Lawrence, "Shop Talk at Thirty," p. 60. Wilson had never been in the White House prior to entering it as president.

29. Baker, *Wilson: Life and Letters* 4, pp. 228–29.

30. Edward Lowry, *Washington Close-Ups*, p. 19.

31. Woodrow Wilson Press Conferences, March 22, 1913; Princeton University Library (microfilm).

32. See L. Ames Brown, "President Wilson and Publicity," *Harper's Weekly* 58 (November 1, 1913):20.

33. Quoted in Link, *New Freedom*, p. 80. His source is a letter from Oliver P. Newman to Ray Stannard Baker, January 13, 1928.

34. Baker, *Wilson: Life and Letters* 4, p. 231.

35. Barry, *Forty Years in Washington*, p. 309.

36. "The Talk of the Town: First Time," *New Yorker* 32 (March 17, 1956):34.

37. Woodrow Wilson Press Conferences, January 29, 1914.

38. See, for example, the front page report in the *New York Times*, September 8, 1914. A fuller account appeared on September 13, 1914.

39. Baker, *Wilson: Life and Letters* 5, p. 280.

40. *New York Times*, September 13, 1914.

41. Kerney, *Political Education of Wilson*, pp. 344–45.

42. Quoted in Link, *New Freedom*, p. 80.

43. Woodrow Wilson Press Conferences, April 9, 1914.

44. Ibid., March 5, 1914.

45. Barry, *Forty Years in Washington*, p. 309.

46. Oswald Garrison Villard, "The Press and the President," *Century* 111 (December 1925):197.

47. "TOBACCO TAX PLAN STARTLES CAPITAL," the *New York Times* headlined its report on June 5, 1913. "SOME CONGRESSMEN THINK MCREYNOLDS' PROPOSAL TO TAX PRODUCTION IS SOCIALISTIC." See also "A Corporation Super-Tax," *The Independent* 74 (June 12,

1913):1318. The following year McReynolds became Wilson's first appointment to the Supreme Court. He served until 1941; in Franklin Roosevelt's administration as one of the justices whose anti-New Deal rulings precipitated the Court Packing controversy.

48. See Arthur Link, ed., *The Papers of Woodrow Wilson* 27, pp. 510–11.

49. L. Ames Brown wrote of press reaction in "Wilson and Publicity." See also David Lawrence, *True Story of Wilson*, pp. 346–47.

50. Cited in Link, *New Freedom*, p. 81n.

51. *New York Times*, May 11, 1915.

52. Ibid., May 12, 1915.

53. Baker, *Wilson: Life and Letters* 5, p. 335.

54. Oswald Garrison Villard claimed that he coined the phrase just two days after he arrived in Washington as correspondent for the *New York Evening Post*, and submitted it to Wilson through Tumulty for possible use in the speech. He said that he was surprised when it appeared verbatim in the text, but without his qualifier, "because there are other and better ways of settling international disputes than by the mass killing of human beings" (see *Fighting Years*, p. 257).

55. McAdoo, *Woodrow Wilsons*, pp. 273–74.

56. Louis Brownlow, *A Passion for Anonymity*, pp. 29–30.

57. Joseph Tumulty described the scene in *Woodrow Wilson as I Knew Him*, pp. 490–91.

58. Woodrow Wilson Press Conferences, March 19, 1914.

59. McAdoo, *Woodrow Wilsons*, p. 275.

60. *New York Times*, December 19, 1916.

61. Lawrence, "Shop Talk at Thirty," p. 60.

62. George Creel, "Woodrow Wilson, the Man Behind the President," *Saturday Evening Post* 203 (March 28, 1931):37.

63. The standing committee did not accept the White House Correspondents' Association without challenge. In 1918 Gus Karger, the committee's chairman, wrote to George Creel to suggest that the presidential press conferences be resumed, only with his organization certifying the participants (see F. B. Marbut, *New From the Capital*, p. 173). One problem with his proposal is that it would have violated the separation of powers doctrine. Although the Standing Committee handles its own day-by-day affairs, it does so under authority delegated by the Rules Committee of the Senate and by the speaker of the House of Representatives. Had it taken over the function of the White House Correspondents' Association, final say over access to the presidential press conference would in effect have rested with Congress (see Fauneil Rinn, *The Presidential Press Conference*, p. 79).

64. Walter Lippmann, "The Job of the Washington Correspondent," *Atlantic Monthly* 205 (January 1960):47–48.

65. *New York World*, June 18, 1920. Joseph Tumulty recommended strongly that Wilson grant the interview, and is said to have helped the reporter draw up his questions, some of which the invalided president rejected (see M. L. Stein, *When Presidents Meet the Press*, p. 66).

66. *New York Times*, May 27, 1913.

67. See J. Frederick Essary, *Covering Washington*, pp. 179–80. Raymond Clapper described Wilson's policy on attribution in "White House Spokesman Mystery Stirs Senate Curiosity At Last," *Editor & Publisher* 59 (January 15, 1927):15.

68. *New York Times*, May 27, 1913.

69. Ibid.

70. Reports on evidence submitted to the Senate Judiciary Committee about the activities of the beet sugar industry appeared in the *New York Times* on June 18 and 19, 1913. For the activities of the Federal Sugar Refining Company, which wanted tariff barriers removed, see the *New York Times*, June 20, 1913.

71. Kerney, *Political Education of Wilson*, pp. 251–52.

72. David Lawrence provided an account of the conversation in *True Story of Wilson,* p. 83.

73. Woodrow Wilson, *The State: Elements of Historical and Practical Politics,* p. 566.

74. David F. Houston, Wilson's secretary of agriculture, wrote of the concern in the cabinet in *Eight Years with Wilson's Cabinet* 1, p. 52.

75. *New York Times,* April 8, 1913.

76. Ibid., April 9, 1913.

77. Houston, *Eight Years With Cabinet* 1, p. 53.

78. *New York Times,* April 9, 1913.

79. Louis Brownlow, *A Passion for Politics,* p. 586.

80. Helen Woodrow Bones to Jessie Woodrow Bones Bower, April 12, 1913. In Link, ed., *Papers of Wilson* 29, p. 556.

81. *New York Times,* April 9, 1913. The paper still questioned the wisdom of such appearances. "Mr. Wilson acquitted himself admirably in his first attempt, but we do not believe that, however favorably his personality impressed Congress, his message will impress the Nation more deeply than it would if it had been sent by messenger and read by a clerk. Meanwhile he has laid himself open to the charge of airing his vanity, which is the worst that can be made in the circumstances." But as the *Times* also conceded, "If he prefers to speak to Congress hereafter, instead of writing to it, Congress will probably submit with good grace."

82. See Henry A. Turner, "Woodrow Wilson and Public Opinion," *Public Opinion Quarterly* 21 (Winter 1957–58):510.

83. See Richard P. Longaker, "Woodrow Wilson and the Presidency," in Earl Latham, ed., *The Philosophy and Policies of Woodrow Wilson,* p. 73.

84. Quoted in "Joe Tumulty Pulls the Strings," *Current Opinion* 54 (April 1913):286.

85. "The Hon. Joseph Tumulty, Human Buffer for the President," *Literary Digest* 64 (January 17, 1920):72.

86. Ibid., pp. 71–72.

87. See John Blum, *Joe Tumulty and the Wilson Era,* p. 64.

88. As Bryan remarked ingenuously to the newsmen at his last conference, "I have been like an old hen. My secrets have been my chickens which I was seeking to protect with my wings while you were trying to get them out from under me" (see Villard, "The Press and the President," p. 198). The attitude did not do much to instill good feelings. "He lacked the dignity and authority to win the respect of all the correspondents," Villard wrote. "In their presence he always seemed to the writer like an old, worn, and shaggy buffalo, surrounded by a pack of lithe, snarling hounds. When he charged them with his horns they were at his heels."

89. Villard described the exchange in *Fighting Years,* pp. 265–66. Quotation marks added.

90. Joseph P. Tumulty, "In the White House Looking Glass," *New York Times,* December 31, 1921. "It was a genuine pleasure for me to meet these 'news-gatherers' after I had learned to know them," the secretary wrote. "In our little daily conferences were cemented friendships that I trust will be lasting."

91. Lawrence, *True Story of Wilson,* p. 89.

92. Tumulty, "In the White House Looking Glass."

93. "Tumulty, Human Buffer for the President," p. 74. Tumulty also commented on the mutual trust between him and reporters. "A candid statement to the newspaper men that the President had done or contemplated doing this or that thing, but that he was not to be quoted, was always received in the spirit in which it was given, and the confidence was never violated" ("In the White House Looking Glass").

94. "Tumulty, Human Buffer for the President," p. 74.

95. Lawrence, *True Story of Wilson,* p. 89.

96. "Tumulty, Human Buffer for the President," p. 74.

97. On this point see Blum, *Tumulty and Wilson Era*, p. 61.

98. Ida M. Tarbell, "A Talk With the President of the United States," *Collier's* 58 (October 28, 1916):6.

99. See Tumulty, *Wilson as I Knew Him*, pp. 236–37.

100. Lawrence, *True Story of Wilson*, p. 88.

101. See Kerney, *Political Education of Wilson*, pp. 252–53.

102. Quoted in Link, *New Freedom*, p. 21.

103. Ibid., p. 142.

104. Quoted in Blum, *Tumulty and Wilson Era*, p. 121.

105. Lawrence, *True Story of Wilson*, p. 334.

106. *New York Times*, January 28, 1914.

107. Ray Stannard Baker, "Wilson," *Collier's* 58 (October 7, 1916):5–6, 41; Tarbell, "Talk with President of United States"; George Creel, "The Next Four Years: An Interview with the President," *Everybody's* 36 (February 1917):129–39.

108. Lawrence, *True Story of Wilson*, p. 215. Lawrence pointed out in a different passage, however, that as a rule he preferred not to see Wilson since the president usually spoke off-the-record on matters a reporter could get independently elsewhere. The result was to suppress news rather than to release it (ibid., pp. 347–48).

109. Kerney, *Political Education of Wilson*, p. 344.

Chapter Seven

1. Quoted in James R. Mock and Cedric Larson, *Words That Won the War*, pp. 50–51.

2. Creel letter to Cedric Larson, July 18, 1938; quoted in Cedric Larson and James R. Mock, "The Lost Files of the Creel Committee of 1917–19," *Public Opinion Quarterly* 3 (January 1939):8.

3. The CPI was organized into two main sections: domestic and foreign. Bureaus within those sections were organized at different times and were occasionally phased out, but several were fundamental to the work of the committee. In addition to the News Division, the Domestic Section included the Official Bulletin, the Foreign Language Newspaper Division, the Division on Civic and Educational Cooperation, the Picture Division, the Film Division, the Bureau of War Expositions, the Bureau of State Fair Exhibits, the Bureau of Cartoons, the Four-Minute Men, and the Division on Syndicated Features. The Foreign Section was organized into the Wireless and Cable Service, the Foreign Press Bureau, and the Foreign Film Division. Overall management came from the Executive Division headed by George Creel.

4. George Creel, *How We Advertised America*, pp. 71–72.

5. "Government Publicity," *Editor & Publisher* 51 (June 15, 1918):22.

6. Robert Lansing, *War Memoirs*, p. 323.

7. Wilson to Breckinridge Long, November 20, 1917; in Ray Stannard Baker, *Woodrow Wilson: Life and Letters* 7, p. 368.

8. *New York Times*, July 4, 1917.

9. Ibid., July 7, 1917.

10. *Washington Post*, July 7, 1917.

11. *New York Times*, July 7, 1917.

12. "Newspapers of Country are Flooded With Publicity Copy from Washington," *Editor & Publisher* 50 (March 16, 1918):7, 29.

13. "The Government Press Matter," *Editor & Publisher* 50 (April 6, 1918):22.

14. Creel, *How We Advertised America*, p. 73.

15. Woodrow Wilson, *Congressional Government: A Study in American Politics*, p. 306.

16. Woodrow Wilson, *Constitutional Government in the United States*, p. 102.

17. Creel, *How We Advertised America*, p. 208.

18. Quoted in Mock and Larson, *Words That Won the War*, p. 94.

19. *New York Times*, March 27, 1918.

20. See Creel, *How We Advertised America*, pp. 45–46.

21. The statement about the picture possibly representing German propaganda appeared in the account of the debate in the *Washington Post*, March 30, 1918. The other comments are all from the report in the *New York Times* of the same date.

22. Wilson to George Creel, March 30, 1918; in Baker, *Wilson: Life and Letters* 8, pp. 65–66.

23. George Creel, *Rebel at Large*, pp. 157–58.

24. Creel to Woodrow Wilson, December 28, 1917; quoted in Elmer Cornwell, *Presidential Leadership of Public Opinion*, p. 55. The point about the CPI's magnifying the name of Woodrow Wilson is developed at length in Cornwell's book. I have benefited enormously from his scholarship.

25. See Mock and Larson, *Words That Won the War*, p. 67.

26. See Cornwell, *Presidential Leadership of Public Opinion*, p. 55.

27. Wilson to Robert Lansing, September 5, 1918; in Baker, *Wilson: Life and Letters* 8, pp. 384–85. The president was mollified to learn that Lippmann's assignment involved the fairly innocuous task of dropping leaflets by balloon behind enemy lines.

28. Quoted in Mock and Larson, *Words That Won the War*, p. 181.

29. Quoted in Cornwell, *Presidential Leadership of Public Opinion*, p. 51.

30. See Creel, *How We Advertised America*, pp. 111–12.

31. See Cornwell, *Presidential Leadership of Public Opinion*, p. 54.

32. Quoted in Mock and Larson, *Words That Won the War*, p. 117.

33. Ibid., p. 125.

34. Cornwell, *Presidential Leadership of Public Opinion*, p. 52.

35. *New York World*, May 13, 1918.

36. Quoted in Mock and Larson, *Words That Won the War*, p. 61; see also Creel, *How We Advertised America*, pp. 60–69.

37. Wilson to Edward B. McLean, July 12, 1917; in Baker, *Wilson: Life and Letters* 7, p. 160.

38. Ibid., p. 167.

39. *Washington Post*, August 10, 1918.

40. Ibid., August 22, 1918.

41. Ibid., September 21, 1918.

42. Quoted in Mock and Larson, *Words That Won the War*, p. 86. The article appeared in the "American Weekly" supplement for Sunday, August 4, and Creel's telegram went out on August 16. It is unclear why he waited almost two weeks to register a complaint.

43. *New York American*, April 24, 1917.

44. See W. A. Swanberg, *Citizen Hearst*, p. 364.

45. *New York Tribune*, May 12, 1918.

46. Wilson to Breckinridge Long, November 20, 1917; in Baker, *Wilson: Life and Letters* 7, p. 368.

47. "Treason's Twilight Zone," *Literary Digest* 54 (June 9, 1917):1765.

48. See Mock and Larson, *Words That Won the War*, p. 83.

49. A reproduction of the ad appears in ibid., facing p. 64.

50. *New York Times*, May 24, 1917.

51. See *New York Times*, April 22, 1917. The statements appeared as editorials in the April 21 issues of those newspapers.

52. See the *New York Times*, May 24, 1917. Opinion was not unanimous on the censorship provisions of the Espionage Act. Among the papers that saw justification for such a step, or at least regarded the prospect with equanimity, were the *Richmond Times-Dispatch*, the

Baltimore Sun, the *New York World,* the *Indianapolis News,* and the *Nashville Tennessean and American.*

53. Wilson to Arthur Brisbane, April 25, 1917; in Baker, *Wilson: Life and Letters* 7, p. 36.

54. Tumulty to Woodrow Wilson, May 9, 1917; ibid., p. 57n.

55. Quoted in Mock and Larson, *Words That Won the War,* p. 42.

56. When the Supreme Court did finally rule on the Espionage Act, it took a notably broad view of the government's power to stifle free speech during wartime. The case involved a Socialist Party member who had been convicted of circulating pamphlets urging resistance to the draft. Writing for the unanimous court in a decision announced March 3, 1919, Oliver Wendell Holmes stressed that First Amendment rights are not absolute. "The most stringent protection of free speech," he said, "would not protect a man in falsely shouting fire in a theatre and causing a panic. . . . When a nation is at war many things that might be said in time of peace are such a hindrance to its effort that their utterance will not be endured so long as men fight, and no court could regard them as protected by any constitutional rights." The justices ruled that words alone could represent an overt act in the meaning of the law, and that the government did not have to prove the defendant had actually dissuaded anyone from service in the armed forces to establish its case. The remote "bad tendency" of the words was proof enough (see *Schenck v. United States,* 249 U.S. 47 [1919]).

57. Roe to Roger Baldwin, June 30, 1917, American Civil Liberties Union Papers, Princeton University Library; quoted in Donald Johnson, "Wilson, Burleson, and Censorship in the First World War," *Journal of Southern History* 28 (February 1962):47.

58. Villard to Joseph Tumulty, September 26, 1917, Wilson to Joseph Tumulty, September 28, 1917, Tumulty to Oswald Garrison Villard, September 28, 1917; quoted in ibid., p. 51.

59. This point was discussed in "Mr. Burleson to Rule the Press," *Literary Digest* 55 (October 6, 1917):12.

60. See the *New York Times,* May 22, 1918, for an example of numbed reaction. The paper ran the story on page seven, at the bottom of column four. The report, in its entirety, read: "President Wilson today signed the Sedition bill, giving the Government wide powers to punish disloyal acts and utterances." As the bill made its way through both houses of Congress and the conference committee not a single report ever appeared on the front page of the *Times.*

61. "The Postmaster-General," the *New York Evening Post* remarked of the latest addition to Burleson's power, "is thus granted, without appeal, the power of life and death over every newspaper and business concern in the country. This would be startling enough even if the recent administration of the post office censorship had been marked by evidence of an ability to understand the difference between honest, well-intentioned criticism and wilfull obstruction" (quoted in Lindsay Rogers, "Freedom of the Press in the United States," *The Living Age* 298 [September 28, 1918]:772).

62. Burleson to postmasters of the first, second, and third classes, June 16, 1917, Post Office Department Files, National Archives; quoted in Johnson, "Wilson, Burleson, and Censorship," p. 48.

63. Zechariah Chafee, *Freedom of Speech,* p. 57.

64. See Frank Luther Mott, *American Journalism,* p. 625.

65. See O. A. Hilton, "Freedom of the Press in Wartime, 1917–19," *Southwestern Social Science Quarterly* 28 (March 1948):352–53. A vivid example of this spirit appeared in *North American Review's War Weekly* in April 1918. "There is no room in America for the Hunnish tongue," the magazine declared. "The rising temper of the American people has been unmistakably disclosed in various communities. . . . They have banned the German-printed press. Some have done it by municipal enactment; which may or may not be constitutional. Some have done it through somewhat strenuous moral suasion. Perhaps there have been other methods. The point is that they have been successful. Sheets in the Hunnish tongue

no longer defile their newsstands (see "Silence Enemy Aliens," *North American Review's War Weekly* 1 [April 27, 1918]:6). Samuel Hopkins Adams, a renowned muckraker before the war and best-selling author afterward, was no less firm in *Everybody's Magazine*. "The great mass of German-language papers, with varying degrees of caution, are disloyal, heart and soul. They are part of the German invasion of America" (see "Poisoning the Press," *Everybody's Magazine* 37 [December 1917]:9–10).

66. See Rogers, "Freedom of Press in the United States," p. 770.

67. John Reed, "Woodrow Wilson," *The Masses* 9 (June 1917):22.

68. Max Eastman, "Socialists and War," *The Masses* 9 (June 1917):24.

69. *The Masses* 9 (July 1917):4.

70. Max Eastman, "Conscription for What?" *The Masses* 9 (July 1917):18.

71. *New York Times*, July 10, 1917.

72. Max Eastman, "The Post Office Censorship," *The Masses*, 9 (September 1917), 24. See also Eastman's *Love and Revolution*, pp. 36–37.

73. See Baker, *Wilson: Life and Letters* 7, p. 165.

74. *Masses Publishing Co. v. Patten*, 244 Fed. 535 (S.D.N.Y., 1917). Accounts of the proceedings appear in the *New York Times* on July 10, 14, 17, 22, 25, 27 and August 7, 1917; see also Zechariah Chafee, *Free Speech in the United States*, pp. 42–46.

75. *New York Times*, September 28, 1917.

76. Ibid., October 25, 1917. According to the paper's account, "Eastman's letter to the Postmaster General promises that he will refrain from publishing any matter detrimental to the interests of the United States in the prosecution of the war, but says the magazine will reserve the right of criticism as far as it does not give aid to the enemy, and that it will discuss the demand for peace with freedom of seas, people and markets, world union, and disarmament."

77. *Masses Publishing Co. v. Patten*, 245 Fed. 102 (C.C.A. 2d, 1917).

78. The editors' personal troubles were far from over, however. In mid-November the government indicted Max Eastman, Floyd Dell, John Reed, business manager Merrill Rogers, cartoonist H. J. Glintenkamp and Josephine Bell (a young woman who had contributed a poem to the magazine) for conspiring to violate the Espionage Act. The indictment cited in evidence material in the August, September, and October issues of the *Masses*. The first trial, in April 1918, resulted in a hung jury. Only after a retrial in November ended in a second hung jury did the Justice Department dismiss the indictment.

79. "There is a limit," the postmaster general told reporters. "And that limit is reached when [a publication] begins to say that this Government got in the war wrong [sic], that it is in it for wrong purposes, or anything that will impugn the motives of the Government for going into the war. They can not say that this Government is the tool of Wall Street or the munitions-makers" (see "Mr. Burleson to Rule the Press," p. 12). Although Burleson denied that he had any animosity against socialist papers as such, the problem with the "limit" he set is that he made such papers automatically seditious.

80. Wilson to Albert Burleson, October 11, 1917; in Baker, *Wilson: Life and Letters* 7, p. 301. Wilson enclosed an editorial from the *Springfield* (Mass.) *Republican* which he asked the postmaster general to read and take to heart. "Increasing uneasiness," the editorial declared, "is to be observed among supporters of the war who hold liberal democratic views concerning the freedom of the press and the unhampered exercise of constitutional rights in legitimate agitation and propaganda because of the postal censorship on the mailable publications of the country." Wilson greatly respected the paper, and he must have been concerned to find even this gentle criticism in it.

81. Wilson to Albert Burleson, October 18, 1917; ibid., p. 313.

82. Wilson to Herbert Croly, October 22, 1917; ibid., p. 318. Four days earlier Wilson responded in similarly reassuring words to an executive of Hearst's International News Service. "I think you have misinterpreted the spirit and purpose of the Postmaster General,"

he wrote. "I have been keeping in close touch with him and I think that he is as anxious as I am to see that freedom of criticism is permitted up to the limit of putting insuperable obstacles in the way of the Government in the prosecution of the war" (Wilson to Grenville S. MacFarland, October 18, 1917; ibid., p. 313).

83. Quoted in Oswald Garrison Villard, *Fighting Years,* p. 357n.

84. William H. Lamar, "The Government's Attitude Toward the Press," *Forum* 59 (February 1918):132.

85. *New York Evening Post,* January 25, 26, 28, 1918. "Naturally because of my having printed those treaties in *The Evening Post,*" Villard wrote, "I have had a deep interest in this question. As I see the evidence, there is no question whatsoever that Wilson deceived the Senators of the Committee on Foreign Relations who called upon him at the White House on August 19, 1919. In that interview the President stated, in reply to a question from Senator Borah, that his own knowledge of the secret treaties 'came after I reached Paris. . . . The whole series of understandings were disclosed to me for the first time then.'. . . Now how was this possible? Not only was *The Evening Post* read daily in the White House but . . . the secret treaties were syndicated in nine other daily newspapers as far West as St. Paul and were then reprinted in pamphlet form and put on sale on the newsstands in New York, Boston, Philadelphia, Chicago, and especially in Washington, as well as other cities" (Villard, *Fighting Years,* p. 470).

86. *New York Times,* September 16, 1918.

87. Villard, *Fighting Years,* p. 327.

88. Albert Nock, "The One Thing Needful," *The Nation* 107 (September 14, 1918):283.

89. Quoted in Villard, *Fighting Years,* p. 355.

90. In its issue the following week, the *New Republic* noted one last twist to the story. "It is an ironical fact," the magazine pointed out, "that just when the American Post Office was threatening to suppress the issue of a journal for criticizing the activities of Mr. Gompers in England, Mr. Gompers himself was offering a resolution to the Allied Labor Conference in favor of an international guaranty of freedom of speech" ("Editorial Note," *New Republic* 16 [September 28, 1918]:240).

91. Norman Thomas was another who benefited from having friends in the right places. In September 1918, the same month Villard ran into trouble, Solicitor Lamar banned his *World Tomorrow,* a publication put out under the auspices of the Fellowship on Reconciliation, because of an article it contained that was critical of American policy toward Russia. Together with John Nevin Sayre, who fortunately happened to be the brother of Wilson's son-in-law, Thomas rushed to Washington to petition higher authority for a reconsideration. Sayre managed to get an appointment with the president, and pointed out to him that Thomas after all was a Princeton man, and had even been enrolled in one of Wilson's courses. The president, in thumbing through a copy of *World Tomorrow,* was unimpressed. "Go and tell Norman Thomas that there is such a thing as the indecent exposure of private opinion in public," he said sourly. But he did write to Burleson on September 16 to "suggest that you treat these men with all possible consideration, for I know they are absolutely sincere and I would not like to see this publication held up unless there is a very clear case indeed." The postal ban was lifted the next day (see Johnson, "Wilson, Burleson, and Censorship," pp. 55–56).

92. "The Week," *The Nation* 107 (September 21, 1918):307.

93. "Never Mind What You Think About the I.W.W.," *New Republic* 15 (June 22, 1918):iii.

94. See Johnson, "Wilson, Burleson, and Censorship," pp. 53–54.

95. "Washington Correspondents," *The Nation* 107 (November 30, 1918):638.

96. Burleson to Woodrow Wilson, September 3, 1920; quoted in Johnson, "Wilson, Burleson, and Censorship," p. 57.

97. *Milwaukee Publishing Company v. Burleson,* 255 U.S. 407 (1921).

Chapter Eight

1. The council that day consisted of representatives of the four major Allied powers: the United States, Great Britain, France, and Italy. On the very next day Japan was included on terms of equality. This body, in turn, evolved into the Council of Ten, consisting (except in the case of Japan) of the heads of state and foreign ministers of the member nations, with other aides sitting in. The Council of Ten remained the focus for the work of the conference until late March, when the heads of state started to meet just between themselves, not even secretaries present, as a Council of Four. The foreign ministers, meanwhile, handled less important details as a Council of Five.

2. *New York Times,* January 13, 1919.

3. Ray Stannard Baker, *Woodrow Wilson and World Settlement* 1, p. 139.

4. Tumulty quoted the message in *Woodrow Wilson as I Knew Him,* p. 158.

5. *Papers Relating to the Foreign Relations of the United States. The Paris Peace Conference, 1919* 3, pp. 543–45. Hereafter referred to as *Peace Conference Papers.*

6. Ibid., p. 550.

7. Ibid., p. 552.

8. Ibid., p. 563.

9. Mark Sullivan, "Back to Truth," *Collier's* 63 (April 26, 1919):6.

10. *New York Times,* January 16, 1919.

11. Tumulty quoted the cable in *Wilson as I Knew Him,* pp. 518–19.

12. Ibid., p. 519.

13. For a complete list of the correspondents registered with Baker's office, see "American Newspaper Men at Peace Gathering Were from Every Part of States," *Editor & Publisher* 51 (March 15, 1919):8.

14. Baker, *Wilson and World Settlement* 1, p. 116.

15. My account relies heavily on Arthur Krock's detailed report on these events written just days after they happened. See "How U.S. Newspaper Men Lifted Press Censorship," *Louisville Courier-Journal,* February 7, 1919.

16. Quoted in Baker, *Wilson and World Settlement* 1, p. 141. Baker incorrectly dated the document to January 14.

17. The ten included Edward Keen of the United Press, J. J. Williams of International News Service, H. C. Probert of the Associated Press, John Nevin representing the Hearst chain, Arthur Krock of the *Louisville Courier-Journal,* Herbert Bayard Swope of the *New York World,* Laurence Hills of the *New York Sun,* Burr Price of the *New York Herald,* Richard Oulahan of the *New York Times,* and Arthur Evans of the *Chicago Tribune.*

18. Part of the reason for confusion in some of the literature as to where Wilson stood on publicity is that his remarks in the Council of Ten sometimes seemed to suggest a greater instinct for openness than in fact was the case. "For [my] part," he declared at the morning meeting on January 15, "[I] would prefer complete publicity, rather than publicity by leak" (*Peace Conference Papers* 3, p. 569). The next day he told the other heads of state that he "doubted whether anything less than complete publicity would satisfy the American public" (ibid., p. 579). On both occasions, however, he was arguing for admitting reporters to the plenary sessions of the conference. Wilson never advocated publicity about the proceedings of the Council of Ten.

19. Ibid., p. 580.

20. See Arthur Krock, *Memoirs,* p. 52.

21. According to the compromise wording, "There being substantial agreement among the British, Italian and American delegations, and that of smaller nations, to recommend equal representation of the press at the Conferences, from which, however, the French delegation dissents, no joint proposal on this point is made, it having been left to the representatives of each nationality to make separate recommendations to their own delegates

on this subject." The document is reprinted in Baker, *Wilson and World Settlement* 3, pp. 50–51.

22. Ibid., p. 51. "American journalists, for one brief night," Mark Sullivan wrote, "wore the mantle of John Milton and wore it not unworthily. One by one the Americans converted all the others except the French, who refused to sign the final resolutions" (see "Back to Truth," p. 6).

23. *Peace Conference Papers* 3, p. 595.

24. Ibid., p. 612.

25. The French rather appreciated that these two men took on the responsibility. "If I wished to be indiscreet I would tell you who drew up that document defining our relations with the press," André Tardieu, the Franco-American high commissioner, declared in a speech dedicating the Interallied Press Club. "But I will limit myself to a half-indiscretion and say that the names of its authors, who are neither of them French, are a guarantee of liberalism which none can dispute and the unanimous welcome given to their proposition by the rest of the assembly proves that this liberalism is shared by all their colleagues" (quoted in "Peace Correspondents Dwell in Marble Halls of $2,500,000 Merchant's Palace," *Editor & Publisher* 51 [March 1, 1919]:7).

26. *Peace Conference Papers* 3, p. 610.

27. Arthur Schlesinger, Jr., *The Imperial Presidency,* p. 337.

28. "TROTZKY BARES RUSSIA'S COMPACTS," the four-column headline in the *Times* blared. Interestingly, the newspaper did not at all approve of such ungentlemanly conduct. "Trotzky is . . . wholly incapable of understanding," an editorial in the same issue declared, "that this is an act of dishonor, that it does infinite harm to Russia as a nation. Governments may change, but the honor of a nation, its good faith, should be zealously safeguarded by whatever party or class happens to be in power; at least that is a principle that has found universal acceptance among nations zealous of their reputation."

29. The full text appeared in the *New York Evening Post* on January 25, 26, 28, 1918. Ray Stannard Baker reported that six other papers printed portions of the treaties (see *Wilson and World Settlement* 1, p. 32n.). According to Oswald Garrison Villard, they appeared in nine other papers (*Fighting Years,* p. 470).

30. On this point see Robert Ferrell, "Woodrow Wilson and Open Diplomacy," in George Anderson, ed., *Issues and Conflicts,* pp. 193–94.

31. House Diary, December 18, 1917.

32. Charles Seymour, *The Intimate Papers of Colonel House* 3, p. 326.

33. Harold Nicholson, *Peacemaking 1919,* pp. 123–24.

34. Seymour, *Intimate Papers of House* 4, p. 193.

35. *Peace Conference Papers* 3, pp. 971–79.

36. Quoted in George Noble, *Policies and Opinions at Paris,* p. 307.

37. *Le Figaro,* February 10, 1919. Quoted in ibid., p. 312.

38. A brief statement on April 2 reported that General Jan Christian Smuts of South Africa had been dispatched to Hungary to look into problems associated with the armistice. The following day a second statement declared that Premier Orlando had stayed away from the council meeting attended by Yugoslav delegates, the only official acknowledgment to date of troubles in drawing the map of that part of Europe.

39. Ray Stannard Baker, *American Chronicle,* p. 375.

40. Edith Bolling Wilson, *My Memoir,* pp. 226–27.

41. See Baker, *Wilson and World Settlement* 1, pp. 123–24.

42. George Creel, *Rebel at Large,* p. 205.

43. Both cables are quoted in John Blum, *Joe Tumulty and the Wilson Era,* p. 171.

44. Wilson's letter to House asking him to undertake such briefings is reprinted in Baker, *Wilson and World Settlement* 1, pp. xxi–xxii.

45. A description of the room in which the briefings occurred appears in Harry Hansen, *The Adventures of the Fourteen Points*, pp. 7–8. Hansen was a correspondent for the *Chicago Daily News*.

46. William Allen White, *Autobiography*, p. 566.

47. Baker, *Wilson and World Settlement* 1, p. 131.

48. "We have been told by a reliable source," the paper declared, "that Mr. Lansing . . . has made the following important declaration: The United States has neither proposed nor agreed to send troops to Poland as *Le Temps* reported last night. To one of the journalists citing *Le Temps'* article, Mr. Lansing categorically replied, 'it is a lie.' Asked about the Interallied High Command's evaluation, alleged by *Le Temps,* of the urgency of sending troops to Poland, Mr. Lansing said 'this is exclusively Marshal Foch's estimate' " (*L'Humanité*, January 14, 1919).

49. Quoted in Reginald Coggeshall, "'Violations of Confidence' at the Paris Peace Conference," *Journalism Quarterly* 22 (June 1945):118.

50. *Washington Post*, January 18, 1919.

51. See the *New York Times*, January 16, 1919.

52. Robert Lansing, *The Peace Negotiations*, p. 216. Ray Stannard Baker noticed his colleague's disenchantment. "I think Lansing had an unhappy time of it at Paris," he wrote. "In common with the other Commissioners he had few real or great responsibilities" (*American Chronicle*, p. 378).

53. Baker, *American Chronicle*, p. 379.

54. *Lousiville Courier-Journal*, February 7, 1919.

55. White, *Autobiography*, p. 566.

56. Baker, *Wilson and World Settlement* 1, p. 131.

57. The British briefings were evidently little better, if better at all. But as is typical of newsmen, reporters from both countries thought the other group more favored. "We of the American press got more from the British press conferences than we did from our own," William Allen White recalled. "They were generally in charge of Lord Robert Cecil, who mouthed and mumbled his words in that one-legged non-rhythm which high-class Britishers use when speaking formally. But he did know what was going on, and he did tell us. It generally checked with the truth. Certainly he never tried to deceive us. The American press respected him" (*Autobiography*, p. 566). Henry Wickham Steed, the respected correspondent for the London *Times*, might have been in an altogether different city. "These conferences became known as 'the daily dope,' " he wrote of the British briefings. "They yielded some enlightenment but more often served to mask rather than to reveal the truth. Though I attended none of them I received reports from most of them and often smiled at the inadequacy of the information given. On the whole, the American press was best treated. . ." (*Through Thirty Years* 2, p. 267).

58. *New York World*, March 11, 1919. He identified his source as "a prominent member of the American delegation."

59. Villard wrote of his relationship with Bullitt in *Fighting Years*, pp. 448–49.

60. J. Frederick Essary, *Covering Washington*, p. 150.

61. See Reginald Coggeshall, "Paris Peace Conference Sources of News," *Journalism Quarterly* 17 (March 1940):5.

62. White, *Autobiography*, p. 554.

63. *New York World*, April 2, 1919. Swope identified House as the source in conversations with friends, and although he later hedged, most observers took him at his original word. About the only other likely possibility would have been Bernard Baruch. Swope had taken leave of absence from the *World* in 1918 to serve under Baruch on the War Industries Board, and the two men became extremely close. At one point it even seemed that Baruch might purchase the *New York Herald* and put Swope in charge. But the financier denied having

anything to do with the leak, and in view of Swope's own testimony, his disclaimer seems convincing. See E. J. Kahn, Jr., *The World of Swope*, p. 226.

64. House Diary, May 21, 1919.

65. See Louis Koenig, *The Invisible Presidency*, p. 246.

66. "For many reasons," Steed wrote in his autobiography, "it would certainly have been better had [Wilson] remained at Washington and had he placed Colonel House at the head of an American delegation on which both of the principal American parties would have been represented. Colonel House knew much of Europe, President Wilson knew little. House had proved his ability to deal successfully with European statesmen of all countries. Wilson was temperamentally unfitted for direct personal intercourse with them. House, though a Democrat, possessed the confidence of many Republican leaders who regarded Wilson with suspicion if not with dislike. Wilson, moreover, was far more of a 'politician' than House, though House was a greater master of the political game than he. House, besides, was unselfish and self-effacing, whereas Wilson was self-assertive" (*Through Thirty Years* 2, p. 292).

67. London *Times*, April 7, 1919. This was not the only occasion when Steed took House's side against Wilson, and as he realized, in doing so likely caused his friend trouble. As he wrote of another such article (one in which he mentioned neither of the principals by name), "Despite all the explanations the President remained convinced that, in some way or other, Colonel House had tried to put pressure upon him through me; and this incident, with others in regard to which the Colonel was equally innocent, may well have helped to turn President Wilson against his wisest, most unselfish and most devoted helper" (*Through Thirty Years* 2, p. 284).

68. It is probably just as well that she didn't know Steed's article would also be syndicated the next day in her hometown newspaper. See *Washington Post*, April 8, 1919.

69. Wilson, *Memoir*, p. 251.

70. David Lawrence, *The True Story of Woodrow Wilson*, pp. 337–38. His source was presumably House himself.

71. Ibid., p. 348.

72. Baker, *Wilson and World Settlement* 1, p. 152.

73. Arthur Krock, in an article which chastised journalists for not taking proper account of the difficulties Wilson labored under, still condemned his isolation from the press. "Devoted as I am personally to the President," Krock wrote, "and sympathizing as I do heartily with his great trials and splendid purposes, I yet must assert that his failure directly to guide the American correspondents on American news is inexcusable" (see "Thinks President Should Have Conferred With Reporters," *Editor & Publisher* 51 [April 26, 1919]:19).

74. See "Says Correspondent Violated Ethics," *Editor & Publisher* 51 (February 22, 1919):6.

75. Quoted in Coggeshall, "'Violations' at Peace Conference," p. 120.

76. *New York Herald*, February 15, 1919.

77. *New York World*, February 15, 1919.

78. Quoted in Coggeshall, "'Violations' at Peace Conference," p. 121.

79. William Allen White, *Woodrow Wilson*, pp. 395–96.

80. Lawrence, *True Story of Wilson*, p. 264.

81. "It is not a rare experience for an American correspondent to meet a French official on the street," Mark Sullivan wrote, "and have the official begin to discuss the correspondent's cablegrams of the day before. The American correspondents permanently located in Paris are so accustomed to this official surveillance that they take it as a matter of course. They tell me that the French Foreign Office keeps a record of the spirit of the cablegrams sent by each, whether pro-French or unsympathetic to the French" (see "Back to Truth," p. 36).

82. *Peace Conference Papers* 3, p. 578.

83. Quoted in Reginald Coggeshall, "Was There Censorship at the Paris Peace Conference?" *Journalism Quarterly* 16 (June 1939):128.

84. *Lord Riddell's Intimate Diary of the Peace Conference and After*, p. 52.

85. *New York World*, April 17, 1919.

86. See Noble, *Policies and Opinions at Paris*, p. 6.

87. Villard, *Fighting Years*, p. 397. On this point, see also "Peace Reporters are Coming With President," *Editor & Publisher* 51 (February 22, 1919):11.

88. Villard, *Fighting Years*, p. 397.

89. White, *Autobiography*, p. 550.

90. Baker, *Wilson and World Settlement* 1, p. 137.

91. H. Wilson Harris, *Peace in the Making*, pp. 12–13.

92. Ibid., p. 13.

93. Italy is reported to have spent 8,000,000 francs purchasing the good will of French journals for hire. "Four hundred thousand for forty-eight lines," an Italian delegate grumbled when a not altogether satisfactory story appeared in one of the leading Paris organs. "That is a bit dear!" (quoted in Noble, *Policies and Opinions at Paris*, p. 351, n.128).

94. *Peace Conference Papers* 3, p. 614.

95. Ibid., pp. 786–87.

96. Ibid. 4, p. 444.

97. Ibid. 3, p. 816.

98. Minutes of the March 18 meeting do not appear in the *Peace Conference Papers*. For Lloyd George's comments on the Danzig question the following day (presumably before the coverage in French newspapers was brought to his attention), see ibid. 4, pp. 414–17.

99. The maps depicted ethnic distribution of people in the Danzig region (see *Le Temps*, March 19, 1919).

100. *Peace Conference Papers* 4, p. 444.

101. Ibid., pp. 444–46.

102. Ibid., pp. 446–47.

103. Although there was never any real choice about where the conference would be held, Paris presented built-in problems. France had suffered as much as any country in the war, and as much as any insisted now on revenge. And Paris, perhaps more than can be said for any other capital city, spoke for France. In such an environment it was obviously difficult to plead for moderation and restraint. Particularly difficult when a news blackout prevented all sides from being heard, and provided opening for selective releases of information calculated to stir up popular feelings. "The fact," a British journalist wrote, "that every delegate, and every member of every commission attached to the delegations, and every journalist charged with interpreting the Conference to his countrymen at home, imbibed morning by morning as the first intellectual diet of his day, the *ex parte* expression of one particular point of view, based on one particular political doctrine and dictated by a particular sectional or national interest, did unquestionably create a force of prejudice and partisanship for whose effects too little allowance has been made" (Harris, *Peace in the Making*, p. 10).

104. "Baker and others of our *entourage*," House wrote in his diary, "have been after me for several days concerning attacks in the French press, not only against the President but against the United States. I told Clemenceau about this and said that I cared nothing about it individually, but I did care about the good relations between the United States and France and I hoped he would stop it" (See Seymour, *Intimate Papers of House* 4, p. 407).

105. Ibid., pp. 407–8.

106. White, *Autobiography*, p. 555.

107. Quoted in Coggeshall, "Peace Conference Sources of News," p. 8.

108. Baker, *Wilson and World Settlement* 1, p. 153. Wilson expressed anger again while sailing back to France after his brief visit to the United States. "The most vehement and indignant comments I heard him make during that voyage," the press attaché wrote, "con-

cerned the control of the French press. He said to me that he had positive evidence of domination of many of the papers by the French Government. . . . He thought this system abominable . . ." (Baker, *American Chronicle,* p. 387).

109. *Le Figaro,* February 10, 1919. Quoted in Charles Thompson, *Peace Conference Day by Day,* pp. 187–88.

110. Quoted in Baker, *Wilson and World Settlement* 2, p. 36.

111. Tumulty, *Wilson As I Knew Him,* p. 350. According to one account, Herbert Bayard Swope later claimed that Grayson—with whom he spent many a pleasant afternoon at the Longchamps race track—told him in confidence that the president had actually suffered a minor stroke. The reporter said he cooperated in keeping the secret because of his concern about what the impact of such news would be on the conference. See Alfred Allan Lewis, *Man of the World,* p. 71.

112. Tumulty, *Wilson As I Knew Him,* p. 524.

113. Richard Oulahan, "Capital Corps Praised," *Editor & Publisher* 63 (April 25, 1931):32. Even with this precaution, signals managed to get sufficiently crossed to create a major flap about alleged British censorship. Oulahan's story arrived on schedule at the *New York Times* on Sunday evening, April 6. When the newspaper attempted to confirm the report with the Navy Department at about 8:00 P.M., it was told—accurately enough—that no order for the sailing of the *George Washington* had been received. It turned out later that Admiral William Benson, the senior naval adviser to the Peace Commission, did not send his message from Paris, routed through London, until 9:00 P.M. Sunday evening, and hence it did not arrive in Washington until 7:50 A.M. the next morning. Moreover, the order instructed the Navy Department to maintain secrecy that such a communication had been received. As a result the denials continued all through Monday. Not until Tuesday, when Benson realized the confusion building up on both sides of the Atlantic and urgently advised Assistant Secretary of the Navy Franklin Roosevelt to publicly acknowledge the president's order, did the story receive official confirmation. In the meantime, newspapers leaped to the conclusion that the British must have held up Benson's cable. And once the tale about perfidious Albion had entered the folklore of American journalism, it proved difficult to dislodge. Five years later William Allen White, one of the most responsible of reporters, still gave it currency in his biography of the president (see *Woodrow Wilson,* p. 422).

114. Baker described having such a conversation with Wilson on March 28 (see *Wilson and World Settlement* 2, p. 40).

115. Oulahan, "Capital Corps Praised," p. 138.

116. *New York Times,* April 7, 1919.

117. *New York World,* April 8, 1919.

118. *Washington Post,* April 8, 1919.

119. *St. Louis Post-Dispatch,* April 9, 1919.

120. *Le Temps,* April 8, 1919.

121. For a summary of how French newspapers handled the story, see Noble, *Policies and Opinions at Paris,* pp. 326–27.

122. The further fact, however, is that no matter how open a country's news system may be, it is almost impossible for an outsider to appeal to people over the head of that nation's leader. Wilson didn't seem to fully appreciate this point, perhaps because he had been misled by the ecstatic reception he received when he first arrived in Europe. He tried the tactic even more directly on April 23 in calling on Italians to repudiate Orlando and accept the Fourteen Points as the basis for resolving the Fiume question. All he accomplished as a result (aside from creating a newspaper sensation) was to solidify his adversary's support at home, which until then had been a bit shaky. Orlando kept the president's statement out of Italian newspapers for twenty-four hours. It ran the following day, but under the premier's stinging response set in bold type. "The step of making a direct appeal to the different peoples certainly is an innovation in international intercourse," Orlando declared. "It is a

great source of regret for me to remember that this procedure, which, up to now, has been used only against enemy Governments, is to-day for the first time being used against a Government which has been, and has tried to be always a loyal friend of the Great American Republic . . .'' (see Baker, *Wilson and World Settlement* 3, pp. 201–2).

123. Tumulty, *Wilson As I Knew Him,* p. 525.

124. See Baker, *Wilson and World Settlement* 2, p. 61; also Allan Nevins, *Henry White: Thirty Years of American Diplomacy,* p. 438. For an opposing view see Seymour, *Intimate Papers of House* 4, p. 404.

125. *Le Temps,* April 8, 1919.

126. Blum, *Tumulty and the Wilson Era,* p. 173.

127. Baker, *American Chronicle,* p. 387.

128. For an account of how the paper secured the treaty see Frazier Hunt, *One American and his Attempt at Education,* pp. 168–71.

129. *New York Times,* June 9, 1919.

130. Ibid., June 10, 1919.

131. For the debate see *Congressional Record,* 66th Congress, 1st Session, vol. 58, part 1, June 9, 1919, pp. 780–802. The treaty itself appears in ibid., pp. 802–57.

CHAPTER NINE

1. "Nation-wide Press-Poll on the League of Nations," *Literary Digest* 61 (April 5, 1919):11–13.

2. For examples of editorial opinion on the League, see James D. Startt, "Early Press Reaction to Wilson's League Proposal," *Journalism Quarterly* 39 (Summer 1962):301–8.

3. Quoted in Nicholas Murray Butler, *Across the Busy Years* 2, p. 201.

4. As part of its campaign against the treaty, the *New Republic* serialized portions of John Maynard Keynes's *The Economic Consequences of the Peace* (see *New Republic* 21 [January 14, 1920]:189–95 and 21 [January 21, 1920]:215–24). Wilson could take comfort, however, that the magazine suffered a heavy loss in circulation because of its stance.

5. For a transcript of the speech, see *Congressional Record,* 66th Congress, 1st Session, vol. 58, part 3, July 10, 1919, pp. 2336–39.

6. *New York Times,* July 11, 1919.

7. Ibid.

8. *Treaty of Peace With Germany.* Report of the Conference between members of the Senate Committee on Foreign Relations and the President of the United States at the White House, Tuesday, August 19, 1919 (Washington, D.C., 1919. 66th Congress, 1st Session; Senate Document 76).

9. Joseph Tumulty, *Wilson As I Knew Him,* p. 423.

10. "Mr. Wilson Testifies," *New Republic* 20 (September 3, 1919):134–35.

11. Tumulty, *Wilson As I Knew Him,* p. 435.

12. Thomas Bailey, for one, raised this point. "One of the most fascinating might-have-beens of history," he wrote, "is to speculate on what would have happened had there been then, as there was to be in a few years, a nation-wide radio hookup. Wilson had a fine voice and splendid diction. He probably would have been even more persuasive over the radio than in person. Sitting quietly in the White House, and needing only several half-hour speeches, he might in a series of 'fireside chats' have informed and aroused the people, while at the same time preserving his health and strength" (*Woodrow Wilson and The Great Betrayal,* p. 104).

13. Hugh Baillie, *High Tension,* p. 53.

14. Ibid., p. 62.

15. Ibid., p. 54.

16. *New York Times,* September 13, 1919. Bullitt based his testimony on a memorandum he dictated to a stenographer immediately following his long conversation with Lansing on the afternoon of May 19. He had been attached to the Intelligence Division of the American Peace Commission, and had achieved temporary prominence when Lansing and House sent him on a special mission to the Soviet Union.

17. Tumulty, *Wilson As I Knew Him,* p. 442.

18. Baillie, *High Tension,* p. 54.

19. Ibid., pp. 55–56.

20. Ibid., pp. 52–53.

21. *Congressional Record,* 66th Congress, 1st Session, vol. 58, part 7, October 6, 1919, p. 6427. The full text of the speeches and rear platform talks appears in the *Record* inserted by Minority Leader Hitchcock a few speeches at a time. See vol. 58, part 5, pp. 4997–5010; part 6, pp. 5585–95, 5937–51, 6175–83, 6234–55; part 7, pp. 6403–27. They can also be found in Ray Stannard Baker and William E. Dodd, eds., *The Public Papers of Woodrow Wilson: War and Peace* 6, pp. 1–416.

22. Quoted in Gene Smith, *When the Cheering Stopped,* p. 87.

23. *New York Times,* September 27, 1919.

24. Ibid. This was the version that appeared the next day in the paper's banner headline: "President Suffers Nervous Breakdown, Tour Cancelled; Speeding Back to Washington for a Needed Rest."

25. See Baillie, *High Tension,* p. 63.

26. Edith Bolling Wilson, *My Memoir,* p. 286.

27. *New York Times,* October 3, 1919.

28. Ibid., October 4, 1919.

29. Ibid., October 5, 1919.

30. Ibid., October 6, 1919.

31. Josephus Daniels, *The Life of Woodrow Wilson,* p. 339.

32. Baillie, *High Tension,* p. 64.

33. J. Frederick Essary, *Covering Washington,* p. 48.

34. See Olive Ewing Clapper, *Washington Tapestry,* p. 53.

35. The statement appears in Baker and Dodd, eds., *Public Papers of Wilson* 6, pp. 420–23.

36. For examples of the medical bulletins, see the box on the front page of the *New York Times* for each issue in the days following the stroke. It is interesting that the press refrained as much as it did from reporting rumors and speculation. Presumably it held back out of awareness that scare stories about the president's physical condition would have enormous political and economic repercussions. They would be all the more controversial if the rumors turned out to be false or even partially false.

37. Essary, *Covering Washington,* p. 49.

38. "The piece of Washington coverage which saw the exchange of black sheets at its zenith was the League of Nations ratification fight in the Senate at the end of the Wilson administration," a veteran reporter wrote. "Senator George H. Moses of New Hampshire plotted the strategy of stealing headlines. . . . Let Senator Gilbert M. Hitchcock of Nebraska, leader of the ratificationists, make a day-long exposition for his cause, and Moses was ready with a statement of strategy fathered by Jim Reed, Borah, Johnson, or Brandegee. It would be sufficiently hot to take the headlines away from Hitchcock from coast to coast" (Bascom Timmons, "This is How it Used to Be," in Cabell Phillips et al., *Dateline: Washington,* pp. 49–50).

39. Quoted in William Rivers, *The Adversaries,* pp. 23–24.

40. *Congressional Record,* 67th Congress, 1st Session, vol. 61, part 1, April 12, 1921, p. 172.

41. For a description of the radio hookup for the broadcast, see Erik Barnouw, *A Tower in Babel,* p. 147.

42. This was Raymond Clapper's description in a column published on November 11, 1943, the twentieth anniversary of that Armistice Day. The column is reprinted in *Watching the World,* pp. 312–13.

43. *New York Times,* November 12, 1923.

Chapter Ten

1. Tom Wicker, "Kennedy as a Public Speakah," *New York Times Magazine* (February 25, 1962), p. 71.

2. Turner Catledge, *My Life and the Times,* p. 165.

3. Max Freedman found the reporter's role in this regard strikingly different from that in his own country when he arrived in Washington as special correspondent for the *Manchester Guardian.* "In Europe," he pointed out, "a big matter of policy is debated in the space of a few hours. The great debate in the British Parliament on Munich took only two days. So a journalist in Europe can't really influence the government. By the time he can write a story, the decision has already been made and the whole thing is over and finished. But here in Washington, the debate goes on for several weeks, and long before the decision is reached the correspondent has a chance to tear the proposal apart in his newspaper and exert pressure on the lawmakers. That's what makes the work of the Washington reporter so exciting and so satisfying, and . . . so important" (quoted in Joe McCarthy, "The Lordly Journalists," *Holiday* 31 [April 1962]:140).

Bibliography

NEWSPAPERS

United States:
  Boston Herald
  Chicago Tribune
  Des Moines Register
  Indianapolis News
  Louisville Courier-Journal
  New York American
  New York Evening Post
  New York Herald
  New York Journal
  New York Times
  New York Tribune
  New York World
  St. Louis Post-Dispatch
  Washington Post
  Washington Star
Overseas:
  Times (London)
  Manchester Guardian
  L'Humanité (Paris)
  Le Temps (Paris)

GOVERNMENT DOCUMENTS

Congressional Record.
Investigation on Panama Canal Matters. Hearing, U.S. Congress. Senate. 59th Congress, 2nd sess., Senate Doc. 401, Serial Set 5098. Washington, D.C.: U.S. Government Printing Office, 1907.
  War Information Series. No. 1. *The War Message and Facts Behind It.* Washington, D.C.: Committee on Public Information, June, 1917.
Red, White and Blue Series. Washington, D.C.: Committee on Public Information.
  No. 1. *How the War Came to America.* June 15, 1917.
  No. 2. *National Service Handbook.* July 30, 1917.
  No. 3. *The Battle Line of Democracy: Prose and Poetry of the World War.* 1917.

No. 4. *The President's Flag Day Address With Evidence of Germany's Plans.* Septemb-
ber 15, 1917.

No. 5. *Conquest and Kultur: Aims of the Germans In Their Own Words.* January, 1918.

No. 6. *German War Practices.* 1918.

No. 7. *War Cyclopedia: A Handbook for Ready Reference on the Great War.* 1918.

No. 8. *German Treatment of Conquered Territory.* March, 1918.

No. 9. *War, Labor and Peace: Some Recent Addresses and Writings of President Wilson.*
March, 1918.

No. 10. *German Plots and Intrigues in the United States During the Period of Our Neutrality.* July, 1918.

Official U.S. Bulletin. May 10, 1917–March 31, 1919. 3 vols. Washington, D.C.: Committee
on Public Information.

*Addresses Delivered by President Wilson on His Western Tour, September 4 to September
25, 1919, on the League of Nations, Treaty of Peace with Germany, Industrial Conditions,
High Cost of Living, Race Riots, etc.* U.S. Congress. Senate. 66th Congress, 1st sess.,
Senate Doc. 120. Washington, D.C.: U.S. Government Printing Office, 1919.

Treaty of Peace With Germany. Report of the Conference Between Members of the Senate
Committee on Foreign Relations and the President of the United States at the White
House, Tuesday, August 19, 1919. U.S. Congress. Senate. 66th Congress, 1st sess., Senate
Document 76. Washington, D.C.: U.S. Government Printing Office, 1919.

The Paris Peace Conference, 1919. 13 vols. Department of State. Papers Relating to the
Foreign Relations of the United States. Washington, D.C.: U.S. Government Printing
Office, 1942–1947.

Historical Statistics of the United States, Colonial Times to 1957. U.S. Bureau of the
Census. Washington, D.C.: U.S. Government Printing Office, 1960.

COURT DECISIONS

United States v. Press Publishing Company, 219 U.S. 1 (1911).

Masses Pub. Co. v. Patten, 244 Fed. 535 (S.D. New York, 1917); 245 Fed. 102 (C.C.A. 2d,
1917); 246 Fed. 24 (C.C.A. 2d, 1917).

Schenck v. United States, 249 U.S. 47 (1919).

Milwaukee Publishing Company v. Burleson, 255 U.S. 407 (1921).

PUBLISHED DOCUMENTS

Abbott, Lawrence F., ed. *The Letters of Archie Butt, Personal Aide to President Roosevelt.*
Garden City, N.Y.: Doubleday, Page & Co., 1924.

Baker, Ray Stannard and William E. Dodd, eds. *The Public Papers of Woodrow Wilson.* 6
vols. New York: Harper & Brothers, 1925–1927.

Bishop, Joseph Bucklin. *Theodore Roosevelt and His Time Shown in His Own Letters.* 2
vols. New York: Charles Scribner's Sons, 1920.

Butt, Archibald W. *Taft and Roosevelt: The Intimate Letters of Archie Butt, Military Aide.*
2 vols. Garden City, N.Y.: Doubleday, Doran and Company, Inc., 1930.

Johnson, Willis Fletcher, ed. *Addresses and Papers of Theodore Roosevelt.* New York: The
Unit Book Publishing Co., 1909.

Link, Arthur S., ed. *The Papers of Woodrow Wilson.* vols. 23–29. Princeton, N.J.: Princeton
University Press, 1977–1979.

Lodge, Henry Cabot and Charles F. Redmond, eds. *Selections from the Correspondence
of Theodore Roosevelt and Henry Cabot Lodge, 1884–1918.* 2 vols. New York: Charles
Scribner's Sons, 1925.

Morison, Elting E., ed. *The Letters of Theodore Roosevelt.* 8 vols. Cambridge, Mass.: Harvard University Press, 1951–1954.

Nicolay, John G. and John Hay, eds. *Abraham Lincoln: Complete Works.* 2 vols. New York: The Century Company, 1894.

Riddell, George. *Lord Riddell's Intimate Diary of the Peace Conference and After, 1918–1923.* New York: Reynal & Hitchcock Inc., 1934.

Roosevelt, Theodore. *Presidential Addresses and State Papers of Theodore Roosevelt.* 4 vols. New York: P. F. Collier & Son, n.d.

———. *Presidential Addresses and State Papers.* 8 vols. New York: The Review of Reviews Company, 1910.

Seymour, Charles, ed. *The Intimate Papers of Colonel House.* 4 vols. Boston: Houghton Mifflin Company, 1926–1928.

Taft, William Howard. *Presidential Addresses and State Papers, March 4, 1909 to March 4, 1910.* New York: Doubleday, Page & Company, 1910.

Unpublished Manuscripts

Rinn, Fauneil J. *The Presidential Press Conference.* Unpublished doctoral dissertation, University of Chicago, 1960.

Taylor, Douglas. *The Masses and the Liberator in Wartime.* Unpublished seminar paper, Indiana University, 1972.

Press Conference Transcripts

Woodrow Wilson Press Conference, March 22, 1913—July 10, 1919. Princeton University Library (on microfilm).

Oral History

Lincoln, Gould. "The President Looks at the Press." Oral History Collection, Gould Lincoln AC 75–52. Lyndon Baines Johnson Library.

Books

Aaron, Daniel. *Men of Good Hope: A Story of American Progressives.* New York: Oxford University Press, 1951.

Abbot, Willis. *Watching the World Go By.* Boston: Little, Brown and Company, 1933.

Alsop, Joseph and Stewart. *The Reporter's Trade.* New York: Reynal & Company, 1958.

Alsop, Stewart. *The Center: People and Power in Political Washington.* New York: Harper & Row, 1968.

Amos, James E. *Theodore Roosevelt: Hero to his Valet.* New York: The John Day Company, 1927.

Anderson, Donald F. *William Howard Taft: A Conservative's Conception of the Presidency.* Ithaca, N.Y.: Cornell University Press, 1968.

Anderson, George L., ed. *Issues and Conflicts: Studies in Twentieth Century American Diplomacy.* Lawrence, Kan.: University of Kansas Press, 1959.

Annin, Robert Edward. *Woodrow Wilson: A Character Study.* New York: Dodd, Mead and Company, 1924.

Baehr, Harry, Jr. *The New York Tribune Since the Civil War.* New York: Dodd, Mead and Company, 1936.

Bailey, Thomas A. *Woodrow Wilson and the Great Betrayal.* New York: The Macmillan Company, 1945.

———. *Woodrow Wilson and the Lost Peace.* New York: The Macmillan Company, 1944.

Baillie, Hugh. *High Tension*. New York: Harper & Brothers, 1959.

Baker, Ray Stannard. *American Chronicle: The Autobiography of Ray Stannard Baker*. New York: Charles Scribner's Sons, 1945.

———. *Woodrow Wilson and World Settlement*. 3 vols. Garden City, N.Y.: Doubleday, Page & Company, 1922–27.

———. *Woodrow Wilson: Life and Letters*. 8 vols.

  Vol. 1. *Youth, 1856–1890*. Garden City, N.Y.: Doubleday, Page & Co., 1927.

  Vol. 2. *Princeton, 1890–1910*. Garden City, N.Y.: Doubleday, Page & Co., 1927.

  Vol. 3. *Governor, 1910–1913*. London: William Heinemann Ltd., 1932.

  Vol. 4. *President, 1913–1914*. London: William Heinemann Ltd., 1932.

  Vol. 5. *Neutrality, 1914–1915*. London: William Heinemann Ltd., 1935.

  Vol. 6. *Facing War, 1915–1917*. Garden City, N.Y.: Doubleday, Doran & Company, Inc., 1937.

  Vol. 7. *War Leader, April 6, 1917–February 28, 1918*. New York: Doubleday, Doran & Company, Inc., 1939.

  Vol. 8. *Armistice, March 1–November 11, 1918*. New York: Doubleday, Doran & Company, Inc., 1939.

Barber, James David. *The Presidential Character: Predicting Performance in the White House*. Englewood Cliffs, N.J.: Prentice-Hall, Inc., 1972.

Barnouw, Erik. *A Tower in Babel: A History of Broadcasting in the United States to 1933*. New York: Oxford University Press, 1966.

Barrett, James Wyman. *Joseph Pulitzer and His World*. New York: The Vanguard Press, 1941.

Barry, David S. *Forty Years in Washington*. Boston: Little Brown, 1924.

Bender, Robert J. *"W.W." Scattered Impressions of a Reporter Who For Eight Years "Covered" the Activities of Woodrow Wilson*. New York: United Press Association, 1924.

Bent, Silas. *Newspaper Crusaders: A Neglected Story*. New York: McGraw-Hill Book Co., Inc., 1939.

Berger, Meyer. *The Story of the New York Times*. New York: Simon & Schuster, 1951.

Bleyer, Willard Grosvenor. *Main Currents in the History of American Journalism*. New York: Houghton Mifflin Co., 1927.

Blum, John M. *Joe Tumulty and the Wilson Era*. Boston: Houghton Mifflin Company, 1951.

———. *The Republican Roosevelt*. Cambridge, Mass.: Harvard University Press, 1954.

Boorstin, Daniel J. *The Image: A Guide to Pseudo-Events in America*. New York: Atheneum, 1962.

Bragdon, Henry Wilkinson. *Woodrow Wilson: The Academic Years*. Cambridge, Mass.: Harvard University Press, 1967.

Brayman, Harold. *The President Speaks Off-The-Record*. Princeton, N.J.: Dow Jones Books, 1976.

Brownlow, Louis. *A Passion for Politics*. Chicago: University of Chicago Press, 1955.

———. *A Passion for Anonymity*. Chicago: University of Chicago Press, 1958.

Bryan, William Jennings and Mary B. *The Memoirs of William Jennings Bryan*. Chicago: The John C. Winston Company, 1925.

Burnham, Walter Dean. *Critical Elections and the Mainsprings of American Politics*. New York: W. W. Norton & Company, Inc., 1970.

Burns, James MacGregor. *Presidential Government*. Boston: Houghton Mifflin Company, 1965.

Busbey, L. White. *Uncle Joe Cannon: The Story of a Pioneer American*. New York: Henry Holt and Company, 1927.

Busch, Noel F. *T.R. The Story of Theodore Roosevelt and His Influence on Our Times*. New York: Reynal & Company, 1963.

Butler, Nicholas Murray. *Across the Busy Years*. 2 vols. New York: C. Scribner's Sons, 1939–1940.

Campbell, Angus and Philip E. Converse, eds. *The Human Meaning of Social Change*. New York: Russell Sage Foundation, 1972.

Cash, Kevin. *Who the Hell Is William Loeb?* Manchester, N.H.: Amoskeag Press, Inc., 1975.

Cater, Douglass. *The Fourth Branch of Government*. Boston: Houghton Mifflin Company, 1959.

Catledge, Turner. *My Life and the Times*. New York: Harper & Row, 1971.

Chafee, Zechariah, Jr. *Free Speech in the United States*. Cambridge, Mass.: Harvard University Press, 1954.

———. *Freedom of Speech*. New York: Harcourt, Brace and Howe, 1920.

Chenery, William L. *So It Seemed*. New York: Harcourt Brace and Company, 1952.

Chessman, G. Wallace. *Theodore Roosevelt and the Politics of Power*. Boston: Little, Brown and Company, 1969.

Clapper, Olive Ewing. *Washington Tapestry*. New York: McGraw-Hill Book Company, Inc., 1946.

Clapper, Raymond. *Watching the World*. New York: McGraw-Hill Book Company, 1944.

Clark, Champ. *My Quarter Century of American Politics*. 2 vols. New York: Harper & Brothers, 1920.

Clark, Delbert. *Washington Dateline*. New York: Frederick A. Stokes Company, 1941.

Coletta, Paolo E. *The Presidency of William Howard Taft*. Lawrence, Kan.: The University Press of Kansas, 1973.

Colman, Edna Mary. *White House Gossip: From Andrew Johnson to Calvin Coolidge*. Garden City, N.Y.: Doubleday, Page & Company, 1927.

Cornwell, Elmer E., Jr. *Presidential Leadership of Public Opinion*. Bloomington, Ind.: Indiana University Press, 1965.

Creel, George. *How We Advertised America*. New York: Harper & Brothers, 1920.

———. *Rebel at Large: Recollections of Fifty Crowded Years*. New York: G. P. Putnam's Sons, 1947.

Crouse, Timothy. *The Boys on the Bus: Riding with the Campaign Press Corps*. New York: Random House, Inc., 1972.

Daniels, Josephus. *The Life of Woodrow Wilson, 1856–1924*. Philadelphia: The John C. Winston Company, 1924.

———. *The Wilson Era: Years of Peace, 1910–1917*. Chapel Hill, N.C.: University of North Carolina Press, 1944.

———. *The Wilson Era: Years of War and After, 1917–1923*. Chapel Hill, N.C.: University of North Carolina Press, 1946.

Davis, Oscar K. *Released for Publication*. Boston: Houghton Mifflin Company, 1925.

Dillon, Emile. *The Inside Story of the Peace Conference*. New York: Harper & Brothers, 1920.

Duffy, Herbert S. *William Howard Taft*. New York: Minton, Balch & Company, 1930.

Dunn, Arthur Wallace. *From Harrison to Harding: A Personal Narrative Covering a Third of a Century, 1888–1921*. 2 vols. New York: G. P. Putnam's Sons, 1922.

———. *Gridiron Nights*. New York: Frederick A. Stokes Company, 1915.

Eastman, Max. *Love and Revolution: My Journey Through an Epoch*. New York: Random House, 1964.

Emery, Edwin and Henry Ladd Smith. *The Press and America*. New York: Prentice-Hall, 1954.

Essary, J. Frederick. *Covering Washington*. Boston: Houghton Mifflin Company, 1927.

Filler, Louis. *Crusaders for American Liberalism: The Story of the Muckrakers*. New York: Harcourt, Brace and Company, Inc., 1939.

———, ed. *The World of Mr. Dooley, Finley Peter Dunne*. New York: Crowell-Collier Publishing Company, 1962.

Finer, Herman. *The Presidency: Crisis and Regeneration*. Chicago: University of Chicago Press, 1960.

Foraker, Joseph Benson. *Notes of a Busy Life*. 2 vols. Cincinnati: Stewart & Kidd Company, 1916.

Gatewood, Willard B., Jr. *Theodore Roosevelt and the Art of Controversy*. Baton Rouge, La.: Louisiana State University Press, 1970.

George, Alexander L. and Juliette L. *Woodrow Wilson and Colonel House: A Personality Study*. New York: The John Day Company, 1956.

Gramling, Oliver. *AP: The Story of News*. New York: Farrar and Rinehart, Inc., 1940.

Hansen, Harry. *The Adventures of the Fourteen Points*. New York: The Century Co., 1919.

Hapgood, Norman. *The Changing Years*. New York: Farrar & Rinehart, Inc., 1930.

Harbaugh, William Henry. *Power and Responsibility: The Life and Times of Theodore Roosevelt*. New York: Farrar, Straus and Cudahy, 1961.

Hargrove, Edwin C. *Presidential Leadership: Personality and Political Style*. New York: The Macmillan Company, 1966.

Harlan, Louis R. *Booker T. Washington: The Making of a Black Leader, 1856–1901*. New York: Oxford University Press, 1972.

Harris, H. Wilson. *The Peace in the Making*. New York: E. P. Dutton & Company, 1920.

Haskins, Charles Homer and Robert Howard Lord. *Some Problems in the Peace Conference*. Cambridge, Mass.: Harvard University Press, 1920.

Heaton, John L. *The Story of a Page*. New York: Harper & Brothers, 1913.

Helm, Edith Benham. *The Captains and the Kings*. New York: G. P. Putnam's Sons, 1954.

Hess, Stephen and Milton Kaplan. *The Ungentlemanly Art: A History of American Political Cartoons*. New York: The Macmillan Company, 1968.

Hoover, Irwin H. *Forty-Two Years in the White House*. Boston: Houghton Mifflin Company, 1934.

Houston, David F. *Eight Years With Wilson's Cabinet*. 2 vols. Garden City, N.Y.: Doubleday, Page & Company, 1926.

Huddleston, Sisley. *In My Times: An Observer's Record of War and Peace*. New York: E. P. Dutton & Co., Inc., 1938.

———. *Peace-Making at Paris*. London: T. Fisher Unwin Ltd., 1919.

Hunt, Frazier. *One American and his Attempt at Education*. New York: Simon and Schuster, 1938.

Hurd, Charles. *The White House: A Biography*. New York: Harper & Brothers, 1940.

Ireland, Alleyne. *Joseph Pulitzer: Reminiscences of a Secretary*. New York: Mitchell Kennerly, 1914.

Jones, Robert W. *Journalism in the United States*. New York: E. P. Dutton & Co., Inc., 1947.

Josephson, Matthew. *The President Makers: The Culture of Politics and Leadership in an Age of Enlightenment, 1896–1919*. New York: Harcourt, Brace & Co., Inc., 1940.

Juergens, George. *Joseph Pulitzer and the New York World*. Princeton, N.J.: Princeton University Press, 1966.

Kahn, E. G., Jr. *The World of Swope*. New York: Simon and Schuster, 1965.

Kane, Joseph Nathan. *Facts About the Presidents*. New York: The H. W. Wilson Company, 1959.

Kelley, Stanley, Jr. *Professional Public Relations and Political Power*. Baltimore: Johns Hopkins University Press, 1956.

Kerney, James. *The Political Education of Woodrow Wilson*. New York: The Century Company, 1926.

Klapp, Orrin E. *Symbolic Leaders: Public Dramas and Public Men*. Chicago: Aldine Publishing Co., 1964.

Knightley, Philip. *The First Casualty. From the Crimea to Vietnam: The War Correspondent as Hero, Propagandist, and Myth Maker*. New York: Harcourt Brace Jovanovich, 1975.

Koenig, Louis W. *The Invisible Presidency*. New York: Rinehart & Company, Inc., 1960.

Kohlsaat, Herman Henry. *From McKinley to Harding: Personal Recollections of Our Presidents*. New York: Charles Scribner's Sons, 1923.

Kolko, Gabriel. *Railroads and Regulation, 1877–1916*. Princeton, N.J.: Princeton University Press, 1965.

Krock, Arthur. *The Consent of the Governed and Other Deceits*. Boston: Little, Brown and Company, 1971.

———. *Memoirs: Sixty Years on the Firing Line*. New York: Funk & Wagnalls, 1968.

La Follette, Belle Case and Fola. *Robert M. La Follette, June 14, 1855–June 18, 1925*. 2 vols. New York: The Macmillan Company, 1953.

La Follette, Robert M. *La Follette's Autobiography: A Personal Narrative of Political Experience*. Madison, Wis.: The Robert M. LaFollette Co., 1913.

Landecker, Manfred. *The President and Public Opinion*. Washington, D.C.: Public Affairs Press, 1968.

Lansing, Robert. *The Peace Negotiations: A Personal Narrative*. Boston: Houghton Mifflin Company, 1921.

———. *War Memoirs of Robert Lansing, Secretary of State*. Indianapolis: The Bobbs-Merrill Company, 1935.

Latham, Earl, ed. *The Philosophy and Policies of Woodrow Wilson*. Chicago: University of Chicago Press, 1958.

Lawrence, David. *The True Story of Woodrow Wilson*. New York: George H. Doran Company, 1924.

Lee, Alfred McClung. *The Daily Newspaper in America*. New York: The Macmillan Company, 1947.

Lee, James Melvin. *History of American Journalism*. New York: Houghton Mifflin Co., 1917.

Lewis, Alfred Allan. *Man of the World*. Indianapolis: The Bobbs-Merrill Company, 1978.

Link, Arthur S. *American Epoch: A History of the United States Since the 1890s*. 3 vols. New York: Alfred A. Knopf, 1967.

———. *Wilson: The Road to the White House*. Princeton, N.J.: Princeton University Press, 1947.

———. *Wilson: The New Freedom*. Princeton, N.J.: Princeton University Press, 1956.

———. *Wilson: The Struggle for Neutrality, 1914–1915*. Princeton, N.J.: Princeton University Press, 1960.

———. *Wilson: Confusions and Crises, 1915–1916*. Princeton, N.J.: Princeton University Press, 1964.

———. *Wilson: Campaigns for Progressivism and Peace, 1916–1917*. Princeton, N.J.: Princeton University Press, 1965.

———. *Woodrow Wilson and the Progressive Era, 1910–1917*. New York: Harper & Brothers, 1954.

Lippmann, Walter. *Public Opinion*. New York: Harcourt, Brace and Company, 1922.

Longworth, Alice Roosevelt. *Crowded Hours*. New York: Charles Scribner's Sons, 1933.

Lowry, Edward. *Washington Close-Ups: Intimate Views of Some Public Figures*. Boston: Houghton Mifflin Company, 1921.

McAdoo, Eleanor Wilson. *The Woodrow Wilsons*. New York: The Macmillan Company, 1937.

McCombs, William F. *Making Woodrow Wilson President*. New York: Fairview Publishing Company, 1921.

McHale, Francis. *President and Chief Justice: The Life and Public Service of William Howard Taft*. Philadelphia: Dorrance & Company, 1931.

McKenzie, Ralph M. *Washington Correspondents Past and Present: Brief Sketches of the Rank and File*. New York: Newspaperdom, 1903.

Manners, William. *TR and Will: A Friendship That Split the Republican Party*. New York: Harcourt, Brace & World, Inc., 1969.

Marbut, F. B. *News From the Capital: The Story of Washington Reporting*. Carbondale, Ill.: Southern Illinois Press, 1971.

Marcosson, Isaac Frederick. *Adventures in Interviewing*. New York: John Lane Company, 1920.

Miller, David Hunter. *The Drafting of the Covenant*. 2 vols. New York: G. P. Putnam's Sons, 1928.

Miller, Hope Ridings. *Scandals in the Highest Office: Facts and Fictions in the Private Lives of Our Presidents*. New York: Random House, 1973.

Milton, George F. *The Use of Presidential Power, 1789–1943*. Boston: Little Brown and Company, 1944.

Mock, James R. and Cedric Larson. *Words That Won the War: The Story of the Committee on Public Information, 1917–1919*. Princeton, N.J.: Princeton University Press, 1939.

Morris, Richard B., ed. *Encyclopedia of American History*. New York: Harper & Row, 1965.

Mott, Frank Luther. *American Journalism*. New York: The Macmillan Company, 1941.

———. *A History of American Magazines*. Cambridge, Mass.: Harvard University Press, 1938.

Mowry, George E. *The Era of Theodore Roosevelt and the Birth of Modern America, 1900–1912*. New York: Harper & Brothers, 1958.

Neale, Walter. *Life of Ambrose Bierce*. New York: Walter Neale, 1929.

Neustadt, Richard. *Presidential Power: The Politics of Leadership*. New York: John Wiley & Sons, Inc., 1960.

Nevins, Allan. *American Press Opinion: A Documentary Record of Editorial Leadership and Criticism, 1785–1927*. Boston: D. C. Heath & Company, 1928.

———. *The Evening Post: A Century of Journalism*. New York: Boni and Liveright, 1922.

———. *Grover Cleveland: A Study in Courage*. New York: Dodd, Mead & Company, 1932.

———. *Henry White: Thirty Years of American Diplomacy*. New York: Harper & Brothers, 1930.

Nicholson, Harold. *Peacemaking 1919*. New York: Harcourt, Brace & World, Inc., 1933.

Nimmo, Dan D. *Newsgathering in Washington: A Study in Political Communication*. New York: Atherton Press, 1964.

Noble, George Bernard. *Policies and Opinions at Paris, 1919*. New York: The Macmillan Company, 1935.

O'Brien, Frank M. *The Story of "The Sun," 1833–1918*. New York: George H. Doran Company, 1918.

Parks, Lillian Rogers. *My Thirty Years Backstairs at the White House*. New York: Fleet Publishing Corporation, 1961.

Pearson, Drew and Robert S. Allen. *Washington Merry-Go-Round*. New York: Horace Liveright Inc., 1931.

Peck, Harry Thurston. *Twenty Years of the Republic, 1885–1905*. New York: Dodd, Mead & Company, 1906.

Peterson, H. C. and Gilbert C. Fite. *Opponents of War 1917–1918*. Madison, Wis.: University of Wisconsin Press, 1957.

Phillips, Cabell, et al., eds. *Dateline: Washington*. Garden City, N.Y.: Doubleday & Company, Inc., 1949.

Phillips, David Graham. *The Treason of the Senate*. Chicago: Quadrangle Books, 1964.

Pimlott, J. A. R. *Public Relations and American Democracy*. Princeton, N.J.: Princeton University Press, 1951.

Pollard, James E. *The Presidents and the Press*. New York: The Macmillan Company, 1947.

Poore, Ben: Perley. *Perley's Reminiscences of Sixty Years in the National Metropolis*. 2 vols. Philadelphia: Hubbard Brothers, 1886.

Pringle, Henry F. *The Life and Times of William Howard Taft*. 2 vols. New York: Farrar & Rinehart, Inc., 1939.

————. *Theodore Roosevelt: A Biography*. New York: Harcourt, Brace and Company, 1931.

Randolph, Mary. *Presidents and First Ladies*. New York: D. Appleton-Century Company, 1936.

Reedy, George E. *The Twilight of the Presidency*. New York: The World Publishing Company, 1970.

Rienow, Robert and Leona T. *The Lonely Quest: The Evolution of Presidential Leadership*. Chicago: Follett Publishing Company, 1966.

Ripley, William Z. *Railroads: Rates and Regulation*. New York: Longmans, Green and Co., 1912.

Rivers, William L. *The Adversaries: Politics and the Press*. Boston: Beacon Press, 1970.

Roosevelt, Theodore. *An Autobiography*. New York: The Macmillan Company, 1913.

Rosebault, Charles J. *When Dana Was the Sun: A Story of Personal Journalism*. New York: Robert M. McBridge & Company, 1931.

Rosenman, Samuel and Dorothy. *Presidential Style: Some Giants and a Pygmy in the White House*. New York: Harper & Row, 1976.

Ross, Ishbel. *Ladies of the Press: The Story of Women in Journalism by an Insider*. New York: Harper & Brothers, 1936.

Rossiter, Clinton. *The American Presidency*. New York: Harcourt, Brace & World, Inc., 1956.

Rosten, Leo C. *The Washington Correspondents*. New York: Harcourt Brace, 1937.

Rourke, Francis Edward. *Secrecy and Publicity: Dilemmas of Democracy*. Baltimore: The Johns Hopkins Press, 1961.

Russell, Charles Edward. *Bare Hands and Stone Walls: Some Recollections of a Side-Line Reformer*. New York: Charles Scribner's Sons, 1933.

Salmon, Lucy Maynard. *The Newspaper and the Historian*. New York: Oxford University Press, 1923.

Schlesinger, Arthur M., Jr. *The Imperial Presidency*. Boston: Houghton Mifflin Company, 1973.

Seitz, Don Carlos. *The James Gordon Bennetts*. Indianapolis: The Bobbs-Merrill Company, 1928.

————. *Joseph Pulitzer: His Life & Letters*. New York: Simon & Schuster, 1924.

Sharfman, Isaiah Leo. *The Interstate Commerce Commission: A Study in Administrative Law and Procedure*. 4 vols. New York: The Commonwealth Fund, 1931–1937.

Shotwell, James T. *At the Paris Peace Conference*. New York: The Macmillan Company, 1937.

Siebert, Fred S., Theodore Peterson, Wilbur Schramm. *Four Theories of the Press*. Urbana, Ill.: University of Illinois Press, 1956.

Sigal, Leon V. *Reporters and Officials: The Organization and Politics of Newsmaking*. Lexington, Mass.: D. C. Heath and Company, 1973.

Smith, Gene. *When the Cheering Stopped: The Last Years of Woodrow Wilson*. New York: William Morrow & Company, Inc., 1964.

Smith, Merriman. *A President is Many Men*. New York: Harper & Brothers, 1948.

Stealey, Orlando Oscar. *Twenty Years in the Press Gallery*. New York: Publishers Printing Company, 1906.

Steed, Henry Wickham. *Through Thirty Years, 1892–1922: A Personal Narrative.* 2 vols. Garden City, N.Y.: Doubleday, Page & Company, 1924.

Steffens, Lincoln. *The Autobiography of Lincoln Steffens.* New York: Harcourt, Brace and Company, 1931.

Stein, M. L. *When Presidents Meet the Press.* New York: Julian Messner, 1969.

Stephenson, George M. *John Lind of Minnesota.* Minneapolis: University of Minnesota Press, 1935.

Stoddard, Henry Luther. *As I Knew Them: Presidents and Politics from Grant to Coolidge.* New York: Harper & Brothers, 1927.

———. *It Costs to be President.* New York: Harper & Brothers, 1938.

Stokes, Thomas L. *Chip Off My Shoulder.* Princeton, N.J.: Princeton University Press, 1940.

Sullivan, Mark. *Our Times, 1900–1925: The Turn of the Century.* New York: Charles Scribner's Sons, 1926.

———. *Our Times, 1900–1925: America Finding Herself.* New York: Charles Scribner's Sons, 1927.

———. *Our Times, 1900–1925: Pre-War America.* New York: Charles Scribner's Sons, 1930.

———. *Our Times, 1900–1925: The War Begins.* New York: Charles Scribner's Sons, 1932.

———. *Our Times, 1900–1925: Over Here.* New York: Charles Scribner's Sons, 1933.

Swanberg, W. A. *Citizen Hearst.* New York: Charles Scribner's Sons, 1961.

———. *Pulitzer.* New York: Charles Scribner's Sons, 1967.

Taft, William Howard. *The Presidency: Its Duties, Its Powers, Its Opportunities and Its Limitations.* New York: Charles Scribner's Sons, 1916.

Taft, Mrs. William Howard. *Recollections of Full Years.* New York: Dodd, Mead & Company, 1914.

Talese, Gay. *The Kingdom and the Power.* New York: World Publishing Company, 1969.

Taussig, Frank W. *The Tariff History of the United States.* New York: G. P. Putnam's Sons, 1931.

Thompson, Charles Thaddeus. *The Peace Conference Day by Day: A Presidential Pilgrimage Leading to the Discovery of Europe.* New York: Brentano's, 1920.

Thompson, Charles Willis. *Presidents I've Known.* Indianapolis: The Bobbs-Merrill Company, 1921.

Thwaites, Norman Graham. *Velvet and Vinegar.* London: Grayson & Grayson, 1932.

Tillman, Seth P. *Anglo-American Relations at the Paris Peace Conference of 1919.* Princeton, N.J.: Princeton University Press, 1961.

Tumulty, Joseph P. *Woodrow Wilson as I Knew Him.* Garden City, N.Y.: Doubleday, Page & Company, 1921.

Turnbull, Laura Shearer. *Woodrow Wilson: A Selected Bibliography of His Published Writings, Addresses and Public Papers.* Princeton, N.J.: Princeton University Press, 1948.

Villard, Oswald Garrison. *Fighting Years: Memoirs of a Liberal Editor.* New York: Harcourt, Brace and Company, 1939.

Watson, James E. *As I Knew Them.* Indianapolis: The Bobbs-Merrill Company, 1936.

Weisberger, Bernard A. *The American Newspaperman.* Chicago: University of Chicago Press, 1961.

White, William Allen. *Autobiography.* New York: The Macmillan Company, 1946.

———. *Masks in a Pageant.* New York: The Macmillan Company, 1928.

———. *Woodrow Wilson: The Man, His Times and His Task.* Boston: Houghton Mifflin Company, 1924.

Wildavsky, Aaron, ed. *The Presidency.* Boston: Little, Brown and Company, 1969.

Wile, Frederic William. *News is Where You Find It: Forty Years' Reporting at Home and Abroad.* Indianapolis: The Bobbs-Merrill Company, 1939.

Wilson, Edith Bolling. *My Memoir.* Indianapolis: The Bobbs-Merrill Company, 1938.

Wilson, Harold S. *McClure's Magazine and the Muckrakers*. Princeton, N.J.: Princeton University Press, 1970.

Wilson, Woodrow. *Congressional Government: A Study in American Politics*. Boston: Houghton, Mifflin and Co., 1885.

———. *Constitutional Government in the United States*. New York: Columbia University Press, 1908.

———. *The New Freedom: A Call for the Emancipation of the Generous Energies of a People*. Garden City, N.Y.: Doubleday, Page & Company, 1913.

———. *The State: Elements of Historical and Practical Politics*. Boston: D. C. Heath & Co., 1896.

Wingate, Charles F., ed. *Views and Interviews on Journalism*. New York: F. B. Patterson, 1875.

Wister, Owen. *Roosevelt: The Story of a Friendship, 1880—1919*. New York: The Macmillan Company, 1930.

Woodward, C. Vann. *Tom Watson: Agrarian Rebel*. New York: The Macmillan Company, 1938.

Young, John Russell. *Men and Memories: Personal Reminiscences*. New York: F. Tennyson Neely, 1901.

ARTICLES

Anon. "The Adulteration of News." *The Nation* 31 (August 12, 1880): 107–8.

Anon. "The Advance of Fifty Years." *Editor & Publisher* 1 (October 5, 1901):4.

Anon. "American Newspaper Men at Peace Gathering Were From Every Part of States." *Editor & Publisher* 51 (March 15, 1919):8.

Anon. "An Average American." *Time* 26 (November 18, 1935):41–42, 44–46.

Anon. "Civil Liberty Dead." *The Nation* 107 (September 14, 1918):282.

Anon. "Concerning Three Articles in This Number of *McClure's,* and a Coincidence That May Set Us Thinking." *McClure's* 20 (January 1903):336.

Anon. "A Corporation Super-Tax." *The Independent* 74 (June 12, 1913):1318.

Anon. "Editorial Note." *New Republic* 16 (September 28, 1918):240.

Anon. "First White House Reporter Dies." *Editor & Publisher* 64 (October 31, 1931):38.

Anon. "The Freight Rate Question—A Simple Resolution." *World's Work* 11 (January 1906):7028.

Anon. "The Government Press Matter." *Editor & Publisher* 50 (April 6, 1918):22.

Anon. "Government Publicity." *Editor & Publisher* 51 (June 15, 1918):22.

Anon. "The Hon. Joseph Tumulty, Human Buffer for the President." *Literary Digest* 64 (January 17, 1920):71–72, 74.

Anon. "Joe Tumulty Pulls the Strings." *Current Opinion* 54 (April 1913):285–86.

Anon. "Journalism." *Public Opinion* 1 (June 12, 1886):173–75.

Anon. "Loeb, The Patient Man." *Current Literature* 44 (February 1908):155–57.

Anon. "Mr. Burleson to Rule the Press." *Literary Digest* 55 (October 6, 1917):12.

Anon. "Mr. Politics of the *Times.*" *Time* 60 (December 22, 1952):58.

Anon. "Mr. Wilson Testifies." *New Republic* 20 (September 3, 1919):134–35.

Anon. "Nation-Wide Press-Poll on the League of Nations." *Literary Digest* 61 (April 5, 1919):13–16 et seq.

Anon. "Never Mind What You Think About the I.W.W." *New Republic* 15 (June 22, 1918):iii.

Anon. "News Leak Has Caused Flurry in Washington." *Editor & Publisher* 49 (January 13, 1917):30.

Anon. "Newspapers of Country Are Flooded With Publicity Copy From Washington." *Editor & Publisher* 50 (March 16, 1918):7, 29.

Anon. "Peace Correspondents Dwell in Marble Halls of $2,500,000 Merchant's Palace."
    Editor & Publisher 51 (March 1, 1919):7.
Anon. "Peace Reporters Are Coming With President." *Editor & Publisher* 51 (February 22,
    1919):11.
Anon. "Picking Flaws in the New Administration." *Literary Digest* 38 (March 20,
    1909):452–53.
Anon. "Says Correspondent Violated Ethics." *Editor & Publisher* 51 (February 22, 1919):6.
Anon. "Secretary Tumulty." *Outlook* 103 (February 15, 1913):331–32.
Anon. "Silence Enemy Aliens." *North American Review's War Weekly* 1 (April 27,
    1918):6–7.
Anon. "Steed Made Editor of London *Times*." *Editor & Publisher* 51 (March 1, 1919):24.
Anon. "Swashbuckler or Scholar!" *North American Review* 202 (October 1915):488–97.
Anon. "Tainted News." *Collier's* 39 (May 4, 1907):13–15.
Anon. "The Talk of the Town: First Time." *New Yorker* 32 (March 17, 1956):34–35.
Anon. "Things Talked Of." *Harper's Weekly* 37 (April 22, 1893):367.
Anon. "The Treason of the Senate: An Editorial Foreword." *Cosmopolitan* 40 (February
    1906):477–80.
Anon. "Treason's Twilight Zone." *Literary Digest* 54 (June 9, 1917):1763–65.
Anon. 'Washington Correspondents." *The Nation* 107 (November 30, 1918):638.
Anon. "Washington Topics." *Editor & Publisher* 13 (September 13, 1913):245, 257.
Anon. "The Wedding at the White House." *Public Opinion* 1 (June 5, 1886):141–44.
Anon. "The Week." *The Nation* 107 (September 21, 1918):307.
Adams, Samuel Hopkins. "Invaded America: Poisoning the Press." *Everybody's* 37 (De-
    cember 1917):9–16, 86.
Baker, Ray Stannard. "The Railroad Rate: A Study in Commercial Autocracy." *McClure's*
    26 (November 1905):47–59.
———. "Railroad Rebates." *McClure's* 26 (December 1905):179–94.
———. "Railroads on Trial: The Private Car and the Beef Trust." *McClure's* 26 (January
    1906):318–31.
———. "Railroads on Trial: Private Cars and the Fruit Industry." *McClure's* 26 (February
    1906):398–411.
———. "Railroads on Trial: How Railroads Make Public Opinion." *McClure's* 26 (March
    1906):535–49.
———. "Following the Color Line." *American Magazine* 63 (April 1907):563–79. Three
    additional articles in series.
———. "Wilson." *Collier's* 58 (October 7, 1916):5–6, 41.
Balk, Alfred et al. "Personal Involvement: A Newsman's Dilemma." *The Quill* 60 (June
    1972):24–32.
Barber, James David. "Adult Identity and Presidential Style: The Rhetorical Emphasis."
    Daedalus 97 (Summer 1968):938–68.
Bingham, Worth and Ward S. Just. "President and the Press." *The Reporter* 26 (April 12,
    1962):18–23.
Bishop, Joseph B. "Newspaper Espionage." *Forum* 1 (August 1886):529–37.
Bloomfield, Douglas M. "Joe Tumulty and the Press." *Journalism Quarterly* 42 (Summer
    1965):413–21.
Blum, John M. "Tumulty and Leavenworth: A Case Study of Rumor." *Journal of Abnormal
    and Social Psychology* 44 (July 1949):411–13.
Boorstin, Daniel J. "Selling the President to the People." *Commentary* 20 (November
    1955):421–27.
Brandt, Raymond P. "The Washington Correspondent." *Journalism Quarterly* 13 (June
    1936):173–76.

Brown, L. Ames. "President Wilson and Publicity." *Harper's Weekly* 58 (November 1, 1913):19–21.

Brown, Junius Henri. " 'Newspaperism' Reviewed." *Lippincott's Magazine* 38 (December 1886):721–28.

Burnham, Walter Dean. "The Changing Shape of the American Political Universe." *American Political Science Review* 59 (March 1965):7–28.

Burroughs, John. "Real and Sham Natural History." *Atlantic Monthly* 91 (March 1903):298–309.

Capple, W. L. "Cartoons That Made and Unmade Presidents." *Editor & Publisher* 73 (July 27, 1940):5, 18.

Carroll, Raymond G. "Reform vs. the Washington Correspondent." *Editor & Publisher* 61 (July 21, 1928):7, 44.

Cater, Douglass. "The Presidents and the Press." *Annals of the American Academy of Political and Social Science* 307 (September 1956):55–65.

———. "How a President Helps Form Public Opinion." *New York Times Magazine* (February 26, 1961):12 et seq.

Clapper, Raymond. "White House Spokesman Mystery Stirs Senate Curiosity At Last." *Editor & Publisher* 59 (January 15, 1927):15.

Clark, Edward B. "Roosevelt on the Nature Fakirs." *Everybody's* 16 (June 1907):770–74.

Coggeshall, Reginald. "Was There Censorship at the Paris Peace Conference?" *Journalism Quarterly* 16 (June 1939):125–35.

———. "Paris Peace Conference Sources of News, 1919." *Journalism Quarterly* 17 (March 1940):1–10.

———. " 'Violations of Confidence' at the Paris Peace Conference." *Journalism Quarterly* 22 (June 1945):115–23.

Colcord, Lincoln. "Why Wilson Was Defeated at Paris." *The Nation* 108 (May 17, 1919):782–84.

Corey, Herbert. "The Presidents and the Press." *Saturday Evening Post* 204 (January 9, 1932):25 et seq.

Cornwell, Elmer E. "Wilson, Creel and the Presidency." *Public Opinion Quarterly* 23 (Summer 1959):189–202.

———. "The Presidential Press Conference: A Study in Institutionalization." *Midwest Journal of Political Science* 4 (November 1960):370–89.

Creel, George. "The Next Four Years: An Interview With the President." *Everybody's* 36 (February 1917):129–39.

———. "Woodrow Wilson, The Man Behind the President." *Saturday Evening Post* 203 (March 28, 1931):37 et seq.

Crowell, Chester T. "American Journalism Today." *The American Mercury* 2 (June 1924):197–204.

Davenport, Walter. "The President and the Press: I." *Collier's* 115 (January 27, 1945):11–12, 46.

———. "The President and the Press: II." *Collier's* 115 (February 3, 1945):16–17, 47.

Davidson, John Wells. "Wilson as Presidential Leader." *Current History* 39 (October 1960):198–202.

Dobie, R. M. "Essary Talks About His 32 Years as Washington Correspondent." *Editor & Publisher* 74 (May 31, 1941):13, 22.

Eastman, Max. "Advertising Democracy." *The Masses* 9 (June 1917):5.

———. "Socialists and War." *The Masses* 9 (June 1917):24.

———. "Conscription for What?" *The Masses* 9 (July 1917):18.

———. "The Post Office Censorship." *The Masses* 9 (September 1917):24.

Essary, J. Frederick. "President, Congress and the Press Correspondents." *American Political Science Review* 22 (November 1928):902–9.

————. "Democracy and the Press." *Annals of the American Academy of Political and Social Science* 169 (September 1933):110–19.

————. "The Presidency and the Press." *Scribner's Magazine* 97 (May 1935):305–7.

George, Charles H. "New York's Newspapers." *The Journalist* 13 (March 21, 1891):5.

Glavis, L. R. "The Whitewashing of Ballinger." *Collier's* 44 (November 13, 1909):15–17, 27.

Godwin, Earl. "White Housekeeping." *Goldfish Bowl* 4 (July 1937):1.

Graff, Henry F. "Life with Father, the President." *New York Times Magazine* (July 14, 1963):10 et seq.

Grantham, Dewey W. "Dinner at the White House: Theodore Roosevelt, Booker T. Washington, and the South." *Tennessee Historical Quarterly* 18 (June 1958):112–30.

Hard, William. "Mr. Burleson, Espionagent." *New Republic* 19 (May 10, 1919):42–45.

Hilton, O. A. "Freedom of the Press in Wartime, 1917–19." *Southwestern Social Science Quarterly* 28 (March 1948):346–61.

Hurd, Charles W. B. "President and Press: A Unique Forum." *New York Times Magazine* (June 9, 1935):3, 19.

Inglis, William. "An Intimate View of Joseph Pulitzer." *Harper's Weekly* 55 (November 11, 1911):7.

Irwin, Will. "The American Newspaper: A Study of Journalism in its Relation to the Public." *Collier's* 46 (January 14, 1911):15–18. Thirteen additional articles in series.

Johnson, Donald. "Wilson, Burleson, and Censorship in the First World War." *Journal of Southern History* 28 (February 1962):46–58.

Jones, John Paul, Jr. "Traces History of Press Relations With Every U.S. President." *American Press* 59 (November 1940):5, 23.

Keynes, John Maynard. "Europe After the Treaty." *New Republic* 21 (January 14, 1920):189–95.

————. "How to Mend the Treaty." *New Republic* 21 (January 21, 1920):215–24.

Krock, Arthur B. "Thinks President Should Have Conferred with Reporters." *Editor & Publisher* 51 (April 26, 1919):19.

Lamar, William H. "The Government's Attitude Toward the Press." *Forum* 59 (February 1918):132.

Larson, Cedric and James R. Mock. "The Lost Files of the Creel Committee of 1917–19." *Public Opinion Quarterly* 3 (January 1939):5–29.

Lawrence, David. "Shop Talk at Thirty." *Editor & Publisher* 77 (May 27, 1944):64, 60.

Lawson, Thomas W. "Frenzied Finance: The Story of Amalgamated." *Everybody's* 11 (July 1904):1–10.

Lee, Alfred McClung. "Violations of Press Freedom in America." *Journalism Quarterly* 15 (March 1938):19–27.

Leupp, Francis E. "President Taft's Own View: An Authorized Interview." *Outlook* 99 (December 2, 1911):811–18.

Lindsey, Judge Ben B. "The Beast and the Jungle." *Everybody's* 21 (October 1909):433–52. Seven additional articles in series.

Lippmann, Walter. "The Job of the Washington Correspondent." *Atlantic Monthly* 205 (January 1960):47–49.

Little, Luther B. "The Printing Press in Politics." *Munsey's Magazine* 23 (September 1900):740–44.

Lowry, Edward G. "The White House Now." *Harper's Weekly* 53 (May 15, 1909):7–8.

————. "Mr. Taft and His Critics." *Harper's Weekly* 54 (August 6, 1910):15, 30.

McCarthy, Joe. "The Lordly Journalists." *Holiday* 31 (April 1962):140 et seq.

McDougall, Walt. "Old Days on *The World*." *The American Mercury* 4 (January 1925):20–28.

————. "Pictures in the Papers." *The American Mercury* 6 (September 1925):67–73.

McGuire, Delbert. "Democracy's Confrontation: The Presidential Press Conference: I." *Journalism Quarterly* 44 (Winter 1967):638–44.

————. "Democracy's Confrontation: The Presidential Press Conference: II." *Journalism Quarterly* 45 (Spring 1968):31–41, 54.

Manning, George H. "Liberalizing of President's Contact with Press Hoped for From Hoover." *Editor & Publisher* 61 (January 12, 1929):5–6.

————. "Bennett Fight Opened Senate to Press." *Editor & Publisher* 67 (July 21, 1934):116, 118.

Marbut, Frederick B. "Early Washington Correspondents: Some Neglected Pioneers." *Journalism Quarterly* 25 (December 1948):369–74, 400.

Markham, Edwin. "The Hoe-Man in the Making." *Cosmopolitan* 41 (September 1906):480–87. Series continues intermittently through July 1907.

Moon, Gordon A., II. "George F. Parker: A 'Near Miss' as First White House Press Chief." *Journalism Quarterly* 41 (Spring 1964):183–90.

Munsterberg, Hugo. "The World Language." *McClure's* 28 (November 1906):102–11.

Needham, Harry Beach. "The Senate—of 'Special Interests.' " *World's Work* 11 (January 1906), 7060–7065.

Nock, Albert. "The One Thing Needful." *The Nation* 107 (September 14, 1918):283.

Oulahan, Richard V. "Capital Corps Praised for Diligence." *Editor & Publisher* 63 (April 25, 1931):32, 138.

Parton, James. "The *New York Herald,* From 1836 to 1866." *North American Review* 102 (April 1866):373–419.

Pew, Marlen. " 'Leak' Inquiry Awakens National Interest." *Editor & Publisher* 49 (February 10, 1917):5–6.

Pollard, James E. "The White House News Conference as a Channel of Communication." *Public Opinion Quarterly* 15 (Winter 1951):663–78.

Poore, Ben: Perley. "Washington News." *Harper's New Monthly Magazine* 48 (January 1874):225–36.

Pringle, Henry F. and Katherine. "Mr. President!" *Saturday Evening Post* 229 (June 15, 1957):32 et seq.

Pulitzer, Joseph. "The College of Journalism." *North American Review* 178 (May 1904):641–80.

Reed, John. "Woodrow Wilson." *The Masses* 9 (June 1917):22.

Richardson, Francis A. "Recollections of a Washington Correspondent." *Records of the Columbia Historical Society* 6 (1903):24–42.

Riggs, Edward G. "The American Newspaper." *The Bookman* 19 (July 1904):476–95.

Rogers, Lindsay. "Freedom of the Press in the United States." *The Living Age* 298 (September 28, 1918):769–74.

————. "The White House 'Spokesman.' " *Virginia Quarterly Review* 2 (July 1926):350–66.

Roosevelt, Theodore. "Nature Fakers." *Everybody's* 17 (September 1907):427–30.

————. "A Disagreeable Duty." *Outlook* 104 (June 14, 1913):316–18.

Rosapepe, Joseph S. "Neither Pinkertons Nor Publicity Men." *Public Relations Journal* 27 (October 1971):12–14 et seq.

Russell, Charles Edward. "The Tenements of Trinity Church." *Everybody's* 19 (July 1908):47–57.

Savage, M. J. "A Profane View of the Sanctum." *North American Review* 141 (August 1885):137–53.

Seligman, Lester G. "The President is Many Men." *Antioch Review* 16 (September 1956):305–18.

————. "The Presidential Office and The President as Party Leader." *Law and Contemporary Problems* 21 (Autumn 1956):724–34.

Sharp, Willis. "President and Press." *Atlantic Monthly* 140 (August 1927):239–45.

Startt, James D. "Early Press Reaction to Wilson's League Proposal." *Journalism Quarterly* 39 (Summer 1962):301–8.

———. "Wilson's Trip to Paris: Profile of Press Response." *Journalism Quarterly* 46 (Winter 1969):737–42.

Steffens, J. Lincoln. "The Business of a Newspaper." *Scribner's Magazine* 22 (October 1897):447–67.

Stockbridge, Frank Parker. "How Woodrow Wilson Won His Nomination." *Current History* 20 (July 1924):561–72.

Sullivan, Mark. "Back to Truth." *Collier's* 63 (April 26, 1919):5–6 et seq.

Tarbell, Ida M. "President McKinley in War Times." *McClure's* 11 (July 1898):208–24.

———. "A Talk With the President of the United States." *Collier's* 58 (October 28, 1916):5–6 et seq.

Thomas, W. I. "The Psychology of Yellow Journalism." *American Magazine* 65 (March 1908):491–97.

Turnbull, George. "Some Notes on the History of the Interview." *Journalism Quarterly* 13 (September 1936):272–79.

Turner, George Kibbe. "How Taft Views His Own Administration: An Interview with the President." *McClure's* 35 (June 1910):211–21.

Turner, Henry A. "Woodrow Wilson and Public Opinion." *Public Opinion Quarterly* 21 (Winter 1957–58):505–20.

Villard, Oswald Garrison. "The Press and the President." *The Century* 111 (December 1925):193–200.

———. "The Waning Power of the Press." *Forum* 86 (September 1931):141–45.

Wicker, Tom. "Kennedy as a Public Speakah." *New York Times Magazine* (February 25, 1962):14, 70–71.

Index